The Great House of Raúl Rodríguez

SONETTE TIPPENS

RED APPLE
PUBLISHING

Copyright © 2015 Sonette Tippens

ISBN: 0994753217
ISBN-13: 978-0994753212

DEDICATION

I wrote this book as a tribute to the love and respect I feel for each person included in this book. For this reason, I would like to have used your real names,but for the sake of your privacy, I did not.

Sonette

CONTENTS

AUTHOR'S NOTE

To intensifying the impact of the moment in my own voice,
I have enveloped the conversations into the paragraphs.

TRIP ONE

TUESDAY, MARCH 19, 2002

1

ENTRANCE

The blank face of the Great House tells you nothing, nothing of Abelardo's murder, nothing of the buried for centuries gold being tunneled for during the darkest hours of the night, the pulsing invasive excavations which are causing four hundred year old stone pillars to shake and collapse, to threaten and expose.

From the ancient Mexican cobblestone street, The House, with its iron bars and balconies, its granite window casings, its red plaster ornamental façade, only allows the stranger the merest curious glimpse of the tantalizing gardens, sunlight glinting on blossoms, flashing on flowering trees, a peek at this inside oasis of luxury as the four hundred year old carriage gates swing briefly open, only to close again.

The first thing that one finds, upon entering a Great House, is safety, and the next is love. I knew that I would find safety and love in this house, but I did not know how much I would come to need them both. My only thoughts were of discovery, and adventure, and fun. I was an innocent, and that very innocence had always led people to trust in me. It was no different now.

A Great House has hidden and secret rooms, and the multi-layered living of many generations. My own generation started shortly before Abelardo's murder.

A murder and the changes it brings to everyone's lives is a break, a rupture, of the chain you thought your life would be, a shift, a wrench, to another chain of events entirely. I didn't know then how this murder would carry me, almost unwittingly, into a deeper and deeper involvement, not just with Abelardo's family, but into the very great heart of what was to become The Great House of Raúl Rodríguez.

2

REMEMBERING WITH MY SKIN,
RAÚL AS MASTER, AND OVERWHELMED

The yearning to return, always just under the surface, has at last been satisfied, and I have arrived at what, to me, will always be Abelardo's house, or so I believe. My husband, Richard, has massaged my feet, then my whole body, in an effort to help me calm down, get adjusted. Every part of me is a-jangle. Every step I take, every voice I hear, every door I open brings me back to Abelardo. And bringing me back to Abelardo means bringing me back to myself, to who I was then, to the beautiful, hopeful, carefree girl who loved everything, while all of life still loved her back.

I am no longer eighteen, as I was when Abelardo first brought me to his house. To return to this Great House, to find it so unchanged and welcoming, after all that could have turned it upside down, is personally startling. Yes, it has always been true that the master of this Great House has kept it constantly and carefully preserved, since its construction was begun in 1640. Yes, San Miguel Allende was long ago designated a national monument, and the entire town has been carefully preserved to stay faithful to the seventeenth century architecture, to look exactly as it did when first founded, when Mexico was still a colony of Spain.

Yes, the streets, and all the houses, and alleyways, and parks, and gardens, every cobblestone, every balcony, every church, even the restaurants, and hotels, and the stores have been preserved. It is not surprising to find the sun still bright, the sky a brilliant blue, the flowers profuse, the chatter, and music, and bustle of the narrow ancient streets unchanged. I knew it would be so. And I knew that this house would be preserved as well. It is not what I see with my eyes that startles me so. It is not what I hear with my ears. It is what I see in my heart, the layers and layers of all that happened to me here, and how clearly it all comes flooding back.

I am remembering with my skin, as the fan we have placed in our suite blows away gently the scorching afternoon Mexican heat. I am remembering with my nose, as the smells, and clanks, and soft voices drift upward to our bedroom while the servants bustle about in the kitchen below. I am remembering with my ears as I hear the flutter of bird wings and soft cooing combining with the accordions of the ranchera music playing from the cook's radio, the voices of the family as they cross from the enormous cool of the patio gardens into the dining room, and people of the household passing up and down the outside stairs across from our open window, the muted voices of the crowds in the streets, the vendors, the beggars. I am remembering being here, in this unchanged room, in lying every afternoon on this very bed, when I lived here as Nita's sister, such a short time after Abelardo's murder.

In my core, I am remembering when my Abelardo first brought me into this house, to the place and people who were going to open to me experiences that would provide hundreds of stories, adventures, discoveries, precious friendships. I have stepped back in time. But I am no longer eighteen. I am fifty-seven years old, retired, have been married for thirty-four years. I am not a college girl. I am not the bride Abelardo hoped to bring to his home. I am here with my American husband. And still, I have been welcomed back, welcomed back as Abelardo's Sonette.

The first time I entered this house, it was Abelardo who brought me here. It was the start of my new life. Am I now, at fifty-seven, starting a new life again? How many times can one start a new life? How many times does one want to? I used to be so fearless, so constantly happy, so ready to embrace all the beauty and wonder of life. Can I get that back? It is still inside me, not even locked away. It is my Sonetteness, and I always get my Sonettness back. I am on fire with happiness to be just exactly here, exactly where I now am, with exactly the people who also are here, to have no plans at all, to be a blank page for whatever comes next.

Our imaginations embellish the past into better than the reality was. In my case, it is the opposite.

Thus, my new life's story begins right here, on March 19, 2002, in this suite which, out of all the many, many rooms in The Great House where we could have been lodged, we find ourselves in the very set of rooms where I had hoped to be placed. I feel better than I had even dared to expect. I hadn't known how great would be the impact of the sameness, the comfort that nothing has been changed, that while I was living my other USA life, so far apart from here, like Sleeping Beauty's castle, everything in San Miguel, everything in Abelardo's house, has been cradled for my return. The Great House has been holding its breath, waiting for me, and that is a secret that is only for me to know.

How many people wish they could go back, be 18 again, and find a secret place where all the characters of your long-ago life, when you were perfect, and when the world was sweet, have been waiting for you, are ready for you, and are welcoming. And in this way, I have stepped back in time.

My first journey here to San Miguel was nothing like the swift air flight of today. My college friends and I set out alone with nothing but our tickets and my five suitcases filled with seven sets of colored high-heeled shoes to match my seven party dresses, and all the other clothes, jewelry, and perfumes that I deemed essential for such a visit to another country.

My mother kissed me good-bye at the train station in Rockford, Illinois on a cold January morning in 1963. The boys, as we called them then, had driven on ahead with our college professor, to prepare a place for us to live in San Miguel. We girls, meeting at the bustling train station in Chicago, blithely waved our hands in the direction of the jumbled stacks of our luggage waiting to be loaded by the porters, and we boarded our train for Saint Louis. Once in St. Louis, we entered our next train, still with comfortable passenger cars, and once again our luggage was dealt with for us.

It was all pleasant, a happy, easy trip, until we came to a stop and were instructed to drag all of our own baggage across many tracks and through a confusing row of waiting trains to the cattle car in which we were to journey from San Antonio to the Mexican border! In those days, young ladies dressed up to travel, pretty coats and dresses, high heeled shoes, matching purses, but for this transfer no smiling porters helped us in our struggle to locate the open boxcar which was to be ours for the next six hours, and no one helped us tug, drag, lift, shove our heavy suitcases, and purses, and paperbacks, and snacks. But we made it.

Not at all unhappy with our situation, we sat in the open doorway of the swaying car, legs dangling over the tracks, as we rattled slowly through dusty Texas, and this is how we got our first greeting from the Mexican border. Trains did not connect then, across the border, and we took taxis to reach our Mexican train. And what a train it was!

If you have seen the movie "The Orient Express", you will visualize the luxury that awaited us. We were assigned compartments paneled in precious woods, with bulging panels in the doors that could be opened by you, inside, and by the porters from the outside. When one retired for the night, your traveling clothes and shoes were to be placed inside this door. In the morning, one found the clothes clean and pressed, and the shoes perfectly polished.

By day, we rode in the luxurious club car, with its carved mahogany bar, plush arm-chairs, and instead of a caboose, there was a balcony at the end of the train where we could stand outside, drink an iced fruit drink, and stand in awe of the land unrolling before us. We dressed in our best for dinner in the magnificent dinning car, and in the morning, refreshed from our first sleep in soft beds with real sheets and pillows, luxuriated in what was served to us by white uniformed waiters who set breakfasts covered by silver domes on the white, crisp linen of our rose vase adorned tables. We were learning quickly to enjoy what is meant by "First Class".

When first my feet touched Mexican soil, I had hopped off the train for just a few minutes while it paused briefly in Monterrey. My soul tingled as I experienced an instant connection to what was so much a foreign country, so different from anything I had ever seen, and I felt, "I should have been born here". A new life started for me then.

Today is March 19, 2002. What will happen? If I started a new life in Mexico at age 18, what will happen to me now, at age 57? How many times can one start a new life? How many times does one want to?

I say that we are in Abelardo's house, the house of my Abelardo, even though the house today should properly be called, The Great House of Raúl Rodriguez. I will go back to the beginning as I discover the new and tell of the old. A new life does have a start, a birth, and today will become exactly that day for me. So I will write it all down, and here is my story.

Richard and I arrived last night at midnight, and Raúl and Richard wrestled with our many heavy bags. Out of Raúl's van, through the entrance that once admitted carriages, through the tiled gardens of the patio, around the old stone fountain, past the arches and porticoes of the patio, past the kitchen and servant's room, and finally up a stone threshold and into the downstairs of our suite. Ever courteous and gracious, Raúl insisted on helping Richard until everything made its way up the stairs and into our bedroom, which is where I am now.

I will describe our section of this great house. We have an airy and bright apartment above the kitchen, an ideal location for my purposes in being here. That is to say, we are in the heart of the home, able to hear all the clatter and voices and tumult of a happy and busy household, and yet hidden away enough to not intrude. From our beds, next to the open window, we see the coming and going of all the family, the visitors, the servants, and the dogs and cats, as they race or trudge or scamper up and down the outside staircase across the narrow courtyard from us. We can hear all the clanging and banging of the giant cathedral bells from each of San Miguel's eleven Colonial era churches. We can hear the explosions and pops of the cojetes, the celebratory firework explosions that go on all day and night during Saint's Days. We can hear the cook's radio tuned to the Mexican ranchero music station. We can hear the shouts and hollers for this and that person to "COME", (Eat), "VEN", (Come now), which calls include us. Yes, including, and that is the beauty for me, this is what I am wanting, once more being part of that precious including.

Our bedroom window is cut out of a wall two feet thick. The metal frame opens from center outward, catches the wind, bangs, clangs, slams shut with ferocity, and hasn't broken ever. Even so, I am always amazed and relieved each time that we still have our window intact. Outside, above the stairs, there is a flat roofed section with little tiled chimneys or air vents which are favorite perches for the birds that chirp and flutter around.

As I write, three servants are busy preparing the 3:00 meal, comida. Another is pouring water into the one hundred huge clay pots that line the patio, filled with enormous ferns, flowers, and other giant plants. With the water spilled and splashed in this process, since a bucket is used to take the water from the central fountain, the tiled floors will be thoroughly washed, as is every floor of this Great House, every day. The sidewalks outside, and the street as well, have already had their morning sweep and wash. Meanwhile another worker, perhaps with his assistant, is toiling away at the endless repair of, currently, the library. I say endless because after a year or two, when this room has been completed, the workman will move to the next room, and then the next, and once the whole house has been put into perfect order, it will be time to begin all over again. This is what it takes to live in and maintain a Great House, to love it, to preserve it, and to provide a cool and gracious haven for yourself, for your family, and for your friends, for today, and for centuries to come. And on this day, I am part of the endless, timeless, turbulent, and peaceful flow.

When we wake up, we go down to the courtyard to sit under the arches of the Patio and have coffee. After a long time, we see the "main maid", the boss of the housekeepers. She has just taken a cup of tea across the Patio to Nita's room.

This is how Nita has always been awakened, by a servant bearing her morning tea. So long ago, when Nita and I were sisters together, sharing her room, which is this one, the one Richard and I have been allowed to use for our visit, I well remember this ritual.

It is now 8:25 AM, and in about an hour Nita will drift out to breakfast.

When I say "maid" or "servant", those are American words which do not really describe the job and the person correctly. Chita is the head cook and the supervisor of the household workers, but more the cook than anything else. Still, her duties include caring for the children, shopping, running errands, taking the children for ice cream, opening the great doors to the street outside, doing the family's wash (by machine and by hand), hanging all the wet clothes on the roof, ironing, helping out in the family's private quarters, so what should I call her? The word used to be criada, which I am now told is not respectful enough. Some say "girl", or "helper", and this isn't correct either. She is never referred to by a title, so I don't know what else it could be. She is simply and always, Chita.

So Chita, seeing Richard and me drinking coffee in the Patio, asks us what we would like for breakfast. We don't know the routine and rhythm of the house yet, nor what is expected of us. So we reply that we already made coffee in our room, but we would like some freshly squeezed orange juice. Chita nods, and soon we see her crossing the Patio and slipping out to the street. She returns with a huge bag of oranges, the fruit market store must be close by, and she enters the kitchen to hand-squeeze all the oranges. Try it sometime. Your wrist and hand will hurt and be worn out and useless way before you can squeeze as much as it takes to fill two large tumblers. We wait, but nothing happens.

Raúl Rodriguez, the owner of this house and our host, is Nita's nephew. Nita is still partial owner, to a degree, in the way that families work out the passage of properties from generation to generation. Raúl finally appears, and we all go into the dining room for a formal breakfast.

We don't realize it, because by our standards it is sort of late in the morning, but by the daily routine here, breakfast is served anywhere between 9:30 and 11:00. All meals are in the high ceilinged, echoing, formal dining room, where first I dined with Abelardo's family as his sweetheart, where later my mother and brother were welcomed, and where, after Abelardo's murder, I still returned, where I still took my meals, but then as Nita's "sister".

Raúl arrives, and with a little bow, after greeting us, and hugging, and much kissing of cheeks, he uses the centuries old family key to unlock the glass paned door. We enter and take our places.

Everything is served by Chita, and we are not supposed to help. She has made a huge pitcher of orange juice, and then she brings us bowls of wonderfully sweet papaya. Next, scrambled eggs with minced ham, refried beans, fresh homemade hot sauce, and a big platter of bolillos cut in halves, spread with butter, and heated in the oven. Bolillos look like small football shapes and are purchased at the last minute from the bakery across the street just before each meal. Last we are served coffee, and this is when Nita arrives, so instead of leaving, we all stay, to keep her company, while Chita repeats the entire cooking and serving process. We talk and have fun, and it is pretty late when we finally leave the table.

Each room of this house is kept locked, so after we go back to the Patio, Raúl carefully locks the dining room. Then Nita says, "Let's go for a walk. Do you want to, eh?" in her cute way. Of course, I always want to go anywhere Nita goes. We are still "sisters", and at last I am back with my sister, although it will be later in my story when I explain why and how I can say that we are sisters.

Nita is the same as she always has been. I wonder if I am too? I am not as innocent as I was, and I have been much disillusioned, but so far I have always gotten my bounce back. It's getting harder and taking longer, but this tale won't go into that.

Here is a better topic: yesterday on the way here, our plane flew right on top of a cloud bank for a long, long time. I mean, right on top, so that it seemed like we were surfing or water skiing over the clouds! It was like flying on a magic carpet. I loved it! I think that the pilots must have a wonderful sense of fun. Also making me feel cheery is that on the plane I started reading a very funny novel.

I have always loved being me, Sonette, and I still do, except that lately being Sonette has been narrowed down a little in spirit, tamped down, clouded over a little. I used to be fearless, and I was very, very free.

Well, we came here with no plan at all, on purpose, so as a new blank page, life will come to us! And I believe that I can get my Sonetteness back again.

On the walk I take with Nita, we traverse the center of the city, but it is not uninterrupted exercise, which is what a walk means back at my home. A walk here is an entirely different experience with an entirely different motive, and there is no one better for taking a walk than with Nita. She is the absolute queen and triumph of how to take a Mexican walk.

The first block out, we come across a parade. It seems to consist of every child in town, from babies up to age six. Each is dressed as a flower, or a clown, or for carnival. There are also high schoolers in a marching band with really loud drums. The parade will stream by for hours, yes, hours, and finally Nita just cuts us across it.

First we go to see the houses that Nita owns, and then those she used to own, and some that her family members currently and formerly owned as well. Each one is rented, and all are beautiful. The facades have been preserved historically while being slightly improved.

Everywhere there are real estate offices with lavish color photos and descriptions posted within and without. San Miguel de Allende had a population of 20,000 in 1963, and we few Americans were still rare enough to be curiosities. Most Americans clustered around the Instituto Allende, the beautiful University of Guanajauto, the artistic branch, where I was enrolled. However, I was one of the rare ones, maybe the only one, who preferred to spend all of my time with my new Mexican friends when not attending classes. Most of the Americans pretty much hung out with other Americans, or at the most with Mexicans who spoke English and liked living the American experience by having American friends with American habits and American social life.

Gradually the American population grew, and now there are one hundred and twenty thousand inhabitants here, with a large percentage being Canadians and Americans. The Americans still have their own hang-outs, which I avoid. But many wonderful changes have been effected due to their influence, particularly in clean water and sanitation. Property values have sky-rocketed, and the city's growth has largely conformed to the graceful and lovely Colonial theme, except glorified and adapted by the skill and talents of the brilliant Mexican architects, designers, and gardeners. Even the oldest of the houses that have been gutted and restructured inside have preserved the look compatible or authentic to the 1600's theme.

Being with Nita means stopping every so many feet to talk amiably with a friend or relative. I was reintroduced to those who knew me so many years ago, and to those who did not, as Abelardo's novia, which earned me instant acceptance and guaranteed my welcome to accompany Nita to any engagement and to accept every invitation. I have not mentioned that I became fluent in Spanish in 1963 due to spending every day and every evening with Abelardo and Nita. Novia means sweetheart, fiancée, bride, and newlywed, in that order. The word could not be separated, because each led inevitably to the next stage.

I had never agreed to more than an intense friendship, but everyone else had a 100% certainty that once begun, Abelardo and I would finish as married. This conviction had inadvertently and unknowingly been reinforced by me when Abelardo gave me a lavish mid-night serenade, in the presence of my mother on one of our later visits, and I opened the shutters of the Posada Quinta Lorretto, where I was staying with my mom, and I looked out and thanked him. From that moment, I was the only one who did not know that his part of the serenade constituted a formal proposal of marriage, which I had already many times declined informally, but which I had now accepted, by opening the shutters and thanking him. I continued our friendship, oblivious to my new status, and no one took my denials of marriage being in my future with any seriousness whatsoever.

Since Abelardo was murdered a couple of years later, everyone's conviction was that I definitely would have eventually become Nita's sister-in-law and moved into The Great House. Thus I have forever after been welcomed into the family as Abelardo's widow and treated with much respect and love and generosity. It is his family's tribute to their beloved Abelardo, and their unstinting gift to me. My husband, Richard, never knew Abelardo, and our marriage, years after Abelardo's death, only served to welcome Richard into the family as well, since he never had been a rival. Everyone agreed that Abelardo would have wanted someone to take care of me. And that is why Nita and I are sisters.

None of this needs explaining to anyone in San Miguel because it was a tiny town when all these events transpired. All the great families knew each other then, and they still do. All of the servants of these great families know each other also, and thus everyone in town learns every scrap of news from someone in the news-and-family network every day. This is actually a very relaxing way to live, accepting, uncritical, and with nothing to hide or pretend about. At least to me, it is a stress free way to just always be yourself, although from my observance of Mexicans, I believe this to mean being your best self, your most loving, and kind, and generous self. I may be wrong, but this is my story of my experiences, and this is how it happened to me.

Our progress through the few streets Nita and I traverse both frustrates and delights me today, as I now resume telling about our first day walk. Frustrating because I am like the kind of dog breed that needs lots of exercise, and for too long I haven't had any. Delightful, because here are faces and families from my past, and

Nita is carefully renewing each old friendship for me and establishing firmly who I am in the community. She sets the stage for me for the duration of our visit, and for any subsequent visits, which now seemed possible and likely.

Finally Nita and I arrive at what Richard and I had always mistakenly called The French Park, and now, even after having been corrected, we feel an intimate sense of comfort in preserving a bit of our shared past by continuing with our habit. The park is of semi-tropical vegetation laced with twisting walkways, pedestrian narrow bridges which crisscross the deep ravines, and steep slopes, as well as gardens covered with lush flowers and palms.

The French park holds special memories for Richard because he and his brother used to play there almost every day when his parents began spending their summers in San Miguel. Richard was 13, and his brother was 14. One of their friends lived permanently in a Great House that faced the French Park. When Richard was 15, the friend's parents went somewhere for the summer, leaving their son in the care of the servants. Richard's parents, not realizing that the other parents had gone away, after giving Richard and his brother permission to stay with the friend's family, Mom and Dad unsuspectingly returned to the States. Thus three teenaged boys had the run of San Miguel, all the freedom they wanted, with their need for food and clean clothes satisfied by the servants. Richard and his brother, Mike, spent most of the bus fare money their parents had given them for their return to their home in Arizona on movies and on having fun. When it came time to go home, they could only afford the cheapest bus and had nothing at all to eat until they reached their parents' house. It wasn't until years later that the brothers revealed what they had done, or perhaps they never did. By then, it didn't matter. Richard always considered the whole thing a wonderful lark.

Something interesting is happening. As Nita and I reach The French Park, I am seeing places I have dreamed about, but they can't be memories. Nita tells me that the bank of houses on this side of the park look as old as the rest of San Miguel, but they are recent constructions. She knows, because one belongs to her cousin and his wife. Can such a thing happen? Can you dream the future? Oh, well, I suppose one can only wonder.

Anyway, I am still writing about Day One! Soon it will be clear how much we are doing, and why I started my story by saying that I am on sensory overload, even though, or because, everything is so great.

For one thing, it is boiling hot, and here women are supposed to wear pants, not shorts. I want to go to my room, lie down on my bed, turn the fan to blow directly onto my hot, tired body, and read my funny book. But Nita says, "No, let's go have a cup of coffee".

We go to the Patio of a former convent, a beautiful old Colonial structure with huge vaulted arches, stone staircases worn to scooped out hollows by centuries of footfalls, lavish courtyard gardens and fountains, a structure that long ago became the city's Palace of Fine Arts. I had spent many hours there, during my very first trip, studying Flamenco dance, and also attending dreamy guitar concerts of Segovia and the great masters with Abelardo, so I already know the Bellas Artes as an oasis of coolness and charm.

When we enter, seated at a table are two women I had known so well when, in 1963, I lived next door at Casa Sautto, their hotel! Nita and these women are friends, and what astonishes and delights me is that they instantly recognize me and greet me by name. Well, I have to say that Teresa does recognize me, and Belinda does not, but it doesn't take her long. And of course being with Nita clarified my position.

In fact, it was Belinda and Teresa who introduced me to Abelardo by giving a party in my little college-abroad-group's honor the second night after we arrived from the States. The bond between Abelardo and me was instant, and although I didn't know why, Nita, as the older sister, was soon sent to accompany us everywhere we went as a chaperone. I really liked Nita and had no feelings of wanting to get away and be just the two of us alone, so we were a trio, except for when Abelardo and I openly strolled around town alone, during daylight hours, almost every day from the party onward. To me, Abelardo was a friend, I cannot describe the depth of the friendship, but a friend, not someone with whom I would like to sneak away and kiss.

Anyway, having coffee with these old friends is not simply a matter of resting for a few minutes for a little refreshment. It is powerfully emotional for me. This whole experience, ever since our mid-night arrival last night, means being given the gift of going back in time to relive being 18 and on my first trip, a six month stay in Mexico. Not only do I get to go back in time, but although nothing outwardly has changed in the town, everyone else is now my age too. I don't want to actually be 18 again and have all my friends so young. Instead, I still get to be me, and at the same time be given back what had been many of the happiest days and months of my life. This is why I say I am on emotional overload. Everything wonderful is happening so fast that I needed time to digest it.

But instead of going home, Nita insists on staying for two hours. Mexican time is not like American time, and I know that, and I know I am being given a wonderful gift, beyond all that I had hoped and dreamed. Yet I also know that Richard has been left behind in our apartment, and I don't know how he will feel about having been left alone for so long. At least he is used to Nita and loves her, and he is used to and loves San Miguel and its ways.

When I am getting terribly impatient and about ready to jump out of my skin, we finally return to the house, and as I said when I started to write this, I do finally lie on my bed, with the fan, and read my funny novel.

We are called to comida, the 3:00 main meal of the day. "Called" means that Raúl stands under our window and calls up, "So nayt, Ree chart, Vamos a comer!" Raúl speaks perfect English, but I write "Ree chart" because we love having our names pronounced Mexican style.

Comida is a monumental procedure, and I have never seen anything to equal it in the United States. The dining room is exceedingly formal, with a gigantic, dark, hand-carved antique table, glass topped, and with massive matching chairs. The other furniture in the room is in the same style, and because of the size of the room and the two-story high ceiling, the result is to provide an excellent sense of proportion. All the furnishings, including the paintings, the cutlery, every detail, is exactly as it was when I first visited and was invited to dine with the family; and after Abelardo's death, when I lived in this house with Nita as her sister during the summers of 1967 and '68. On my next visit to the family, after receiving the terrible black rimmed death notice, Nita had offered, "Why you don't come back for the summer, eh? You can stay here with me, in my room?" Instantly I accepted and enrolled again in the Instituto Allende to immerse myself in

15

studying portrait painting and Spanish. And I am glad, so glad, to sit at this giant heavy table again, even if it is Raúl who presides now, and not Abelardo's father, even if it will be Raúl's cheery children seated here, and not Abelardo. Abelardo will always be beside me, and I don't need to see him to know that.

To begin comida today, Raúl takes his seat at the head of the table, which is the end closest to the kitchen. It is the father's responsibility to holler constantly at the cook to let her know what should be served, and to whom, at each stage of the meal. Since Ree chart and I have been doing basically nothing except waiting to be called to eat, we come immediately. Daughter, Conchita, and son, Raulito, enter, kiss their father, kiss and greet both of us, and take their places. They have just returned from school, and this is our first meeting.

Raulito is an energetic boy, an exact replica of his father. Not only that, but Raulito is the same age that Raúl Padre (Senior) was the last time Richard and I lived here. Raúl padre lived in an upstairs apartment with his mother (Nita's sister) and his father. In fact, even the parrot in the Patio is the same parrot (they live for over one hundred years), and one of the current dogs has the same name as the family dog has always had, Turipitis, sometimes shortened to Turis. See what I mean? Everything is the same!

Daughter Conchita is also in grade school, eleven years old. She is a beautiful age, the age I always think of myself as still being, and she is a beautiful girl with exceptionally satiny dark coloring and hair as long, and curly, and abundant as my own daughter's.

Delfina, their mother, enters next, with more kissing of each person as she welcomes us to her home. We have never met Delfina until now. She too is beautiful, generous, and we are to find that her throaty laugh and unusual voice are charming and give a pleasant feeling to all of her conversations. Finally Nita arrives, of course kisses everyone, and is in turn warmly greeted.

Nita is called Tía, (Aunt), when she is present, or La Tía (The Aunt), when she is not present. I become Señora Sonette (Mrs. Sonette), or La Señora (The Mrs.), when I am not there. At last we are ready, and La Comida, the three o'clock main meal of each day, begins.

First we are served bowls of fruit. Because I have been trained to believe that one should wait until the entire table is served, Raúl is forced to urge me repeatedly to "Eat now, right now". It takes me several days to reason out the system of constant clearing and serving that Chita the cook must follow, so that finally I become fully cooperative. Raúl oversees everyone's progress by calling to Chita in the kitchen the name of the person who is ready for the next course, which is large, deep plates of chicken noodle soup into which one squeezes fresh limes. The tortillero has been filled with fresh, soft, hot corn tortillas, and the container is passed to everyone. Some rip tortillas into bits to add to the soup. I slather mine with a great quantity of the dark reddish-purple hot chiles sauce. Everyone but Richard and Nita are astonished and urge caution, but R. and N. assure them that Sonette has an iron stomach and eats more chiles than a Mexican. Still they watch to see if this can possibly be true, and there is a lot of funny and happy chatter about what and how much I eat. I happen to be a very slender five foot two, so amazement about my eating is common, and I am used to it.

As soup is cleared, we each receive a dinner plate with two meatballs. Bowls of boiled white rice and bowls of boiled beans are placed on the table. These are nothing like the refried beans and the red, greasy rice of the Mexican restaurants in the USA. Delfina and Raúl are very healthy eaters and avoid the lard frying Americans have come to associate with Mexican cooking.

Oh, I forgot to add that Raúl also personally dished out to each of us a salad course as well. The lettuce and vegetables here have a sweeter, juicier, and crispier flavor and texture than what we are used to in Wisconsin.

Only Raulito drinks a bit of milk from his favorite little kid's decorated cup. The rest of us have been served huge glasses of fruit water. This is made daily by some variety of fruit blended in the liquadora (blender) with water and a bit of sugar. I have never seen Mexicans drink glasses of milk the way we do in the USA. Neither have I ever seen milk sold in larger than a one liter container.

Dessert is flan, custard cooked long enough to be very heavy, which I like a lot. Nita had brought a large, deluxe box of chocolates from Canada, where she has lived for many years with her Canadian husband. The chocolates are passed around, but I don't like sweets, so I don't take any.

Raúl calls for the coffee. The children have sat through the whole two hour ritual of the daily meal, and I have greatly enjoyed their happy chatter. Their school is bilingual, so they want to practice their English on me, but with their own family, they speak Spanish. I am still adjusting to understanding and speaking because it has been long years since I have been here. Also, kid slang and family talk use words and expressions that I don't always know. Finally restless, the children ask their father to be excused, say the polite "Con permiso" to all, kiss each of us again, and run out to play. We adults linger long over coffee.

When we finally finish, we kiss each other good-bye and leave the dining room, which Raúl again locks with his ancient key. It is now 5:00, so Richard and I take another walk through what I will continue to call The French Park, even though, as I already said, I now know that the correct name is something else. We see a great number of white egrets high up in the tree tops where they are building their nests. The birds call to each other in a cry unusual to our ears. Large bundles of sticks have been placed near the tree tops for their nest-making projects.

The French Park is exotic and comforting to my Wisconsin eyes. The vegetation consists of planned gardens containing many varieties of plantings, and of trees between intersecting paths. However the lush profusion which characterizes the semi-tropical growth gives the impression of being over-grown, over-blown, over-the-top in every way: in color, in variety, in texture, and in the sounds. The sounds are of the birds, the many children playing, the sports games of the young men and teens, the vendors, the dogs being walked, the cars creeping by up the narrow, steep, cobble-stoned roads. The walking paths are wide, maybe fifteen or twenty feet, and are made of hard-packed trampled dirt. More bringing back our memories of the old days as the gardeners constantly are sweeping away the fallen petals, dried leaves, and debris, still using twig brooms.

Wide, round, flat fountains mark the intersections of the paths, giving you a feeling of having reached a secluded oasis in this hot, dusty, sunbaked town, during hot March, marking another dry, dry day after months already into the dry season. The low stone walls of the flat reflecting ponds encircle carved stone fountains and are used by the doggies for a drink, and for little children to throw in petals or poke chubby fingers into the water. Stone walls high enough to be used as benches surround the wide paths that ring each fountain, and in each bower there is usually a couple kissing, enjoying their romance away from mamá y papá y la familia. We avert our eyes as we interrupt their private, precious interlude, and we go our way, seeking a stone bench in the shade, from which we can watch the families seated on other benches and eating lunches brought from home, or the strollers, like us, or the joggers, or anything at all.

The foliage, so lush, conceals enough of the park at all times to make us feel that it is far more large and complex than it actually is. The ground and floors of the gardens are kept so clean that no sticks would be available for the birds if someone or some organization did not provide them. Sounds are sweetly muffled by the plants, the palms, the flowers, and the vines, even by the stone walls that surround the park, so that the constant mummers flow as a stream. There is nothing sharp here, not even a harsh word. This is where everyone comes for some kind of love, love of their children, love of nature, love of peace, or as we do, for love of the gentle companionship of strangers.

On our way back we go to a little tienda (small store) and buy some cheap red wine, vino tinto. Our last stop is the bakery, La Colmena, across the street from "our" house. Our plan is to go up to the roof at nine p.m. and watch all the lights of the town come on, that is after I return from the eight o'clock mass with Nita. Also, Richard and I decide that we shouldn't eat the evening meal with the family because they might get sick of us always intruding upon their family time.

Richard has no interest in mass, so I put on a black dress, and Nita and I walk the distance of one little block and turn the corner to El Oratorio. I wish Richard were here to see this living spectacle! This is the first of the "Semana Santa", Holy Week, events.

All of the nearby churches are lavishly illuminated. People are everywhere, walking, sitting, selling special foods for St. Joseph's Day, and two bands are playing. One band is dance music, and one is the banging of electronic drums in disco music, so loud that I am worried about my internal organs! What a lot of vibrating is going on inside our bodies from that so-called music. There are no musical notes at all, and I can find no other word except banging.

We see a procession coming out of the church. Old ladies and a few old men are carrying an altar with the life-sized figure of St. Joseph which has been all dressed up in real robes. After going around the churchyard once, they begin again, so we join in by following them.

After a while, St. Joseph is carried to the front of the church inside, and his long cape is held up by old ladies and young boys so that we can walk under it. "Do you want to walk under?" asks Nita. "You are supposed to ask St. Joseph for a beautiful death". (As in not dying painfully over a long time? I wonder, or as in not dying from a possible string of calamities?) "Sure", I say because I always like doing things like this, entering into someone else's world.

We kneel and stand many times during the mass. I will not kneel anymore the next time because my knees have no padding, and the kneeling kills you with pain, and then I can't concentrate on why I am really there. I try to be respectful of every religion, but I don't like hurting.

Once outside, we see fireworks, and then Nita asks if I would like her to buy me some candy sold by a little old lady. "No", I say. "I don't feel like candy. I don't like sweets". "Oh, but you must, Sonette. It is really special for this day. It is really, really good". "No", I say. "I don't like candy. I don't like sweets". "Ah, but this is different, it is made of mint". "No, I say, "I don't want any".

No means nothing to Nita. So Nita "buys" some for both of us. But it turns out Nita doesn't have any money. I don't either because I only brought what I needed to put into the collection plate. So this poor little old lady has to just give us the candy for free because Mexicans are very generous and polite.

I am feeling that this is very unfair, and then I remember that there is always more to each story, even though sometimes I find out the more, and sometimes I don't. In this case, Nita may have known this exact same old lady candy seller for her whole life, perhaps buying, and thus supporting, the little señora for many years. That could be why Nita wanted to buy candy from her, and why the candy was properly given as a gift this time. Nita and her mother, sisters, friends, had always attended El Oratorio, and their relationship with this tiny vendor, although unknown to me, could have been a long and close one. I do know that everyone in town, from all the Great Houses, the servants, the trades-people, everyone I ever meet, all their lives have known Nita.

But I still am not going to eat candy, even just four or five little tiny pieces. I really, really hate candy, and in my new recently made vow to myself, to not get pushed into what I say no to, I have already decided that in my heart, when necessary, I will now be tough and never get forced to say yes when I mean no, at least to never eat stuff I hate.

The celebration with St. Joseph and the mass is all wonderful, and after hearing my descriptions, Richard agrees to go to the next one. He says he thought it was going to be an ordinary mass. But how could mass be ordinary here? Seeing the church, built centuries ago, all lit up outside, covered with gold, and statues, and mosaics, and tiles, and paintings, and chandeliers, and altars, and side rooms, and a thousand nooks and crannies, and oddities, and relics, and filled with shuffling, and coughing, and praying, and babies crying, and old ladies wrapped in shawls, and beautiful young girls, and families, and with glass coffins containing dead saints; with the praying, and the chanting, and the singing, how could that be ordinary? It is sure not like my own home church back in Lake Geneva, Wisconsin!

All this time, Richard has been waiting for me. It is now nine p m. Nine P M and we are still on Day One of our visit! That is how much happens here in just one day!

Richard and I go up to the rooftop with drinks, which we have to sip using tumblers from our bathroom. I haven't drunk even one inch when we are called for merienda with the family. They have prepared for us and are expecting us, so we go down for the late evening meal.

It is very good, of course. The cook has her own room and bath in the house, in the back, across from the kitchen, so she is still around, but she does not serve this meal. We have juice, bolillos (Mexican rolls from the bakery) spread with soft beans and melted cheese. I am not hungry, but the food is irresistible anyway, so I eat it, and we have fun.

Instead of coffee, we have tea that is supposed to make you sleep well. Leaves have been picked from the orange tree that grows in the courtyard, and boiling water is poured over them. I guess it works, because I sleep until 7:00 AM, although I always get up a few times to use the bathroom. Never-the-less, each time I go back to sleep. And for me, such a sleep is a real treat.

3

COZY

Inside our own little apartment, our nest, we have our own blue and white tiled bathroom, with a window identical to the one in the bedroom, on the same wall, opening to the same view. The tile, the plaster walls, the details of the room have not changed at all since I lived here with Nita. Every worn spot, every chip of a tile, each peculiarity of a light switch coming loose from the plaster wall, its identical, unchanging sameness, are comforting to me. Whenever I am here, I feel a much remembered, unconditional, all-encompassing love. I relax. I only am myself. I never have to achieve. I never have to perform. I have already lived up to all expectations, simply by being me. No one flies into a rage at me. No one has any expectations at all. Nothing I do is ever wrong.

The bedroom part of our suite extends into a living room. There are closets, dresser, tables, chairs, couch, lamps, and an open stairway leading to the downstairs living room. Richard and I start to re-arrange. We remove the television set we will never watch and hide it in a corner. This frees up a table that will now become my painting table, squeezed into a space we make between my bed and the window. The window's ledge becomes my still-life set-up center. Next we reconfigure the living room, creating a place for our luggage behind the couch. This means Richard has a place to read, while I prefer to recline on my bed by the window for reading or writing. We have sectioned the room so that our close proximity for the next six weeks will still afford us our own spaces.

In our downstairs, we again move the furniture to our liking. The large antique, free-standing wardrobe and the dresser are shoved away from the French doors, whose glassed panes provide the only light. This area becomes Richard's painting area. We store the little refrigerator, which we will never open, under the stairs, and a heavy trunk under the painting table. Now we each have a painting studio. Richard believes that my painting spot is better, and I agree, yet he is always generous, and he gives the best to me.

Unpacking will take many days. I have brought a great quantity of items of every sort for the maids. It has long been my custom, when traveling to anywhere in Mexico, Costa Rica, or Peru, to bring everything I could for our hosts, or for the maids, or to give to a school to be distributed to children and their families by the teachers. I prefer to return home with almost nothing, so unpacking is not a simple matter. We will not tackle this today.

Our floors, up and down, are of Mexican hand-made tiles, but not at all what that description calls to mind. It seems to be the Americans who love the hand-painted, hand-woven, hand-carved furnishings which we identify as Mexican. Mexicans like what we think of as American, that is to say, factory made. I have even seen a Mexican family have their onyx floors pulled out and replaced by American linoleum tiles from Sears. So it is no surprise that the floors in our apartment have been designed to look like linoleum tiles. They are a dull glaze of a murky blue which appear to have had white glaze squeezed out from a bottle in lines, and then these lines were raked with a comb into a zig-zag pattern. This "modernity" is here because Nita's apartment was added to the back part of the house around the nineteen forties or fifties.

I must not give the impression that a Great House is static or frozen in time. What was original remains original, but additions can be made in or on top of unused space, and there is a lot of such construction here.

I brought a fan with us, which is positioned next to my art things on the ledge of our open, unscreened window. We know from experience that during mosquito season, which March is not, an insect invasion can be torture. And we like the constant, gentle breeze of the fan, especially at night. Good thing, too, because in our honor, the entire suite was painted yesterday, and if not for the open windows, the fumes would be more than bothersome.

The construction of this house was begun in 1640, and it is located only one block from the original central plaza, called The Jardín. The law demands the preservation of the purity of architecture of the Colonial Era, the era when Mexico was a colony of Spain, named New Spain. So we are surrounded by other Great Houses, churches dating back hundreds of years, and with cobble-stoned streets and sidewalks, the sidewalks so narrow that one person must step off into the street to let another pass. Streets are the width of accommodating a carriage pulled by horses. Nita's apartment was probably built into the space where the horses were kept.

When last I lived here, I counted seventeen rooms used by the family. Now I could count more, but one cannot tell how many there may be in total because the construction of a Great House is not like what we in the USA are used to. First floor rooms often have their own inside stairways leading to rooms above that are not seen from the downstairs courtyard. Doors do not always connect adjacent rooms; in fact, the norm is for doorways to open only onto the courtyard. To go from the dining room to the library, one goes first to the courtyard. There is one change since 1963; Raúl had a door inserted for passage from the dining room to the kitchen. Until Raúl and his wife, Delfina, became the heads of household, there was no need for a family member to go into the kitchen. The cook served and cleared everything while the family remained seated in the dining room for every meal.

The kitchen used to be very dark and still had the cement or adobe wall-length type of cooking area that had little square grills in the cement counter used as cooking spots. There were openings for charcoal sticks underneath the little grills, and open storage for mesquite firewood, and large clay bowls below that. It was common for cooks to prefer to cook in huge clay bowls, saying that the flavors were better, and that was the way the people were used to cooking.

Delfina had the whole kitchen modernized to a beautiful, bright, efficient plan, even though it is still the cook and her assistants who do all of the cooking, serving, washing, and every other kitchen duty. Refrigerators used to be not used for much besides keeping fruit drinks cool for the family, so a family that had a refrigerator kept it in the dining room. The cook bought all the day's food in the market, so everything was always fresh and didn't need to be stored. Today the refrigerator is in the new kitchen, along with the most modern and beautiful of appliances, but purchasing food ingredients is still done by the cook before each meal.

The salon, library, and dining room are very large, with exterior walls two and one half feet thick, apparently made of granite blocks. The windows are hand-carved wooden French doors if leading to the street, or windows covered with beautifully carved wooden grills like fancy bars if opening onto the Patio. Naturally all exterior windows are covered with iron bars, if at street level, and have iron grillwork balconies if higher up. From the inside, heavy, wooden, solid shutters can be closed for quiet, or privacy, or safety. The ceilings are two stories high and have hand-carved beams. There is a massive stone fireplace in the salon.

The courtyard has a patio in the center, is filled with flowers and fruit trees, has a stone fountain in the middle, and is ringed by a two story high arcade, under which one goes from room to room when it rains, and under which everyone sits in the beauty of the cool shade on hot, dry days. This is where we have our breakfast coffee, where we wait for each other, and where later on in our trip I will sometimes paint. The ceiling under the arcade is made of red bricks laid over hand-carved, dark beams, which means that to hold the bricks in place there are many of these beams, and that they are close together. The arched walls of the patio are supported by stone pillars with a sort of Ionic design for the bases and capitals. Some of the pillars are original, while a few have had to be replaced, because from 1650 to 2002 is a long time!

The interior of the house is white, smooth, chalky plaster. Around the base of the patio, the walls are painted a deep red going up elbow high. Above that, to the ceiling, it all is painted white. The floor is of small hand-painted, hand-glazed tiles, yellow and orange, in geometric designs. There is a thick low wall, knee high, connecting the pillars, on which are set a great number of huge, dark clay pots filled with flowers and plants. This low, thick wall is also covered with differently patterned glazed tiles of a pale yellow. Flowers and leaves spill over the walls in great fullness, casting complex patterns of ever-changing shadows.

There is only one entrance to most Great Houses, and this entrance is as I described, originally used for the carriage. The space of the entrance is big enough that Raúl sometimes keeps his car in it. The double wooden doors are massive, the original iron tracks are still embedded in the floor, and the big doors are opened by rolling on these curved rails. For people, one of the huge doors has a smaller door cut into it.

Until recently, no one could enter without someone inside unlocking to admit you, including to admit the family members themselves. Today it is no longer as unusual to have a key of your own if you live there, but not everyone bothers to take along a key, so there is frequent pounding of the brass knocker or pulling of the cord to ring the gigantic, heavy cooper bell for admittance. After you pound or ring, a maid comes running to let you in, just an ordinary part of daily life. Running to let you in may mean running down three flights of stairs from the rooftop laundry, or from doing some other task in the far reaches of the house, so letting someone in is far more involved than what Americans would be used to.

I unpack all of the dresses I have brought, and I let Nita pick what she wants. This part is good. But the next part makes me really, really mad. Before I came, I asked Nita what she would like, and Nita had said for me to bring her beautiful lingerie, which I was happy to do. Richard and I went all the way to Milwaukee looking in many stores to find things with lots of lace and of excellent quality. Here is a list of what we bought: a nightgown of pink satin with lots of pink lace, a turquoise bra and panties set of pure lace, a white lace set of camisole and darling shorts type panties, a silk pale turquoise robe, and a pale tangerine softie robe.

Then, I don't know why, but a little later in the day, Nita tells me that she gave it all to Conchita for playing dress-up! Conchita is only eleven years old! I would be happy if Nita gave it to Delfina if she didn't want these fancy things herself, but why did she ask me to go to all that trouble only to give it away for a child to play with? I would love to give gifts made for a child to a child, but not this! Adult lingerie from Fredrick's of Hollywood!

I was to find that on this trip Nita would sometimes exasperate me. She would contradict me, and it wasn't until years later that I learned that she was often right after all. Any disagreement with Nita, or something she would do that I didn't like, would upset me terribly. It was a long time before I figured out that because I loved Nita so much, I thought that we should always get along in perfect harmony. When anything went wrong between us, I felt terribly disloyal, so I never wanted to let it show that I could consider her less than perfect in every way. It took me many years and many life-lessons to learn that everyone has ups and downs, and disagreements do not mean we don't love those who are so important to us.

But I didn't know that then, and I never felt that I had the right to get mad about anything. So I squelched my anger every time, and that squeezing of my little annoyances inside me created my own frustrations, and this is how I could get mad. All I knew then was that I loved Nita so much, and I owed so much of the good in my life to her, that I had no idea how to deal with anything less than perfect behavior on both of our parts.

Thankfully, our disagreements are not too many, and neither of us every wants anything but the best for each other. But the little incident of Nita giving away all the gifts that I had thought she would like bothers me at the time that it happens.

I have written out my thoughts about this because I have decided to include the bad times with the good times as I write my story. At first I thought that I couldn't because saying anything seemingly against my friends would be so disloyal. But the more I thought of it, I realized that I never have said or written anything "against ". If nothing ever went wrong, we would not be real people, and my story is every bit true, written each day just as it all happened.

We have brought gifts for the whole family, so we go on passing them all out. For the toys that I brought for the children, I went to a toy store at home and found a dad with a seven year old boy, Raulito's age, and asked the dad to help me. Raulito considers his gift a great one. I also give to Raulito a back-pack, which evokes very little interest, but the toy is a big hit.

I give Conchita a Disney-Land sweater that is a perfect fit, and some other gift, but I can't remember what.

To Raúl a large bottle of Jack Daniels, which is very expensive in Mexico, but it turns out that he is a reformed alcoholic and very active in A.A., so Richard and I are embarrassed. However Raúl is self-confident and friendly and says it can be for offering to his guests, and pretty soon he has us feeling better! To Delfina, a T shirt with "Wonderful!" written on it in many languages. I guess that also was kind of a flop because the next day Raúl wore it to breakfast. But although it doesn't suit Delfina, the family is acting very gracious about using the gift happily in a different way.

Everyone thanks us heartily because all know that when you have not met people yet, it is not easy to figure out what they would like, and it's always the thought that counts. So everyone ends up happy.

I also brought stuffed toys to give to Raulito and Conchita at Easter, but on our tour of the house, I see that Conchita has about two hundred of these already! There are so many that they are held in nets on the ceiling! It looks cute, and Conchita is such a dear, we love her already.

And I brought two conversion sliders for the kids, metric to USA measurements. These converters slide back and forth and are easy to read; all the measurements you can think of are on them. So if the children don't already have some, it will be great for their use at bilingual school.

The children are absolutely darling. They are the perfect ages that I enjoy. Good manners, happy, lively. This morning we were shown photos of them on cruises and foreign travels, and I think that at their young ages they have gone almost everywhere in the world already.

Richard gets very hot on our morning walk and wants to stop for coffee. We are only one block from our house. I want to come on home and relax and have a cool drink in our apartment. I am afraid I am not very nice about it, and I am sorry that I spoil his fun, although we do stop where he wants. So to try to make up for it, I propose that today in the evening, we will get a little dressed up, I will set my hair and fix my nails, and we will walk up the hill to a swanky place above The French Park and have a tiny cena. (Cena is a more elegant dinner than merienda, which is the casual fare we have before bed when we join the family.) I don't really want anything to eat, but I think a little cena should be more fun than having another cup of coffee somewhere which we have free in our own apartment about one hundred times a day.

Now it is Wed, 10:30 P.M, and we are waiting for my tea to steep. You pick five leaves from the orange tree in the patio, wash them, because they are covered with dust, put them in water, and boil for twenty minutes. I am remembering that I drank this last night and had a very good sleep, which is rare for me and greatly to be desired.

4

THE FIRST OF THE PARTIES

This morning we have another bang-up breakfast. Then lots of nice walking with Nita. San Miguel is built on the side of a very steep slope, the side of a mountain really. Anyway, the streets are not at all suitable for driving because they are so narrow and crowded, so it is far easier to walk. Also the cobblestones of the streets wear out your car's shocks and rattle your teeth. Who would want to go in a car here anyway, when walking is so beautiful and fun? Walking everywhere is a great part of the pleasure of living in San Miguel, and a car is pretty much a nuisance.

Our walk is followed by resting and writing up here in our room. I am rarely in the downstairs of our apartment. I like being up here where it is so airy and bright, where the life of the house drifts up to me by sounds, or everyone passes up and down the stairs outside our window. We have comida at 3:00, and then I go to a baby shower with Nita at 5:00. Five o'clock is afternoon here. Evening does not begin until eight, at the earliest.

The house of the baby shower is newly built, using the characteristics distinctive to Colonial architecture in new ways to make an extraordinarily beautiful and unusual home. The baby shower house is worth one million dollars or more! Richard and I are astonished at the prices here in SMA now.

There are lots of very nice ladies and babies present. Of course I am the only American. I am always disappointed if there are other Americans because I prefer to speak only Spanish and live the completely Mexican life, which I love, and which is the reason that we are here.

Two cooks in very pretty uniforms serve a beautiful meal (which I skip because of already having finished an enormous comida) and then heavy chocolate cake, the kind I would have liked to eat, but I also skip it for the same reason.

I start to get worried about Richard having been left alone for so long. I come home, dress up, and then we go out so R. can have dinner and we can have a walk. It is about a mile on up-hill cobblestone streets in high heels, and I don't care. I always take Richard's arm, and we are used to going around San Miguel all dressed up. In fact, we have always been champions at getting dressed up, going out to dinner night after night, and then topping off the evening with dancing. This is what we hope to do on this trip as well.

Nine o'clock is about the time to leave for going out for dinner, so it is late when Richard and I finish in the restaurant and return home. That is, late by Wisconsin standards. Nita and the cook are in the kitchen, the cook still working! She does every kind of job all day, and I guess all night too. Her only break is her day off, Sunday.

5

LUXURY AT HOME, AND
FINDING THE YELLOW HOUSE

Last night Richard picked the five leaves for me, and after drinking two cups of the tea, I sleep a wonderful sleep, except that Richard gets up very early. He is trying not to wake me, but I hear a lot of banging and pounding. I think, why are the workmen starting so early? But I am hearing the squeak, and bang, and clang of the metal doors to the bathroom that neither Richard nor anyone else can prevent. Oh, well. I get up and do more sorting and hanging of the clothes that I brought.

Wow, do we have a great breakfast, and a feast of conversation as well as of food. We have the marvelous hand-squeezed orange juice, extra-sweet honeydew melon, and huevos rancheros, to perfection! I dearly love huevos rancheros, which are prepared one plate at a time for each person while we are eating our fruit. Chita first goes out and gets the fresh tortillas each morning from the tortillería down the street. To cook them, she puts them one at a time into a frying pan of hot corn oil. Even earlier that morning she will have made fresh tomato sauce, using plum tomatoes (also purchased that morning), chopped onions, and I don't know what else.

Two tortillas go side -by-side on a plate, next, eggs sunny-side-up on top of the tortillas, then generous amounts of sauce over the top. This is trotted out to you as soon as you are ready, and then Chita scoots back to the kitchen to cook for the next person. Lastly we have such good coffee that I think it has cinnamon in it, but it does not.

Cookies are then offered by the daughter, Conchita. (Since both the cook and the daughter actually have the same name, Conchita is used for the daughter, and Chita is used to refer to the cook. The distinction is made by me, so it is easier to follow who says and does what in my journal. In reality, both are called by both names, so you have to just somehow know which one is meant, and it is not always easy to figure out. Sometimes two people are talking for quite a while before one says, "Oh, you mean the cook!" or, "Oh, you mean Conchita hija", which means, Conchita the daughter.

Conchita had gone to the store to buy "polvorones", powder cookies, to show her contribution to our breakfast. There are also little flat cookies from the store like American baby cookies. I don't like any cookies, but everyone else eats them. We have so much fun talking that we remain at the breakfast table until eleven o'clock.

Here are parts of our conversations: Telling all the stories anyone knows about dog bites. I have a really good one to tell about a lady I knew right there in SMA whose nose end got bitten off by a dog. It turned out great because she became very pretty as previously she had a too big nose.

Next, bullies, and raising children. Naturally everyone has a story about that. Then about Nita's houses that she owns here. Also about the antique furniture that Delfina's mother is trying to sell from her own Great House. No one will buy it because it is so large and fancy that it won't fit anywhere except in another Great House, and there are fewer of these left each year. Yes, the structures are still there, but the houses are becoming divided up inside and used for other purposes. Not everyone can afford the servants and expenses of maintaining living in a Great House anymore. It has seemed either more practical or more necessary for the owners to sell and take the three or four million dollars, American dollars!, or to rent out the houses in pieces to banks, or realtors, or shops, or restaurants.

And if I write all that we talked about, you will think that there are no topics left for the next meal.

The first time I experienced Semana Santa was here in San Miguel with Nita and Abelardo in 1963. They took me to the Good Friday mass, and we walked from house to house, being invited in to drink "the waters". The waters are blends of fruit and sugar mixed with lots of water. We were also given ice creams and cookies. This is in reverence to when Jesus carried the cross and was crucified and was very thirsty, and no one would give him a drink. And this was also a definite test of faith, because Americans were strictly advised never, never, never to drink the water. Of course I did anyway, so that tells you something about either me or about San Miguel. But other than for this celebration and in Abelardo's house, you were considered crazy to drink Mexican water.

We were invited into the houses because everyone loved Nita and Abelardo. We even went up to roof-top gardens for cookies- oops, that was at Christmas time. I got it mixed up. Semana Santa is very solemn, and the Christmas walking through the streets and visiting houses is very jolly and is entirely different.

For Semana Santa a woman needs black dresses, which I learned long ago, so I have brought several for such occasions. Here many activities take place in the streets, and one needs to dress respectfully and formally even for the street, when it is some religious devotion that is taking place.

I have brought a gift of black patent-leather flats with black gross-grained ribbons, dressy, but good for the hours of walking that will happen this week. Nita likes them and wears them. She also likes the black and white striped pants I give her that are very soft and never wrinkle. They fit her beautifully and are very much in style. For myself I did not bring my most stylish clothes, because when I go home, I will leave all my clothes here, and how would one of the maids get much use from my fancy ladies luncheon suits, or outfits for dinner at the Yacht Club?

Richard and I tried to change our traveler's checks to pesos yesterday, but the Cambios (money changing places) will not accept traveler's checks until April! Of course, there is always somewhere glad to exchange our traveler's checks for pesos, but their exchange rate is not good for us. So what to do? I use my calculator to figure how much we would lose by going to the other places, and it is at least ten dollars for every hundred! Bah, that is bad, bad. So we will try to go to places that take our credit card. There are places you can use machines, but you can't know the rate of exchange until you put your card in and finalize the transaction. We don't know if the machines also charge a fee, we don't really know how it any of it works, and we don't want to use the machines blind.

Nita, and Richard, and I walk, or rather amble, all over, talking to her friends. That means stopping for ten or fifteen minutes about three times per block. This is a good thing once you re-set your American hurry-up mind to your adopted Mexican mind, but this cannot be done by a force of will. It is an adjustment that has to just gradually happen by itself. Finally you get to really enjoy your re-found attitude. You do not sigh to yourself, "Oh, No, not again," as another friend greets Nita. Instead you think, "Oh, good, this is so much fun". I am remembering old friends and making new friends, and hearing everyone catch Nita up on all the family news is like living in a novel.

We go to mass at El Oratorio, and then we wander all through the market. After a while we find a place that washes laundry for three dollars or $3.50 per load. Nita says that is cheap, cheaper than the other laundries, but it doesn't sound cheap to me.

Richard and I decide to wash our own and divide it like this: I will wash my socks, panties, and light blouses in our bathroom sink. Richard will wash his socks and underpants. His big heavy Levis and other pants can go to the laundry. We will have to figure out how to iron. Darn, we forgot our travel iron. I am so neat and orderly that I always know exactly where everything is, but I put all the accumulated stuff belonging to our son, Bob, into a long cubby-hole at home, and the iron must have gotten pushed to the back. In fact, we used to have two travel irons. Anyway, we didn't bring one, not really thinking much about it.

Nita takes us to where I can get a new watchband and crystal for twenty dollars. It will be ready tomorrow. The band is really pretty. In the states the jewelers all said they don't make that size to fit my watch anymore. I knew I could get it done here. The watch repair shop is very tiny, about the width of a bit more than your out-stretched arms. It has a little glass counter, rows and rows of watches in flat glass cases along the walls, and a dark cluttered tunnel going far back, which I suppose is the repair part, the watch workshop. Little shops like these that do all their own work are called "talleres", and I wouldn't be surprised if they would even build you a watch from scratch. I love these little talleres, and if you find one, you will get a bargain price and excellent workmanship on what you are told is impossible, or costs a fortune, and has to be sent away somewhere for weeks, if you go to repair shops or watch and jewelry shops in the States.

Then Richard and I set out alone to take a "real walk", an exercise walk. We are used to walking for several hours every day.

When we come back, to make friends with Conchita and Raulito, I play cards with them. We play Fish, the American game, which I teach them. I do not know many card games, but we have a lot of fun at Fish.

Delfina and Raúl come to get the kids to take them to Querétaro to see Conchita's nutritionist. They say that it is really working because she used to be fat and is now normal and very pretty, also sweet. I like the children a lot.

Even though comida is only Nita, Richard, and me, we are still served formally, in the dining room of course, and it takes three cooks just to make and serve our meal! Here is the menu:

- Purple "water" made from boiled purple flowers. It tastes like lime juice, or cranberry, or something a little bit sour. Very refreshing.
- Watermelon, which is super-sweet and juicy.
- Cheese soup, very rich.
- A plate of four red enchiladas sprinkled with white goat cheese and minced onions. On the side of the plate are also potatoes and carrots, nopales (chopped cactus of the flat leaf type, if you can say that a cactus has leaves), tiny green hot peppers soaked in olive oil and vinegar.
- A huge salad of lettuce and tomatoes.
- Coffee
- Offers of lots of desserts and other foods which, by now, I am so full, that I cannot eat even one single bite.

Richard is so exhausted by all the walking and eating that he goes right straight up to our room and falls asleep, which is what he is doing now, while I sit on my bed by the window with the fan on me, and I write.

We are very comfortable here in our luxury suite. The bathroom is very funny and makes me laugh. The toilet seat, which is made of plastic and is hollow, doesn't fit right, it is too small for the toilet, and every time you sit down, it slides over, so much that, be careful, or you end up on the floor. Also, the windows open directly upon the person who is seated, giving a view of you like a picture in a frame, to anyone going up or down the outside stairs. These stairs are in use by the people who live in the upstairs apartments, the maids who clean upstairs, do the laundry scrubbing, or hang up the wash on the roof. The children run up and down to see their friends, retrieve balls and toys, and just because they have a lot of energy. The family's two dogs race all over the house, including up and down to see the people and chase the cats, and the workmen and delivery people come and go as well. So we have to remember to keep the "privacy pattern etched" bathroom windows closed. There are no curtains, and that is fine as we don't want any. We like the parade each day, but of course when sitting on the toilet, we don't wish to become part of the entertainment.

At noon Nita and I go to mass. Richard has lost interest in the Holy Week spectacle already. A tiny, elderly lady comes into the church, and naturally she knows Nita. She is dressed entirely in lavender. Her clothes are very stylish, lavender shoes, lavender hat, lavender silk suit, lavender scarf over one shoulder, jewelry, and lots, lots, lots of make-up, but so well done that she looks like a miniature fashion-plate doll. She is about four and a half feet tall, she has a limp, and yet she still presents a portrait of loveliness and grace.

Almost everyone else at mass wears pants and T shirts. For the women who wear jeans, the majority, the jeans are so tight that how can they bear it? The old ladies wear long cotton print dresses, checkered aprons, and rebozos. A "rebozo" is a Mexican long scarf-like shawl, and you can tell a lot about a woman by her rebozo. Modern women wear sweaters or jackets now, but servants and the elderly still use the rebozo. Younger poor women do too. They are good for carrying around the babies that poorer women take everywhere and have to carry all day and night, whatever they are doing. A utilitarian rebozo is usually black rayon woven with a few colored threads, but if you have money, you can buy all colors and qualities for dressy occasions.

There are hardly any Americans or upper-class Mexicans at this mass. It is in El Oratorio again, and I get a warm feeling of all of us there together, especially I feel very included when they do the shaking of hands all around.

Nita will be going to a card party today, after she calls her husband, Jackson, who stayed home in Canada. She forgot to bring a bunch of stuff, and he is supposed to send it down here to her via two of her friends who will be coming here in a couple of days. Nita will call to us so we can walk with her to the party place, and then we will walk around by ourselves. I had planned to start painting today, to get back into practice, but that may have to wait until tomorrow. When Nita returns here, around nine PM, she wants to eat salads together. The cooks have already made the salads, and a friend brought a Jello to Nita that she has been trying to get me to eat. I am sure it will be good. It is made with Carnation Evaporated Milk (which everyone here just calls Carnation, "Do you want some Carnation in your coffee?" like we would say, "Do you want a Coke?"), and also pineapple is in the Jello. There is a big dish of it waiting. It will be very rich, not a salad to me, a dessert is more what I would call it. I am weakening in my resolve not to eat what I don't like, and I do not like desserts and sweets, but Nita is so determined that I should love this so-called salad. What shall I do? I suppose I will take one tiny politeness bite of whatever is put on my plate.

I want to walk and walk. This city is called "Mexican Hill Town" in a very old photographic book we have from the sixties, or from the fifties. Wherever you go, it is either up or down.

Richard and I were planning to go out to dinner tonight, like last night, but since Nita is expecting us to be here, we will stay here and wait for her. We thought that her card party included dinner, but that must have changed.

Last night we walked around looking for a fancy place to just have wine and bread. Then Richard decided he didn't want to walk home in the dark, so after a lot of searching, we ended up going right across the street from our house to a new restaurant. Richard likes to have three huge meals per day, so he ordered a Cuba Libre, a dinner of pork tacos, a red wine, and bread. I had only the bread. Just right. The boiled citrus tree leaves tea ended our wonderful day yesterday. There was enough tea left over for Chita to put into a jar for me and keep it in the refrigerator for tonight. Goodie, not because I like the slimy thickness of the brew, but because of the results. If we are out late, the kitchen will be locked, so before we go anywhere, I will find the jar of tea in the refrigerator and put it in our room. I must be sure that I remember to get it!

Nita calls for us, and we set out for the card party. We walk down deep into a gully many blocks away from our house, and then up, up, up through a very humble section to where a few new multi-million dollar houses are starting to spring up. These so-called streets are packed-down mud, dusty and blowing right now. There are no square blocks or street signs, and all Nita knows is that we are looking for a yellow house. After much searching, we find it, although I don't understand how because it is not yellow, it is red.

We don't care because we had a great walk and an adventure into new territory. Nita doesn't care because here there is no such thing as "late", particularly for Nita. Nita's friend, Isabel, who is really, really pretty and glamorous, invites us in to meet the card club and to see her house. A very well-dressed and friendly group of seventy year old ladies are seated around a special Bingo-Poker table, with snacks everywhere. No one is in the least bothered that Nita is two hours late.

The house is indescribably beautiful. Each room opens to a courtyard filled with glorious flowers, statuary, tiles, grass, fountains, and benches. When I say "opens to", there is actually one whole wall missing from each room. All are open to the free air.

There are many rooms, each furnished in a contemporary elegance, a very comfortable style. We are taken through the many levels up to the third floor where the husband has his art studio. He is a painter who uses a fresh style to create beautiful landscapes. Larry is a former lawyer from Canada, and like his wife, he too is very good looking. Isabel is Mexican, but blond, and is darling in every way. We have a great visit while the ladies remain at their games.

You might wonder how each room that we have seen has one wall entirely open to the free air. Privacy and safety are obtained by the giant walls that surround the entire house. I am not sure, but it is possible that no windows at all open to the street. The only windows in the house face their own multi-layered courtyards. Some of the courtyards are small, some larger. All are of odd shapes, narrow rectangles and triangles, with stairways here and there. There are fountains, many flowering vines, small trees, and endless pots of lavishly flowering, brilliant blossoms. And from the roof-top studio, you can see to the mountains in the distance.

From the street, one sees only three-story high walls, solid and plain. Only the quality of the construction and the strangeness of such a grand structure in a wind-swept, dusty neighborhood gives a clue that inside is a house of wealth and beauty.

While Nita stays, Larry offers to drive Richard and me home, but we want to walk, and this is the right decision. It is warm, and there is a strong breeze. I can see now why all of the women we see have long straight hair, or else the short "I don't want to bother" cuts. It is because the winds blow dust into your hair all day long, so a shampoo is required almost every day. A set would have to be repeated each morning, and that is too bad for me, because I would prefer to have my hair a little bit curled for the style that I think suits me.

Walking back to the house, we decide that Nita probably won't get back from the party until nine, even though she said seven. So we go up to the Jardín (remember, everywhere is either up or down), to sit in front of the cathedral, La Paróquia, for a while. The giant bells are clanging, and there is also a concert of some kind outdoors in front of El Oratorio. The amplified men's voices drift towards us over the three blocks away distance and still are powerful enough to mix with the church bells, as well as with the general hubbub of the town's principal gathering place in the evening. I am wearing a black silk dress, sort of long, with a flounced hem. It has tiny dots of pink, purple, and yellow, and I think it is quite jolly. The evening is fun.

We wait and wait, but no Nita. It is exactly as I have suspected, she never comes. She had insisted so much that, yes, she was coming back, and she wanted to eat with us. We remember that we must give up our Wisconsin ideas about appointments and taking them too seriously.

Finally we go into the kitchen. I am hoping to find some fruit, but instead I find the delicious red sauce left over from the enchiladas at comida. I mix it with ripped up tortillas and heat it in the microwave, but this is a poor substitute for the way the cook makes them, and I am disappointed with what I was drooling for until I tasted it. I give up and don't eat it. Richard eats the Jello made with Carnation. Chita comes in to clean up after us. "Oh, no", I say, "I will do it". "No, no, Señora." She won't hear of it. It is her job, day or night.

So we write a note to Nita telling her where to meet us, that we are going to the Bougainvillea restaurant. When we open the great wooden doors to go out to the street, there, ten inches from our faces, are La Tuna. La Tuna is a wildly popular singing group. They are young men, supposed to be university students, dressed in the satin cloaks and velvet bloomers and tights of the style of university students in Spain in the 1500's. They wear huge, floppy velvet hats, and they carry golden satin embroidered banners. They wander through the streets singing and playing their guitars. They also carry wineskins which make a stream of wine go into the mouth, when desired. People join and follow the group through the streets, so for a little while, we do to. The Instituto Allende here in town is a branch of the University of Guanajuato, and the large, formal university itself, the headquarters, are in the city of Guanajuato, state of Guanajuato, an hour and a half away. Maybe these really are students from the big school.

Nita never comes to join us at the restaurant. When we return home, the family has just arrived from Querétaro, and Nita is there too. She has already changed clothes, but did not notice the big huge note we had stuck on her bedroom door. It doesn't matter, she doesn't care. She had fun, as we did, and we are all in good spirits, sharing our stories.

Chita is also on hand, having opened the big outside doors for the family so that they could bring the van in. They have gone shopping in Querétaro, and Chita hurries to help the family carry in all the stuff. It is now eleven PM. We think that is late, but a servant's day starts around seven in the morning and ends when the family goes to sleep, or maybe later because of cleaning up. This is the way for nannies, housekeepers, and cooks. "Our" family is very good to Chita, and they love her a lot. Never-the-less, we can't help still seeing with Wisconsin eyes and Wisconsin ideas, so to us, her day seems very long.

6

STREET VENDORS, CONCHITA'S ENGLISH LESSONS, AND THE DRINKING OF THE WATERS

We really need to get some money changed! I did not pack any toiletries, thinking that it would be silly to carry all that weight and bulk. I didn't realize that here in San Miguel, lotions, soaps, shampoo, etc. cost double of what it costs in the USA. We are not going to spend our declining cash on that stuff yet, but I need lotion. My hands are so dry.

We go to the Jardín to sit under the trees on the wrought iron benches. Well, not really wrought iron, which means heated, twisted, soldered bars. These benches are iron but are somehow poured into molds, like garden furniture back home. The trees have had their leaves and branches clipped for many years into the shapes of drums on top of trunks. The tree tops are covered with netting to keep the birds out and off. We are disappointed because the calling of the birds, their presence and flutter in the park, are dear to us from all of our previous times here. The new city boss or park boss thinks birds are dirty and doesn't want birds here. There are still a few pigeons strutting around, looking for specks of dropped food, but that is all. The previous bird inhabitants of this park were in multitudes, and their cacophony was one of the "sounds and sights" famous in San Miguel. Combined with the clanging and banging of the church bells, it made a symphony that we treasured, even dreamt about back in the USA.

Also gone are the vendors shouts of "Paletas" (frozen milk and fruit bars on a stick), "Nee uus" (meaning the newspaper in English for Gringos), and "Fresas" (the house to house selling of strawberries, the sweet kind just picked in the fields).

Vendors used to go through the streets every day crying out their products. "Leche" meant tiny metal cups, soup can size containers of goat's milk, all you could get years ago. Goat's milk

THE GREAT HOUSE OF RAÚL RODRÍGUEZ

is relatively disease free, unlike cow's milk. Milk was used for cooking, not drinking, as far as I ever saw. People didn't have refrigeration back then, and cow's milk would have been risky.

"Championes" are fresh, whole mushrooms. "Aspara gooos" shouted out for whole, long, gigantic, fresh spears. Bread was carried up and down the streets for sale in an enormous Mexican hat (worn on the head of course). The brim was turned up at the edges so the hat could be filled with rolls, "Bolillos". Now I guess that in this section of the town, there must be so many rich people that they can send their cooks to the market to do the shopping because we don't see or hear vendors like we used to.

It is not like in Wisconsin to go to the store. There are vegetables, fruits, and eggs for sale at little places every few blocks. Same with bakeries, tortilla making places, and tiny stores that sell rice, and soap, and herbs, and candy. About every three or four blocks there will be one. Cooking and shopping are a major part of the joy of life, done daily, or even more often, and no one appears to think that this is in any way a nuisance. I don't either. I love it. I even love to go to the little store two blocks from here and buy some coffee or a bar of soap, whereas back in the states shopping is a chore- too big, too much, a lot to unload, and a lot to put away. Here items are sold in tiny quantities, for use today, and a standard request of a produce seller is to give you fruit "para hoy", suitable to be served today.

At nine AM I go in to breakfast. Richard is already there having a nice visit with Raúl and Raulito. For breakfast we have OJ, watermelon, heavenly whole-wheat pancakes, and perfectly crisp bacon. Last of all, Nita decides to make her own recipe for pancakes, adding to her batter cottage cheese, zest of lime, and eggs. These are so good that we eat more, even though we supposedly had finished eating breakfast already.

Conchita, Raulito, and I play Fish again. Conchita teaches me about homophones vs. homographs, which I write down in my notebook for our daughter Mary, who is also a Spanish teacher, as I was. Conchita's explanation is about the English language and has nothing to do with Spanish, but I think Mary will get a kick out of what Mexican kids learn when they study English in school.

Here is what Conchita carefully prints out for Mary:

Homophones are words spelled differently, but they sound the same.

Ex: *ate and eight*

Homographs are words spelled the same and sound the same but have different meanings.

Ex:

Sow: Feminine pig.

Sow: To put seed.

Dove: A bird.

Dove: Past of dive.

Row: A confusion.

Row: To move a conuu.

I know, these example words do not sound the same, but I am showing what Conchita wrote, and I think she did pretty well. The word that might puzzle you, conuu, is canoe. Cute! Also she made tiny illustrations of each example.

I plan to play with the children a little each day because I like them, and also our playtime will be when we practice English. They are eager to practice English, and of course I prefer to speak Spanish all the time, so this compromise makes everybody happy. At their school, which naturally is private, morning classes are in English, and the second section of the school day is in Spanish.

Nita and Conchita and I go to noon mass at the same church as before. There is a children's choir in the balcony, an ancient, rickety structure that groans and squeaks. There is an organ playing too, and the combination is ethereal, beautiful, entrancing. The music and chanting go on all through the mass. The sun is streaming in, and next the whole congregation is singing and chanting too. It is hypnotic, dreamy, otherworldly.

Back outside, we shop for more nopales, which Nita craves. She also wants to buy tennis shoes. Nita and Conchita stop to buy sweet yogurt drinks, but I go back home to find Richard and to go for a walk. We go to the French Park.

When Richard and I return to the house, Chita the cook tells me that we will have Chile Rellenos for lunch! Oh, yippee! We love those.

We finish lunch, and I resolve that I must stop eating all that I am served. The food is so good that I have been eating double, maybe triple, of what I have at home. We are served many courses here, and each one is so big. Just one of the courses served here would be an entire meal back in Wisconsin. Yet we are served three or four courses for breakfast (plus orange juice, the juice of several oranges per glass), five courses for comida, and then we eat again at merienda, the nine o'clock evening meal. And juices or fruit waters at comida and merienda. I eat everything, everything, until my stomach hurts.

So you will understand, here is today's meal:

- Grapefruit halves.
- Orange juice.
- Mussels on crackers.
- A chile relleno with rice and beans on the side.
- Hot tortillas.
- Dessert – the only part I ever skip.

Oh, well, now we are going walking, which is really strolling, to "Tomar las Aguas" to "Drink the Waters". These will be the sweetened juices mixed with water in a blender, and we will also be served ice creams and cookies. Not at just one home, but at all the homes that we visit! Here is how this outside ritual works, and it takes many hours, from now until late evening. Because everyone in town can participate, the pace of the activities varies from family to family.

First we go to a different church, not El Oratorio. This time Richard is with us because all of the family has come. Nita shows us how to buy offerings for the special mass. During the mass, each time the choir sings, a group walks down the aisle and puts their offerings on the tables in the front to be blessed and then used by the priests. Our offering is wine. In between each offering and the singing there are sermons, in total, a lot of sermons. I can understand sermons when there is not too much echo, and when the microphones do not scratch and squeal, so I enjoy all of this service. I have supposed that this service is a mass, but then I find out that this lengthy ceremony is just a prelude to the mass.

The offerings are brought almost one hundred per cent by little old ladies and women of my age, and a few little girls who are holding their grandmother's hands. Not until the end do the men come forward, and then only a very few. I guess men are not very religious.

The choices of offerings to buy and put on the tables are:

- Charcoal.
- Incense.
- Candles (large red ones).
- Rose petals and little watering cans filled with cologne, a lot of which gets spilled, so the church smells quite sweet.
- Wine for the mass, for the sacrament. We come forward with this group.
- Lilies.
- Palm leaves about ten feet tall.

Mass starts off in quite a leisurely way, but after an hour and twenty minutes, the priest says, "Bring everything down now. It is getting late". So the end is a hurried rush forward like a grand finale.

Richard has already skipped out, not wanting to hear the mass that he will not understand, plus we are not Catholic, but he comes back in time to see us do our part at the big finish.

On our way home, we pass beautiful altars and people give us paletas. We have to take a break from today's ritual and go home because Conchita, the daughter, is making home-made pizza. I help a little.

Conchita is so sweet, and she asks me what I like, then makes the pizza that way. Mozzarella cheese, sour white goat cheese covered with black something (which gives the pizza a great flavor) sliced turkey hot dogs (which causes a lot of controversy at the table-- are the hot dogs forbidden, or aren't they, on the Friday of María Dolorosa? Is turkey a meat (forbidden) or not? I guess not, because everybody eats it. Also pizza sauce, sliced tomatoes, "Y qué más?", What else? I don't know, because I go upstairs to put on warm pants and a sweater for our night's walk.

The pizza is so thick that it takes much longer than expected to cook, so by the time we finish eating, and the whole family is assembled together, it is probably 9:30 instead of 8:00. I don't care because Conchita went to so much work that I like it that everyone honors her by not complaining that we are running pretty late. Also, the pizza is delicious.

We all set out together, finally, to Take the Waters: Delfina, Raúl, Conchita, Raulito, Nita, Richard, and I. Altars have been made all over town. Some are little and are viewed through the bars of an open window, the altar being in the family's living room. Others are big, occupying an entire patio or a whole of a living room. Since everyone in town is invited to enter wherever there is a display, the houses are crowded to bursting with people trying to get in and see the displays, then to get out again. There are lines and crowds around the outsides of the houses too. Therefore, I am surprised by how long Nita and Delfina linger inside each house, with the rest of us staying too, to be polite. This is sincere devotion and not a time to hurry. Nita cries at just about every altar, because of how religious she is, or sentimental, or both.

A basic altar is like this, with infinite variations:

The Virgin Mary crying. She can be life-sized or little, a statue or a painting, an antique owned by the church, or belonging to the family, or new.

Jesus on the cross, or leaning against a pillar being whipped, or carrying the cross, or anything from the crucifixion drama.

Other Biblical characters, such as Romans or saints.

Lots of candles, all lit.

Sour oranges, which represent bitterness, which I suppose is gall.

Tiny wild daisies, Manzanilla, in huge profusion, laid out flat on the floor. These smell wonderful and the flower heads are later boiled to make a stomach ache remedy tea.

Roses, long stemmed, large. Roses represent the Virgin Mary.

Very little trays of dirt growing tall wheat which is still yellow because it is young. Wheat represents the bread of communion, The Last Supper.

Music playing, which is the choir and the organ from the mass in church on the Day of Santa María Dolorosa. This is the same song sung everywhere, sung only on this day each year. I didn't understand the words, but it is very pretty and haunting.

Some houses have floors with "carpets" made of spread out sand, and then covered with colored sawdust.

Other things too. I don't remember what. Oh, yes, golden flags on toothpicks stuck into the bitter oranges, representing The

Ascension? The Annunciation?

We walk all over, up and down many streets, and we see about fifteen altars. We all agree on which ones are our favorites.

High up on Barranca Street, is a very old tableaux, home-made, using many scenes from the Bible. The figures are little, about ten inches high, made by hand, and moved by someone crawling under the table and pulling strings or turning a crank. It is primitive, sincere, and complex. What a contrast to the first visit, near our house, another Great House, owned by a cousin of the family. In this, the whole patio has just a beautiful Virgin Mary, almost life-sized, surrounded by lots and lots of candles, flowers, with lights on the patio's fountain, creating an elegant and lovely spiritual atmosphere- of Heaven?

About eleven thirty we come home. Nita is quite disappointed that we hadn't started at eight o'clock because by the time we got there, many of the altars were already closed. But to me, I liked everything exactly the way it was. I fall asleep in bed, after hearing the cathedral's great bells, announcing that it is midnight.

7

WHAT DAY IS IT?

Yesterday was not Good Friday! That will be next week! Because of all the ceremonies and fuss, I thought that it must have been Good Friday. I just go wherever Nita says to go and do whatever she does. I am like a baby. I guess that Holy Week lasts for two weeks here. At home all we do is go to church on Easter, and then my family gets together for a giant ham dinner with lemon meringue pies that I make for dessert. So I don't have any Holy Week calendar in my head. Holy Week is called "Semana Santa", which I will say from now on. Anyway, the name of yesterday was "María Dolorosa", or "La Virgin Dolorosa", or something like that. "Dolorosa" means painful, The Suffering of the Virgin Mary.

It is a nice idea. The celebration is all about how Jesus' mother must have suffered to see her son beaten, misunderstood, tortured on the cross, and killed. This is true. No one but Jesus could have known of his final triumph over death and the glory of his continued and still continuing mission.

After the mass, we see the most darling, little, tiny, short, stout lady. She is of the old style, wearing a servant's apron and a rebozo, her white hair in a long thick braid down her back, and she is carrying a brightly colored plastic woven shopping bag, the kind all criadas used to carry.

Nita recognizes her, and we all hug a great deal. Richard kisses her hand in a very courtly style. She is so happy about this gesture that she gets a huge smile, grabs his hand, and rubs it all over her face. So sweet! Then she takes my hands and holds them for a long while. She is very warm.

I want to buy her a new cane because the one she has is broken and taped together with duct tape, and I can't stand duct tape, even though it often saves the day. But like so many things that I want to do, I can't figure out how to buy her one on the spur of the moment.

Later today I am surprised and happy to see her sitting on the ledge of a building near the church, eating a torta and drinking a bottle of cheap red sugar water. I stop and say, "Oh, Buenos Días", and she says, "Oh, please excuse my eating. I have not eaten yet today".

I say, "Hay necesidad?" which means, "Are you too poor to afford the basic necessities?" She says yes, in a very round-about-way. We don't have enough change to be of any use, so we give her a twenty peso bill, about two dollars and twenty cents, US. She is so grateful that it is hard for me not to cry. To pay us back, she tells me about the masses that will be held today, although I don't try to remember it all because Nita will tell me everything, and by now we want to go home. Richard is not interested in masses, and I am, but only "hasta cierto punto", to a certain point.

8

OLD LADIES, BEGGARS, AND MUSICIANS

First we have another great breakfast, of course. O.J., the sweetest, juiciest papaya, scrambled eggs with chopped tomatoes in them, tortillas, hot green sauce (hot means "picante", burns your tongue), and "bolillos calientes", buns (heated), split, and spread with butter, which I don't take, but Richard takes two. Coffee at the end, from the new coffee maker, with everyone giving an opinion on how many spoons of coffee will make the most perfect result.

Then we walk with Nita as she goes to the hairdresser for a perm. The beauty shop is far in the back of a beautiful restaurant which is in a hidden courtyard with three stories of balconies completely surrounding the patio. The balconies are all of black wrought iron, and every foot of the railings have attached to them hundreds, yes, I think hundreds, of clay pots containing a million bright flowers and cascading vines. The rooms behind the balconies are private apartments. What a great chance for us to discover another secret, beautiful place!

But Nita decides that she wants to go home to take her insulin instead of getting a perm and goes to the hair dresser to tell her to scratch the appointment. Richard and I say we will walk to the tip-top of the town. We wander around some very steep streets until we get to the very top, which is predictably being built with new rich people's houses. Very swanky. It is wonderful that this entire town preserves the traditional Colonial architecture. There is a great view, and we find a little place where we can sit on someone's step and admire it. The return down the hill only takes about ten minutes, after the climb that seemed so long.

We go shopping. We buy one small bag of powdered laundry soap, one shampoo, one notebook, and one small shaving cream. It costs eighty pesos! The average poor working person earns three hundred pesos per week, Raúl has told us. How can they live? This is terrible.

We give money all the time to beggars, who usually are old women. We usually give two pesos, which means twenty-five cents U S currency. We see a very old lady with a cane picking up glasses of fruit water left here and there around the street from last night. She is drinking what is left in them. Imagine! I say to Richard, please give me five pesos for her, so he does, of course.

On one hand, we think that we can't go around giving a total of about five American dollars to beggars every single day. But on the other hand, why can't we? I figure it out. That would only come to two hundred and ten dollars by the end of our time in San Miguel. At home I give fifty dollars per week to my church, so I guess I can afford two hundred and ten dollars to give a tiny bit of help for a tiny minute to some poor, gnarled, weather-beaten, poverty-stricken, pathetic old, very old, ladies.

Richard gets change for me every day, for giving away, and then I forget to bring it, and then I have to ask him for more. I guess I better go to the bank and get my own change and start being more responsible.

We look at adding this new expense to our budget like this-- we buy some plastic hangers, and we will now wash all of our underwear and socks ourselves, so that saves the three dollars from the laundromat, "la lavandería".

I also pick up my watch from getting fixed, and it costs thirty pesos less than what they told me it would be. I can't figure out why. It is perfect! In the U S A I had taken the watch to jewelry stores, and all said, "Impossible, out of date". Naturally I knew that they could fix it here, so I brought it with me. It was an expensive watch. The gold band broke, and so did the crystal after being run over by cars in the parking lot of Frank's Foods for three days. (I kept praying that someone would find my lost watch and turn it in to the store, and the store would call me, and finally they did.) It still runs fine, and now it looks gorgeous with a fine new band of beautiful, delicate, flat gold to match the brushed gold watch.

So see, giving to a poor old lady has already been paid back to me, and more, five minutes after the deed was done! That is how the world gives to us.

Lunch is another big hit.

- Fruit water of something unknown heretofore.
- Jícama - juicy, sweet, crispy. Over it we squeeze fresh limes and add salt and red chile powder. Jícama looks sort of like a potato. It is peeled and sliced and eaten raw.
- Soup of gazpacho made like this: Thin, tasty tomato broth. Bowls of add-it-yourself chopped green peppers, chopped hard boiled eggs, chopped cucumbers. You squeeze in limes and add a little vinegar.
- White sour goat cheese on soda crackers.
- Stew of ground beef with onions, potatoes, and a long, narrow, sweet, red chile.
- White rice.
- Boiled beans.
- Tortillas with chopped nopales, onions, and tomatoes. Add lime juice and chile powder.
- Coffee.

Then I give the metric converters to the kids, and we play conversions. It is fun. Conchita helps me with her computer to make my own email address. It takes a long time and costs twenty dollars per year. I hope that she doesn't accidentally sign me up to buy other things because I don't understand how to avoid all the offers that come onto the screen while one is trying to send a letter. I send a letter to Bob, our son, and free (I hope free) Easter cards to Bob and Mary, and then a letter to Mary, our daughter.

We go walking, Richard, Nita, Conchita, and I. I ask Conchita to walk us to her school, and she does. We go through Casa Sautto to show them where I used to live while a college student. I am thrilled to see my old room is still the same. All of Casa Sautto is the same. And since it looked at least two hundred years old back in the sixties, I am guessing that "still the same" is all the more impressive. This makes me feel nice, nice, nice. Raulito has joined us during this part.

We come back home to wait for supper. But we decide to go out to a restaurant together. We like dressing up and going out. Nita joins us, and we have in mind somewhere beautiful, popular, tranquil, but this is not to be. Crossing through the Jardín, in front of La Paróquia (the cathedral) are many people, all very happy.

Mariachis lean against the wall, hoping to be hired. Other Mariachis have been paid and are playing, and the music is beautiful. Nita is excited and keeps hoping that they will play "El Mariachi Loco Quiere Bailar", in which all the musicians jump forward, backward, and around. They don't play it, but we feel great anyway.

Richard says, "Here comes a procession". It is another group of Tunas, followed by a crowd. They go up to the bandstand in the center of the Jardin and play on the steps. But they don't play the usual Tuna songs, which I don't particularly like. Instead they play in the style of " Trío Los Panchos", which I love.

When I hear Trío Los Panchos, I am always with Abelardo again, having a very late steak dinner at El Patio, the only luxury restaurant in San Miguel at that time. The courtyard was open to the stars, filled with flowers and gentle breezes, we were always dressed up and eating by candle light, and the trio of guitarists who sang Trío Los Panchos style would approach our table and serenade us. Then Abelardo would ask me to dance, and we would sway and step upon the rough stones of the garden floor.

If you don't know about Trío Los Panchos, they had three guitars. One a little tiny one that is plucked to sound like a harp. The second, a giant, a guitarón. And the third, regular, for the melody. All sang, and I would advise you to listen to their music if you want to know anything about the romantic soul of the Mexicans.

El Patio once hosted two famous guests, Bridget Bardot and Jeanne Moreau, and I know this is true because someone came running up to Abelardo and me one hot afternoon excitedly telling us that if we wanted to see the most famous of the movie star beauties to get over to El Patio right now! We did and were seated at the table next to them. Abelardo ordered comida for us, and we got to bask in the wonder of their presence. I even saw La Bardot up close when she came into the ladies room while I was washing my hands. Naturally Abelardo assured me that I was far more beautiful than even those two famous ones, but all that I can claim is that I was certainly more innocent. Such was the charm of El Patio that everyone in town took it for granted that it would be exactly the place where a movie star should come. And lucky for the movie stars if they did!

Naturally, with these memories and more, I am delighted that La Tuna is playing in the Jardín tonight, as I have described, in the style of Trío Los Panchos. Members of La Tuna, always in their costumes, are passing around and selling little white ceramic jugs with a spout. They pour wine into the spout, and one drinks by tipping the jug so the wine flows into your open, greedy mouth. The wine always seems to be red, and young men think it is funny to glug down a lot, choke a little bit, have the mess splash over your face and clothes, or if you are really able, to open the throat and let the whole jug get emptied right down into your stomach with no interruptions. And no pleasure, from my point of view, plus I would never drink from a spout that is getting passed around from one stranger to another! Ugh! But the music is beautiful, and everyone is having fun.

Nita wants us to eat at the restaurant Mama Mía. We can hear the electronic boom, boom, boom, thump, thump, thump from a block away. "No, Nita", I say. "It is too loud."

"Oh, no", says Nita. "It will be fine. It is very nice."

"No", I say. "No, no, no. We don't like this."

"Oh, it will be good", says Nita. "Let's go in, eh?"

This arguing goes on and on and ends with Nita going in despite anything we say, so we have to follow her, so not to be rude. "Look", I say, "All these are very young. This is not our kind of place. We don't like it". It is crowded with twenty-five year olds pouring in, blasting electronic music, of the kind Richard and I have never liked, even when we were twenty-five year olds ourselves. Now don't get me wrong, we both love rock-and-roll, and we still like the new, live rock bands, but not this music, and especially, since we have never been bar people, we don't like this atmosphere.

"No", I say, "We have to leave". And I win!

But I don't win by much. She goes into the restaurant right next door. It is not very pretty, and not our kind of place either, but Nita is very determined and forceful, and of course she is my sister and my friend, and that is why I say ok so much. This place has very shrill, jazzy, recorded flute music. Richard can't stand it anymore than I can, and now there is a struggle. We are happy that Nita is having such a good time, but that is not enough for her. We have to be convinced to admit that we really love this music as fervently as she does. This is too much.

"Nita", I say, "Everyone does not have to like the same thing." We are butting heads.

"Well, I like everything!" Nita has the last word.

Things get worse. Live musicians start, and we are right in front of them, and also right in front of the amplifier. The music is the same flute jazz, playing right into the microphone, so we can't hear to talk. That is, I am the one who can't hear Nita talk, because she completely ignores Richard and talks only to me. I try and try to bring Richard into the conversation, but it doesn't work.

So I say, "I am so sleepy. Let's go home" On the way I think, we simply need to get more adjusted to each other, but in retrospect I think that the typical best friends thing has happened. You like each other so well that you spend all of your time together, and all of a sudden you have over-done it, so you create a break of your relationship so that you can take a break from each other. Not a good-bye, but a rest, a time apart. But I don't see that at this moment, and I decide that I must relax more and forget about "my way" or "her way". Richard gets lots of breaks from both of us, so it is not such an issue for him.

9

PALM SUNDAY, AND, OH, NO,
I MAKE CONCHITA CRY!

Yes, it really is Palm Sunday, not like when I thought it was Good Friday but it really wasn't. This time I knew to ask.

Nita says that at seven this evening there will be a procession of palm fronds and carrying the statue of Jesus Riding the Burro through the streets - Jesus entering Jerusalem. I say, "Oh, it will be fun". This hurts Nita's feelings, and she says, "Well, for me it is not fun. It is serious. It is devotion." I explain, "Well, fun to me is joyous, and God's glory and love are joyous. That is what I mean by fun." Then Nita feels fine and says, "Oh, ok, I can see that. Ok, I agree."

Although I am not Catholic and do not agree with all their doctrine, I feel united anyway. I love the Spirit of Love that "they" and "we" are all seeking and trying to express. I love the churches, and the ceremonies, and the people as a beautiful, creative, imaginative way of expressing and sharing gratitude, a love of goodness, an appreciation of beauty. And the Catholics are so generous to share all that they have, all of these activities, with everyone who wants to look, listen, or participate. I love being invited and going with Nita. If it weren't for her, I would not know where to go, or when, plus also I like doing all the doings together. On anything religious or "típico" (typical of native customs), I like to be the follower and do what I am told, like a little child. All of the Holy Week stuff is on Nita's territory, and I am grateful and very much enjoy being included. It's hard to explain to her that my own religion leans to the rejoicing but pretty much does not include a lot of religious crying. I think on the rest of it, we are more or less united.

The maids are on vacation. I guess they took the bus to the Ranchos where they live. I believe they took with them the clothes that I gave them. I hope the clothes will be gifts that they enjoy.

Conchita plans to prepare the breakfast today. She asked me last night if I would like pancakes made with chocolate chips and syrup. I say, "No, but you go ahead and make them, and I will have a taste". Then she suggests oatmeal. I say, "For me, just papaya because I can't get it in the States. But for everyone else, you cook what you want. You cook, and I will wash the dishes". So that is our plan. Especially after I find out that the pants that I brought to give away because they were way too loose are now tight. Oh, no. These "loose" pants are now all I can even squeeze into. Yipe!

It is 9:30 AM. Richard and I awaken usually at 6:30. I read my Christian Science Bible Lesson, we drink coffee, talk, shower, etc. I have plenty of time to write in my journal, and about 9:00 we come down and wait for breakfast. I have the feeling that today the family will sleep pretty late. Usually Raúl and Delfina are barely awake at 9:00, although every day the kids have been leaving for school in time for the classes which start at 8:30. Maybe Delfina gets up and does all the getting them ready and then goes back to bed? I do not know.

I am all dressed up for mass. I love all of the music, and singing, and chanting, and babies crying, and people sounds of entering and leaving, kneeling, standing, sitting, the drone of the priest, the birds trapped and flying high in the nave, the street sounds slightly drifting in, the echoes. I love the sounds that are all at once, but complement each other.

I love the look of it all, the splendor of the churches, which to me are far more wonderful than the cathedrals of Europe. The Mexican churches are like the European cathedrals in their structure, enormity, design, floor plan, soaring heights, dropped chandeliers, pillars, columns, domes, vaulted arches, buttresses outside, and decorations.

The Mexican Colonial churches are different though, in that they are more exuberant, lavish, more covered with gold, altogether more intense, be it with having more dead people stuff, such as glass coffins displaying dead saints covered with wax, painted, and fully clothed, or more really bloody crucifixes, or more statues of saints and martyrs. Also, the Mexican churches are more darling in colors - baby pinks, pastel lime greens, and lavender stone for the pillars and walls. Pinks and whites and yellows are in the tiles (azuelos). There are many, many cherubs and angels, huge golden frames, highly decorated altars everywhere you look, each laden with burning candles, flowers, oranges, and offerings.

The enormous oil paintings that are hung high up, including near the tops of the domes, are usually antiquities painted in somber colors of solemn personages, maybe saints? Famous Catholics?

To me, it is the best show in town, to go to the most attended of the masses at the biggest, fanciest of the churches. I love it! And that is where we will go today.

Meanwhile, it is a beautiful, warm day. Richard and I are seated in the patio of the house listening to the caged parrots and to the birds that fly around freely. One of the parrots is young, and the other is over one hundred years old. Raúl knows for sure because the family already had that parrot when his mother's mother was born, around 1905, like my own mom. The parrot is still just fine, except to me it is a sin to put a bird, or any other creature, into a cage.

To me sin means doing anything without Love, because I am using Love as a synonym for God. "Do unto others" includes every living creature—birds, animals, insects, snakes, all. "Sin" in Spanish means "without". I think "sin" in English means acting without Love. Would I like to be a "pet", kept in a cage? How can anyone think that a captive actually likes it?

We should have told the family that we did not need to have breakfast today, because maybe they don't usually eat breakfast on Sundays? Maybe this is their only day to sleep late? Next Saturday, we decide, we will buy a papaya and take knives, forks, and plates to our room. Then when we wake up on Sunday, we can have a breakfast of coffee and papaya on the roof and not bother anyone. Hmmm.

Nita went to the bakery across the street yesterday to get pan (bread) for today's breakfast. She said they were totally sold out! She bought the few items they had left which were three huge whole-wheat triangles, really light and delicious, and several large round cookies made of lard and coconut, which of course I would not eat, and that is because of all the lard and sugar, not because of the coconut. No, I would not eat those on a bet.

Today Conchita wants to take me to the market. I don't want to buy anything, but I will enjoy looking and being with her. I don't like to drag Richard along to where he doesn't want to go, nor do I like to leave him alone to just hang around and wait for me. Maybe he can do his art. I want Richard to have fun. He has the right to decide where we go and what we do at least half the time. It seems like I am always deciding everything whenever Nita is not making the plans. I feel like I am treating him out of balance.

There are two darling pet doggies here. One, Turis (Turipitis) is named after the dog from when Richard and I had our apartment here on the roof the summer of 1969. The other is Max. Turis is a puppy, but he is so calm and good that it is hard to believe that he is a puppy. Turis is golden and looks like a sheared cocker spaniel. Max is black and old and looks just like Turis, except Max is smaller.

The doggies are best friends and play, greet everyone, follow people around up and down the stairs, and hang out in the patio. They can never leave the house because the outside is way too busy and is filled with car traffic every minute. The streets are one car wide with sidewalks that accommodate one person only, yet they are crammed with single-file pedestrians, moms and babies, grandmothers also carrying one baby and holding the hand of another child, and everyone is always stepping down into the traffic all the time. No one cares, no one honks, and all drivers stop constantly and politely gesture for you to cross in front of them wherever and whenever you wish. All people are gentle and kind to each other, at least as far as who we see and meet.

The family comes out of their private apartment which is on the other side of the patio from the dining room. It is ten o'clock. Everyone seems to be helping with breakfast, since as I said, all the servants are gone. There are no oranges, so Raulito and Conchita take me with them to the nearby frutería. We buy two bags full of oranges, full, full, full, to the point where Raulito decides that this is exactly how much he can carry. I also want a papaya, and Conchita wants two avocados. The bill is forty-four pesos, and this is just for one day's breakfast, not including the cost of the eggs, pan (bread), and tortillas. Remember that the average daily wage is 300 pesos per week, and that is for an eight hour day, five days per week, which often even include extra hours. Such a Mexican worker would have to support a whole family on this little income. Yet Americans still believe that Mexico is cheap, and that is why it is ok for servants to be paid practically nothing. Well, just go into any store and buy food, or soap, or the cheapest clothes and shoes in the market, and see how "cheap" it is.

We bring the food into the kitchen. Nita is wearing the new robe that I bought for her over her clothes. She is cooking omelets with cheese, and the robe has huge grease spots all over it. Each spot is orange and looks suspiciously like long finger wipes culminating in big hand marks. Darn! That robe was very fine. It is white with tiny rosebuds, has lace trim all around the neck and front, and is threaded with pink silk ribbons. Why would you wear that, brand new, for wiping your hands on like an apron while you are cooking omelets? Naturally you can tell how I feel about that, but once a gift is given, the giver cannot dictate about it, even if the giver (me), would really like to!

Conchita, Raulito, and I make a production line for fixing the orange juice. Conchita washes one of the bags of oranges with soap and water, and I cut them in half. Raúl squeezes them with the little spinning electric squeezer and throws the rinds in the garbage. I pour the juice into the big serving jar each time the juicer machine container fills up.

Conchita washes an apple and a pear. Here everything is washed with soap and water and a little scrubber before doing anything else, even though now the apple and pear will be peeled. Nita cuts up this fruit and puts it into three large, shallow bowls. She covers the fruit with dry oatmeal and then adds condensed milk. These are cooked in the microwave. I consider the portions huge. They are for Nita, Conchita, and Raulito, except Raulito changes his mind once his is ready and doesn't want his. No one cares at all.

I cut up the papaya, and Conchita gives the seeds to the one hundred year old parrot. Nita says not to give fruit or seeds to the parrot. (Remember that this was Nita's home for all of her life, and the parrot was her parrot too.) Conchita says they always give the seeds and fruit to the parrot. Delfina says that she doesn't know what the parrots eat.

Nita makes an omelet for Richard but then sees that he hasn't eaten his papaya yet. He still mistakenly believes that we are to wait for everyone to be served. "No", she says, "You must eat your papaya first". She whisks away his omelet and puts it at Raulito's place, even though Raulito has not entered the dining room yet. We think this is strange, but that is because we haven't caught on to proper etiquette yet. After all, we want to be taught, so we better pay attention, but at this moment we are still baffled. As soon as Richard obediently eats his papaya, Nita makes him an excellent new omelet. The point is to prepare each dish for the optimum perfection, a great courtesy and expression of caring and good manners.

I know that the omelet is delicious because I always take a bite of his food if I am not having any myself. I have to decline because my buttons are stretching and straining from eating so much every day. I have juice and papaya. Delfina comes in and has hot cakes and syrup. No one here cares how much work it is to cook so many different things. We think that is nice. At home, I always cook three different dinners, because I really like to please everybody, even though no one demands it, so I am not particularly surprised by all of today's extra trouble.

It is a wonderful day! Except there is one sad part that I will tell in a minute. Well, I hope that it is not too sad.

First, though, we go to the noon mass at La Paróquia: Nita, Conchita, Raulito, and I. Conchita tells me we should buy palm fronds to take into the church. When the palms have holy water put on them by the priest, then you take them home and put them by the door, and you won't have burglars. I will have to find out why palm leaves prevent robbers from coming into your house.

The old-fashioned types of Mexican men and women are sitting on the flat stone sidewalk in front of the church and in the church courtyard. They are selling palm leaves and the same flowers as during María Dolorosa, "Manzanilla", the tiny white flowers that smell so good.

By "old-fashioned", I mean the way Mexicans used to look back in 1963. They are very small, very dark, with thick black hair and beautiful eyes. The children and babies with the venders are also very tiny and beautiful. I, who am only 5' 2", used to be taller than most of the Mexican men in the old markets. I think two things:

The smallest people were from small-bodied original Indian

groups, called indigenous peoples.

Food now, especially milk, makes middle and upper-class children grow much taller, because we see it happening all over the world.

Another thing I mean about old-fashioned is dress. These women that I am seeing here today still wear a dress style that has a fitted bodice and a long, gathered skirt. Or a flower print blouse with a plaid skirt. Over this is an apron that covers the shoulders, bust, and front of the skirt. These are of little checks in red and white, green and white, or blue and white. I have several of these aprons myself and want to buy more. They are for the serious cook, or here for keeping the clothes from having to be washed so often. You would wear this protection too if you had to wash all of your clothes by hand.

Hair for old-fashioned women of any age is worn in two braids, often tied at the ends of the braids in back with a ribbon so the braids don't flop forward. Little girls' hair is straight, long,g and pulled back in pony tails.

What everyone is selling today are palm fronds which have been braided, twisted, and woven into a multitude of fantastic designs, sort of the way we used to weave flat plastic strips into whistle chains and bracelets in Brownie Day Camp when I was little. Except the palm creations are complicated and fanciful. They cost five pesos, or small simple crosses cost only three pesos. Some are elaborate, or covered with glitter, or religious ornaments are glued on. It seems like everyone in the crowds buys one, or maybe one per family. Conchita buys one for herself, one for her brother, and one for me. She also buys handfuls of the flowers.

There are huge crowds trying to get into La Paróquia. We finally sneak past everyone, led by Nita, and walk all the way down the aisle to the front, looking for seats. Of course there aren't any. Nita walks right up to the railing of the platform that is for giving the mass, where we put the kids in front of us along with all the other little kids who have been sent forward to get a better view. I tower over the standing-room-only ladies and feel like a giant. Many must only be four feet tall, judging by their heights compared to me.

Mass has already started. In the center of the stage (really it is the big altar platform, but I don't know the specific name for that) are seated, left-to-right, a youngish priest in an all-white cassock, a white-haired "major player" type priest in a red cassock over a white shirt. Two other older dark-haired priests are next and are dressed the same. Seated along the right wall are older women dressed in red blouses and white skirts (or maybe vice versa). On the left wall, standing or leaning, are altar boys of various ages, also in red and white. They are chubby darlings.

The three major priests stand and take turns reading the Bible. The microphones are good, and the priests speak clearly. Plus I already am very familiar with the chapters they are reading, so it is easy to follow. It is all regarding Jesus' entrance into Jerusalem on Palm Sunday and continues on through the crucifixion.

When it is kneeling time, Nita and I join the group of children in kneeling on the floor, and for sitting time, we sit on the floor too. Except now "we" means the children and me. I do not know that I am the only adult who sits during times when the children are sitting. When I see that the other adults are standing, I stand too. And I finally understand what they are saying when everyone stretches out their arms, palms upward. It is The Lord's Prayer, so I stretch out my arms too, and it feels great, because I have often prayed like that when I am alone.

Raulito thinks it is funny that I am getting the sitting-kneeling-standing requirements all wrong and plays a cute little-kid trick on me. A priest comes up to the railing, where we are, swinging the incense and producing clouds of smoke. Raulito tells me, "Now you must put your hand into the smoke". So I believe him and I do so, because my back is to everyone else, and I can't see whatever the other people do. But no one else does it, and Raulito laughs. I laugh too, because I like practical jokes.

The service is very long with lots of prayers and singing and Bible. I love it. Afterwards I ask Nita what red and white means. She says, "Joy".

We enter the Jardín, and Conchita wants to buy me some candy. There is a tiny stand selling all kinds of candy for children, and the one Conchita picks is the kind that I have told her Mary likes.

We sent Mary to Puebla to live with a Mexican family and attend Mexican school and Mexican Catholic catechism classes when she was ten years old. People are shocked by that for many reasons. "Are you going to send a little child away from her home and family all by herself to live in a foreign country? You are not Catholic, why would you let her go to a different church than your own religion? Aren't you afraid that she will convert? Get lost? Cry all the time and be lonely? Do you want to get rid of her? Why won't you miss her? How do you dare let her miss school at home? Did you get permission?" friends and strangers asked us.

When Mary turned ten, we had a little imp of an eleven year old Mexican girl live at our house for a school year, and she and Mary became best friends. Naturally I got to know the parents by phone, and when the family invited Mary to come home with Emi, we said, "Sure, great, and be sure to do the whole thing, go to Mexican school, Mexican church, eat what the family eats, and be a little Mexican girl for a few months!" Mary loved it, and in a few weeks she really did start to be a little Mexican kid in every way, which began stories in themselves, about Mary's international life while still a child.

Conchita by now knows all of this and is very interested in Mary. So Conchita wants to buy her a present. The candy selected is popular with fourth and fifth graders. It is hot chili powder mixed with powdered Jello. One shakes it together, pours some on the palm, and licks it up.

Conchita is in fifth grade and eats it herself, so she thinks I should try it. Conchita doesn't have any money, so the vendor says, "Take it, as a gift. Take it". Nita tries to pay, but the man says, "No, it is a gift". I am not carrying money, but I say, "The candy is for me. I will come back and bring some money and pay". "No, no", and finally we take it. This man is very old. He has about two teeth, gnarled hands, very humble clothing, and feet that show that he has probably grown up not being able to afford shoes. His candy stand is so little, tiny, and yet he is generous.

This generosity is typical. I have never seen Mexicans take out an item of food or drink for themselves without offering it all around to share first. This is not an empty gesture. Others will take of what is offered, even if it means ripping one stick of gum into enough pieces for everyone. I once sat on a third class bus next to a very poor person. It was a long trip. He unwrapped his little torta from its clean bandana wrapping, ripped the torta in half, and handed half to me, even though that would be all he had to eat for the entire trip. It would be mean to refuse. When I could, in response to such a gesture, because this happens often, I would then try to purchase something for the two of us, but usually I was taken unaware, and nothing was available for me to buy and share.

(If you are wondering, a sandwich is made with sliced bread, and a torta is a bolillo cut in half. The typical torta has ham, cheese, lettuce, mayonnaise. But a poor person's torta will be filled only with mashed beans - cheap and nutritious. Tortas are preferred by poor people because you can purchase bolillos one at a time, instead of having to buy an entire loaf of bread, so tortas are cheaper.)

After the candy, we come home. I say to Nita that Richard has been waiting for so long that I will take a walk with him. "When should we be back?" I ask. "Four o'clock", she says.

Richard and I walk all over, staying on the shady sides of the streets. At four o'clock we are back. I put on my dress and sandals because the day before Nita has told us that we will all be going out to eat enchiladas at a little lonchería because the cook has the day off. But when Raúl comes out, he says that we are all going to a party at a farm, a rancho. Finally I will tell the sad part. I will later feel so bad that I will be awake for two nights thinking about it.

Here is what I do wrong. I say, "Oh, we didn't know about the party. We don't want to intrude on your family time. You go ahead and spend a nice afternoon with your family and relatives". Of course they say, "No, Come", and I say, "No, you need some time away from us, to be private, with your family".

So they leave. You see, I am thinking very American, that you can get tired of strangers coming with you everywhere every minute. I don't realize that we are being treated like real family, and I have not been polite, I have hurt everyone's feelings. I was offered something wonderful, a gift from Raúl's family, to be a part of their entire, extended family. And I rejected it.

When they return, I am told that Conchita cried and cried because all the time she was expecting me to come. Conchita even wanted to get out of the car and stay with us. Now I see the mistake I have made, and I feel so mean and stupid. What hurt has my blunder caused? I can't find a way to not feel so bad and guilty.

But, not understanding, oblivious to the hurt we are causing, we wave good-bye, thinking we have done the right thing. We don't exactly know what to do with ourselves, so we walk around town looking for somewhere more elegant than the lonchería. Nita has stayed behind from the family party to keep us company (and thus missed the family party because of me). We go looking for enchiladas, but not too expensive. We find a beautiful open courtyard restaurant with stone arched balconies, flowering vines all over the place, beautiful small trees, paintings, and fancy cast-iron tables and chairs. The place is full of Mexican San Miguel families, so everyone knows Nita. And because of her, they know who I am too.

We eat and then stroll around the Jardín, listening to the bands and seeing the crowds in the church courtyard. There are masses every hour, all day, because of today being Palm Sunday. People are crowded into the Jardín, the park, under all the archways that surround the Jardín, in front of all the stores and restaurants, on the sidewalks, and in the streets. We are feeling the hot sun and then finally the cool shade of seven o'clock.

We come back to the house and fix coffee which we drink in the darkening patio. Nita tells us lots of tales, and we feel cozy.

I jump up. "Hey, we forgot about seven o'clock mass!" By now it is eight o'clock. "Hurry, let's go, there is a procession right now!" Nita says. We hurry, and we arrive exactly as the faithful are carrying the "Jesus on the Donkey" altar out of El Oratorio. A band of tubas and trumpets (old men) is playing. A choir of about fifty grade school children (regular clothes) and little kids are singing. Their director is a priest dressed in white with a black cassock. The church bells are clanging to beat the band (ha, ha, a joke, because the bells are at the same time as the trumpet and tuba band). All the people line up on either side of the procession and wave their palms as "Jesus on the Burro" is carried around, supported on the backs of men bent over and slowly walking.

A man next to me is seated on the ground, on the large flat stones of the churchyard, selling his woven palm fronds. He is holding his little baby which is dressed in pajamas. The little baby reaches out his sweet hand to pat me, so I buy a palm. Imagine sitting so patiently, so hopefully, by the door of the church, to sell a few palms for a very few pesos. Nita and I hold the palm I just bought with both our hands together and wave it like everyone else. Then Richard joins his big hand with our little hands, and we feel very nice.

One can feel what it must have been like to have stood by the road in Jerusalem, welcoming Jesus. It is a good idea to have these re-enactments to get the physical, emotional impact of the real event. I like it.

Leaving the church, we once again walk to the Jardín, and we walk around and around the circle that the path makes as we listen to the bandstand music. The music is great! Real Latin with rumba rhythms and drums. One man is dancing with his wife. "Watch his feet", I say to Richard. "We can do that". "Ha, ha", says Richard.

Benches the size of love-seats are everywhere in the Jardín. They enable you to sit and watch the parade of people who circulate through on their way to somewhere else, or the people who have chosen the park for their destination. I say benches, but I don't know how well this describes the fancy, filigreed cast iron seats. They look like fancy out-door garden furniture, which I guess is what they really are, this being the town's main garden. Instead of the traditional white or black, the seats are painted the fashionable dark green so popular lately. Everything is occupied during Holy Week, even the less popular spots directly in the sun, and tonight is no exception. Little children are running back and forth in front of their seated parents, balloons and toys are being sold by strolling vendors, food is being purchased, sweethearts walk arm-in-arm, and oldies are taking a rest and observing it all. We finally locate a bench, and we sit, listening to that great band.

Nita likes to tell us stories about her childhood because we are such an appreciative audience. We always beg for more, and her stories are great, from another time, from another world. They were eight children, and every night from five until eleven P M they would all sit in their own patio, no lights, enjoying the coming of dusk and the dark that finally engulfed them, while their father told stories. The stories were about old San Miguel, or about their relatives. Sometimes they roasted marshmallows. I can't remember the rest. She says she loved it. I think any child would.

Finally we come home and raid the refrigerator. We find papaya. I drink my boiled orange leaves water, and we go to bed.

10

CONCHITA AND RAULITO
MAKE A NOPALES RESTAURANT

Nita leaves early to get the perm she skipped yesterday. All of the rest of us fix breakfast together, much like yesterday. We start fixing at nine, eat at ten, and finish at eleven. Conchita takes Richard and me to the market. She shows us where to buy a lime squeezer, since we intend to use lime juice at home, now that we are getting used to how good limes are squeezed into and onto so many foods. I buy a large package of toy money Mexican pesos for Mary to give out to her Spanish students. I am tempted to buy some of the little hand-made toys that delight me, but the first week of a trip is a silly time for shopping if you are staying for six weeks.

Conchita buys nopales and huraches, which are like thick tortillas, so named because they are thick and tough, like the soles of Mexican peasant sandals called huaraches. I am guessing that is why. Conchita plans to cook "Nopales Estilo Mexicano Con Salsa Roja" tonight and set up a little restaurant in the entryway of their house. I say that Richard and I will come and eat in her restaurant. I have to confess that I do not like nopales. They taste a little like green beans, but they are very slimy. However, if anyone can make them taste good, I suppose that Chita can, and it is she who will be supervising the kitchen adventure that the two children are planning.

Conchita tells me to buy orange blossom buds from a tiny old lady seated in a doorway. The lady and Conchita say that these make a good sleeping tea. Then we find that the bakery finally has opened, so Richard buys six different sweet breads. Here instead of the sweet rolls that we have in the USA, they have pan dulce, which is bread with sugar in the dough and on top also. He loves soft pan dulces. Good thing he buys it now, because later we see that the bakery has closed again.

In a Mexican bakery, called a panadería (which means a bread bakery, not a pie and cake bakery) you are given a large, round metal tray and large metal pinchers. You walk around and pick up what you want and then pay. All the breads are good. They are called bread, but Americans would call them large rolls. Loaves of bread I have never seen, and sliced commercial bread is only sold in "tiendas", stores. All of the cookies are made with lots of lard and are very rich, although maybe not especially sweet, and seldom have frosting. Most people like these, but I don't.

We return home, and Conchita starts cutting up the nopales. She quickly abandons this task because the frog which Raulito caught yesterday at the ranch has escaped. The kids put rocks and water in the three hundred and fifty year old fountain in the center of the patio and call for me to see the frog, which keeps climbing out, getting re-captured, and thrown back in. I hope that he doesn't get hurt. Oh, I should explain, the kids are home for Easter break. That is why they are still around at this time of day. Maybe the servants are at their homes for the week also?

Richard and I walk up a long way to the top of a different ridge. On the way down, we pass a mask store, and I find what I want for Bob and our son-in-law, Jason. Still, I only will remember and return later, keeping to my plan to not buy take-home gifts this early in the trip. For Mary, I plan to look for nativity figures. Mary picked out a tiny clay glaze painted set on her first visit to Puerto Vallarta with me when she was about six years old. She has always loved it, so I gave it to her last Christmas as a gift for her own home. I know she'd like a bigger one from Mexico. Jason loves cats, so his gift will be a cat mask. For Bob I have in mind a mask of a man with shoe-polish type slick black hair, rosy puffy cheeks, and angle's wings. The masks are made of paper maché.

My plan is to start painting after comida today. However comida is so many delicious courses that I am stuffed and need to walk. Just when my pants started to get comfortably loose, I have to go and eat everything again. Oh, well, the comida is great!

- Fresh fruits cut up: grapes, cantaloupe, papaya, kiwi.
- Soup of tomatoes, chicken broth, and little tiny pastas.
- Salad of lettuce and tomatoes.

- Rolled up fried tortillas filled with chicken and carrots

Conchita also prepares her restaurant food and gives me both Nopales A La Mexicana Con Salsa Roja (which turns out to be delicious), and green chiles cut into strips and covered with thick cream , fresh mushrooms added, served on a hot tortilla. See why I think I have to go walking until it all packs down?

We have fun for a long time talking at the table, as usual. Richard asks Raúl about the trips and cruises they have taken. Raúl tells a lot, and he and Richard have such a laughing good time and are enjoying this. Raúl tells that he and Delfina went on a three month cruise for their honeymoon, all over Europe! I don't exactly understand what kind of cruise that could be, but whatever it was, it was long and thorough!

Raúl goes and gets their trip scrapbook which is carefully done, with lots of personal notes and descriptions, including all their tickets to here and there, this event and that. It is a wonderful moment, and I am sure they enjoy the re-reading and the telling, which makes for the re-living of those wonderful days.

Oh, I forgot to say that Chita is back here again, and besides cooking the comida, she "helped" Conchita and Raulito to cook for and set up their restaurant (which means that Chita finishes everything the children started). The best of the restaurant fare is still cooking on the stove. It looks and smells delicious.

I want to order everything from the children once they are set up, but I am so full that I have to figure out a plan. I will buy some of everything, taste it all, wrap up the rest, and put it in the refrigerator for later. Tomorrow we are invited to Nita's friends' ranch for swimming. That could turn out to be an eating affair too. If so, I will eat Conchita's restaurant food on Wed. It is too good to miss.

A bit of time has passed, and I am dressed up in a cute yellow sundress with stockings and white sandals. We will:

- Go to the Jardín and hang around.
- Eat in Raulito and Conchita's restaurant
- Go to Holy Monday ceremony at El Oratorio, which I hope takes place at eight thirty, as I read on the list of Holy Week ceremonies posted on the door of another church.

- Come back here, and Richard will take me (and Nita too if she has returned) for a "copa" (a glass of red wine) at somewhere beautiful.
- Sit more in the Jardin? There will probably be music since it is Semana Santa and therefore crowded with extra people starting to come to town.

For their restaurant, Conchita has made a sign of menu items and prices. It has been taped outside of the open front door, and the tables are set up in the entryway, waiting for customers. The children have all the food (which has taken the entire afternoon to cook) on display in pans.

- Frijoles - beans refried with onions, garlic, and cumin.
- Papas Rojas con Nopales y Salsa Roja - potatoes with chopped cactus leaves and red sauce.
- Rajas Con Champiñones y Crema - strips of green chiles with mushrooms and cream.
- En Gorditas o En Huaraches - served on fat blue corn tortillas or on thick yellow corn tortillas.

Chita sets up the microwave out by the kids. At eight o'clock we are the first customers. (The next day they will tell us that they got two more customers. Far from considering this a scanty crowd, they are so happy that they decide to open up every day of Semana Santa.) We take our loaded paper plates outside, after tasting everything in front of the children and praising it all. It is easy to praise, because the food truly is wonderful.

However, we are both still full from comida, so I think up a plan. I will carry the plates around through the streets and give them to the old lady beggars who sit huddled and tattered in doorways. But tonight I don't see any! Where did they go? I find two boys, about ten years old, alone and sitting on the edge of a fountain.

"Excuse me", I say. "I bought too much of this food and can't eat it. Would you like some?" Their faces light up in big smiles, they say thank you, take the plates, and eagerly begin to eat. "Good", I think, "Éxito!" (Éxito means success!)

The religious ceremony for tonight was listed for eight thirty. I go alone and get there at eight twenty, but it seems to be half finished because there are lots of children dressed as angels who don't do anything, so their part must be over. Also there are tall young men dressed in robes (acolytes?) carrying candles which are in lanterns stuck onto long black poles. They don't do anything either. The part I see is the priest telling the Bible story and Judas (dressed in costume, and looking really sinister) who kissed the statue of Jesus leaning over the column. The bloody, whipped, lashed statue of Jesus is then carried through the streets, followed by the crowd.

I return to the house for Richard, and we go to the Jardín. We listen to the music and then walk towards the French Park looking for a beautiful restaurant for a little drink, not dinner, no more food for tonight, please, but one must buy something, and we want to go out. Most restaurants are closed, to our surprise. We finally find one that is open and is beautiful, but hardly anyone is there, and there is a loud TV playing, so we don't stay.

Instead we go on farther to the hotel at the top, highest point, of the French park because we think that hotel restaurants are always open for the convenience of their guests. Not one person is actually in the restaurant, but it is gorgeous, so we don't care. A large patio, stone floor, is surrounded by stone arches. There is a stone fountain in the center, probably carved granite, which is typical. There are flowering trees, flowering vines, flowers growing in little crannies, flowers in pots. There is lots of art, there are masks, and there are fine paintings. All lighting is from the candles on the tables, torches and lanterns under the arches. The patio is open to the starry night sky. Around the walls are doors to the hotel rooms. The tops of the doors are arched as well, and the doors and woodwork are made of fine, dark, highly polished wood, with brass numbers and brass knobs and knockers. The patio tables and chairs are of mesquite wood and leather. Music is playing, and we dance. We have a good time.

11

THE GARDEN POOL PARTY, AND
THE DUSTY DESERT PARTY

Today I want to go to the church of San Francisco and copy down the information from a poster that is nailed to the door and tells the what and the where of the events for Semana Santa. Also it tells the Catholic name for every one of the Holy Days of the week, which I find interesting. That way we won't miss anything, or at least we will have a chance at it.

Nita tells us that we are invited to go to the house of a friend of hers for lunch and swimming out in the country, but we have to take a taxi both ways, and that it could be expensive. We don't want to go because:

- We like it here where we are.
- We don't want to pay for a very expensive taxi both ways.
- Nita's friend is married to an American man, and I don't want to get trapped into speaking any more English and go looking to meet Americans.

But we will go anyway. Raúl offers to drive us, and since the children are on vacation, they can come too. The drive takes us very far out of town, and I guess no one here gets too hot, like I sure do, because the car windows are always closed, the air conditioning never on, and everyone seems perfectly comfortable. I try to act as if I am comfortable too, so as not to be a complainer, although I am so hot I can hardly breathe.

It is a beautiful ride through the mountains, and Raúl is a saint of patience and kindness. He drops us off, saying he will come back at 1:45 to bring Richard, who doesn't want to swim. Then Raúl will take the kids home, and drive us to yet another of Nita's friends for lunch. I haven't brought any nice clothes because, as often happens, I didn't fully understand the plan.

by Sonetto Tippans

The Great House of Raul Rodríguez

The Great House of Raúl Rodríguez

The true story of an American college student abroad in picturesque San Miguel de Allende, Mexico, as she unknowingly accepts a proposal of marriage during a midnight serenade. Complications arise when two years later her 'fiancé' is murdered.

Far from stopping Sonette, the ties of this presumed future marriage now forever bind her to Abelardo's family. The story of their romance is revealed in rich detail as she returns to San Miguel to take her place in the family home, one of the few Great Houses still occupied since 1640, as the 'widow' of Abelardo.

Embraced by Abelardo's only remaining sister as a sister-in-law, Sonette is on hand during the drama of mysterious digging which is undermining the house, presumably in a search for gold hidden under the stables centuries ago. Suspected and gradually confirmed, the mid-night excavations cause a portion of the upper stories to collapse, the one witness willing to testify is found mysteriously dead in his apartment across the street, and the family is menaced and threatened.

Meanwhile Sonette describes the joys of becoming a part of the daily life of a wealthy and prestigious family's routines as well as their adventures, using her painter's eye to portray in words of colorful detail all who dwell in, or enter, "The Great House of Raúl Rodríguez". She shares her blunders and angers as well as her delights with realistic honesty as, however loved and accepted by the family, she is still a stranger in a strange land.

The first place, where we swim, is a private home. It has several swimming pools, all heated by natural hot springs. One is small, for soaking, very hot; one very, very large for swimming, warm. And more pools here and there, for the geese! And for the ducks! And even a peacock, which lacks having his own pool only because I don't think peacocks are swimmers.

The house is large. The part facing the pool has a long row of arches painted white on the sides and Virgin Mary blue (sort of an electric blue named for The Blessed Mother) on the undersides. From the arches extends an enormous patio, all tiled, where they have dancing and huge parties, as big as for a hotel. Steps lead down to the largest pool, the swimming one.

The steps do not connect directly to the pool. There is an expanse of mown green grass, which is not common in this area of dry rocks, hills, and mountains. Farther away, the property contains many pine trees, tall and lovely, and mimosas.

Present are the great-grandmother (age ninety-two), the grandmother, Aldonza (Nita's friend and the mistress of the house), Aldonza's married children, all of Aldonza's little grandchildren, and lots of babies. Almost everyone is in the pool. Everyone is so friendly and gentle to each other. We change into our bathing suits in the pool dressing rooms that they have in the house, which are spacious and pretty, one for men and one for women.

We enter the pool, and I play a lot with Raulito and Conchita. We jump around and cavort, and I try to be a good water playmate. Since as an adult, I don't exactly know how to play anymore, the children tell me what to do, and I am glad for all their ideas. When my fingers have gotten all white and wrinkly, I get out, and the children join the other kids for a wonderful time of jumping, diving, swimming, and water games.

Plates of snacks are brought out and placed by the edge of the pool so the children can re-fuel without leaving the water. The snacks are bright orange corn curls, fresh oranges cut into wedges and sprinkled with red chili powder, fresh green garbanzos covered with fresh lime juice and sprinkled with red chili powder. The garbanzos are in green pods, like peas, except that there is only one bean per pod. You chew up the whole thing, and a plate is provided for spitting out the husks.

We are invited to stay for comida, which is to be "carne asada"—meat roasted in the outdoors. But of course we cannot accept because we are going somewhere else for comida. The maids are trotting around bringing out beautiful hand-painted ceramic plates, hand-blown glassware, and setting up five tables on the patio which is so big that the tables hardly take up any room at all.

You can barely see that there are four more houses among the trees, maybe one for each of the married children when they visit? No one else lives with our hostess full-time except the great-grandmother and the grandmother, and of course servants, if I understand correctly. Besides the trees, there are flowers near each house, and near all of the pools, along with flowering shrubs and tall flower covered bushes and vines.

Inside the house, right in the living room, is a Jacuzzi. It looks like a huge, greenish plastic bathtub to me. I bet during the cold Mexican winters (January and February get into the thirties most nights, and very few houses are heated in any way whatsoever), this heated inside spa would be quite a treat.

The house is comfortable and obviously geared for having lots of children there. And much entertaining goes on here too, I surmise. Yesterday Nita was here from one PM until very late for Aldonza's birthday party, celebrated by one hundred guests! I'm sure it was a spectacular event! Nita says it was eating, and dancing, and lots of fun. I believe it. This family is really friendly.

Raúl comes back for us, bringing Richard. We drive over all kinds of dirt roads, trails really, searching for the place where we are invited for comida. We drive over rocks, we drive through gullies, we drive through dust, and sand, and cactus, with only the vaguest of directions to guide us. Finally we find the right house by the process of Raúl asking some little kids that he sees standing around, kicking at the dust while they watch us, "Where does the gringo live?" Everybody knows the answer to that, so soon we find the house.

Our hostess has prepared some wonderful appetizers—guacamole and fried tortillas, all kinds of hot vegetables, chunks of fatty-looking sausages that I don't try, and wine or beer. We happily dig right in.

After a lot of visiting, we go into their house where the table has been set in the kitchen, but set in a very beautiful way, with Talavera hand-painted pottery and hand-blown glasses. We have:

- Vegetable soup (Every soup I have ever seen in Mexico is made from scratch. Fresh vegetables washed, chopped, peeled, and boiled).
- Red Mexican rice with peas, and chicken baked in mole. Yum, yum (If you don't know, mole is made from ground nuts, ground hot peppers, ground pumpkin seeds, chocolate, sugar, chicken broth, cinnamon, nutmeg, and lots of other ingredients. We love it!).
- Very fresh, soft, hot corn tortillas. (These have to be heated one at a time and placed in a clean napkin in a special tortilla basket to be kept warm).
- Salad of all different fresh, raw vegetables.
- Mexican-style bread pudding made like this - Fry bread in lard or butter. Get your husband to chisel off a chunk of piloncillo, and melt it to pour over the bottom of a cake pan. "Piloncillo" is shaped in a cone and consists of rock-hard molasses. Well, not exactly molasses in that it is almost granulated, but smashed together or melted so tightly that it is almost impossible to break off a chunk. That is why you need a hammer and chisel. After you have conquered the piloncillo, you can layer sticks of cinnamon on the bottom of the pan over the melted piloncillo, and then add almonds or pecans if you don't have any pine nuts, which you are supposed to use. Isabel did not have pine nuts, and that is how we know that you can substitute almonds or pecans. (This is a different Isabel from Larry's wife, the couple in town. This Isabel is Rob's wife).
- Red wine from Chile.
- Lime-aid made from lots of fresh key-limes, sugar, and water.

(If you think it odd for me to write the meals as lists rather than in paragraph form, it is because I do not know of Americans who would serve so many different items at each meal, especially when each dish is made not only from scratch, but with the added chore of using ingredients just purchased that day for optimum color, freshness, and taste.)

Finally we are finished with the fantastic meal. Isabel says, "Let's have coffee in the living room". I say, "Could we sit on your patio for the view and the breeze?" So we do.

Their property is near the top of a big hill overlooking San Miguel from miles away. The view of the near-by mountains is spectacular. Isabel and Rob have four horses and two big friendly dogs. We are not supposed to pet the dogs because they are intended to be mean guard dogs, but I kiss the mean dogs a lot and pet them anyway, and they lick me with delight. I don't feed them, because I am told not to. I think, privately, that your dogs will guard you and your house even if you pet them, maybe they will even care for you more, if you do pet them. But I don't speak that idea aloud. For once I show a little restraint!

At seven PM Nita says that we should go home, and she asks Rob to drive us! Yea!, I think, because we don't know how to send for a taxi. How could a taxi ever find this place? Anyway, Rob can't tell Nita no, so we have a nice ride home.

Conchita has been waiting for me, so we play cards. We play Fish, War, and Twenty-one, almost the only games I know. Well, I guess I also know Concentration and Poker, but three games are enough. Then Raulito and I shoot a few baskets on the roof.

I make my sleepy tea. Richard and I walk all around the Jardín while the family eats merienda. We are still way too full. I do eat one fat banana, and I drink three cups of tea before bed. I can't sleep past six AM and would love to sleep a lot later. Oh, well.

12

THE BELL RINGERS IN THE TOWERS, AND WHAT ARE EASTER BUNNIES?

Today, starting at eight-thirty in the morning, all the church bells really go at it. It is wonderful. The clanging seems to be picked up by one church after another and lasts until after nine o'clock. Nita says this is to announce the special mass that is held each morning during Semana Santa. I love these bells!

When I was eighteen, some local boy who worked in the main church, La Paróquia, took me up the stone, spiral staircase that leads to the bell towers. The bill ringers sit way up there to do the ringing, rather than standing down on the floor of the entryway and tugging on long, dangling ropes. These bell ringers must all be deaf after the first couple of weeks on the job. It was one of the cold months when I was up there, January or February, and you could see that these men kept little fires going to warm their hands. There were comic books around, to pass the time in between ring duties, I suppose. From this high spot, you could see all over San Miguel, and out into the mountains and valleys. When I am cozy in my bed, and I hear the ringing of these gigantic bells, I like to think of the men all over town, high up in their towers, eating their tortas and galletas and reading their comic books.

I think about the men all-knowing each other. Do they discuss the order of ringing, and the number of rings, and which of the bells to clang in whatever sequence? Or do they get orders from the priests? Or has the tradition been the same since the churches were first built?

El Oratorio has a lintel that says construction was started in 1606. La Paróquia is the newest and was built by local Indios after someone saw a postcard of one of the greatest cathedrals of Europe, so the legend goes. That means it dates from the age of photography. But the other churches are from the 1600's, or maybe the 1700's, judging from their appearances and locations. I suppose I could find out.

But I am not interested in doing the least bit of historical research. I like someone local and friendly to tell me their lore directly, and if it turns out to be inaccurate, I don't really care at all, because that is how all the stories I tell are. That means, accurate to the best of my knowledge, but often far off the mark because I can't remember gossip at all, and if I feel that changing something a little bit to keep the pace better, or giving the punch line a better punch, then that is literary license, the same as in a painting one exaggerates the light a little, or in photography gets rid of the TV antennas or the plant that appears to be growing out of someone's head. Since the stories are my stories, then I get to tell them. They are just stories, not an accounting to be audited by the IRS! These experiences of mine are not court documents, they are me telling about my experiences and what I think really happened. But that doesn't mean that I can't be wrong! OK?

I read the autobiography of some famous author, in which he related that as a boy, he used to write stories. His religiously over-zealous grandmother beat him whenever she found one, saying, "Are they true?" "No", Grandma, "they are stories". "If they are not true, then they are lies!", and Bang, she would hit him.

Breakfast is OJ, huevos rancheros, "piña" (pineapple so sweet and juicy that slicing leaves a big puddle of delicious juice, and still the fruit yields satisfying bursts of more and more juice at every bite). Then Richard and I go to the bakery across the street. He gets pan dulces. Richard likes to eat three sweet breads, pan dulces, each day. I guess he eats them when I am out with Nita or the kids. For myself, I like one half of one before I go to sleep.

I go into the Botica and give Perla three hundred dollars in travelers' checks which Raúl says she will exchange for us. I have not explained yet about the Botica (Raúl's pharmacy), nor about Perla, the manager. Perla will turn our travelers' checks in at the bank because she goes every day to turn in the days' cash intake. She therefore can get pesos for us at the best rate. We ask this of her because the best-rate Cambio here still will not cash travelers' checks. We don't need more pesos yet, but we will if the banks close for Good Friday and the week-end.

While I am hanging around the Botica, I chat with Perla, except she is usually too busy with customers. I ask Perla how many kids she has. Three, all boys, ages fourteen, sixteen, and eighteen. Richard selects three CDs from the ones we brought as gifts. The new one of romantic piano music will be for Perla herself. We buy wrapping paper at the wrapping paper store around the corner. Here in Mexico you buy wrapping paper by the sheet, and ribbon by the meter. It is not cheap. I think it costs more than in the USA. Paper is normally expensive in Mexico.

A very poor old lady is sitting in the doorway of our Botica when we come back, so instead of giving her coins, I go to the bakery where I buy for her the two biggest, heaviest, filled pan dulces I can find, to give them to her still in the bag, for now or for later. But when I come out, she is gone! I go looking, up and down each street, but she is gone. There were a police man and police woman on the corner. I wonder if they chase beggars away? Darn.

As I said earlier, I brought stuffed toys, darling ones. The maid who cleans our room is also named Nita. Her kids are seven and ten. I tell her that on my bed I will put two Easter bunnies and a fancy Easter gift bag for her to carry them home to her children and give to them on Sunday. I explain our custom, because they don't have Easter Bunny type of fables in their celebrations here.

Richard thinks I go overboard on caring so much about everyone. Of course I go overboard! I am an overboard type person! I love to go overboard!

13

SEMANA, SEMANA SWALLOWS US UP, AND I AM A WILLING VICTIM

Ah, the cozy family life. Outside it is boiling hot, the sky is brilliantly clear, and tourists are pouring into the city. We know because we just got back into the sanctuary of our wonderfully comfortable suite. I keep the windows wide open at all times. We could turn on the fan, but we like the sounds drifting in through the windows as I lie on my bed, and Richard reads a hand-out given to him in the Jardin, "Restaurant Guide to San Miguel".

The cook's radio is playing a mass. Raulito is banging doors and calling to someone in his sweet eight year old voice. Someone (Raulito probably) is by turns bouncing a ball and running around the patio. Church bells gong from time to time. The doves are cooing.

We are drinking ice water that I just brought up from the kitchen. It is ten before three, and while in the kitchen I saw a huge pot of vegetable stew simmering. Fresh spinach and other ingredients such as whole white mushrooms are on the counter, ready for something.

Out in the front entryway, a man who just arrived this morning for breakfast is setting up tables, lots of long tables piled high with blue jeans which instantly began to sell like hot cakes. Raúl is uneasy about having his patio and house so exposed to the public, (and I agree with him) but this fellow is a friend of the family, and Raúl is generous in helping his friends.

Conchita is probably still at her computer. She helped me check for replies to my emails, but the only one who replied was my brother. I didn't realize that by pushing delete I would lose his address. Maybe we can set it up again, and I will try sending another message to everybody.

Nita is wearing another of the new dresses I gave her. It is a very fine long silk skirt with a matching silk sweater, scooped neck, and short sleeves. Even so, I don't see how she can stand it in this heat. Yet I am really happy to see how well she looks in it and that she likes it. Also, she wore a new, soft tangerine bathrobe that I bought for her to breakfast. She loves it, and that makes me glad.

Raúl and Delfina are working in the Botica, as is Perla. Raúl has told me that he hated working in the Botica as a child and teen, but he started to really like it as soon as he realized that it would "earn his food", as he put it. The Botica seems to be a thriving business. It is no small thing to have a life-long apprenticeship and then to be handed the business as its owner!

Also, the Botica is an old-fashioned apothecary, and it was stocked with a full inventory when Raúl was given it to take over. Some of the medical ingredients are left from the 1700's when they were shipped here from Italy, can't be obtained any more, and so have a high value.

Before breakfast this morning, I washed more clothes in our little bathroom sink. If you ever wash clothes by hand yourself, you will be astounded at how much dirt is left in the water from just one garment that you thought wasn't all that dirty!

Richard and I are a team at washing. I plug up the sink with a squashed up plastic bag (my idea, because there is no stopper). Then I add hot tap water and some boiling water from our hot-pot. Next some of the granulated laundry soap which I swish around while wearing rubber gloves. Starting with the littlest and cleanest, I squeeze garments one at a time in soapy water, then throw them on the floor of the shower. After all are soaped, I rinse them in the sink, one at a time, and hand them to Richard who squeezes them out and puts them on hangers, which he hangs on the shower rod. After the worst of the dripping has abated, we can carry them to the clothes-line on the roof where the scorching sun will dry them quick as a wink.

For us, doing our little hand washing is a lark. But what if you live here always, and have a family, and sheets and towels, and all the etc. to contend with? Leave it to the servants, is that your guess?

Having servants, if you are the mom of the household, is a lot of work. You have to interview, hire, train, tell what to do, what to buy—there is a lot to it. Especially if you realize that the servants probably live in a house that has no appliances, and maybe not even running water, so training is from the ground up.

But when one is a guest, as we are, having someone else clean our rooms from top to bottom every single day is a dream! And having another someone do all of the shopping, cooking, meal-planning, serving, and clean-up, work that takes all day and on into the night, is also unbeatable! That is, from the point of view of the guest.

This entire house is swept and wet-moped every morning. Besides all the rooms I have already described, there are stairways everywhere, inside and outside. I know of seven, and there could be more. Also, there are all the terraces, walkways, patios, and roofs. On the top of the house, there are two clothes washing rooms that have cement sinks with built-in slanted, ridged, wash scrub boards. Then there are two clothes drying roofs. These have wire for hanging up the clothes. So to wash all of the floors of the house every day, including all of the stairs, all of the inside rooms, and all of the outside rooms, is a major job. Oh, and also the sidewalks and streets are swept and washed each morning as well!

There are five bathrooms that I know about, and these are scrubbed every inch every day. Besides the cook, there are three women whom I see here each day, to do the cleaning. The cook lives here, but the others come from a long, long way off.

It is time to go to the mass of The Last Supper. Nita, Conchita, and I go to El Oratorio. Since there is a full house, Nita leads right past all the people who have been waiting for hours and puts us right to the very front again. We sit on the step that is right next to the rail that prevents people like us from coming even closer and plopping ourselves down on the altar itself. We can see perfectly when twelve little boys of three or four years old, dressed in beautifully colored satin robes worn over white satin tunics, and wearing sandals, are brought in by their moms and grandmothers. They are seated on two benches which face each other, directly in front of us. Their little short legs dangle, causing frequent slipping off of sandals, and one boy giggles and elbows his friends quite a bit. The others are awed and still.

After some singing, and prayers, and Bible readings about The Last Supper, the main priest comes to the boys, kneels down, and washes their feet. Carried by the other priests are: a bar of Zest soap, lying on its wrapper, a towel, a pitcher of water, and a basin. It is all very moving and sweet. I like the touch of using ordinary soap, which means to me that the significance of humility and service is for us and is for today.

There are more prayers, singing, and Bible readings about the significance of the bread and the wine, and then big round loaves, maybe made in the bakery across the street from our house, are given to the boys. Each loaf has one golden coin poked into the center. The little children carefully hold the loaves until it is time to go up to the altar and carry the bread here and there as part of the ritual. All the little ones shake hands with the one hundred year old priest who is seated on the platform of the altar. Not only is he one hundred, he is still giving masses, which we all think is great!

Now everyone lines up to take communion, so I think that this is my chance to go home and go to the bathroom. The mass has already lasted one hour, so I think that it is over. But Nita tells me later that after I left, there was still more. Part of the next half hour was passing out buns and salt which had been blessed. Nita brings me home buns and tiny bags of salt. We eat the little buns, and they are good.

Next we are supposed to go to seven more churches to see the seven holy altars that are specially prepared for this day. We make it to five. The altars are spectacular! One is a statue of Jesus blindfolded and in jail. One is a tableau reaching to the ceiling of the church, all made of white roses in beautiful vases. There is a fountain bubbling in the center of the arrangement, I suppose signifying Jesus as The Living Water.

I am intrigued with all the tables in each church where miniature holy souvenirs are sold, such as a piece of purple yarn to wear around your neck, or all different kinds of crosses, or little laminated pictures.

The last church must have been the oldest, maybe dating from the late 1500's. Outside there are rows of women seated in a line on the sidewalk. They are frying small "empanadas" (dough filled with piloncillo and hot red pepper powder), and also frying "gorditas" (extra fat tortillas). Then there are rows and rows of women selling cut up fruits. Next are rows and rows of men. They are selling boiled corn on the cob. The ears are large and white. It is not like USA sweet corn. Nita tells me that when she and her mom and dad, and her one sister, and her six brothers all used to come here, everyone sold lettuce. It was a big treat, and everyone bought it and ate it because they always came at night, and the nights were very hot and dry. "Lettuce cools you off", Nita says.

All of the selling places are lit only by candle-light. Families are sitting in the surrounding gardens, eating. It seems like everyone in town comes to see all the churches. The atmosphere seems kind, friendly, quiet, and good. I like it.

Nita has forgotten her insulin, so she decides to go home before visiting the remaining churches. Richard says he has had all the churches he can stand, so we get back to the house, and he and I go to the Boganvilla restaurant. He orders quesadillas, and we are brought hot rolls, fried tortillas, and really hot red "pico de gallo" (chopped tomatoes, onions, and jalapeños).

We arrive home at ten thirty, and the Botica is still open! Richard and I go to bed. Nita and the family leave the house at eleven thirty to go out for tacos! This astounds us, because we think eleven thirty is very late for dinner. In fact, we think that eleven thirty is very late period!

14

SEMANA SANTA IS NOW RULING OUR LIVES, AND RICHARD IS NOT LIKING IT

We check the list of events as posted on the entrance doors at San Francisco Iglesia, and it tells us that today at four o'clock is the mass at El Oratorio, and at five o'clock the procession leaves from there. I will go there as soon as we finish comida. Nita went to noon mass, I think, if all went as planned. I did not accompany her because I wanted to spend time with Richard.

I help Conchita translate her Barbie magazine into English for our English practice session of the day. The magazine is so cute, and we have fun, because all the characters talk baby-talk, and the baby says, "Gou", and we have to learn the American sounds of "Goo", and also "Bow-wow", and "Meow". The Spanish is "Gau, gau" and "Miau". I like learning little kid stuff.

As Richard and I set out for the French Park and another walk, we see that the town is filling up to be stuffed with tourists. This is of only passing interest to us, since our own cozy home territory is a fortress, a quiet refuge. Once we enter and the big doors are shut, we are in our own quiet, safe, tranquil little world.

That is how we feel today, and every day, as we go home, and we eat comida.

- Pineapple- very sweet chunks.
- Soup of chopped cabbage and chicken broth sprinkled with parmesan cheese, and adding cheesy round crackers if you wish.
- Blue corn gorditas filled with nopales, potatoes, and red sauce. I hope we don't have nopales anymore, but we probably will because Nita is crazy for them. That's ok.
- Strawberries in real cream, meaning straight from the cow, not pasteurized, not homogenized, thick real cream spooned from the top of a big jar.

- Mango water.
- Coffee.

Nita and I arrive at the procession of today at five o'clock, when it is scheduled to start. In the street is a police car with flashing lights, ready to clear the way. A black van with loudspeakers is broadcasting very loudly read and musically accompanied Genesis, The Story of Creation. The line-up for the procession starts at the street, goes through the court-yard, and all the way to the altar of the church. Everyone is ready for the command to begin, which will be when the priest says to ring the bells.

Tall young men dressed in cassocks and carrying incense in censers dangling from chains are first.

Next, older women, and beautiful young women, all dressed in their best very elegant black dresses. Many wear splendid jewelry like big pearl collars, extra-large rhinestone earrings and necklaces, (no doubt some are wearing real diamonds) and tiaras. Almost all are made-up with lipstick, rouge, and lots of eye make-up to look their best. And they do. All wear some variety of large lace black mantillas. Also black dress shoes with fashionably high heels, which are still on the feet of the young ones, while the older ones have taken off their shoes before even getting started.

Since the procession will take three hours of walking over cobble-stoned streets, I wonder how many will be barefoot before everything ends. But I have not counted on the measure of their devotion, and I will realize at the completion of the whole long event, that shoes are still on, no matter what. The return to the church won't be the end either. The procession will come back to this same church, and then there will be a mass, and no one would ever think of taking off her shoes during mass!

Each of the first of the women dressed in black is carrying something significant on a tray. A hammer, huge tongs, and long spiked nails. Baskets of grapes (representing wine). A basket of apples (man's first sin). A tray of thirty silver pesos and items like a ruby ring, but I can't remember what else. A wooden, painted, life-sized rooster. Fancy portraits of Jesus. Baskets filled with rose petals. Full sized Mexican Charro hats made of sugar, yes, made of sugar, which pretty young women dressed in black wear by tying purple scarves over their heads first, you can understand why. (A "Charro" hat is what you see Mariachi musicians wear, gigantic, and almost too heavy to lift.)

Trays full of fruits made of sugar. The crown of thorns. "El Rostro" (the face of Jesus in blood on a handkerchief). The pointed lance. The jar of tears shed by "La Dolorosa", which is the Virgin Mary dressed in purple. The sponge on a pole. The dice. The ladder. The rope (which Judas will make into a noose).

Next in line are little girls dressed in white as angels wearing marabou or gold on the edges of their wings. Then a row of young girls dressed in First Communion dresses holding bread. Followed by a row of teenagers dressed beautifully in white.

Now the men, starting with twelve or eleven year olds carrying unlit candles in lanterns. A group of teenaged boys dressed as Roman soldiers. One is playing a loud, slow drum, and all the soldiers walk in time to this beat.

An altar of Jesus carrying the cross. This altar, and all the other altars, are carried on the shoulders of adult men, wearing fine black suits. Except that the altar of the Virgin Mary and the female saints are carried by women. The altars all have poles at the four corners for support. Four women walk next to these poles and are carrying black step-ladders for resting the altars upon when the women get to step out from their burden every time the procession stops for the Stations of the Cross throughout the winding steep streets of the city.

There is a lot more to this procession. I am only listing what I personally remember.

We hear that the procession will go right down the street to Nita's (Raúl's) house, to their Botica, the family's drugstore. So we hurry down there. No, correction, it is I who hurry. Nita never hurries. I want to tell Richard to come down, he must see this!

It is a splendid sight, especially because the procession descends the hill as it comes towards us, so we can see the whole thing at once, like an aerial view. The great swaying, solemn, endless group reaches us, the pace is somber and draggy, and at our corner it heads to the Jardín. We have plenty of time to accompany it, with other people who are watching, but not as many as you might think. The black van with the recorded Bible story is leading it all, and we hear the voice echoing through the narrow stone streets.

We arrive in front of La Paróquia, the boys carrying the tall candles on posts form a circle, and the main priest gives a sermon in which he tells us that this particular statue of Jesus, named "El Cristo de La Columna", has performed many miracles, and that all who accompany the procession should stand in front of it, not behind. Then a big man in regular street clothes, a fine suit, lights the candles that the boys are carrying. After some prayers, the procession starts up the hill.

Meanwhile, in the Jardín, adjacent to where all this praying has been taking place, musicians are playing popular songs, vendors are selling balloons, toys, candies, foods, ice creams. People are sitting on the benches and talking, little kids are running around, people are sitting in the out-door cafes eating and talking, and each group, although in touching distance, is oblivious of the other. I guess you focus only on what you personally care about.

In the old days, everyone along the parade route would have been dressed in black, and when the procession first appeared around the corner, the whole street full would have knelt in silence until the procession disappeared. I decide that I don't care which way it is done. Both seem ok to me.

I intend to continue following the slowly moving drama, even though it has started to rain a little bit. This is too much for Richard, so he goes home. But I too get bored, after I remember that there will be a lot of long stopping in each block, for three hours, and my interest in seeing how it all ends does not hold sufficient promise for me to stick it out, so I leave.

Going home, I find that Richard and Nita want to go out for a little copa. We find a beautiful little restaurant only two blocks away, sit in its patio surrounded by flowers: flowers growing in dirt, flowers in trees, flowers on vines, balconies covered with pots of flowers, with a fountain bubbling in the center, open sky overhead, soft guitar music, and candles on the tables for light.

Richard orders Cuba Libre. Nita has lime juice with carbonated water. I have Piña Colada. Everyone eats peanuts. We speak English for Richard's sake, and we tell every joke we know to get him out of his mood which has become downcast. Probably so much religion is seeming like less and less fun, and since it is not even meant to be fun, who can blame him? I think he is being really patient, because his interests must lie more with the people in the Jardín who had seen as much as they cared to about religion on other occasions and have opted for eating ice cream and listening to the bands, or going to the bars, or to dances.

We give it a try anyway to be jolly. Here are Nita's jokes that I want to remember. Nita can be so funny that she really gets you laughing. (At least she really gets me laughing.)

A Mexican truck driver is driving along, singing,

"Yo soy Ramón, y éste es mi camión, y tengo viejecitas por el montón."

He sees an old nun hitch-hiking and stops for her.

"Madre, qué te pasó?"

"Pues, el camión me dejó, y voy a Vera Cruz."

"Bien, pero tienes que saber que yo soy Ramón, y ....(etc)"

("I am Ramón, and this is my truck, and I have as many old ladies as I want". He stops and gives her a ride. "Mother, what happened to you?" " Well, the bus left me, and I am going to Vera Cruz.")

At night the truck driver stops and beckons to the nun to cuddle up and have sex. She says "No", that she's a virgin. He says, "But I will do it so no one will notice, not even you". (That is the part that I think is really funny.)

So the nun says, "In that case, OK." (This strikes me as funny too.)

The next morning everything is fine, and he drops her off in Vera Cruz, saying, "Well, here we are. And remember, I warned you that you should know that "Yo soy Ramón... etc."

So the nun gets out and says, "That's OK. But I think you should know that "Yo soy Pascual, Y voy a Vera Cruz, Para Carnival". (Because if you didn't get it, beware of people wearing costumes for Carnival.)

Ja, Ja. (Ha, Ha.)

I plan to write down all of the jokes, but by the time we get home, I have forgotten all the rest, so this is the only bit of our wonderful humor that gets recorded.

It is twenty minutes before nine when we get back to the house, and the procession is supposed to return to El Oratorio at nine o'clock. Nita says, "Let's go, So nay tay", (using an old pet pronunciation of my name that hardly anyone uses any more. It shows that Nita is in a good mood, like I am). Richard doesn't want to come along, of course. But Raúl saves the day by inviting us all to go for tacos at a restaurant with his family. Richard is meant to go with Raúl, and that is what we think he does. Conchita wants to go to El Oratorio with Nita and me, so Raúl says to drop her off at the restaurant after church.

When we get to the church, everything has been over and done with for a long time, so we go directly to the restaurant to drop Conchita off. Well, not exactly directly because as we head towards the restaurant, we get side-tracked by meeting a different procession, and we follow it to the four hundred year old church which is connected and perpendicular to La Paróquia. We swarm in with everyone else and sit in the front row. We watch as a different altar of Jesus is carried up to the front, near us, where it is placed (IT? HE?) in a little spot made to look like the Garden of Gethsemane.

Then we drop off Conchita at the restaurant and start home. Richard had changed his mind and was out looking for us at El Oratorio. He is very irritated to see us coming home from a different direction. We thought he was having a swell time with Raúl, but no, and we feel bad, but it was a misunderstanding. Nita and I fix ourselves gorditas, and finally Richard comes down to the kitchen, and I make him beans and cheese and hot sauce.

I try to explain like this, "Coming to San Miguel for Semana Santa and then not liking to see the religious stuff is like going to Acapulco and saying, "I don't like the beach, it is too hot". When you do that, you have placed yourself in the wrong place at the wrong time".

I continue explaining that in Mexico you can't always know what is going to take place, or where or when, so we have to just sort of drift along with Nita and see what happens. He says, "I guess so".

In retrospect I will see that neither he, nor anyone who hasn't been through it, can understand in advance what the mood and the activities of Holy Week would be like, the intensity of it. But like many things, I didn't know that an entire week of religious activities, actually ten days in all, would get so boring for him. For me it was like living in the midst of a thrilling drama, like the most magical and lavish opera, and I didn't want to miss a single minute. Richard understood this about me, and I will come to recognize how patient he was with my enthusiasm. That was his gift to me.

15

GOOD FRIDAY,
THE EPIC PROPORTIONED OPERATIC
PROCESSION OF BLOOD, AND GOLD AND
DIAMONDS AND DEVOTION

This is the big day, the major day of the year. All the other days have been gearing up to this. One could think that The Resurrection would be the major event to celebrate, but it is not.

We take an early walk, before breakfast. Our usual routine is to hang around in our rooms. Richard takes his coffee up to the roof, if I am not awake, or we both have coffee in our rooms. I read the Christian Science Bible lesson, and then I write in my journals. Richard reads his novels. But today we cannot sit still. Probably no one can. Excitement must be in the air. We go for a walk. It is already hot.

Breakfast is orange juice, mixed fresh fruits, scrambled eggs with tomatoes and onions, hot bolillos, hot tortillas, and coffee. As usual, the conversation is so interesting that we don't finish until eleven o'clock. Richard and I take another short walk and come back to pick up Nita and go together to the noon procession.

There are huge crowds everywhere. At the Jardin, purple ribbons and purple cords mark the parade route, I mean the religous procession route, to keep the crowds back. The full width of the street will be needed. Purple flags are hanging from buildings. Finally everything starts, and we are right up at the front of the crowd for a perfect view.

This will be the most long and elaborate procession of all. Instead of describing it, I consider buying a video which the owner of the Boganvilla restaurant recommended to us last night. She says we can buy it at Videomundo (Video World), and that it shows the Semana Santa processions very well.

At first the whole town is like a jolly fair. People are dressed in bright colors, buying a million things, talking, eating. When the procession starts, everyone quiets a little, but there is still talking and whispering. But by the time some of the men who are dressed as prisoners to be crucified walk by, what we see seems so real and horrible that a silence falls over the whole town. Men who are dressed in just loincloths have their hands tied to logs behind their backs. They are being whipped by Roman guards while they are forced to march along. The blood looks pretty real, and it gives a dramatic impact in a sense of the times and the events that really took place.

The altars that are carried by groups of men and women are so huge and heavy that you can see the men's shoulders quivering before the group gets even one block away from the church. The altars have to be stopped and rested on ladders every so often, or everyone would collapse.

The stone pavement is scalding hot, and many men and boys walk barefoot, believing for some reason that God will like them to suffer and burn their feet in His honor. To me, if you want to make a sacrifice in His honor, then let the captive birds out of their cages, or go out into the country-sides and pick up the trash in honor of God's beautiful world. Or give up some entertainments and use the money for the poor old lady beggars to have food and new canes. Well, no one is asking me, but this is what I am thinking.

We have to move back from our places at the front because we are getting so hot and burned. We have to get into the shade. But as soon as we move, I wish we hadn't, because if you are not up right in the front with no one between you and the living, passing panorama, it just looks like a parade and loses its intimate sincerity.

Finally we return home. I make myself iced lime juice with water and visit with Chita, the cook, in the kitchen. In all these years, she has never seen any of what we have been seeing. She always has to cook or work. Of course that is her job, and she has never asked to be let off, but I feel something for her.

Comida will be at three thirty, and after that, Conchita will wear her white First Communion dress and be in another, yes, another pageant-procession-drama. This one we can watch from right here in front of the house because we are on the route! Yea!

Richard and I had planned to go walking before comida, but he is asleep.

Comida is another WOW. Raúl is using his mother's recipe for "Coctel de Camarones", shrimp cocktail made of giant shrimps. Years ago, Raúl's parents owned the restaurant Hostería del Parque, and I have so many fond memories from there. Richard and I went many times when we were first married.

When you entered, someone was always playing guitar in a sort of bar-salon. As you came in, you were handed a Latin rhythm instrument, so all guests played and sang along while they had their drinks. When you were ready, you proceeded into one of the small dining rooms, and the food was outstanding.

Raúl was a small boy then, and the last time I saw him was in this very house, where he and his parents lived in an apartment on the roof. It was the night of Nita's wedding, in which I was a bride's maid, that we came to the house for the reception. Raul opened the door and shouted to his family, "It is the Americans! They are all so punctual!" And indeed, none of the other guests arrived for over an hour, plus the family was nowhere to be seen either, presumably still getting ready. Raúl was the exact age then that Raulito is now. The looks of each boy, the dad and the son, were, or are, so identical that that is another reason we feel we have stepped back into the past.

We eat the Coctel de Camarones with great enjoyment. Raúl describes how it is made. "You need large, fresh shrimp. They are added to a red sauce into which you mix minced onions and jalapeños", but he doesn't tell more details. This is served to us in fine, etched crystal cups. Soda crackers and hot sauce are added to the top and then garnished with a slice of perfect, sweet, soft avocado.

We have also been served crispy sliced jícama, juicy and crunchy. Raúl asks if we want more Coctel de Camarones. We conclude that this must be the main course today, so we say yes. But when we finish, here comes the soup! There are vegetables and greens in the broth, and of course it is delicious. Now we know we are in for it-- a whole meal will be served, and we already filled up on shrimp cocktail! The main entrée is a huge plate of buttered rice with three enormous garlic and butter fried shrimp. Raúl comes around and offers, "Who wants the scrapings from the frying pan?", and the answer from me is, "I do". Yummy! At last it is dessert. I don't mean "at last", as in "I have been waiting and waiting for this". I mean as in, "How many more courses will there be? I am so stuffed that I don't think I can swallow anything more." So, finally, here is the dessert. It is large, sweet strawberries with cream.

I do not understand a lot of where we are going, and when, and how, and what will happen when we get there. It is not that I don't understand the Spanish. It is that the style of attending events is very different. Here is an example.

We have been told that this evening's procession, in which Conchita will take part, will pass by the Botica at seven or seven thirty. We are just finishing dinner, at four forty-five, when Nita says, "Come on, let's go to El Oratorio, the procession is starting now".

"Now?" I say.

"Yes, come on, let's go, hurry up!" says Nita.

When we get there it has already started, even though we only came from two blocks away. The procession has proceeded well down the street. So Nita says we should go take a walk to the downtown. "Don't worry, it will be very slow before they get there", says Nita.

How can that be? I wonder. But we do as she says. The center of town, where the procession is headed, is only a few blocks away. Nita is right, of course. There is no sign of them yet.

We find a good spot where we can sit on the curb or lean against the wall to be out of the sun, and we wait. We see the procession come around a corner and start down the hill towards us, only to stop. Then it comes, then it stops. It is stopped for so long that I go to the Holandia ice cream parlor and buy a cone.

I can't imagine how I can begin to describe this procession. It involves many hundreds of participants, altars, flowers, decorations, choirs, musicians, and costumes. There are Roman soldiers, Jesus crucified, Jesus in a glass coffin, priests clustered and slowly walking under a golden, red-fringed and tasseled canopy, children dressed in purple, girls in white, women wearing black dresses, pearls and diamond jewelry, black high heels, black stockings, black lace mantillas, and white gloves. Men in black suits, young priests in white and black cassocks, men carrying tall, black, candle-lit lanterns, or tall, elaborate, shiny brass lanterns, and women also carrying the same.

From start to finish, the procession goes from 4:45 to 8:00. After seeing almost the whole thing, we kind of split up. I don't know where Richard goes. Nita is going to her apartment and invites me to watch the whole thing come by again from walking out through her tall window and standing on her balcony.

Instead, I go up to the roof (four stories high) to watch and to see the entire panorama fill the length of the street. It is wonderful. Dusk is coming, all the oldest churches (which look like cathedrals) are visible from the roof. One by one their lights go on, illuminating their gorgeous elaborate domes, spires, towers, and decorations, while below the procession makes its slow, laborious progress. Sounds from the Romans' drums lead from the front, beating out the pace for all, and I hear the children's choir, with the adult men's choir, and at the very rear, the orchestra. All the sounds are muted, mellowed by the height of my vantage point, and the sounds mingle enough to encompass the past and the present.

I am seated on the edge of the stone parapet at the top of the house, and I twist and wiggle until I can see straight down, and I must manage not to topple off. There is nothing to hold on to. I have excellent balance and love heights, yet being this high up and seated at the edge of a four story drop gives one a sort of vertigo, a sense of maybe leaning over just an inch too far, and then a terrible plop!

After a while I have the feeling that I could find Richard about now, and get him to come up and see this other-worldly spectacle. So I leave my spot and go to look for him. Just then, I look down from where I am into the heart of the house, the patio, and I see him crossing through it. I call to him, and he comes up. It almost always happens to me that whoever I need to see crosses my path just right without me having to do running and searching.

We get back to the roof exactly in time to see Conchita's group of about forty girls who are wearing white communion dresses. They are carrying four different altars of little angels, and they stop right below us. Just as I figure out which one is Conchita, she looks up at the roof. I wave, and she waves back.

When everything has passed by and finished, I get dressed up in a black dress and heels. Richard likes to go somewhere fancy, and we invite Nita. When she sees me, she says, "Why didn't you wear that to the procession, eh?" (I had been wearing shorts when she told us to hurry away from comida.) "Well", I say, "I didn't know that we were leaving so soon, because you had told us it started a lot later. I don't always understand all the plans". "Well, I already tell you, Sonette. Oh, it doesn't matter because you were ok for a tourist."

We go to a beautiful restaurant near the French Park. It consists of gorgeous little rooms, all in pastel salmon and pinks, with hand painted, hand-carved white and pink furniture. There are lots of linens, brass, silver ornaments, tiny fireplaces, a piano inside, and white cast-iron furniture, and fountains, and flowers. The trees are covered with fairy lights, and there are flowering vines all over the outside patio, where we chose to sit. This is a hotel owned by the husband of Estela Sautto, the sister of the Sauttos that I know.

I met Belinda, Teresa, Jose Luis, and Juan Alfonso Sautto when I first arrived in San Miguel for the semester when I came with my college group. We students all started out by living in the hotel, named the Casa Sautto, which is still going strong, although it has removed its swimming pools, communal dining room, and perhaps does not any longer raise its own chickens. But the bedrooms, gardens, patios, and general atmosphere are essentially the same. I will try later to describe the beauty and tranquility of the Casa Sautto. I would say my five months of residing in this inn, together with the other kids from my Beloit College group, with also an aristocratic and strikingly beautiful Mexican mother with her lively daughter, a polished and immaculate military Colonel from the next door Mexican army headquarters, and a few other gentle, refined Mexican long-term guests, were at the top of the list of the happiest days of my life. And I suppose at some point I will be able to tell you why. It's not exactly, or only, because of what happened, but more of the feelings I had about everything all put together.

Anyway, Estela Sautto is older, and I do not remember her as being a part of Casa Sautto at that time. It turns out that it is Estela who hosted the baby shower, or was it a bridal shower, the one where Nita took me. The Sauttos are enormously successful, it is evident. I should be so happy for them, but I confess that I am struggling with a great sense of failure in my own life. Will there ever be an end to the flop I have made of what I expected to be and do? Since I have not accomplished or fulfilled any of my hopes, dreams, and expectations, I have turned my life into one of service, so at least there is some little point to my life, but—well, why dwell on old, unresolved, seemingly hopeless riddles? I am not writing an introspective. I am telling my Mexico story, just as it happened, which is so easy, because the Mexico parts of my life are good.

(In case my children read this, don't worry. I am not giving anything away to say that years later I will decide that it all turned out great. The real story is not in knowing what my life turned out to be. The real story is in the how. So as I tell about today, about now, I am being honest. I am describing how I feel at this time, age 56, married to Richard, on our return to stay once again in Nita's house, in Nita's rooms, in this Great House.)

16

SATURDAY BEFORE EASTER,
HAPPY DAY ENDS IN A FIGHT

We took an early walk. It is now ten o'clock, and no sign of anyone from Raúl's family being awake yet. The maids are busy, as usual. I decide to go back to our room and read my book until they call for us.

Just as I decide that, Raúl appears, then Raulito, then Nita. They are the nicest people you could ever meet, I think once again. After thirty years of living with screaming anger, pointing anger, bullying anger, rage anger, silent stomping away anger, it is almost impossible for me to believe that I am spending days, which are turning into weeks, without being subjected to any kind of anger at all!

Everyone except the little kids come to breakfast in their sleep-wear, which look like sweat suits to me. Breakfast is OJ, cantaloupe, fried eggs, tortillas, hot sauce (red), buttered toast of pan Bimbo (commercial, sliced white bread), bacon, beans. The reason pan Bimbo is served today, instead of bolillos, is because yesterday whoever at the bakery who makes the bolillos got the day off, being Good Friday. The bakeries won't have bolillos today until after one PM.

Apparently we are served different beans each day. They all look exactly the same, boiled and served without being mashed or fried. The markets all sell a wide selection of beans, and that is another thing that is so healthy and delicious about Mexican cooking, that variety is constant.

About eleven o'clock, when we finish eating, everyone goes to shower and dress. In this family they are all very nice dressers with excellent haircuts, beautiful skin, exemplary posture and bearing, perfect manners, and elegantly gracious. We all kiss upon first greeting, and for good-byes, hellos, and for the good-nights

Except today Nita has friends coming over, so her hair is still in rollers, and she is in her robe. So Richard and I make our own plan for today.

- I will wash some blouses and the shorts that I wore yesterday to sit on the parapet of the roof. The shorts are grimy, because the parapet is the one and only place that the maids do not wash every day!
- I will mend Richard's orange shirt. (I always have with me my sewing kit of braided thread that my Beloit College sweetheart. brought me from his trip to Germany in 1962, along with a set of three pairs of fine scissors in a leather case, which were soon stolen from my dorm room in college. As he presented them to me proudly, he said, "I brought you something which every woman wants and will last a life-time". Since he had proposed when we were both freshmen, and I had accepted, I thought he meant a ring to finalize our pledge, but instead the gift was scissors and thread. And although my dashed expectation made it hard for me to be as joyous over scissors and thread as he anticipated, yet he was right iabout this thread braid lasting my entire life. It is comprised of every possible color, and it will probably last through Mary's life-time as well.)
- I will relax around in our suite, drink coffee, read my book, and write in my journal.
- After that, go up on the roof and hang up the clothes once they stop dripping.
- If Conchita comes home, ask her to help me send more email to my brother and to Mary. I'll try Bob's again too. Maybe adding a dot after com will help.
- And of course, walk around town, also buy post-cards, and write home.

Then probably go walk around even more. It is too hot to stay out for three hours in a row walking. Plus I always have to come back to use the toilet.

I have seen public toilets only in the market. Where do poor people who have to be in town all day selling things go to the bathroom? The market toilets cost, and cost a lot. If you are a woman vender with your three little kids, or a beggar man or woman with your little kids accompanying you, what do you do? And the thousands of tourists? What do they use for toilets? It would be impossible for them all to use the facilities in the restaurants. And surely they would need to go several times a day?

The irony is that if you look rich, you can walk in anywhere, to the best hotels and restaurants, and use the bathrooms. But if you look poor, you have to walk all over town to find the one public toilet which you have to pay for with money that you don't have, plus it will be nauseatingly filthy to boot!

Being in our room is very pleasant. Sunshine floods the wall on the other side of the outside staircase and patio, making a cheery view of a brilliant, shining white wall, with a view of rooftops beyond. Inside, we are in shadow, so we are nice and cool, and our windows are always open. We've got it made! Every sound of the city and the household comes to us, but muffled, so it is indeed very pleasant.

As we walk around town, the crowded atmosphere reminds us of Great America, which I love, but without the rides. It is boiling hot, there are nice people everywhere, families with children, and many, many babies.

For comida we have more shrimp cocktail. Then chicken tacos with red sauce, rice, and beans. Dessert is some kind of huge pan dulce, sliced. Delfina and Raúl get into a very hot discussion about who works harder, men or women? And who runs the family, men or women? Enrique (the friend who is selling Levis in the front entry) says men work harder, and women run everything. Needless to say, Delfina and I do not agree with his opinion! Enrique thinks that men help with half the child care and half the baby care, etc. We women say, "Ha, ha!"

Nita and Richard and I stroll around town, ending at a beautiful restaurant that used to be a church. Or a cloister? Or a hacienda? The gardens are beyond description, multi-leveled, little pools, cascades of flowers mixed with bushes and palms, but so different from most, established centuries ago? The outdoors flows indoors in a setting filled with the most unusual plant arrangements, all growing in such peace with their surroundings.

The place is so lovely that we decide to dress up more and come back. But when we arrive back there, all spiffed up and excited, things go very wrong with our seating and our treatment, and I end up making a self-righteous fuss, during which I feel humiliated and stupid. Nita tries to tell me that these are her friends, and I am embarrassing her. Selfishly I don't care, because I am too mad to care.

Nita catches my bad mood, and although we leave and go somewhere else that also is beautiful, Nita refuses to order anything because she only wanted a special drink that the other restaurant served, and she only wanted a special item on the menu that the other place had, plus, the other place served peanuts with their drinks, and where we are now does not serve peanuts, and why don't they serve peanuts anyway? So she calls the waiter over three times and orders peanuts. Each time he says, "We don't have peanuts".

She says there is nothing on this menu that she can eat because she has diabetes. I say, "You eat candy often. Oh well, try one of these." I give her the appetizer menu, then the dessert menu. I say, "Look, they have petit fours, just like you love from the bakery. Try those". "No", she says. She only wants peanuts and nothing else on the menu will do.

Several more times the waiter approaches our table to bring us this and that, and Nita wonders to him why they can't send somebody out to the store, or to anywhere, to buy peanuts. We are the only people there, and our waiter seems to be the only staff on duty, so who would they send? And it is late, so where would anyone buy? But when you are mad, logic does not rule.

Richard tries telling jokes, and telling about adventures while taking his students to Rome, and asking her questions to get her mind off her miff. Nothing helps. I go into the bathroom and cry. I pull myself together until we get home, but then all my terrible feelings about the ruined evening turn into anger, which erupts into me writing in my journal of how unfair I think this and that have been in my life. I don't express any of this to anyone, but I write it down, stomach clenched, furious and still wanting to cry. My writing gets big and scratchy and sharp, I pour it all out, I am mad about the past, and what can I do? I am like Nita, who stayed mad and couldn't stop.

Many days later I will realize that I was wrong, behaved badly, am sorry. Too late. In things like this, one just has to hope to forget and be forgiven. But I know that I can never go back to that restaurant. They will be nice to me, but they will remember, and I will remember, and no one will enjoy anything.

17

EASTER SUNDAY
WE EAT TOO MUCH, AND SEE TOO MUCH,
AND WE ARE GLAD WE DID

Richard wakes, as usual, at six thirty. He wanted to go up on the roof and wash his Levis, and his opening of the cupboard door to get the detergent woke me because the cupboard is right next to my bed, and sticks, and therefore makes a racket. Since I was now awake too, we went for a cool early walk for about an hour or so. We return and sit in our room, drinking coffee, reading, and waiting for the family.

But we wait and wait until finally it is ten thirty AM. Usually breakfast is at nine. We were pretty sure that Raúl and the family would sleep late today, so we do not go down to the patio, which we feel would be like urging them to get up and feed us. This is cook's and maids' day off, so no one else is stirring. Soon Raúl stands below our window and calls out to us. He kindly invites us to go out to breakfast with the family. I do not feel comfortable to do that. Raúl says he will unlock the kitchen for us, and he does. But because of last night I am not in the mood for anything, no matter what.

So, knowing that Richard loves to eat out in restaurants, and trying to behave better, not so gloomy, I say, "Let's go out to breakfast somewhere by ourselves, and afterwards go to the markets and buy a plastic sheet or drop-cloths for the floor so we can get started at painting". We have been too busy with all the processions and celebrations, and we haven't done more than put our painting tables into good spots.

We don't know where to go for breakfast. Raúl has told us that there are three hundred and fifty restaurants in San Miguel. We chose one, sit down, order, eat, and just as we are finishing, guess who comes in! Yes, Raúl and his family!

I say that we were just finishing, and what was it that we ate? I will tell you, and we really, truly did eat all of this. I can hardly believe it myself. It is even too long to write in my usual list form! Ok, here goes.

We had freshly squeezed grapefruit juice, so sweet that I had three tall glasses. Then a glass of milk. Super sweet pineapple. A plate of chilaquiles with green sauce. Pork in dark, spicy gravy. Re-fried black beans with goat cheese. Scrambled eggs in dark brownish purple ancho chiles sauce. Hot tortillas. Veal in dark chiles and gravy sauce. Sweet scrambled eggs with tomatoes, onions, and sliced bright red hot dogs. We were also offered hotcakes, and various dry cereals, but by then we were full and didn't want any.

Now we should be hurting from stretched stomachs, but we are not. We are happy. We go to our room because I need my hat and sunglasses. We make coffee and make our plan - walking, market, more walking.

We go to the Jardín and see two separate dance groups, both indigenous Indians. One is Yaqui and one is Aztecas. Yaquis are like apaches, and Aztecas are like you see in the Ballet Folklórico in Mexico City, peoples who lived around the great central pyramids. Both groups are dancing at the same time, while their drummers beat loudly at their own separate rhythms. Except since they are right next to each other in the street in front of La Paróquia, nothing sounds very separate. No matter, like a mother recognizing her own children, the dancers recognize their own beats. I love cacophony, so I find this a most pleasing racket.

I also love, love the drumming, heavy, thumping, repetitive beats. I mentally figure out the Yaqui dance steps, well enough that I could have joined right in. "Indian" dancing is participatory, hypnotic, usually involves repeating only one basic step per dance. It is not designed to be particularly a performance. I watch and watch, wishing I could get right in there with them, being reminded of as a child jumping Double-Dutch jump rope, two heavy ropes turning at once. It is the same dreamy feeling one gets from repetitious, slow movements, over-and-over, one foot, other foot, one foot, other foot.

I hand the boss dancer fifty pesos and ask him to buy sodas for the dancers. I thank him for sharing his wonderful heritage.

Now comes a Cumbia band! They are great. Oh, how I wish that everyone would dance in the street so that we can too, but no one does.

Soon the scorching hot sun makes standing in the street not so fun anymore. We decide to walk down to the Instituto to see the Art Fair.

The Art Fair is both very nice and very awful. Nice because of the lovely, lovely arts and crafts on display, the hopefulness of the sellers, the happiness of the viewers, the camaraderie of all who sell the huge variety of international foods, drinks, and desserts, the beauty of a Mexican Mariachi band playing, and the ambience of the site—a former monastery turned into an art and cultural institute.

Awful in the way of all such displays of stuff, stuff, stuff. At fairs, in malls, in stores, everywhere you look. Too many material possessions are being created, no matter how much money there is to buy it all. To have one hundred or one thousand times more than we need, whereas many people in this world don't even have water, or shoes, or bits of firewood to cook their skimpy food—it gets me down.

I think, I used to be so in love with the world. Why do I have to be such a black philosopher, getting so darkly upset when I get overwhelmed with gross materialism? How can I rise above such a negative take, go back into the happy person I used to be, the sunshiny dispositioned person people used to love seeing coming? In situations like this, where everyone else sees all this stuff, stuff, stuff as a sign of abundance, whereas I feel choked, smothered, and frightened by it, in order to be even tolerably polite, I have to bite my tongue. How terrible if I have become too overly concerned, and feel so personably responsible for conditions not of my own making.

We walk home and have cool water, hot coffee, and sit in front of our fan before going on to the market.

In the market we look for a tablecloth for me to buy, and for something to set up as a still-life for me to paint. I don't find anything that I want to paint. I'd rather paint landscapes or portraits, but the idea of carrying all the equipment I'd need, and of having passers-by watching me, hanging around, asking questions—I can't. It is just too daunting.

I find an ad in the local paper saying "Studio Space for Rent, plus art lessons included, at one hundred eighty dollars per month. But Richard says he wants to come too, share the space, and take the lessons along with me. There is nothing wrong with that, except I need to be alone, to get entirely lost in the painting and become oblivious to everything else. So if we are going to be together, why not just paint here? We are big supporters of each other's work, but here will be better because we will each have our private spaces, me upstairs, and he down.

You would think that we would not want anything more to eat today, after the giant breakfast. However, when we get back to the house from the market, we find that comida will not be served either, so Richard and I go back to the restaurant we like by the French Park. Now it is evening, and I think that I should try to remember this restaurant's name because possibly we will be coming back here a lot. We order green enchiladas, and red enchiladas, sharing by splitting our plates because we both love each type. The meal is very good. Then we walk around the Jardín and hear the town band playing in the bandstand. Everything is locked up and empty looking at the house when we return, no one is around, and we go to bed early.

18

THE BABY CLOTHES-APRONS-UMBRELLAS-CLOTHS SHOP

Chita has not come back from her rancho yet. (Rancho means the tiny town where her family lives, not ranch like in cowboy movies). So Nita makes breakfast. We have OJ, papaya, scrambled eggs with ham, beans, salsa, and fresh whole bolillos. We do not have tortillas because tortillas require going to the tortillería before each meal, and then heating each one on the comal over the open flame of the gas stove, continuously, throughout the meal, so they will be hot and soft. None of us wants to do that much work, and all the hopping up and down, and all the running from table to stove.

We thought that the kids would be back in school now that Easter is over. But they are here. I ask Raulito when school will start again. He says he doesn't know. Wouldn't it be great to be so unconcerned about your obligations!

Nita knows where to buy everything. Why does this matter? Because shops are tiny, and everywhere, and sell only one specialty, so the fun of it is going to all these fascinating little places where the displays of goods are worth a trip to see even if you didn't want to buy anything. We are going to the plastic shop. This tienda only sells plastic of every kind necessary for wrapping, flat sheets. A different plastic shop sells plastic buckets, glasses, plates, and the like. See how specialized they are? Anyway, we will finally buy plastic to cover the floors while we paint.

There are many cloth tiendas, and I want cloth as a back-drop to the still-life I hope to paint. Do I want plain, commercial cloth, like at Wal-Mart at home? That is in one tienda. Do I want heavy, beautiful, expensive, laboriously hand-woven, intricate, short lengths of cloth? There are two or more tourist fancy stores for that. Do I want something that I don't even know exists yet? Yes.

So we will go to the cloth, and baby clothes, and aprons store. It takes lots of walking and looking, and every shopkeeper is Nita's friend, so we also take a lot of fun-time talking. In the baby clothes-aprons-umbrellas-cloths shop, I spy exactly what I want, way in the back. It is a big bolt of trapo! "Trapo" means rag. This cloth is used for tying onto a pole and washing the floor. Or for throwing down in front of an inside doorway when it is raining outside, and everyone can step on it first instead of on the clean floor. Or for many ugly or humble jobs.

But I see trapo as beautifully soft, buttery yellow, hand woven, or so loosely woven as to give that illusion, and there are red and blue threads running parallel to each edge. This will be perfect! I am so enthused that I want to buy many meters, thinking how beautiful it would be for something, somewhere, back home.

It is deceptive to meet the shop owners here. They look like clerks in these very humble, old, shadowy stores. But like Raúl, they can be men and women of important wealthy families, owning a great deal of expensive property, owning beautiful homes, and traveling all over the world. This particular cloth shop owner is the one whose house, kitty-corner from Nita's, had the beautifully decorated patio with just the Virgin Mary statue, music, and flowers. His is one of the finest of houses, another Great House.

We drop off our purchases and take another walk. When we get back, Nita has made comida. I don't know why, because Chita is back. Raúl and Delfina have taken the kids to Querétaro. We are only three people eating comida, but we are served by two servants!

We sit grandly in the large, echoing space of the dining room, so quiet with everyone gone. We have a lovely, friendly comida. We have:

- Watermelon cubes - extra sweet and extra red.
- Water made from boiling purple flowers. It is a very dark purple water and tastes sour, like limes. Nita tells the cooks that it isn't sour enough. What can they do?
- Salad of lettuce, tomatoes, and avocados.
- So-called "Hamburgers" that are really filets. Why are they called hamburgers? Maybe because the cooks don't really

know what hamburgers are?
- Tiny boiled potatoes rolled in olive oil and garlic with mustard and herbs. Delicious!
- Beans.

Nita tells us stories about when she was little, and her family all sat at this same table in this same room. Four children sat on each side of the table, with mamá y papá at each end. Her dad each night read to them: almost all of Shakespeare's works, the entire !!!! "Arabian Nights", "A Child's Garden of Knowledge" (a sort of set of children's encyclopedias), and much else.

It makes me remember my mother reading to my brother and me each night as we were tucked into bed. Dickens usually, or a set of classic children's fairy tales (horrible and long, not like today's cartoony stories), and from a huge, many volumed set of children's stories.

It is after five o'clock, and Nita has to meet with Perla, and then some other friends. Richard and I take a long, rambling walk, going nowhere in particular, just hither and thither. We end at La Colmena and buy some bolillios, then find mangos somewhere else. We cut everything up, making a type of fruit and sandwich plate, and we take this, along with chairs, to the roof. It is precious and sweet, enjoying the view of the distant hills and mountains while the church domes become lighted, one by one. Then we head to our rooms for an early bed-time.

But what a night of racket! First there is a lot of shouting around eleven when the family returns for a late merienda., calling for the dogs, and general family clamor. We don't mind this at all, in fact it is kind of fun.

But at one AM the cat starts to scream and yowl. He stays outside our window and yowls with tremendous energy and volume every hour, and we know this for sure because of course we wake up and look at the clock each time. We both give up on sleep at five thirty.

Finally the endless, sleepless night is finally over, and we start Tuesday.

19

THE PATHETIC FAMILY, THE DESPERATE PARROT, AND THE TWIN DOGGIES

We shower, shampoo, make coffee, I read my Bible Lesson, and as is becoming our routine, we go outside and walk in the cool early air. A young woman with two little children and a baby is trying to sell nopales door-to-door. Anyone who has to do that must be down to her last resources. Here is why.

She would have to have picked those spiney cactus leaves somewhere far out of town early this morning, taking her little children with her, all the while carrying her baby. Then she has to carry the baby and all of the prickly bundles back into town, including her knife and another bag of meager possessions to get herself and her little family through the day. She has to find somewhere to sit and cut off all the spines, and last she has to find someone to buy her nopales.

As we walk by, the little daughter holds out her hand, and I give her three pesos (about forty cents). We continue our walk, but I am thinking, "What if I had to do that? What if our daughter had to do that?" I am feeling terrible, so we turn around.

We look for a bakery, but there is none around where we are. I spy a man with a truck-load of fresh rolls. They are very large and destined for some hotel or restaurant to serve for breakfast. The man lets me buy five, and we walk towards where we think we will find the woman and her little ones.

We find them seated on a curb, and some nice lady from one of the houses where the woman is trying to sell her nopales, has come out with two tin cups of milk. This compassionate woman gives the cups of milk to the mamá, and all start to share and drink. The whole scene makes me cry, for their desperation, and for the kindness of the giver of the milk, who is very humbly dressed herself. We give the mamá the rolls and the three more pesos, which is all we are carrying, and she thanks us. We go our way.

Today we have big plans, ha ha. We will wash our clothes, start our paintings, and as usual, take lots of walks. I must, must get an email off to my brother today. Nothing else is getting through. Yesterday, Monday, was April first. Our pensions are on automatic deposit, so timing of mailing out the bills is very important. Before we left, I wrote out all the bill payments, put them in stamped, addressed envelopes. Our son, Bob, was supposed to mail them right on the first of each month. This is so important because our insurance on house and cars is due on the fourth. Jason (Mary's husband) intends to borrow our truck and camper for the coming week-end. I have to enlist my brother's help to phone our son and verify that the task is or will be done. The reason I am in limbo about being able to find out what is happening about the bills is that our son's email came back undeliverable, and Conchita has been at her cousin's house all week-end and can't help me. I hope she comes back soon.

No one is around yet, so we go for our second pre-breakfast walk. The streets in the French Park are shady until ten or nine thirty AM. It is fresh and airy. We feel wonderful, enjoying the plants that in the States come in little pots, which here are huge trees. Vines reach up through patios, over the roof edges, and spill down towards the streets, heavily covered with blossoms. Many of the balconies, all of which are wrought iron, contain large, beautifully painted, glazed pots full of more brilliant blooms. Even the cobble-stone streets are bright with the fallen blossoms, every color mingled together.

The houses surrounding the park are made of stone with little sharp shards of broken pieces pushed into the spaces between larger flat sided stones. If not of stone, the walls are of a very rough type of plaster made by holding up a coarse screen and then throwing trowels full of colored plaster or cement with enough force to penetrate the screen and stick to the wall. Exterior walls are of brilliant colors, the colors of tropical fruits and flowers. The doors are of hand-carved wood with brilliantly polished, fanciful brass door-knockers. Windows are covered by black iron bars, doorways and window frames are heavy squares and rectangles of granite blocks. Some windows are wooden, many-paneled, and glass paned French doors also swing open to reveal billowing white curtains within. Each twisty street sings to us with flashing color and beauty.

Maybe it is time for breakfast by now, so we head towards home, passing through the downtown. Even in the Jardín, the flat square stones of the street are washed each day, mopped by hand, using buckets. Morning walking is so lovely because the daily cleaning has been accomplished, and the day's accumulation of dog poop, discarded wrappers, plastic bottles, and general junk has not yet begun.

We return, but only Nita is around. We go to our rooms, and I have the urge to start painting, right now. But I know that the air is so dry that in twenty minutes all the paint I need to squeeze out onto my pallet will have dried, and the call to breakfast could be at any time. What else to do?

I can't pass the time by using Conchita's computer, because to do so I would have to go into her parents' private quarters. They are so gracious that they always say, "Oh, yes, oh certainly, go right ahead". But I think it is rude to go in when none of their family is with me. And certainly I cannot enter while they might be still asleep or getting dressed.

We sit down on a bench outside of the locked dining room with Nita, and she tells us that Raúl will be taking his family to Acapulco for three days. After that they will go to Zacatecas, which is ten hours away by train. What wonderful plans. The family had to stay here for Semana Santa because of all the extra business from the tourists. We are not told what date they will be leaving to go on these little, short trips. Although the trips will be short, they don't seem little to me. They seem major because of being so exotic.

Richard and I were in Zacatecas about ten years ago. We were living in Durango, Durango and attending the Romance Language Institute, which I loved. We lived with Consuelo and Jose Piedra for a month. We went to Zacatecas on a week-end excursion given by our school. The town is Colonial and therefore a lot like San Miguel, except it is a much smaller.

While we are sitting in the patio and talking, Raúl awakens and comes out of his apartment. He says breakfast will be in a few minutes. The cook has been in the kitchen for quite a while, and the radio is playing softly. Lots of other workers have been busy too. Up in the rafters of the portico above where we sit, the swallows that live up there are flying around and chirping. The one hundred year old parrot is out free. He sticks around his cage. The young parrot is never let out because he so desperately wants to escape and fly. That is terribly sad to me.

At our feet are the little brown doggie and the little black doggie. They race around everywhere together, side-by-side. In fact their sides are actually touching as they dash up and down the stairs, skid around the patio, follow Raulito, or anyone who comes by. They are like a darling set of living toys. And they are cuddly and curly.

We leave the dogs, and the swallows, and the parrots, and the radio sounds, and the workers and go into the dining room for breakfast. It is OJ, papaya, chilaquiles with onions, scrambled eggs, and beans with goat cheese. No tortillas, because chilaquiles are made from tortillas. You rip them up or cut, then add to a wonderful labor-intensive sauce made of green tomatillos and chiles, and then add cheese to melt in, or else goat cheese crumbled over the top. Oh, so delicious.

Conchita has returned for breakfast, and she helps me receive and send my email. Wow! There is one from Mary! She asks me to save realia for her classes. I will start saving food labels and maybe get some posters. Mary writes that it was hard to figure out how to reply to our Mexican system.

We decide to first walk once again, and then we will paint.

For our third walk of the day, we do not go back to the French Park. Instead, we walk way, way up. We come across four small children who have just been sent out of the door of their home carrying large, heavy, black plastic bags. Two girls struggle to carry one bag together, each holding up one side, and two little, little boys are trying to carry the other. The littlest boy is having a very hard time, so I say, "Les ayudo? Can I help you?" "Yes!" accepts the boy who is actually ten but looks seven. The four year old runs ahead to help his sisters, and I take his place. How could that little one carry this sack? It is very heavy, even for me. We walk for several blocks and have a nice chat.

We return home. Here is what I paint, and it starts out fine. On the window sill, I put a plant that we bought in the market on our walk after breakfast. I put a colorful Mexican ceramic plate under the plant, and the beautiful yellow trapo cloth under the plate, all bunched up and wrinkly the way I like to paint. A lot of my paintings are about cloth and how it looks—shadows, valleys, ridges, patterns. I use the table which was intended for the TV to spread out my paper and pallet. My start at the painting is pretty pinchy and tight, but instead of thinking that I will begin with good results, all I am expecting for a while is to get back the feeling of loving to paint, loving the feel of the brush, loving spreading the paint onto the paper.

I don't have the right red. What I brought with me is one tube of cherry red. There is no way to make it into pink. It turns into salmon. Also, Richard did not pack a pallet knife. Therefore we must go to the art supply store here. I resist doing that because at home we have huge supplies of everything under the sun, and it is just sitting there to dry up before we get home. Here everything is so expensive. "Ni modo", which means never-the-less, we have to do it.

Enough painting for now, because Raúl calls us for comida. I stick my brush in the empty yogurt plastic cup that Chita the cook has found for me to use as a water-can. We go downstairs and eat:

- Ochata. Cantaloupe seeds and cantaloupe ground up in the blender with water. This is a delicious drink that (if you don't know how it is made) you won't say "Dis gust ing". You will like it.
- Soup of shell macaronis in chicken broth, and you squeeze limes into it.
- Goat cheese in cubes.
- Tortillas.
- Slices of fried baby zucchini.
- Tomatoes and avocados over shredded beef, topped by onions, olive oil, and vinegar.

Raúl tells us that he is not taking the family to Acapulco. He is going by himself because it is a pharmaceutical convention. Also the train for the trip to Zacatecas doesn't have all of its parts put together yet, so that excursion is postponed.

Conchita asks me to help her practice percentages for math class, so I do, and then she teaches me the binary system.

Interesting! Next she wants me to see her project, and to help a little bit. It is to make a flannel blanket for her cat. It has to be fitted to a basket to be a cat bed. We cut and sew and have a lot of fun. Everything about sewing is still new to her, and I get to see threading a needle, poking it through the fabric and getting it out again, making a knot, through her fresh eyes.

Time has drifted on, Richard and I walk to the Instituto and back, we go up to the roof for a while and talk, and now we hear the rattle and clamor of making the nine PM merienda. I will go help.

To me it is very strange to go out shopping now, in the dark, at this hour of the night, but Nita wants to go to the bakery and get empanadas. These are little half-circle fried pies, in this case filled with tuna. Conchita comes too, and we walk far, to the only open bakery in town. It is such a beautiful, soft night that the walk is wonderful. On the way back, Nita wants to hear the Mariachis playing in the Jardín. We stay there until ten o'clock. Finally we are back at the house, and we all eat.

We go upstairs, I boil my sleepy-time tea, and we go to bed.

20

FUN RUNS AMUCK

I wake up, and I am not sure, but I think today is Wed. Fun Runs Amuck.

Comida today is just Delfina, Richard, and me. Raúl and Raulito have gone to Celaya to get a tire fixed. Nita is attending a women's luncheon. Conchita is at her grandmother's. Even though we are only three, our comida is still royal. Delfina does not take over the responsibility of yelling at the cook, like little Raulito did when his papá wasn't here, but Chita delivers everything at exactly the right moment anyway. All we have to do is talk, and eat, and enjoy.

- Pineapple, dripping with sugary juice.
- Tamarindo water. "Tamarindo" looks like a long, lumpy, downy, brown pod which I think grows on trees. Somehow it is boiled, and the liquid tastes like apricots.
- Cold, red gazpacho soup with a number of bowls filled with add-your-own chopped eggs, chopped green peppers, chopped cucumbers.
- Rice and butter.
- A long, purple, sweet chili cooked with vegetables.
- And fresh hot tortillas.

There are also hot butter beans, which I love, but Delfina is telling us such interesting things that I forget to take any.

She says that Nita's blood sugar is way up. Delfina and I have told her that it is because she eats so many sweet things like sweet rolls (pan dulce), candy, fried pies. Nita always answers, "No". She has decided now that the cause of her high blood sugar is the vegetable soups and the fresh juices, so she will be giving these up. We can't convince her of anything, so I am trying to talk myself into being more respectful of her own intelligence as an adult, to not interfere with advice she doesn't want, but it sure goes against my nature (because I usually do interfere and give advice). She is doing what she believes is right, it is her body, her home, her town, and she has a right to select her own diet. I know this, but it will take a lot of restraint to not comment, or at least sigh, or frown, or betray somehow how I feel when she eats the candies and all the rest!

When we finish eating, Richard and I will leave for an exciting adventure of buying clothes pins and hangers. Then we will do our wash. Also, since it is now April, we may try again to change some money at the Cambio. They are supposed to have money now. Or maybe it is just that now that tourist season is over, they are willing to accept traveler's checks again. We got in line to change some this morning, and when we finally arrived in front, we had forgotten to bring the checks! Oh, dear.

A cool wind is coming up, and it is cloudy, so I am eager to get going. I had to put on brand new underpants this morning because all the others were dirty. What if it rains? I want my underwear washed and dried before that happens.

This evening I belive is going to be so much fun, but it runs amuck. Like this. I am taking a walk, and I see a sign in a very nice restaurant, near to our house, and it says, "Margaritas, Two for One". "Oh", I think, "how great. Richard likes to go out every night, and he will love this place. We can invite Nita, and then we will go home after our two drinks for merienda". So I rush home and tell Richard. He says, "Great, sure, go invite Nita".

So OK, I do, except I enter her apartment to invite her, and I don't realize that behind the door is Nita's friend, whom I have met and like, but don't particularly know. Mexican style, Nita invites the friend, and also the friend's husband (who is American) to join us, and the friend accepts. We start out looking up and down the streets, but we can't find this particular restaurant, so the friend takes us to a restaurant she likes, where, unbeknownst to us, Nita had already made a plan to meet this same woman friend and her husband for dinner later tonight.

The waiter who takes our order for Margaritas brings everyone their two-for-one, both at once. This naturally gets everyone to drinking too fast, because the drinks are right there, two in front of each person instead of one. Some American man that nobody knows leaves his barstool and asks if he can join us. He is perfectly nice, fun actually, but now I am starting to not like this because the conversation has shifted to English for the stranger's sake and also for the friend's husband, who does not speak Spanish either. The drinks bill comes, and because we had invited Nita, and the whole bill is on one tab, the entire thing is given to Richard. Naturally he cannot say, 'Wait a minute, I only invited Nita". No one else says, "Oh, let me pay my share", not even the stranger. This is a more deluxe restaurant than the place I had seen, and the bill is really high. Now I am even more so not liking this, but oh, well, cocktail hour is over, and we can go home. Or that's what I think. But, no. Ha, ha. If only.

No, we cannot go home. Richard is having fun and wants to stay because everyone is urging us to not leave and to eat dinner here. I don't want to at all, but since Richard almost always does whatever I want, or whatever Nita or the family wants, of course I tell Richard, "Sure".

Everyone except us orders lots more drinks, lots more food, appetizers, and desserts, while we only order something simple, inexpensive, and no more drinks. Everyone is still speaking English because mostly Americans are patrons of this restaurant. When the bill comes, it is given to Richard again, yes, again, and everyone's food and drinks are on it. Richard is laughing and smiling and pays the whole thing. But what is even more bothering me is that I have not been able to speak Spanish.

This new couple is very nice, and I really like them. Everything about them is better than fine, EXCEPT that I do not want to get into a friendship, or a companionship, or anything at all that involves spending time with Americans and speaking English while I am here in Mexico. I can attend many cocktail parties, and dinners, and social stuff right in my own town any day of the week. When I am in Mexico, which is so rare and so short, I want to be with Mexicans, think and speak in Spanish, feel Latin, breath the soul of this city. For me to come here and not speak Spanish would be like for someone else, saving all year for some exotic expensive vacation and then spending all of it in the hotel room watching TV, if that will explain how cheated I feel, how I am missing out on the reason for being here. It has already been very hard for me because so much of the daily talk is in English.

Richard speaks English to me. Others speak English when they are with me for the sake of Richard. I feel so frustrated by this prospective shift from the reason I am here (to be Mexican for six weeks), to an endless circuit of drinking, and American cocktail parties, and American-style dinners in American hang-outs, and American types of parties and- Oh, to explain it sounds so selfish.

And I feel really selfish, but before we decided to make this trip together, Richard agreed that he understood how much it meant to me to "live Mexican", so to speak. He agreed to just listen or to do something else when everything was in Spanish. And he has been really supportive that way. It is not Richard who promotes all this English speaking which bothers and frustrates me so much. He really understands and tries to switch everything back into Spanish whenever he can. But now what! We have a date to meet with this couple at their house tomorrow at three o'clock!

Not only I don't want to get this started, but also I don't want to miss comida with the family. It would be so easy if I didn't like these new, friendly people, but I do, and I feel like some events have to be for Richard's sake after all he endured about Holy Week. Oh, dear, oh, dear, oh dearie me.

21

WORRIED ABOUT BAD ME, AND
I MAKE UP FOR IT

I went to sleep, sort of, still in turmoil. And I awake in turmoil still.

I could not sleep last night because for hours I worried about something I failed to do during the evening. This is what it was.

As Richard and I were walking all over the place, trying to find the originally selected "Margaritas, Two-For-One" restaurant (before we got ensnared in all the night's events that I just described), we passed an old woman sitting in a doorway, holding out her hand for a coin or two. Usually I carry coins for just that purpose, and I would never pass anyone by. But up until then I hadn't seen anyone begging after six o'clock, and this old lady was sitting in her begging spot still at eight o'clock, and I hadn't thought it necessary to bring coins.

Richard had already given all his coins to me that day, so he had none either. This old lady was skinny, bony, dressed the shabbiest, and she had one deformed hand. I should have gotten a big bill from him, gone to a restaurant or store, bought some little anything, and then I would have had coins. But it is awful that when you are in a hurry on your own business, you don't take enough time about someone else's plight. How could I have been so self-centered?

Another no sleep worry was that not intending to stay out for dinner last night, I had not let the cook know that we wouldn't be back. I should have phoned Delfina and told her. What if they were waiting for us? I stewed and stewed over what an irresponsible, bad person I was, with no way to make up for it.

But yippee! When Raúl wakes up, he says not to worry about not showing up for dinner because he knew we were with Tía Nita, and that that means that anything can happen.

Richard awakened early and has already gone up to the roof to wash his clothes. Our hangers and clothes pins will help, because sometimes the wind was blowing our clean wet clothes right down onto the dust of the roof before or after they dried.

So I go for a snappy walk by myself before breakfast. Richard's attempts to quietly gather his wash and the soap and all that he needed woke me never-the-less, so I am awake, but I am groggy, and a walk will help to clear my head.

At ten o'clock, Conchita asks me what I want for breakfast. I say, "Huevos rancheros"! We also have OJ, papaya, and warm bolillos with melted butter. Only Raúl and Raulito are here, and although we speak all English, this time it is for the sake of little Raulito, so this time it is fun.

In a few days Raúl will go to Acapulco for the convention. I tell him about the last couple of times we stayed at Fiesta Americana on the beachfront. We love that hotel, so luxurious and almost entirely Mexican. But the beach front, like all beaches in Mexico, is open to the public. That part is very good, but there is tremendous crowding, and there are no public bathrooms except for one about a mile away. So naturally one must think of the results to the beautiful water in which you are swimming. Two times my children got terrible infections from the beach water, and on the first day of the vacations, and the result was that they couldn't swim at all for the whole trip! What do you do on a boiling hot tropical vacation in a luxury ocean-front hotel vacation if your kids can't go swimming?

So I spoke to the manager and said that all people, rich or poor, deserve bathroom facilities on the beach, and that also it would be in the best interest of his guests. He was very agreeable and said he would take it up with the hotel association.

Later I was delighted to receive a big, thick letter from the manager saying that all had gone well, and that the hotel had built a bathroom, free, for use of the people on the beach in front of the hotel. So I ask Raúl to go there and check to see if it is true. Raúl says he will.

The whole family will be gone for the rest of today, until late tomorrow. Chita, the cook, asks me what we would like for our meals. I say that we like anything involving tortillas and sauces, and that we like everything that she makes. She suggests enchiladas today, and chile rellenos tomorrow, knowing that these are my favorites. "Oh, yes, yes with all my heart!" Chita is so thoughtful.

I tell Chita that we can make our own sandwiches for merienda, and that Nita wants us to go out for breakfast tomorrow morning. This is good because it will give Chita a bit of a break. Also this is bad because we are meeting Nita's English speaking friends for breakfast, and I am discouraged about more English. But what can I do? The husband is a wonderful artist, and it is only he who is American. So I think, "Fine, he and Richard can speak English, and Nita and the Mexican wife and I can have fun speaking Spanish", and since I really do like them both, I feel happy.

But not everything is rosy. We have been going out in the evenings more and more, and now Richard wants to go out a lot with our new friends. Before we came on the trip, we budgeted for going out for dinner three times a week. All our meals here in the house are included in what we are paying, so we would never need to go out at all, but Richard quickly changed the plan to every night out, and drinks and dinner in restaurants every night is eating up our money fast. It is fun, so it is not a bad thing, but it is pretty different from our original plan. We have to figure out something about money. We have spent one half of our money in just two weeks, and now we have four weeks left. Plus now that Richard is enthusiastic about going out with our new friends, they select American hang-outs with higher prices and a lot more drinking. No simple enchiladas and a glass of vino tinto where we will be going.

I should explain that we are not poor people. It is that we only brought so much in traveler's checks, and there is no way to access our money in the USA from here. We don't know how, and neither does anybody else.

Oh, well, we shall see. There is one invitation from the American husband that I would love to accept, but we can't. It is to go out to the country and do landscape painting, but we don't have the proper equipment. It would be nice if Richard could figure out how to go. The two men would have a great time.

I tell myself that it is time to stop worrying and be grateful, so I do.

Thanks to Mary I have plenty of books. Thanks to Richard, I have plenty of paint. Thanks to Nita, we have plenty of food and our wonderful home. Thanks to Chita, who is saving empty food packages for Mary, I will have plenty of realia to take to her for her classes. So we are in good shape.

We eat comida:

- Watermelon water.
- Grapefruits.
- Yellow butter beans
- Chili rellenos.
- Rice.
- Hot tortillas.

Heavenly!

Nita did not accompany the family on their outing, so she is eating comida with us too, and she tells us wonderful stories about first meeting Jackson. He proposed the third day after they met! Jackson's mom set it all up. Señora Gleason had lived here for many years, having a beautiful house two blocks away. She liked Nita so much that she sent for Jackson to come from Australia, where he had been living for the last ten years. When Señora Gleason introduced Jackson to Nita, he said it was love at first sight. Here is how he proposed.

Señora Gleason (did I mention that she was Canadian?) invited Nita to comida. After comida, Jackson asked Nita if he could spend the rest of the day with her. The day passed well, and not wanting it to end, Jackson invited Nita to go out for dinner at nine PM. During the dinner, Nita said that she liked the dessert that his mom had made for lunch. Nita said, "Do you think she will give me the recipe?" Jackson answered, "Yes, after we are married, she will give you all her recipes". What do you think of that!

Their courtship was one month in person. After that Jackson went back to Australia, and their courtship was by letter until he returned for their wedding. I was a bride's maid in her wedding, which I must tell about at some point. It was a real fairy-tale, taking place in the greatest of San Miguel's churches. Anyway, she still loves him, and he still loves her.

Richard and I decide to walk to the top of San Miguel to enjoy the breath-taking view. We start for home, and Richard suggests coming back to a beautiful restaurant that we pass, one that also has two-for-one Margaritas. We go home to get dressed up. I have been looking frumpy, so I cut my hair. Now I look good and feel good. We go back to the place we saw, and we have a great time.

Then we walk home, amidst thunder and lightning, which we love, and we fix tortas for our merienda. We use whole wheat rolls from the bakery, cheese, sliced ham, and hot chiles. I select a banana for dessert, and Richard chooses a fried pie.

We go to our room, and having eaten, I now boil my sleepy tea. Richard reads the paper, "The News", from Mexico City. We will read in bed, listen to the thunder, and go to sleep early. Goodie, because I hardly slept at all last night, and I awoke with one blood-shot eye. But I am fine now.

Nita told us not to wait up because she went to her five o'clock Girl-Friends-Thursday-Night-Group where every week they play poker, Old Maid, and Bingo, eat pretzels and junk food, and finish whenever they feel like it.

I get drowsy and cozy and think about my painting, which I believe turned out fine, considering just getting started at painting again after a too long interval of being too busy to paint.

I run over my blessings of today and thank God for answering my prayers. This means that I saw the beggar lady on the street today and was able to give her some money. She was in an entirely different place, and we just happened upon her! Maybe you think that I am just a silly sucker. I'd rather be a silly sucker than repeat what has happened to me in the past.

Many years ago I passed by an old lady and old man begging. I was going in their same direction. I only had enough coins in my pocket to go swimming, it was really hot, and I just went on my way. On my way back from swimming I saw them. Guess where they had gone? Into a corner of the market where the day's remainder of spoiled produce is thrown into a huge pile. They climbed up the rotting slope, with their poor broken sandals on their poor, calloused, old feet, and they picked through the refuse, eating whatever bits they could find. How much do you think I enjoyed that swimming day? How happy was I with the choice I made in not giving my coins to them?

Another time, I passed by an ancient tiny woman, with her little gnarled hand out, and I didn't give to her. She went into a little tienda, and I saw the owner give her a cookie. The lady was so relieved and grateful as she immediately ate it, making the sign of the cross, and bowing her thank you.

So what would you do? How worried would you be that the beggar who asks you might be bilking you out of a nickel and not really needing or deserving your help? A good night's sleep with a clear conscience means more to me. And that's what I will have right now, with the thunder as my lullaby.

22

I CRY BECAUSE NO ONE SPEAKS SPANISH WITH ME, THE SOLUTION IS RICHARD, AND THE WHIPS OF ATOTINILCO

When we get up, Nita tells us that there was a hard rain last night. I am surprised and must have been very soundly asleep to have not noticed. Nita invites us to accompany her to breakfast at La Paróquia restaurant and meet Larry and Isabel. This will give Chita a break from cooking, and also Nita loves to go out. I would have said no, because I don't want to speak more English, but Chita is not my employee, and if Nita suggests eating out, then we will eat out.

At the restaurant, we meet Isabel and Larry, as Nita had arranged. I like them a lot, but a Canadian woman has been invited too. "Oh, no", I think, "another time of speaking English". I feel so frustrated that I don't know what to do.

Nita and Isabel talk exclusively to each other, in Spanish, Richard talks with Larry, in English naturally, and I get stuck speaking English with the Canadian. She too is very nice, but I yearn to speak Spanish. It is like being at a banquet with your favorite foods surrounding you, but you are only served oatmeal. Here I am in Mexico, living with a Mexican family, and I can't get anyone to speak Spanish with me. The breakfast lasts for four hours, and I start to cry with frustration. I go to the bathroom and cry, come back to the table, try again with Spanish, get nowhere, go back to the bathroom and cry, and I come up with a plan.

I try interrupting Nita and Isabel and explaining how much I want to converse in Spanish. They will understand and help, or so I think. But they don't understand, or don't care. They offer me an absurd "solution". I should go to the public library, which has lots of helping-people-programs, and teach English! Their other idea is that I should follow the maids around the house as they do their work and speak Spanish with them.

When we finally come home, I put on shorts and go for a long walk by myself. I am crying, and praying, and trying to come up with some solution. I get one idea. I can go to the tiny stores and try to find someone I can pay to go on walks with me and speak Spanish, perhaps for one or two hours each day after comida. This is what I did in Durango.

When Mary was eleven, I took her to our favorite Mexican hotel right on the ocean front in Puerto Vallarta for a week. We had a wonderful time. Then we went by bus to Puebla, where she was once again going to stay with a Mexican family for a month or so (although this time it turned out to be for five months). I stayed for three days to make sure that she was happy with the family, and then I took the bus north to the city of Durango, where I enrolled at the Romance Language Institute. While there, I lived with a delightful Mexican family and spoke exclusively Spanish for the whole month. It was a beautiful, happy time for me. And the Institute provided tutors for each of us.

Every day my tutor and I walked and talked, one-on-one, for two hours. My tutor was an intelligent, beautiful, interesting young woman, a university student. By spending so much time together, I learned a great deal about the life of a young, Mexican, single woman, as well as practicing Spanish. So that is how I have gotten this idea now, of looking for someone to walk and talk with me.

I don't "need" to know more Spanish. I am retired from teaching, and I have no one to speak with back home, except my daughter. But speaking Spanish and being here in Mexico is something I love to do. I have spent a lot of time and money for this purpose, and yet it just is not happening, and I don't know what to do.

If it had been under other circumstances, I really would have enjoyed my talk with Sally, the Canadian. She had a lot of interesting information to relate, and she is quite likeable. She said that the Colonial era Spaniards made it a law that every house had to have a street-front store so that the Spaniards could collect taxes. That explains the look and construction of Mexican towns, even to this day. Only new houses built by rich Canadians and Americans ignore this old rule.

Sally is a Presbyterian, and her church has a huge "Feed the

Hungry" program, a large, free hot lunch, which is the comida, and comida is the main meal of the day throughout Mexico. For many of these children, this is the only meal of the day that they have. I understand that all of the people involved in this charity are Americans or Canadians.

Isabel says that there is some Mexican government program which provides medical and dental care and free lawyers to the very poor.

And Sally unveils a mystery. There are many tunnels under the oldest part of San Miguel. The tunnels were built in 1810, around the time of the first Mexican revolution and were used for the rebels to escape. Apparently the tunnels are all clogged with dirt right now. Sally gives historical tours, and all these interesting facts and places would be explained or visited, and I do like such tidbits of lore, but that is for when I feel like being an English speaking tourist on an English speaking tour, definitely not what I want right now, on this trip. In fact, I have gone on so many trips to Europe and Mexico, taken so many tours, listened to so many well-informed guides, that I have really had my fill.

I only want one thing! To be in Mexico with Mexicans, not with Canadians, not with Americans, only with Mexicans! And not to speak English, to speak Spanish! And not to go places run by and for Americans, but to do Mexican things in Mexican places! Is that so odd? Is that too much to ask? Is it impossible? I am upset!

Since our breakfast ends very late, 1:30, I ask Nita if we can have Chita serve comida later, not at the usual 3:30. " No", she says, "because then, 'the girls' (meaning the servants) would all have to eat late". I had forgotten, but that is true.

Each day, after serving us, "las muchachas", the three women who work here as cooks and cleaners, eat in the kitchen, usually standing up and while running back and forth serving us. There is a little table in the kitchen, and I wish they could sit down and eat in a relaxed way, but it is not my business.

The custom is, that whatever the family eats, the servants eat. This is good, because then everyone eats very good food, and I suppose it is an incentive also to put a lot of care into preparing this very good food!

When Richard and I had our first apartment here (on the roof of this very house) in 1970, it was the custom for the cook to take home all of the leftovers for her family's dinner, and that meant purchasing enough for that purpose. It was an excellent custom because a cook would get home very late and tired, probably 8:00 PM, and her home most likely didn't have a stove or running water, let alone time for shopping, or money for purchases, or time to cook. For that reason, there were special multi-layered pails for carrying home various foods separated from each other in one convenient pan or pot. That is probably all the cook's family lived on.

Our maid, Tecla, was twenty-eight years old, and her husband was twenty-one. They already had four little kids, and she was heavily pregnant. Tecla had to spend her entire pay-check (from us) each week to get her husband out of jail for getting drunk. I said to just leave him in jail, but she didn't dare. So I let her bring all her children to work each day and gave them peanut butter and jelly sandwiches for lunch, which they ate while Richard and I were being served our comida. I told Tecla to always buy and cook enough to take home for everyone's supper. Of course, Tecla also did all of the shopping, and I let her select the menus, just telling her to make everything typically Mexican. She was a great cook.

Also Tecla cleaned our little apartment and hand-washed our clothes. Usually the children sat quietly on the steps, and I never heard any fussing or chatter, never saw any games, but then we were only home for comida. For what we paid, we were entitled to have her stay, and cook, and serve suppers, wash the supper dishes too, and again clean the kitchen. The amount she received seemed so tiny to us that we said to go home after doing the lunch dishes. We wanted to pay more, but then our Mexican friends and neighbors said that all those who hire servants, meaning everyone we knew, would resent it, because then everyone would just want to work for Americans. So letting Tecla go home early every day, and making sure her dinner pails were full, was the best we could do.

Back to the present and what to do about all the English, English, English. I guess all my walking and crying helped, followed by me writing it all down, letting it out in my journal, all my frustrations and dashed hopes about speaking Spanish, because now I feel better. And now comes the biggest help of all. I finally remember that in Mexico the man is the boss. I say to Richard, who is entirely on my side but doesn't know what to do either, "I think I've got it! You tell Raúl and the family that YOU want me to speak as much Spanish as possible. As the man, you are the boss over our trip. Will you try it?" Of course he agrees, and he does this, and it instantly works! Suddenly it is Spanish, Spanish, Spanish for Sonette.

The next big help in lifting my spirits is a spectacular lunch served by Chita. We have:

- Ochata for our water.
- Cantaloupe (Which I almost never chose at home where it is unappetizingly pale, hard, dry, and without flavor. Here it is the delicious, drippy, sweet fruit I remember from childhood, before food turned into an industrial product).
- Zucchini soup in heavy cream.
- Real Mexican enchiladas with red sauce, goat cheese, and onions. (I say real because the meat-filled or hugely cheese-stuffed enchiladas of the USA are not the same at all).
- Potatoes and carrots on-the-side, cubed and boiled together.
- And strawberry and yogurt dessert, made from fresh ingredients, not needing sugar.

And all of this is just for Nita, Richard, and me! I still am amazed that so few people merit such arduous attention.

At last Nita is making great efforts to speak Spanish to me and vows to speak even more from now on. And there is yet another delight! Ignacio is feeling well enough for Nita and me to go over and see him tonight.

Ignacio is Nita's older brother, the only one of the eight children left besides her. Ignacio was my dear friend.

I used to go to Ignacio's Botica, which is only one block from here, each evening at seven. He would tell his very pretty young girl assistant to take over, and we would go up the stairs to his over-head apartment to dance, and dance, and dance. He was fabulous, playing fox trots on his record player and leading me in complicated steps and twirls all around the coffee table, and avoiding the lamps and chairs as we swirled joyously through his living room. This, of course, was after Abelardo's death, and before I started going out with Richard.

Ignacio was never my sweetheart. He was a loved and important friend. I knew Ignacio from the first, as Abelardo's older brother. The Mexican custom was for all family members to buy their own houses as close as possible to the family home, and in this case the family already owned other houses that could be parceled out to the grown children. And if not married, the sons ate comida every day at their family home, so I saw Ignacio often. Of course, when I say adult children moved out and into their own homes, I mean that an unmarried daughter stayed at home until married, and then she and her new husband would establish their own home, being careful to buy their house as close as possible to the bride's parental home, preferably only one block away. (Abelardo even started in on plans to do that for me, another Great House, of course.) Before marriage, young women would not leave home and live alone. That is why, back in those days, we were always a jolly big group whenever I joined the family for comida.

As I remember all this, and anticipate seeing my friend tonight, I am thanking God because during my long crying walk I was asking God to help me, and He did. I feel like everything has changed.

Before we do anything else, Nita wants to go buy cards for tomorrow's baptism, to which we are invited. Richard goes to the bank to get new bills to enclose in the cards as gifts for the twin baby girls. We ask Nita how much to give to each, and she says one hundred and fifty pesos.

Finally we go to Ignacio's. I meet his wife Fernanda whom I instantly like. They still live in not only the same apartment where I used to visit and dance, but every smidgen of their kitchen has remained intact, exactly as Ignacio had it when I first met him (and probably since he first moved in) the same to the tiniest detail. There is the instant coffee on the little shelf over the stove. We sit at the same little kitchen table wedged into the corner. Except for the date, the calendar on the wall is identical. They are getting excellent service out of the stove and refrigerator, because they appear to still be the same ones from 1963, and they may have been old then.

We never leave the kitchen, on this or any other visit, and I get the feeling that this is their nest, where they spend all of their time. Ignacio's living room used to be very formal, and I remember him proudly showing me his new blue brocade French Provincial furniture back in our dancing days. Fernanda and Ignacio do not look now like people who would sit on French Provincial furniture, or even crave the formality of any room other than the kitchen. But of course, I am only surmising.

Ignacio and Fernanda are intellectuals of the highest order. They are very comfortable with each other and with us. I can discuss topics that interest me greatly, and they have plenty to contribute. I believe they are very well informed on esoteric matters, which thrills me, for I love to enter into the world of ideas. The world of ideas irritates and bores most people, and I am used to being brushed aside while the conversation gets changed to the ordinary, to agreement with whatever drivel the popular media is telling everyone. So I am extremely refreshed and delighted by the company and conversations of Ignacio and Fernanda. Apparently they allow very few people into their house and rarely go out, so I guess they like my company and conversations too.

Ignacio right away wants to know all about Christian Science. Fernanda says she likes all the ideas I present. I tell them that I have brought copies of Science and Health with Key to the Scriptures, by Mary Baker Eddy, for anyone who might want them. They say that they would each like to have a copy as they are voracious readers and would like to pursue these ideas in extensive detail. I say, "Sure, great. But Fernanda, they are in English". She says that although she does not speak English, she reads it, so that will be fine. They also want the weekly and monthly magazines, The Christian Science Sentinel and The Christian Science Journal, and also the Spanish Heraldo de la Ciencia Cristiana, so I say I will bring these on my next visit.

Richard, knowing of my desire to speak Spanish, has considerately said that he would visit the couple next time, so that no one would speak English for his sake. Also it is a good thing that he did not come on this visit, because all the topics we discussed would have been what he calls "heavy". Whenever he thinks the conversation gets "heavy", he side-tracks it with jokes and a new topic, and he believes he is doing everyone present a favor by "saving" them from me. I know this because he tells me so.

All of a sudden it is eight o'clock. I hurry home to where

Richard is waiting, and he and I and Nita go out for a copa. We go right across the street. The live music for tonight is a harpist playing the music of Vera Cruz. This is thrilling to me, full of trills and impossibly high, tiny, fast notes, harmonies, very full, danceable melodies. I have loved the music of Vera Cruz from the first. We have lots of fun visiting and talking.

When we come back, there is more food. Chita has prepared plates of enchiladas and potatoes and carrots. She knows how much I love this food and is always doing something special and extra. We end with bananas, and Chita has even prepared sleepy tea which Nita, Conchita, and I all share. Before leaving the table, Nita and I decide what to wear for the big event tomorrow.

Nita plans to wear one of the beautiful silk dresses I brought her. I decide upon something not nearly as dressy but much cooler. A baptism will take place at hot, dry, dusty Atotinilco. Raúl will drive us all. There were several pilgrimages to Atotinilco during Holy Week, and I could have gone. It takes four hours of walking, carrying statues of Jesus, and hundreds or thousands of people participate, starting from here in San Miguel at four AM.

Atotinilco is a tiny village consisting mostly of an incredibly old vast church, a warren of rooms, and altars, and passageways, and high adobe and stone walls. It is famous all over Mexico, and you can buy postcards or books of excellent and detailed color photos showing its old and astonishing interior, exterior, and architectural details, plus relics and statuary of saints. I believe that huge crowds also walk all the way from Mexico City, a distance of three hours by car. At least, they used to. Perhaps today they come by bus.

I considered going on the walk that left from here at four AM. Free buses are provided for the return trip. But I asked about bathrooms along the way, and nothing is provided. With hundreds or thousands of people around me, I couldn't even sneak off behind a bush, so for certain I could not make it. Even when the crowd arrives at the church, there still are no bathrooms, and how long might you have to wait to get on one of the busses shuttling everyone back to town? With those numbers, I think you better plan on maybe waiting all day. So my decision had to be not to go.

Also four hours of walking seemed daunting. It is true that old women and little children do make it, and I suppose that progress is very slow because of carrying all the heavy altars, but would I, an American woman alone, or sort of alone by way of being unaccompanied by a man, be safe? Probably. But no bathrooms is what seals the deal.

Atotinilco, when I first saw it in 1963, looked probably exactly as it did in the 1500's or 1600's, or whenever it was built. The church and the few dusty, crumbling buildings that comprised the village were not a bit tidied up, or prettified, or restored, or changed in any way. This made it of great interest because I felt that I had entered a little piece of the past. No one was around, pigs slept in the street, a few pine trees gave a bit of shade in the courtyard, and the wind blew lazily all around. The interior of the church was clammy cold. Somehow we, meaning my college professor and fellow students, were given a tour.

Like most churches in Mexico, the edifice contains many rooms, far more than I had ever suspected, having been raised as I was in the Presbyterian church of Rockford, Illinois, where, to me, a church consisted of the worshiping part, the Sunday School, the pot-luck supper area, the kitchen, and the bathrooms. I was unprepared for Atotinilco!

Our tour revealed rooms that would have shocked Rockford. There was one room full of crowns of thorns, real thorn bushes twisted into crowns, and bearing the brown stains of dried blood on the sharp thorns. The room was piled to the ceiling, ready for use by penitents. Although I think self-mutilation dishonors creation, the penitent does not at all agree, vigorously whipping his own back with one of the thorn equipped whips I saw stored in the whips room.

Another room was also filled to the top, but this time with empty cans of Pet Evaporated Milk. Evidently those who bring babies or young children need this, as there is not much of a place to buy food or supplies around here, and why the empty cans are still here is a mystery, unless it was so hard to get someone to come here and haul out the refuse that it was only done once in a while?

There was another room, of so-called toilets. The room was built over a near-by stream and contained rows and rows of benches with holes in them, and you can guess the rest. "Things are probably much different now", I say. "Oh, no, Sonette, it was never like that", says Nita. But Raúl has come back and is talking with us, and he confirms that everything I said was true. He had seen it himself.

There is a beautiful book about Atotinilco for sale in Raúl's Botica, as I said, but it is too big and heavy to take home, and it has so much writing and detailed explanations about everything that I would never read it and would feel guilty. So I don't buy it.

One more idea before I sleep. It is to call Ignacio and Fernanda and ask when I can come again. Fernanda is "green", and so am I. I like her, and I like to talk.

23

CHRISTENING OF THE NOT TWINS AT NOT ATOTINILCO, BAPTISM AT YES ATOTINILCO, AND PARTIES AT A RESORT

I don't exactly know who it is that has the two baby girls, and I was wrong to say that they are twins. The grandmother, or maybe the mom, is Delfina's sister, or else niece, whose daughters were born ten months apart! The baptism is not at Atotinilco. It is at La Paróquia. I find out that La Paróquia means simply whichever is the principal church of each town. The baptismal ceremony takes place at nine AM. For the celebration, we go to a breakfast which is as fancy as a wedding reception at a resort.

The resort is breathtakingly beautiful. It is out in the country, on top of a hill, with many hills and mountains in the distance. The rooms for lodging are of the most beautiful construction, two storied, and very individualized with white walls, and heavy dark wooden doors. Each room opens to cool balconies with flowers spilling over the railings in profusion, and there are beautiful hand-painted tiles set into the walls, there are pillars at all angles, and there are various set-backs, all to the purpose of avoiding a flat industrial look.

We see many separate buildings, each for a kind of game, or for dining, for dancing, for towel service, bar and restaurant, indoor pools, and an aviary. There is a large out-door pool with groupings of tables and chairs sheltered by palapas. All of these are connected by gardens and paths, a few expanses of grass, and shaded by flowering trees and shade trees. There is no cement used anywhere. Even the long, long drive from the road to the hotel is made entirely of cobble-stones.

The celebration breakfast is served in a large room with huge open windows, that is, no glass, and each window frames a scenic view, like a gallery of magnificent landscape paintings. Lots of large round tables are set with pretty linens. On each table is a platter of tiny home-made cookies. The waiters bring delicious coffee made with cinnamon. Each table is given baskets of fresh bolillos and plates filled with butter and cherry preserves. Nita always reminds us that she can't eat this and that because of diabetes, but she rarely follows her own dictum, and she eats five cookies and one bolillo heavy with butter and cherry preserves before breakfast is even served.

Tall glasses of freshly squeezed orange juice are brought to us (requiring someone to squeeze a mountain of oranges). We are given plates of chilaquiles with sour cream, beans, and gigantic omelets with red sauce. Lastly comes the cake-- huge slices of layer-cake using a thick spreading of light, fluffy butter frosting, covered with almonds.

Nita eats everything served, and then more cookies followed by another bolillo and jam. Does that seem like a lot? Indeed it is, and not only that, right before we left home to come to this breakfast, she had a bowl of All-Bran, a banana, and one half of a sweet roll. I am a size four or two, and Nita fits into all the size fours that I brought for her. She is a miracle of eating. She stays tiny and eats even more, and more often, than I do, and that is saying a lot, because my appetite is known politely as hardy!

Breakfast is over, and this is when we proceed to Atotinilco, for the ceremony of First Communion of Carl, the son of Delfina's other sister. The children younger than twelve have wisely been left at the resort to swim under the care of Raúl, Richard, and a couple of moms during the second church service. I like being in the old church, to be part of a ceremony that keeps this structure from being a tourist attraction or a museum. And of course, like everything else that pleases me so much, Atotinilco and its tiny town have not changed at all. It is still the moldering, crumbly, wind-swept, isolated place that it always has been.

We return to the resort to pick up the children and everyone else who stayed there instead of coming to the First Communion. We linger by the pool under a palapa drinking iced diet cokes and water until late in the day. I feel so happy to have spoken Spanish all day, including with all the other guests, and with the people seated at our table.

The minute we get back to the house, the family invites us to accompany them to go out to dinner. Dinner!! We are astonished because we ate the same as everyone else, and we are still full beyond comfort. How can they go anywhere and eat still more? So we decline. The very thought of more eating is impossible.

Instead we decide to walk about a mile to a little store to buy more instant coffee and a bar of soap. Nita has told us that she will be back in one hour and wants to walk with us. We wait, but she doesn't come. I suggest leaving a note on our door saying to meet us at the Jardín. This is Saturday evening, and we can hear the sounds of the Yaqui Indians pounding drums in the square, which means they will also be dancing, and we want to go and watch. Richard finishes drinking his coffee, and we mosey back to the Jardín. That is, after he gives me a wonderful foot massage. After standing for a long time on cobblestones, sharp, pointy, hard little rocks, in my thin-soled dressy high heels, my feet feel abused. The massage feels terrific.

We receive an invitation by telephone to accompany Nita tonight. Some friends of hers want us to meet somewhere at ten PM for dinner and dancing. Thank heavens Richard doesn't want to go. It will be Canadians and Americans speaking English, it starts too late for us, and the restaurant mentioned is expensive. I would have said yes for Richard's sake if he had wanted to go, but in the long ago past we had been part of the Ex-Pat cocktail circuit, and we are definitely not here to do that again. Nita says it is ok, she can go alone and meet her friends anyway. So that worked out nicely. Plus my feet hurt too much for dancing, even though the massage helped a lot.

I am ok for walking though, so we go to the Jardín. After enjoying the Jardín, we get up and go home to dress up and walk to above the French Park to the Hotel Molinas for a copa. I have described it before, and it is one of our favorite places. As we are enjoying the beautiful outdoor restaurant, we hear big thunder and see lightening. We think to escape a deluge and hurry home. But if the rains are to come at all, it will have to be after we are asleep, because not a drop falls before we go to bed.

24

THE ORDEAL OF THE ORANGES, AND THE FIVE HOUR SOUP

We walk around town until ten o'clock. When we return, we see Nita in the kitchen, so I go in to help. She is fixing papaya, Mexican style scrambled eggs, beans, tortillas, and hot sauce. Richard goes to the fruit tienda to buy the oranges. We need two large bags every day.

Nita wants me to squeeze the oranges by hand on the little glass squeezer which has a dome of ridges and a circular trough for catching the juice. I have tried this at home and know how hard it is, so I want to use the electric machine, which really is the same, except instead of you twisting the orange half as you press, the machine twirls the ridged dome around, and you just press. Even the machine is hard to use, but the hand squeezer is much worse. Still, I try to please her by doing what she says, but soon I say, "I can't. This hurts my wrist too much, and I'm hardly making any progress. There are still so many oranges to go". "No, Sonette", she says, "It is not hard". I say, "Yes it is", and she says, "No, it is not". After a few "Is", and "Is not's", Nita says she will do it. It is not very long before she says, "Yes, it is too hard", and we get out the machine.

Luckily there are only four of us for breakfast this morning. I take a glass of juice out to the Botica where Delfina is working. Raúl has taken the children somewhere, so that means three fewer glasses to squeeze. Nita, Richard, and I settle into the dining room for our wonderful breakfast, and that is our adventure for "Cook's Day Off".

We finish eating and wash the dishes, and now it is noon. We immediately start cooking comida! We are boiling chickens. As soon as the chickens are safely in the water, I escape to walk with Richard. I am thinking that when I get back, the chickens will be sort of cooked, and I will be available to help again. But when we return at three o'clock, I find that Nita has never left the kitchen, except to buy two huge bags of vegetables to make a caldo (soup) to add to the chicken broth.

Daughter Conchita and I immediately start helping by peeling and chopping, yet even after two hours, we have only finally finished our part in making the soup! That is, for Conchita and me, it took two hours. But for Nita, she has worked from noon until five, and all just to make one soup!

Everyone is there for our late comida. It is fantastic, and we have so much fun eating and talking. Now I will describe the five hour soup:

- Chicken broth with large chunks of chicken. (The bones are usually left in, and today is no exception.)
- Green beans.
- Carrots.
- Zucchini.
- A green pear-shaped vegetable.
- Cilantro.

That is what is cooked into the soup. To add at the table, there are bowls of fresh ingredients, all chopped or diced.

- Cilantro.
- Onions.
- Avocado.
- Ancho chiles. (These are large purple dried chiles that Nita had to wash, seed, boil until soft, puree half in the blender, and dice the other half to add to the puree.
- Limes to be squeezed into the broth.

For our water, we have limeade. (This is much easier than the trial by oranges ordeal of the morning. Limes have their own metal squeezer that works like a press.)

At seven thirty, we have finished eating and are cleaning the kitchen. We didn't eat by courses, because there are no maids here today to serve us. So there are not as many separate plates and bowls as usual. But there are still pots, and the blender, and many serving bowls, and it seems like a lot of everything. We don't mind, but it makes us appreciate the cook.

Some of Raúl's and Delfina's friends drop in, so Richard and I decide to go walking. First Conchita tells me to come, she will help me with my email. It takes a long time because although I would just type a message and click "send", Conchita wants us to go to a free greeting card site. She finds lots of possibilities, all of which I am supposed to pay careful attention to, before finally at last I can select one. This is so much fun, because without a child, one forgets to play.

Conchita is serious about teaching me, and if I make any mistakes, she erases everything up to that point, and I have to start over. Maybe this is how she learns in school. Then she sets up a chat site so she and I can chat after I return to the States. I vow to learn everything so we can chat. So far, I am a very raw beginner at chatting. I don't even know how to enter the site or anything at all about how it works. But I really like Conchita and would love to keep up our friendship by internet or by anything.

My lesson with Conchita having ended, Richard and I go walking. We buy pan for something to eat before bed and leave it in our room. Nita joins us to go to the Jardín, and we listen to Peruvian music at the bandstand. It is a nice family night with lots of grandparents and little kids. Saturday nights are for couples, and Sundays are for families. The churches are all lit up, lanterns are lighting the streets, and the atmosphere is cozy and sweet.

Around 9:30 we leave the Jardín to go to Tío Lucas, which Nita likes, and arrive home by 10:30, eat our bread, and I brew my sleepy tea.

25

RETURN OF THE KIDNAPPED PUPPY, BIGAMIST ON THE RANCHO, AND THE DEAD RIVER

There are two major events today. One is that the children return to school. They loved their two and a half weeks of vacation, and they love school too, so going back was fine with them.

The other is more dramatic. Turis, the puppy, is back! He escaped from the house on Friday evening, and everyone was fervently hoping that he would somehow come home again. When I wake up this morning, I hear talking under my window that Turis has been returned. I look out, and sure enough, there he is. Apparently someone found him, and on Saturday it was announced on the San Miguel radio station that the man who had found the doggie was there at the radio station, dog in hand, or dog on leash, and that he would wait for one hour for someone to come and claim him.

Naturally no one here was listening to the radio, so the opportunity passed by. The man left with the dog, did not have a phone, and did not leave an address. So our family offered a reward via radio. Finally everyone got together, and now Turis is back. It cost the family almost forty dollars US currency. You have to give a "reward", or you will not get your doggie back. (That is more than the Mexican minimum wage for a week of eight hour days, or longer.) Everyone here is so excited, especially I am, and we all keep petting and hugging him. Max, the old dog, has his playmate again. Yea!

I have slept late, until 9:30, whereas I usually awaken around six thirty. When I go downstairs, Nita is already in the kitchen making the OJ. I head for the presser, not the squeezer, since by hanging around Chita the cook, which I do often in order to talk, and make her laugh, and observe all her cooking methods, I have learned that there actually is an orange presser which can be screwed onto the counter top. The presser doesn't get out as much juice, but if I have to use the squeezer, I won't get out any juice at all, because it hurts my wrist too much, and I just can't do it. Richard is very strong, so when he comes into the kitchen, he takes over and smashes those oranges into juice in a jiffy. I cut up the fruit, and Delfina comes in, makes the scrambled eggs, and heats the tortillas, helped by Nita.

Breakfast lasts until 11:30 because we always have a lot to talk about. Today I learn about a servant whose husband left her and her two children to go to the USA and earn money. When he came back, he brought another wife. If that's not bad enough, he came back to their same rancho (which means little village in the country), ignores his real wife and kids totally, pays nothing for the children's support, and everyone takes the bum's side because they consider him to have a lot of money! The first wife can't do anything because there are no laws against what he is doing, and even if there were, she doesn't dare speak up because his whole family live in the rancho, and they would "do bad things to her and her family". Yipe!

Everyone here likes the aggrieved woman very well and has high praise for her work in cleaning and general helping, and they say she takes wonderful care of her children who are always immaculately clean. This in spite of being so poor, living far from here, and having very little access to water, hand washing all her own and her children's clothes, and having the many obstacles of being poor. Plus to send your children to school, the parents have to purchase all the books, their paper, and so forth. It seems overwhelming and impossible to me, especially because I know how much she earns and how far away she lives, and other hardship details of her life because I am interested, and I have made friends with her too.

We are very sorry to hear this terrible tale, but what can we do? So we take another walk and start our day.

First to the French Park. Then to the Instituto. My plan after this is to start another painting, wash clothes, go to the Post Office, and buy stamps. We have been here for three weeks and have not mailed one card, although we have emailed as much as we could, reaching my brother and my neighborhood friend, Diane. I think I got through to our son, Bob, this time. We were worried about not having enough money, because everything here is as expensive, or more expensive, as at home in Wisconsin. So we asked Bob to mail us one blank check.

However, we don't think we will need it. It is all the nightly going out for copas, and sometimes dinners, that is taking so much money. However, even though I don't care that much about going, Richard does. I want to go and have a good time with him each night, especially because all day he puts up with me speaking Spanish, which is finally starting to happen more.

It is time for comida, the servants are back, and we enjoy being served again.

- Mixed fruits.
- Lime and sugar water.
- Vegetable soup.
- Chicken tacos with red and green sauces.
- Rice with butter
- Beans.
- Tortillas.

Yummy, and we sit and visit until five thirty. Our conversations could make a book by themselves. Today Raúl and Delfina tell us that they would like to show us a movie titled "Callejón de Milagros". "Calle" means street, and "jón" added to the end means ugly. Or alley. Milagros means Miracles. It is about the life of Mexican poor people and political corruption. It is believed that this movie so greatly opened people's eyes that it caused the electoral defeat of the PRI, the ruling party for the last seventy years, roughly. Anyway, they think it would be a good movie for us to see, so some night they will show it to us.

And that is the end to serious grown-up talk for a while, because Conchita would like help with her math story problems. I enjoy the kids, and I help her for two hours. The story problems are in English because the school is bi-lingual. It is not a horrible task, doing such a long homework, as it would be if confined to some stuffy classroom or at a desk. Instead we sit in the beautiful patio surrounded by all the loveliness and freshness of the late afternoon. We have a good time. When I leave her, I go upstairs and paint until Richard is ready to go out walking.

On our walk, on a back street, we pass a little, teeny, tiny old woman walking with two canes. She looks so old and tired and poor that I turn around, run across the street, and put a ten peso coin into her hand. I shake hands, speak to her respectfully. She is so happy that it is heart-breaking, or heart-rending. She thanks me over and over and keeps making the Sign of the Cross . Her little tiny hands are work hardened, almost sharp with calluses, and yet warm, and papery, and gentle.

Then we see a tiny old man dragging a huge tree branch down another narrow street. He has a strap around his wrist to help it along. He can only drag for two steps, then he has to rest, two steps, rest. The task is harder yet because this street, like all streets, is made of bumpy cobblestones. "Can we help you?' we ask. "No, thank you, I can do it alone." "OK", we say, and on we go, on we go.

Once we get home, we decide to go up to the roof and enjoy the dusk. I go downstairs to help make merienda, and Chita, the cook, shows me how to make whole wheat rolls spread with beans and cheese, and then toasted. We have become friends, and while we cook, she tells me tales of life in her village because I like to hear about her life with her family.

At her rancho, rich people upstream blocked off all the water from the river that runs (or used to run) through her village. Now her whole rancho of poor families have to share one well, and that is all they have for water. There is no longer the river for swimming, or washing bodies and clothes, no water for raising animals. Everything is dead. All the people who can want to leave there and go to the United States to earn a living.

But for Richard and me, the day is over. We leave behind the troubles of other people, we go upstairs to our comfy room, we turn on the fan, lie down on clean sheets on soft beds in a safe, secure house. We have no troubles, and we relax, reading, listening to the evening sounds, until time to fall asleep.

26

CHITA'S KITCHEN, AND
TIPS FOR A BLABBER MOUTH

I sleep until 8:30! Qué milagro! For me, to sleep so late is a miracle! Because of the late start, we do not take our morning walk. I hear Chita working in the kitchen, so I go down and wash and cut the oranges. All fruits and vegetables have to be washed with soap and water before being handled, except I have not seen washing of bananas or pineapple. But everything else, yes.

Then Richard comes down to the kitchen and squeezes the oranges using the press, and he is quick as a wink because he is as strong as the Hulk. He likes Chita too, so sometimes he comes in to make her giggle with his bits of Spanish and his attempts to tease her. At home we laugh about Richard because, being so strong, he over-tightens everything, sometimes until things break. Whenever we cannot undo something, even a jar, we say, "Oh, Dad must have tightened this". Here, for squeezing oranges, this strength is, "What an asset!"

Nita arises and makes herself her usual bowl of oatmeal with apples and milk. This is to sustain her until the real breakfast is served, which will be in about fifteen minutes. Her oatmeal is always in a very big bowl too.

Chita finishes, we gather at the table, and we are served:
- Orange juice.
- Cantaloupe.
- Chilaquiles. (Eggs scrambled with ripped up fried tortillas)
- Green hot sauce.
- Beans.

After eating all of this second breakfast, Nita goes across the street to the bakery, buys and brings to us a huge plate of cookies, but she is the only one who eats them. Then she leaves to go and get dressed because she is going out with her madrina (God-mother) to guess where? Out to breakfast!

Nita says that she has to eat so much because of being diabetic. Being diabetic also makes you sleep like a rock for twelve hours straight each night. It is very hard to see anything very terrible about being a diabetic, if you judge by observing Nita.

We have exhausted breakfast, meaning that the food has been eaten, the coffee served, the conversations finished, and probably even the mountain of dishes clattering in the kitchen have been washed and put away by now, so leave taking begins. This is always a formal and loving ritual. It consists of one person saying something like, "Well, I must now..." the cue for the rest of us to stand. All kiss each other good-bye until lunch, and we depart.

Richard and I go upstairs to tidy our rooms. What started out to seem orderly has become chaotic, to my eye, and I need to hide, store, re-organize, do something to eliminate the clutter. After all, we use our rooms for more than just sleeping and dressing. Lately, upon entering, I have begun to think "Pig Pen".

I clean and organize best by dumping everything loose into a big pile, maybe on a bed, maybe on a rug. Then each item gets picked up only once. To set it down, the article needs to be placed in its new, logical, useful, unobtrusive "home". The new home can be a garbage can, a bag for the maid, a drawer. There are many miscellaneous that belong returned to the suitcases until further notice, but everything in categories, not all in a jumble.

Finally the room is under control with almost nothing "out" or lying around because it doesn't have its own designated spot, like before. The suitcases are then stored behind the sofa, and with a little artful trial-and-error rearranging of the living room section, the suitcases disappear, and the bedroom is separate from the living room, the extra couch is no longer a dumping ground for clothes that are not dirty enough to wash, or not wrinkled enough to iron, but not clean enough to put away. Under the couch is not where the shoes will be kept. On the nightstand is not where the pencils, and change, and maps, and ticket stubs, and travelers checks, and money folders are set, nor where empty glasses can rest until tomorrow. Now I can breathe. Now there is order. And this brings us to comida.

The gathering for comida consists only of the children and us.

Conchita has helped in the kitchen by pressing the rice into little molds, inverted onto our plates looking very special.

- Mango water.
- Cantaloupe.
- Cream of green vegetables soup.
- Meatballs in red sauce, Conchita's rice on the side.
- Beans.
- Various sauces.
- Tortillas.

Anyone who thinks it is becoming tiresome to read every menu for every meal needs better visualization techniques, and that is the job of the author. For example, "Various sauces" is not like saying "bottles of catsup and mustard". Each sauce is made in our own kitchen by our own Chita who had to go to the proper store this morning for each ingredient for everything served today. That includes deciding upon the exact, correct, chile pepper for the menu, selecting from maybe fifty kinds of chile peppers of every size, shape, color, flavor, and hotness. Each has to be washed with soap and water, deseeded, chopped, browned in the skillet or on the comal, and then ground in the blender with all the other fresh ingredients for the sauce. Then the blender has to be dismantled, hand washed and dried, reassembled (even the base and the cord have to be washed until the whole thing looks "store new"). Next put it back into its original box of purchase, and back onto the proper shelf in the proper cupboard, ready to repeat its same duty tomorrow. And as I said today, there are sometimes several sauces for one day, or for one meal. Also the blender is used for making all the fruit waters which we are served each day for comidas.

This describes the process. To give the feel of entering the empty, cool kitchen, and seeing bags of fresh purchases, while I take a drink of lime-water, and then noticing Chita coming down from the roof, or in from the hot laundry room where she has been ironing clothes, and seeing her face break into a slow shy smile because I am there, and we can laugh and talk for a little while as she gets ready to cook, that is part of making the "various sauces", or whatever we will eat for comida. To watch the cute doggies try to squeeze in through the slamming kitchen screen door behind

Delfina or one of the children as they stroll in with a message or request, that is part of the sound of the making of the "various sauces". To hear Raulito bouncing his ball on the roof of his play spot just above the outside stairs across from the kitchen, and to hear his cheery child-voice responding to the friendly chatter from the people who live up-stairs in the apartments, that is part of being part of the making of the "various sauces". So you see? When I describe the food, I am describing the life. The life of just one of the servants living in The Great House of Raúl Rodriguez.

In fact, I am hanging out in the kitchen right now, at the request of Conchita. She has an interest in making desserts (and eating them, but not in washing dishes or cleaning up). After all, Conchita is only eleven, and why would an eleven year old clean up when the cook will do it for you? Plus when you are eleven and believe that because the cook sincerely loves you, and you really love her, and because you are a child, and the cook always does all of the work anyway, you imagine that she also really loves doing your clean up as well.

So here I am, because Conchita came and got me and wanted me to make the choice for tonight's rice pudding which she will make for merienda. "Which do you want in the pudding, Sonette, apples or raisins?" "Apples", I say. And I know it will be good.

While Conchita is getting out bowls, and pans, and the beater, and the eggs, and generally getting a start on the pudding, Richard and I take a walk. We return after a long while, and Conchita has finished with the pudding part. She abandons the clean-up part with a perfect excuse. Will I help her with her math?

"Sure", I say, and we spend another pleasant time in the patio with the math book and the story problems. Conchita is very smart and probably doesn't need help, but we like doing things together, and this is another good way for her to practice her English with me. I am glad to do this because of our arrangement that we will speak Spanish all the time, except for one or two hours per day while I am helping the kids do their homework.

The afternoon unfolds slowly. Richard and I have time to do our laundry and write a few postcards before Nita returns (from breakfast with her madrina). I ask Nita, "Let's call and see if we can visit Ignacio again". She says, "Great", so she calls, he says yes, and Nita, Richard, and I go over. This time Fernanda serves us nuts and fried tortilla snacks. We have a great time.

When it becomes nine o'clock, Nita lingers on, but Richard and I go home because Conchita is waiting for us to eat her rice pudding. It is delicious, and Conchita is proud and happy that we like it. At nine thirty there is still no sign of Raúl and Delfina for merienda, so we go upstairs. We are waiting to be called, but the call never comes. We know that Nita bought empanadas at the bakery for tonight's merienda, so hunger drives us down to the kitchen. Conchita heats up the empanadas de atún (tuna fish stuffed fried pies). We take them to our room to eat because for us it is late.

While we eat, Richard gives me some good advice. Nita has been contradicting everything I say, no matter what it is. It has become noticeable to everyone. He tells me that I should talk less and listen more because this is her house, with her family, in her town. The friends we make are her friends, and I might be seen as taking over the conversations, which no one likes. He is right, and I am glad that he has told me this. He says, "You can talk, but not too much, and don't offer any opinions unless someone asks you". You would think I would be embarrassed and ashamed of myself upon hearing this, but actually I am relieved because I see his point, and it will solve a problem that I didn't realize I was creating. But I guess I was. Blabbermouth! Oh, well!

Instead of reading in bed, I decide to describe something of what we are experiencing when I say, "We take another walk". The worst walks I can imagine are in a gym, on a treadmill, in an inside room, maybe hooked up to some kind of exercise monitor for burning calories, or heart rate, or speed, or some other clinical rat-in-a-trap approach to walking. As far as I know, this is not common in Mexico.

No, no, no, a walk here is outside, airy, breezy, full of adventures, sounds, smells- a sensual feast. This evening's walk was up, up, up, each street steeper than the last. The houses we passed were all in the Colonial style, but individualized. The richest and newest often have nothing street-side except a two story high cement wall painted in one solid color. There is nothing to be seen that hints of what may be inside.

After you pass those, and go still higher, there are other new houses that are composed of the most creative combinations of triangles, balconies, outside stairs, exposed patios and gardens, curves, and angles. Nothing is a box with windows. All display spectacular architectural skills which harmonize completely with the rugged mountainside into which they are built. The houses cling to, or spring from, or nestle into, gullies, hills, drop-offs. Streets are curvy, winding, twisting, very narrow, and of course are made of smooth, slippery, lumpy cobblestones. We can barely walk and don't want to even think about driving a car. Taxis cost only two dollars per ride to anywhere in the city limits, and that is San Miguel's answer to not needing or wanting a car.

Flowers and trees are of such brilliant colors that I have no way to describe them. They are all clustered together, or in some cases planted in patterns. Every low window is covered with iron grills, and the higher up windows all have iron balconies full of clay pots overflowing with flowers, dripping down the walls which are painted in clear, sharp, bold, hot colors. Where we in Wisconsin would have wooden trim, or aluminum, here in San Miguel there are granite chiseled stone doorways, window edges, and window sills. Sometimes you do see wood, but it is very brightly painted wood, or sometimes it is a deeply polished, glowing mahogany. Trees are allowed to grow right in the middle of the sidewalks, in the gutters of streets, in little nooks notched out of walls. The branches of the trees arch over the streets giving welcome shade and grace even to the humblest of neighborhoods.

In contrast to the streets, the sidewalks consist of large flat stones, and the total width of a sidewalk is about one foot. Consistency is not considered to be a particular virtue, and streets often widen and then narrow again to some degree. The same with sidewalks which sometimes even disappear or turn into steep stairs for a while. Walking where there are many people means everyone is stepping up or down off of the sidewalk to let someone pass or to be passed.

You can always orient yourself by looking for the towers or domes of churches that you know. No house is higher than three stories, and there are no offices, factories, or businesses, other than the little house-front tiendas, or restaurants, or workshops. And you ought to know that if you just went up, then you need to go down to get home. You may wind all over the place, and go up and down many times as the streets traverse gullies and ridges, but still you can look for and find the churches.

There are no parking lots, malls, shopping centers, or big stores. Garages are hidden behind house walls. I guess there are some parking lots hidden in the downtown behind massive, ancient, wooden doors. Such parking areas appear to be housed in old stables or churchyards where a car spot can be rented.

There are, actually, some industries and one big store, but these are far out of town, so they don't count, if like me, you don't want to go there or know about this intrusion of the industrial world. Probably there are more places like that which I am glad not to know about.

And each day, each walk is different. There are many routes in this tiny city. There are our favorites to be savored again and again. There are even zones that are too quiet, menacing, and we feel wisdom says, "Turn around". There are people, different every time. There are glimpses into other lives and other ways of life— through an open door always heretofore closed. Through a passageway unnoticed, except today someone enters, granting us a swift glimpse of the unknown. Through happening upon a well-dressed someone who is passing through the door to a particularly beautiful shop which had never before attracted our attention. Through smells of cooking, and children's chatter, as uniformed school kids are delivered home by the family servant.

These are our walks, and remember that we are artists. We walk to fill our eyes as much as to stretch our legs, and fill our lungs, and move our feet.

27

THE FANCY MOVIE PLACE, AND MY PLAN X

On our nice fresh morning walk in the French Park, we encounter Nita and her two walking friends. She has been urging me to join them for a seven AM walk each morning, but I don't want to be ready that early, and anyway at ten AM Nita is usually still in her bathrobe. So I never went because I figured the seven AM walks were a kind of dream, or goal, or are hit-and-miss, and I wasn't about to hurry up and be ready for maybe nothing.

We are wearing shorts and T shirts and are uncomfortably hot already. Nita wears a blouse and pants, a long-sleeved sweater, and a huge heavy woolen wrap-around shawl. She says she is still freezing, even after having walked for forty-five minutes already. She gives me her hands to prove it by her icy fingers. Living in Canada must be miserable for her for most of the year.

Nita tells us that she will be up early every day now for her early morning walks. She was just being polite by sleeping late because the kids' vacation meant that the family slept later and she didn't want to wake anyone up. Nita sleeps with Conchita so that Richard and I can have the use of her apartment. She really does so much for us that I must never forget that there are reasons for everything that she does. Anyway, now that school has started, everyone in the house gets up and going early, I am told. Actually, Nita could be given her own room, but Conchita loves Tía Nita and wants her to stay in the same room together. They laugh and giggle and whisper until late. The love of a child is precious, and childhood is short.

I suppose that since school has started and everything will start earlier, I could now tell Nita to call to me outside my window each morning, but I don't know if I might sleep late, so I don't accept the offer of walking with her friends. Also our present arrangement gives me the early mornings with Richard. And, Nita shares most of her friends with me, so it is good for her to have a few friends who are hers alone.

We go home and find that making breakfast today is to be a cooperative effort. Chita helps me clean our hot pot which gets water scaled, and when it does, it loses its efficiency. I have tried to clean it, and I always fail, but Chita succeeds. Richard squeezes the oranges, of which there are only a few. But there are a lot of limes, which he is also told to squeeze for breakfast because of the lack of oranges. Chita has already prepared papaya, and Nita is heating up empanadas. Just for me, Chita is fixing eggs Mexican style because fried pies for breakfast is not what I want. If we had no other choices, I still would not eat fried pies. I would have only tortillas and hot sauce. But Chita and I have become friends, and she is very considerate about accommodating me. She knows that I would not like to put her to extra trouble, so she does all these special things without asking me.

During breakfast, Nita talks exclusively to Raúl, not even glancing at us. So I think that Richard is right, she wants to have her family time without interruptions from us. Previously I would have considered that kind of behavior very rude because to me, everyone at the table (even including strangers if you are at a big party) should be included in the conversation. That is a hallmark of gracious consideration.

However, now that I have attended a few Mexican gatherings and have seen that pals talk exclusively to each other and leave everyone else out, I suppose that such behavior is correct according to this culture. Thus, maybe what I consider as an important social skill, wherein I try to address everyone and draw the shy person into the general conversation, could here be regarded as "butting in". I am now guessing that here when friends or relatives talk only to each other, one is supposed to leave them alone to enjoy each other's company.

Understanding other people's cultures is interesting, but it is not always easy!

As breakfast is served, mysteriously the lime juice has transformed into plenty of orange juice. There wasn't time, and there weren't enough oranges to make all this, so what happened? And where is all the lime juice? Richard squeezed twenty-five limes! What happened?

We have invited Nita to attend her friend's "theater-bar" at their beautiful, ritzy restaurant hotel, where we have gone a couple of times for copas. We will go tonight, as the showings are only on Thursdays. Nita is delighted with the invitation. She wanted us to go there on the first night we arrived in San Miguel, but we were not up to so much on the first day. So now she answers "Yes", as her face lights up with delight. The movie for this week is "Tortilla Soup", and all three of us are excited. Evidently the ticket price includes one drink from the bar.

Of course Richard and I go for another long after-breakfast walk. We return to our rooms where Richard boils water for coffee while I squeeze paints onto my pallet. First I take off my tennies and put on the flip flops, which I bought for the trip Mary and I took to Puerto Vallarta when she was six years old. My tennis shoes need to air out and do not look good with skirts or dresses. I would rather wear sun dresses for our walks instead of pants which are so hot, but I would have to wear sandals to look decent, and we do so much walking that without socks my feet would be rubbed raw by sandal straps. Socks with sandals would be dirty by the end of the first block. I am too vain to wear tennis shoes with a dress, because that looks like a cleaning lady waiting for the bus to get started on someone's house. Even the maids here care too much about how they look to make that fashion mistake. One of the maids here always wears a nice skirt and blouse, and although she can't afford stockings, and it is too hot anyway, she wears flats or pumps. Chita wears pants with tennis shoes, and so does the other helper woman. Nita almost always wears dresses and dress shoes or else sandals. Delfina wears beautifully tailored slacks with a matching sweater and elegant flats.

We explore lots of beautiful streets. We are trying to find the place where one summer we rented an apartment from Nita, but in a different house. We can't decide which one it was, although we know it was very near-by to this one. It is really Richard who wants to find it. His memories of that summer are happier than mine.

During the walk, I am thinking about my "secret plan" for myself when I get old. If I can't care for myself, here is my idea. It is to pay a Mexican family for me to live with them and take care of me. My pension and social security would be ample. What I would like would be a family with a beautiful house and large courtyard and gardens. My room would have to be on the main floor, open to the patio and gardens.

The family should not be too rich because they must think that the money from taking care of me was very important so that they would want me to stay healthy, happy, and remain with them. I'd want some shelter on the patio so that I could be outside all day, hot or chilly, rain or shine. Lots of coming and going, a family with children and several generations under one roof. I'd want to eat with the family at all meals, and me be a grandmother type to the children.

I'd want enough maids around so that taking care of me would not be a burden. I'd want to sometimes be taken to parks to see birds and hear music, maybe to pretty out-door restaurants. To go out of the house at least twice a week. I'd want to go for a ride in the country at least once a week to see the mountains.

For food, just like this family. Everything fresh and Mexican. At each breakfast and comida, fresh OJ, fruits, fresh soups and tortillas, and Mexican style main courses. No desserts, or packaged food, or sweets, hardly any meat or chicken. Lots of beans, and rice, and eggs. For the evening meriendas, fruits, or bolillos, or both. My sleepy tea also.

If my children ever read this, I hope it is in time to make it happen for me, in case I ever need it. I think about this because I had to put my mother in a nursing home (at age ninety-two), and although it was an excellent place in every respect, and she grew to like it there, I have never seen a nursing home that takes the residents outside. I visited my mother every single day for two years and always took her outside, sometimes carrying her breakfast or lunch trays outside too. In rain I covered her with a large plastic bag, face cut out (because you can't push a wheelchair and also hold an umbrella). I tried to take her to concerts, public gardens, and dinner theater every couple of weeks. I carried a snow shovel and broom for walking her when the sidewalks were drifted closed. So she was happy. But I can't count on my children to be able to do all of that for me. That is why I have thought up my "Plan X'. Plan A is to never need care away from my own steam, away from living where and how I want to.

I couldn't really, literally, visit my mother every single day, but almost, and when I could not, either Bob or Mary went in my place and always took Grandmother Barbara outside, or at least to some event. For my own "Plan X", I even think that there would be enough of my savings left so that Bob and Mary could fly down to visit me twice a year, staying for as long as they want. They both love Mexico and are always wonderful to me, so I think they would do this.

Maybe they will read this, and maybe they won't. I will read everything I have written here when I am old and want to re-live my fun. My mother kept occasional diaries and shared them with me. They were sketchy, and short, and sporadic. I think one was of attending Wellesley College, and one was later when she went gold prospecting, or treasure hunting in the desserts with Cousin Harry, and when she went to Hollywood, and went to movie star parties on their yachts. I wish she had written a lot more, but she told everything out loud instead, in wonderful stories.

Comida. Why didn't I know that we would have lime-aid for lunch? How obvious. Naturally I love everything served except the slimy nopales, which instead of I eat lots of tortillas in red sauce. We finish with the last of Conchita's rice pudding, and then I help her with her homework. She is very smart and doesn't need me at all, but it is an excuse to be together and to be a team. I finish my second painting, start a third, and it is time to dress for the movie.

Nita, Richard, and I leave at seven PM, walk to the beautiful hotel next to the French Park, the one owned by Estela Sautto. The movie is "Tortilla Soup" which is peopled by mean, self-centered characters, but contains lots of scenes of good Mexican cooking which all of us enjoy watching. The screen is big, there is a dome overhead with a crystal chandelier, we are seated at round tables with linens, and the waiter brings you any drink you want, plus bags of popcorn! This is a far cry from the freezing cold, overly-loud, sticky-floored theaters we are used to in Wisconsin!

Delfina met us just before the movie started, and now that it is over, Raúl joins us, as well as the owner's son, whose name I think is Harry. We sit in the hotel's luxurious dining room and get to know Harry as we order dinner. He is most interesting, and we like him. He is a very fine painter who is currently making exceptionally complex and high quality stained glass because it is too hard to sell paintings. Just like our Bob!

We have a lot of fun talking. Nita says she will treat. Raúl and Delfina order pie, chicken wings, and shrimp salad. Richard and I order nothing because we don't want Nita to have a big bill, and I think that we have bread from the bakery in our room. But when we leave the restaurant and go home, I find that Richard had eaten all of it while I helped Conchita. That explains why he didn't order dinner. So I go to bed hungry. Richard too is feeling hungry by now, the kitchen of course is locked, the bakery is closed, and, oh, well, it was still a nice evening. Raúl had come by car, so he drove us all home, and we accepted the ride because it was 12:30, not a good hour to be out walking by the park. Night, night.

28

STREET SELLER BRINGS ME A GIFT, RICHARD GOES PAINTING WITH LARRY, AND I WANT TO BOIL A HARMONICA

There is a tiny, wizened lady with very few teeth who waits outside for me most days, hoping for a few coins. She is probably not very old but has had a hard, hard life. I think I already explained how all this woman can do to earn money, like many desperately poor people, is to cut a few cactus leaves way out in the country and bring them to town during the early hours. Then she finds a doorway to sit in, cuts off the sharp spines, and tries to sell them. I always give her a few coins, as she is trying hard to earn a living by her own work.

This morning as I come out of the house for my early pre-breakfast walk, she is waiting for me. She beckons to me, calls me "amiga", and from her bag of daily needs supply, she brings out a little bowl of something she has cooked for me. It is cactus with chopped onions, still warm, and she is so proud of her gift. Of course I eat some right then, so as not to disparage her sweet generosity. That bit of onion could have been precious to her, seeing how little she earns, and how much things cost here, not to mention the fuel it used for cooking, and I think of how she has waited for me and timed it so her gift would still be hot.

Poor people, and street people, have very little access to water and soap, so it is not wise to eat street food, unless you are very sure about its conditions of preparation. But I think, "She did something wonderful. God certainly could not let me get sick because of her inability to fulfill ideal sanitary conditions". She wants me to finish it all, but I say I do not want to take her bowl. She has brought a tiny plastic bag, so I say, "Give me la mitad" (a one half portion). I take it, put it into my pocket, and give her ten pesos (although she hasn't asked for anything). I say I am taking it inside to finish and re-enter the house.

When I come out a few minutes later with Richard, she is just leaving. I say, "Wait!" Richard and I go into the bakery to choose a tray-full for her, the most nutritious of what they have to offer—a tuna fish empanada, a bean and sausage empanada, and two bolillos. When I come out, I show her what is in the bakery bag, and we tuck it into her woven plastic carry-all. She shows me a tiny plant she has brought with her today, and she says she is now going to the market to try to sell it. It is good for curing stomach aches.

As she moves along in her daily struggle with life, I return to eat our splendid, abundant breakfast in the company of a lively, loving, prosperous family, attended by the cook and the other women servants. The humble cactus bits cooked with onion does not find its way onto my plate, but it has found its way into my heart, corny as that sounds, because it should be obvious that I am a corny person myself, plus sentimental.

But our breakfast is served very late this morning, and by the time it is, Richard has already left to go landscape painting out in the country with Larry. All the family is upset because Richard left with no breakfast. "Well", I say to Raúl, "I said to Richard, "Drink the fresh orange juice that is waiting on the counter, and go across to the bakery, and buy an empanada", but he wouldn't do it". "Why not?" Raúl is bewildered. "I don't know, but Richard doesn't like to be a bother. He is shy". Raúl is so funny and quick. He says, "I am shy too, but I still eat breakfast".

Our breakfast is the usual wonderful stuff, plus "synchronized ham", "jamón sincranizado". That is a funny name for chopped ham, tomatoes, and onions between two fried tortillas. Nita and Raúl talk, mostly to each other, and it is good listening practice for me because their vocabulary exceeds mine, as does their speed when they really get going. Still, they speak very clearly. Breakfast is not over until the cathedral bells clang and clang to announce noon. Nita leaves immediately to go have lunch with Isabel.

I go walking past the Instituto. When out walking, I have to stay in range of a bathroom and a drink of water, and the Instituto supplies both. True, water at the Instituto comes from a big upside-down glass bottle-jug set out on the patio, and the water is dispensed into little, tiny, pointy, flimsy paper cups, a trickle at a time, but still it is water, and better than nothing.

Passing the Instituto, I come to the dusty shops on the outskirts of town. In a ceramics shop of bright hand-painted plates, platters, cups, pots, and even bathroom sinks, I buy an unusually shaped jug thing for keeping water on your bed-side table. It looks like a vase that you smacked flat on two sides, leaving the middle section curvy. It has a long neck, and a matching cup which is meant to be placed upside down over the opening to keep the bugs out until you get thirsty. It is really pretty. I would buy lots of them, but how to get them home? I can use this as part of a still-life to paint, and afterwards take it home to put on our own patio.

Delfina's parents come over. They are so much fun and really nice. We have:

- Juice of boiled flowers, purple and sour.
- Papayas and bananas.
- Bowls of gazpacho and add-your-own chopped eggs, cucumbers, and green peppers.
- Bowls of hot soup with beef chunks and broth, with cucumbers added just before serving.
- A platter of cooked carrots, potatoes, and zucchini with shredded lettuce on top and crumbled goat cheese.
- Corn tortillas.

Raúl knows how I love hot chiles, so he puts a special sauce on my plate, and also he has bought me a yellow hot pepper. Very Good! Instead of thinking what a glutton I am for hot sauces, and how much work it is to make them, the whole family is very proud of me and say that I am "more Mexican than a Mexican", loving my delight in all foods "picante", tongue-burning hot. (My mother always said that my tolerance was probably because once I started my hot sauces indulgences, I had quickly burned all my taste-buds off.)

As we finish comida at our usual 5:00, Nita returns from her lunch date with Isabel and flutters into the dining room looking radiant, and pretty, and excited. She has had a very good time, kisses us all hello and good-bye, and sets out for her 5:00 Bingo and Games Club. Obviously she will be late arriving there, but in Mexico there really is no such thing as "late", especially for Nita.

Richard returns also from his day of painting with Isabel's husband and says he needs to phone Larry to set the time for tomorrow as he will paint with Larry again, and we have just been informed that tomorrow at 1:30 we are all invited for tacos at the home of some of Raúl and Delfina's friends. Everyone departs the dining room for their own afternoon activities. "Afternoon" in Mexico means "until dark", and dusk starts around eight PM.

Richard and I take a walk until all of a sudden the banging and clanging of the cathedral bells tell us that it is already 7:45. I haven't even squeezed out my paints yet today, so we hurry home. Our plan is to paint until dark and then go up to the roof with tortas and wine for merienda. So this is what we do.

When we get to the roof it is not quite dark, and we hear the harmonica of the blind man who always sits across the street from the Botica. Richard says he looks exactly like the same blind man who used to beg the same way back in 1968, and it is true, he does! He sits on the corner, playing his harmonica, with his tin cup on his left, and passers-by toss in coins. (Except I do not because I don't like him.) Even inside the house, when I stand by my window to paint, I am tortured by his harmonica. He only knows one song, "Cielito Lindo", and only the first few bars of that. I have been thinking of buying his harmonica and boiling it, and then taking it to some distant part of town to give to a little poor kid as a toy. All that stops me is that the man would just go buy another and start his musical torture all over again.

Tonight, from the roof-top, his unbearable song sounds even louder. I look over the high edge of the roof. Usually I am seated on the edge, but this position is so precarious that I could not dare to turn around and look down at him, so I have to stand on tip-toe on the roof itself and lean over on my chest to get a glimpse of him. There he is, of course, accompanied by the unfortunate little boy who sits next to him all day, every day, and on into the night, to guard the money and run errands, I suppose. I feel so sorry for this little seven year old. (I am guessing his age.) What a horrible fate if this man is his father or uncle or something, or if this is a grotesque job, or if he is paid. Can you imagine how this little fellow must feel, never running, or playing, or reading, or doing anything at all but sitting on the sidewalk for twelve hours each day? Does he get to go to school? Even if he does, he would still be here every day from 2:30 until nine PM and all day on weekends.

This makes me think about the famous Spanish novel, "Lazarillo" which I assigned to my students in Spanish IV. Lazarro is from Lazuras. Lazarito would mean cute little Lazarus. But Lazarillo means just common and little, ordinary, not cute, not special at all. Lazarillo in the novel is owned by a mean beggar, blind, like the man across the street, and Lazarillo doesn't get much to eat, he gets hit, beaten, he can't escape, etc.

Still looking down from the roof, thinking about Lazarillo, and this tragic little boy, I look at my watch. The bakery will be open until 9:00, five minutes from now. "Quick, Richard, money!", and he gives it to me. I run down all the stairs, out of the house, across the street, and into the bakery. I buy huge pan dulces, sweet breads, hand one directly to the little boy (to be sure the man doesn't take it), and give one to the blind man. Also five pesos and the bag with more bread in it. I don't want to give anything to this awful man who uses this child as a captive, but like all adults of my type, I still feel sorry for the boy and want to help him in the only way I know how. That's why beggars use children, everyone knows it, everyone suspects that giving makes more people take more children captive, and yet one feels sorry for this kid, this one particular kid, this right-before-your-eyes kid. Which is exactly how I feel, and is exactly why I have done what I have done.

I climb back the stairs to the roof, look over to see if the boy is eating, and how hungry he appears to be, and…As soon as all the restaurants and stores are closed, which means no more tourist foot traffic, the man hails a taxi! He opens the door and gets in and goes home!

Richard laughs and laughs. The man has a real racket going, earning enough, we are to later observe, to arrive by taxi every morning and take a taxi home every night. I am outraged, then bewildered, then thoughtful, and then I give up. Why should I be upset because a fellow human being can afford a taxi? But the little boy, he is trapped.

29

SURPRISE LUNCHEON AT THE VILLA

Richard goes painting with Larry. I go for a walk. I have a plan for the morning. I always have a plan. When I do not have a plan for the day, I feel weepy, or frightened, or jittery, or, let's say I do better when I have a plan. For one thing, I feel so grateful to be alive and in this wonderful universe that I don't want to waste it. Even if my plan is to sit in the sun, read a book, write in my journal. The plan does not have to be grand. But it has to be a plan.

Today's plan is grand though, and I don't understand just how grand until it all unfolds. It starts out simply:

1. Paint.
2. Wash and set my hair.
3. Get dressed up.
4. Leave here with Richard and all the family to go to the home of friends of Raúl and Delfina for comida, departing from here in Raúl's car at two thirty.

I have plenty of time. Oh, ha, ha, I always think that I have plenty of time, with very little to do, and all of a sudden, it is night.

I paint a little, set hair, and put on a good silk dress and a pair of fashionable high heels. We go to the most wonderful place! Raúl drives us up, up, up through tiny angular alleyways, to "the top of San Miguel", and then winds us down a little, again through alleys, to a great, closed, metal door with an intercom. We are on a mysteriously named street, a dusty beat-up looking lane really.

We are admitted as the doors are swung open by a uniformed man, Raúl is shown to a place inside the compound where he can safely park the van, and we find ourselves in a beautiful Arabic style courtyard. This is the entrance to the villa, the home of Estela, and I do not know it, I have no inkling, but Estela is going to become a close, close friend, and she will become a major part of my life. All I see now is what is before me, the gardens, the villa, and Estela, beautiful, intelligent, talented, and brimming with life.

Estela speaks seven languages, not ordinary ones, and she learned all of them by living in the countries where these languages are spoken. She is fluent in each. Her husband is Middle-Eastern. They are very much in love and have a son and daughter.

Estela's son is great pals with Raulito, and that is how the two families became such close friends. When I first met Estela, in the dining room of Raúl's house, I liked her instantly and was impressed with her knowing so many languages. She is very lively and down-to-earth, and I believed her to be a high-up language tutor for important business men. Now I am surprised that she is so much more than that. She is easy to know and is a wonderful person, not at all assuming, or pompous, or anything that would indicate, "I am above the rest". She is exceptionally talented as an architect, designer, business woman, and much more.

We are ushered through a garden door that has been cut through a huge red wall. We enter a large patio with lots of tables with umbrellas, each filled with guests. On one side is a rocky cliff covered with palm trees, pines, vines, flowers. Paths are carved out through the rocks and wind up and down past pools of water, stone stairs, over little bridges. On the other side of the garden are beautiful buildings, and tables brimming with food.

Each table holds lots of fresh toppings of diced vegetables, sauces, crispy, crunchy, and round large yellow tortillas made of yellow corn, which is unusual, as Mexicans prefer white corn. We are offered a variety of fruit drinks or soda pop. We chose the purple water, tangy, made of boiled flowers. I have to remember the name of this because I am seeing it on more and more occasions.

A beautiful, well-dressed young woman comes to our table. Clearly she is not a servant. She brings us course after course of:

- Beans cooked with bacon and seasonings.
- Tortillas patted out from fresh masa (dough) right before our eyes, and cooked on a comal (flat piece of metal with fire under).

- Chopped, diced, fried steak to fill the tortillas. Cooked at the long outside grills by men dressed in white who are busy chopping, and stirring, and searing to get it all just right.
- Chopped, diced, fried lamb, also to stuff into folded tortillas.
- Last of all, a heavenly cake, Pastel de Tres Leches (cake of three milks). The three milks are regular milk, evaporated, and condensed, which is heavy and sweet, with the consistency of a pudding. The cake is a huge hit with everyone, being a favorite dessert of most Mexicans, and of me too.

Conchita takes fresh limes, covers them with chile pepper, and sucks out the tangy juice. When Anna Marie Henry, my childhood friend, was eleven years old, like Conchita is now, she fixed lemons with salt just this way, and we used to sit by the river in back of her house to enjoy them. Anna Marie's mother was Mexican, at the time when someone from Mexico living in Rockford, Illinois was a rare and interesting phenomenon, and was what my mother called "A true beauty, from a very high-class family". Emma Henry was my mother's best friend. I wonder if it was Anna Marie's mother who taught her about this Mexican children's treat? No one else I knew ever tried it.

Estela chooses us, out of all her many guests, to sit with. When lunch is finished, a big wind tips the table over, spilling a bowl of chile beans onto a chair. I admire her aplomb as she calmly places the cushion on the ground, calls the family dog, and then proceeds to put all of the serving bowls, with their delicious contents, on the floor next to the dog. Everyone is delighted by the dog's happiness. It makes an accident turn into a very happy scene.

We start to help by picking up the fallen paper-ware and plastic forks. The servants run over and quickly finish the job.

I tell Estela what a beautiful view of SMA we had on the way to her house. "Oh", she says, "would you like to see a really pretty view?" She goes up to her house, which can barely be seen from the party area where we are, brings down the keys, and invites us to take a tour.

So beautifully and cleverly landscaped are the multi-leveled gardens, that we were unaware that within these walls are five more houses, stepped down from one another. We have been entranced by our surroundings, which also include a band-stand, a sixteenth century fountain and stone wall, and indescribable semi-tropical gardens. The five houses are up the ridge, behind us. Estela has designed them all and supervised their construction and placement. She hired local artists, and craftsmen, and workmen, together creating these extraordinary guest houses.

Inside the casitas, each one has domed ceilings made of red clay bricks with white mortar. There are stone walls and stucco walls, fieldstone walls, hand-painted tile walls, and walls covered with tromp d' ole murals. Ceilings let in light by capillas (tiny bell towers). Some ceilings have beams as well as bricks. Other ceilings are surrounded by twelve-inch molding painted by hand in blends of soft pinks and greens.

Bathrooms and kitchens are abundantly decorated with hand-painted tiles, painted to order and imported from Puebla, the town of tile and ceramic masters of the country. Ceramic sinks of elaborate hand-painted patterns and pictures, with golden fish for faucets and spouts. Mirrors surrounded by stained glass. Everywhere Jacuzzis, hot tubs, showers and baths painted with fanciful designs, all made of the finest ceramic.

Windows protected, instead of with the traditional iron bars, with sculpted grills of black iron leaves and flowers. Patios, terraces, balconies everywhere, harmonizing, but no two alike, nothing at the same level, all with views spectacular of San Miguel below, and the blue, and golden, and purple mountains in the distance. Each room is filled with windows, splashing brilliant light, but no glare, nothing edgy, just light bouncing through flowers, and trees, and palms, and vines. All floors are tiled, shining and scrubbed every inch every day. Hand-carved furniture with brightly striped or pastel striped hand-woven fabrics, rugs hand-made to match. Art, pottery, and ornamentation have all been commissioned from local artists and artisans.

Estela says it takes her employees four hours each day just to sweep and wash all the patios. This does not even count the labor for the insides of the house floors, or the rest of the cleaning of the houses, and it is all done again and again, each and every day.

Last we go to see Estela's own personal house, which is just like everything I have already described, except it is bigger, and even more elaborate and grand.

Everyone is particularly nice to me. I can't figure out why. In any case, Estela is a wonderful person, and of course Raúl and Delfina are just tops. Lots of Delfina's relatives are here too, so I know quite a few of the crowd. They all have the most perfect and gracious manners, which make me feel very comfortable, because that is the way I grew up. USA behavior has become so harsh over the years, so much so that I feel an enormous sense of relief when here in Mexico where kindness, liveliness, and thoughtfulness are still a way of life. Getting back to the way life used to be for me, after so many years of a gradual but steep decline in the importance, or even the presence of niceties, makes me realize how much I have missed this gentelness, and why I feel more at home here in San Miguel than I do in my own house, in my own state, in my own country.

Speaking of such things, there are several retired American couples attending the party also. They are all vacationing in Estela's guest houses, casitas, for one or several months.

30

THE SCARY MUMMIES OF GUANAJUATO, AND A SCARY RESTAURANT BILL

At 8:45 AM we all pile into Raúl's van for a trip to Guanajuato. On the way we pass Raúl's and Nita's aunt's ranch, which is a huge, huge ranch, which includes a whole village, a lake, and land, who knows how much, but lots, lots of land. Raúl tells us that this aunt was so generous that she gifted a deed to a house to each tenant who lives here and works the land. The main huge hacienda is now just one dot in the middle of an artificial lake, as decreed by the government which confiscated the aunt's land. The "dot" is the round top of a campanilla (a bell tower) of the family's private chapel.

I start thinking about 1966. I was a very young and new teacher of Spanish and art. My students loved my stories of San Miguel, so I brought fourteen of them here for twelve days of Christmas vacation. Or maybe twelve students for fourteen days. Anyway, Nita invited all of us to this very spot which was at that time still their fabulous, huge, old, old, old hacienda. The aunt's servants roasted for us a whole goat, on a spit, cooked all day outside. The goat was intact in the way of still having head, hair, hoofs. That produced quite a sensation for the kids. Tables were set up inside the courtyard, and we were served a wonderful feast. Everyone was so friendly and lovely.

Looking at the flooded spot that used to be her aunt's home, Nita tells us that every year her aunt would fill her car to overflowing with toys and clothes for all the children who lived on her land and personally give them out for Christmas, or maybe on Three Kings' Day, the traditional Mexican gift giving day. I believe this story because Nita's whole family is of people who are very modest and do not exaggerate. And I guess the aunt gave much, more than just the things for children.

I have not been out of town since our arrival, and now we are driving through spectacular panoramic vistas of the mountains, hills, and valleys that I have loved since first sight. Yippee.

We stop in a small village for "breakfast", which of course is not cereal, or toast, or pop-tarts, but is a monumental Mexican assortment of marvels. This is a road-side, open-air restaurant of the type that Americans are taught to fear and avoid, and sometimes for good reason because of the lack of clean water. That can create trouble for the American digestive system. But in a free-wheeling, haphazard way, these are the cutest and most authentic places to eat, and Raúl knows very well which places are perfectly safe, if not sanitary exactly, but close enough.

There are three women cooking in the open air, tending huge clay pots of all kinds of meats, sausages, stews, eggs, sauces, and fried vegetables, already prepared. It is a buffet, ladled generously onto our plates by the women, and also includes home-made tortillas and gorditas.

There are three tables between the cooks and the road, and a few more tables under the shelter of the open-fronted structure. Nita wants to sit inside, so we do. I have a little of everything plus a huge glass of orange juice. Richard has café a la olla (coffee boiled with piloncillo and cinnamon and served in an orange clay cup, sort of a little jar).

Naturally I have to use the restaurant's bathroom, which is also the family's personal bathroom, evidenced by the shower, tub, and toothbrushes. In case the restaurant patrons need to look in to see if the bathroom is occupied, there is a nice view from the restaurant through a window that has a screen but no curtains or glass. You just glance over, and you can easily see that someone is using the toilet, and you and think, "Oh, well, I'd better wait a minute". No fussing about modesty, I guess. The bathroom is only for toilet purposes, where customers are concerned. For hand washing, there is an out-side sink mounted on a wall on the sidewalk.

After a breakfast that should last us for the whole day, we continue to Guanajuato. We drive through all the tunnels, old and new. The old tunnels were built hundreds of years ago, gradually were abandoned and filled up with dirt, and then eventually cleared out and put back into use in 1963, which I know because I was here and saw the beginning of the excavations.

Later the government dynamited out new tunnels, blasted out of solid black granite. It is easy to see which are which, as the old are arched and carefully bricked, and the new are chunky solid rock, not smoothed or covered. One can traverse almost the entire downtown by car or on foot using these speedy tunnels.

We park and walk, sightseers now, and stroll towards "The Alley of The Kiss". This is a famous so-called street (only one person wide). On each side is a balcony, so close to each other that one somebody could lean over to the other for a kiss. Of course tourists are clustered all around, some up on the balconies kissing while friends take photos. There are little boys hanging about, acting as guides. They are chanting out the memorized legends and explaining "The Ten Kinds of Kisses", one of which is the microwave kiss—it leaves you hot. Other kiss descriptions are pretty earthy or highly descriptive, and because these boys are so little, everything seems funny, the crowd is laughing, and the boys are raking in tips. We are hearing startling recitations!

Next stop is a famous, huge, covered market in the heart of the city. Its structure reminds me of L'Orangerie (a former train station) in Paris. The framework is iron, and the walls are mostly of glass, very high, and the market is jam-packed with every type of Mexican trinket, souvenir, curiosity, necessity, food, flowers, music, toys - the list is endless.

In contrast, the next building we visit is a huge box-like structure, as drab as the market was florid. The flat walls contain tiny regimented windows, as befits the strong-hold of military government power, into which the ruling Spaniards fled in order to fire at the insurgents during the first revolution. Nita wants to take the tour, for which one has to pay. We find this prospect duller than dull, so we escape, but not for long. Nita is determined that we should take some type of educational tour, so at the theater, Teatro Juarez, she insists upon paying our way to hear a lecture. The lecture is fine, and the theater is splendid, but Richard and I have taken so many students on so many tours, and seen so many sights, and heard so many lectures, that we would gladly be the ones to pay if we could just NOT hear another lecture. We would run away if we could, but we do not want to offend our very well-intentioned friend.

There is one funny anecdote that we are told that makes the tour worthwhile. The rich women who attended the opera back in those days had so many servants and were so restricted in their lives that they all became hugely fat. Thus the invention of the corset. After being mercilessly squeezed, and yanked, and tied into a semblance of having a waist, all the fat rose to the top, giving the illusion of huge and temptingly displayed bosoms. Many a man suffered a terrible disappointment after the marriage when his sweetheart's corsets were removed and the breasts collapsed and the stomach burst forth in all its natural enormity. Probably the disappointed husbands were able to seek solace elsewhere, while the wives were forced to continue with isolated, idle lives within the confines of their homes, and conforming to the strict rules of the day.

Even Nita, up until age twenty-six, was not allowed to leave the house without her father's permission. Wearing pants, even at home, was also forbidden. A strict father defined a careful, loving father, so went the belief. I, as a foreigner, could go where I wished, but even I, in 1963, would not have been allowed to wear pants on the street. It would have created the same stir and fuss as if someone in the States today appeared in church wearing bra and panties. It was just not done! I even remember a shocked policeman sending a pants-clad woman home, as she crossed a downtown street in San Miguel, saying, "Oh, Señora, you forgot your skirt!"

Guanajuato has mostly preserved its architectural heritage, of the Colonial period, as well as in its gardens and streets. Each view, from anywhere, is charming, picturesque, colorful, authentic. People now are crowding the streets, are bustling around, probably because it is Saturday, and I suppose that everyone has some purpose in mind. One can also see the surrounding rounded hills, still in their untouched natural beauty, from anywhere downtown.

We go back to the car and drive up to see Guanajuato's mummies. Richard and I do not descend to view the long underground hallway lined with propped up dried bodies in glass cases, to squeeze through with other viewers, looking from side to side at the awful spectacle. The mummy site is a highly commercialized spot with a formal entrance and a turn-style. It is like descending to a subway. Above are tourist shops, maybe thirty or forty, bursting with trinkets of every kind. You could call it better, or worse, than a carnival, depending on how much you like carnivals.

Richard and I had already seen the mummies under far different conditions, before it was generally known that there were any. I can't remember if I was the first to show Richard, but I do remember that it was Abelardo who took me on the long, winding, mountain road bus ride to Guanajuato, precisely to show me the desolate spot, marked only by a small wooden trap door on the flat dessert, deserted, wind-swept, lonely place. No one was anywhere in sight, except the cab driver Abelardo had guided over barren hills towards where we now stood. Abelardo lifted the trap door, a door out in nowhere leading to nowhere, except below there was revealed a rickety ladder. We climbed down, and by only the illumination of the open little square of sunlight above, gazed at the propped up dead people, desiccated, dried out. Wrinkled, distorted bodies of men, women, children. Most still wore a remnant of a ghoulishly preserved garment. A man, one black sock. Another, shoes. Another, a suit. And worst of all, a baby, still wearing the crumbling remainder of rubber pants. Nothing separated the visitors from the mummies, except the instinctive abhorrence or respect which would keep one from touching the dead.

The bus ride to return to San Miguel was the same one as to get there, but now it did not seem the same. On the way there, I was looking straight down the steep, steep, sheer drop-off on the other side of the road at the crashed buses and cars that had been left at the bottom because it was impossible to retrieve them. The roads then were only wide enough for two vehicles to squeeze by each other, there were no edges to the road beds in mountains, and everyone followed the custom of driving at break-neck speed. The matter of passing on curves and at the crests of blind hills was resolved by whoever honked first, in day-time, or whoever turned on headlights first. (Drivers did not use their headlights for night driving then, preferring the purity of the stars and the moon for illumination, I guess.) Well, those signals meant, "Here I come. Get out of the way, because whether you do or you don't, I am coming through". Naturally this style of driving caught my attention.

But on the way back, all you could think of were the mummies. Especially if someone had taken you, like Abelardo had taken me, to somewhere where they sold mummy candy, and if you had bought some, like Abelardo did for me, and if you were trying to decide whether or not to eat it.

Evidently, with the passing of years, teenagers (the ones suspected always of every type of irreverence) were found to have taken fingers or flesh home as souvenirs, and fearing the ruin of these dead-people-objects, a more formal presentation was begun, starting with glass cases and escalating to a semi-commercial, semi-museum establishment.

Why were the mummies there at all? Where did they come from? I never hesitate to take from my experiences and jump to conclusions, so here is my guess. Mexican graveyards are very small and crowded. Spaces for dead bodies are rented, and when you (of course I mean someone on your behalf) are not paying, out you go. There is a pile of not quite disintegrated hair, and bones, and remnants over in the corner somewhere, and that is where you end up, if there is something left. These piles I have seen with my own eyes long ago, but it has been a long time since I cared to enter a graveyard, so I am not an authority on today's customs.

But we are not talking about today's customs when we talk about the mummies. Evidently in some places the soil preserves dead flesh and bones fairly well, and my guess is that when the rent was overdue for these folks, who are now the mummies, they looked too good to waste and were propped up underground because...? Respect? Curiosities? Would look too ugly if tossed on the old bone pile in the corner? I confess that I do not know, but I do know that the mummies were not created on purpose. No matter, there they are!

For Raulito, eight being the perfect age to be scared, but not too scared, seeing the mummies has long been anticipated. Raúl and Delfina accompany him to the cool underground, while we wait above in the scorching heat. It is fun to think of Raulito's creepy delight. And of course, naturally, for sure, we know that Raulito must have heard of mummy candy, made of some brownish parchment-like sugary stuff, and rolled and twisted and shaped to look like a mummy, so when you eat it, it flakes and crumbles like the dead skin you just saw, naturally we know that Raulito must buy and eat "a dead mummy".

To the refuge of the car, (but not to air conditioning), we leave the mummies and head for Leon. The route is a horrible ten miles of road-side clap-trap construction, a tumble of garages, stores, low rent apartments and houses, just like so many towns today, in Mexico, in the USA, and maybe everywhere. Leon is not a Colonial town. It is industrial and known for shoe manufacturing. You can like it because nice people live there, but I don't think you could admire it for its beauty. It has a few streets made bearable by pockets of trees and flowers, but for architecture, it is too much of a stretch to call these mundane buildings "architecture".

But, as I said, some very nice people live here, some of them being this family's relatives. Lorencio and his wife Eufemia, and their two very young daughters meet us on the corner where Raúl has taken us to get the very best jícama and fresh fruit, as he says, "In anywhere". Mine was chopped jícama with diced onions, lime and vinegar, salt, hot chile powder, and garlic. Raúl selects the same, therefore so does Raulito. Nita has a plate of watermelon and pineapple. Delfina has watermelon. All are large servings, but even so, after finishing all the jícama, Raúl orders a plate of watermelon. We are en route to comida, so I am astonished by how much everyone consumes.

Back through the ugly streets we drive to a restaurant that has a jam-packed outside line, and an inside line, and a one and a half hour wait. Thank God! Because although Richard and I are sorry to see everyone's great disappointment, here is what this restaurant is like. No one is over thirty. The music is louder than sitting close up to a rock band. In fact, the music, which is neither Mexican nor rock, is so loud that you can't even tell what kind of music it is. The theme of the restaurant could be cute. It is a bull ring with a round balcony hugging the upper wall for additional seating. However the tables are teeny-tiny in order to jam in as many people as possible, the secondary theme apparently being, "It is fun to be crowded". There are even people standing in the miniscule spaces between the tables.

Nita loves it and insists on staying. Raúl is a superb diplomat and gets her into the van by explaining how difficult it would be for Eufemia to wait in line in the scalding sun for one and a half hours (a modest estimate) with two very little girls to carry and control. We could hardly expect the young mom to think that this is really a good time.

Lorencio, the papá, directs us to a different restaurant where a wedding reception is in progress. From the spill-over of the music, it sounds like the party to end all parties. So I peek in to look at this party, more than once, but only one couple at a time is ever dancing. Too bad.

We are seated in a different part of the restaurant at a long, long table. Richard and I are placed between a high planter and the two little tots. We were hoping to get to know Eufemia and Lorencio, but probably the cousins all want to reconnect and catch up, naturally, and we are unable to hear any of the conversation, so at least we are not interrupting anything. We all have a good time, and the little girls are well behaved.

Richard and I order the only remotely Mexican choice on the menu, which is steak plate for two. We receive little flat tasty, fried steaks, little grilled chicken breasts, grilled onions and peppers, and lots of rolls. We had told Raúl before we left on this excursion that we would pay for both breakfast and lunch for everybody. We start to get scared as the ordering begins, because for one thing, we did not know that four other people would be joining us. In Mexico it would be extremely rude to say that other people should pay for their own, and we would never consider doing so. But we have brought every bit of the money that we have left for the remaining two weeks, and it looks like even this will not cover the bill. We may have to suffer the embarrassment of not having enough. And even if we do somehow, miraculously, have enough to cover the bill, how will we pay for the rest of the trip? (We have already paid Raúl for room and board, but one needs money for some things anyway. We do not know of a way to get more money from the States. What will we do?)

Here is how the ordering goes, and here is why we are starting to get scared. Everyone is hot and thirsty and orders several fruit drinks each. Soup is a-la-carte, and everyone orders some, even the children. Next appetizers which are huge beef bones split down the middle so you can dig out the marrow, which is globby, slimy, fat to smear on tortillas. This treat is a big hit with everyone. (Or let's say everyone except us.) Each person now, including the little children, orders a complete dinner of roasted lamb, except for Delfina, who orders spaghetti. Lastly each orders a dessert. Then coffee. Of course each item is an extra for the bill.

I am super tense, and I go into the bathroom and pray. I say to God, "Dear God, please let this all be ok, to injure no man, but to bless all mankind. I'm leaving it up to you. If this takes all our money, I know you will take care of us some other way". Then I cry and cry in a release of fear and tension. I wash my face, step outside to the garden, breath the fresh garden perfumed air, and then walk back in.

I come back in to find that Raúl has already paid the whole bill! I say to Richard, "Please go outside with Raúl and give him enough for the bill because we did offer to pay, and we both like to keep our word". Richard doesn't mind at all and says, "Oh, sure, don't worry. This is just like going on a trip, and the car breaks down, and you have to pay for something you hadn't foreseen, and you just pay it, and then you forget it". He knows just what to say to make me feel alright. He will solve everything. Richard takes Raúl outside and makes the offer.

Raúl says, "No, you pay next time, when it is just our family. You do not pay for my relatives". We are relieved and feel better, because we do have enough money budgeted for that. And as I said, we did at least pay for this morning's breakfast. It was very inexpensive, but as they say, it shows our good intentions.

It is time to proceed to the home of the relatives. I do not understand who they are, but the elderly lady who owns the house says she knows me, and she says how glad she is to finally meet Abelardo's sweetheart. She is a very sweet intelligent woman, and it is explained to me that she is the wife of Abelardo's and Nita's oldest brother, so of course this aunt did know all about me.

Even in this town, where at first I don't understand and connect people and places, everyone continues to treat me as Abelardo's chosen one in an enormous generosity of spirit, showing how much they all loved Abelardo by doing for me what they think he would have wished. And I do feel his presence with me often, as if he has decided to stay by me all through my life and to help me. It is strange to feel this way because I do not believe in ghosts, or spirits, or saints, or anything about dead people hanging around. Never-the-less, I feel what I feel, and the feeling is fine, comfortable, normal, a part of my life.

So we women sit in the little kitchen and drink Coca-cola while Raúl and Lorencio disappear for hours. Nita wants to talk with her sister-in-law, so Richard joins us and we all listen. The sister-in-law relates lots of family gossip which solves several family riddles and mysteries of old relationships, so it is interesting to Delfina as well as to me. Poor Richard doesn't care, in fact I have forgotten that we are speaking Spanish, which means that Richard has not understood anything and is also very tired. When will Raúl and Lorencio return? It is so late.

Richard goes to the living room and tries to sleep on the couch. But the family parrot is energized by the company, keeps up incessant chattering and whistling, and Richard gives up. At 9:30 the two men return. We say good-bye and get into the van. It is sweltering because the windows are all rolled up. No one else notices the heat. After forty-five minutes I feel like I can't breathe and ask Richard to roll down his window, as I am seated behind him. It helps, except that Nita complains that dust will get into her eyes until Raúl rolls it up all except for a tiny crack. With only the tiniest of a slit for air to enter, Nita puts on her sweater and then a huge heavy shawl and starts to cough, saying it is from the cold draft! I am almost sick with the heat, and we have two more hours to go, but I have to stand it.

It is dark, and since I can't see anything, then I need to think about something. If I can't see out the window, then I have to see with my mind's eye, right? So I pick thinking about how much I admire Raúl. He arranged for something for every one of us to enjoy today. It turns out that he and Lorencio were attending an important meeting of volunteer work. Raúl has kept his kind and gentle spirit throughout the whole day, and even after this long journey and all the things we have done, he still is just as jolly and sweet natured as when we started. So is Delfina. They never utter a word against anyone.

When we arrive home, it is mid-night. Raúl backs the van into the front entryway, the tightest of fits, lots of maneuvering required. He comes within an eighth of an inch of scraping his back fender on the four hundred year old pillars. I know because we have to get out before the van fits into its tiny slot, and I am watching. Raúl says, "It is ok, Sonette. I know you are scared for me. I am scared too, but I know everything is gonna be ok". And he is right, "A miss is as good as a mile", and an eighth of an inch is a miss, even though it's not by much.

31

ESTELA, AND OUR FRIENDSHIP BEGINS

I slept! Richard did not snore. And although I always go to the bathroom many, many times during each night, every time I got up last night, I went back to sleep! Until seven AM! Yea!

We take our time with coffee and showers. I had told Raúl and Delfina not to think about meals for us today, believing that they need time alone with just their own family.

Richard and I walk up to El Mirador (Look-out View). Then we walk downward through tiny alleys, and then to a beautiful garden restaurant far back in an old courtyard, quite hidden from view from the street. It is near the church El Oratorio and by all the common people's little shops and cafes. We enter and order. Richard, omelet of three eggs with cheese and ham, fried potatoes, OJ, and coffee. For me, huevos rancheros, fried potatoes, beans, OJ, and coffee. Before bringing us our orders, they serve us a whole loaf of fresh hot bakery bread, a tub of butter, and home-made peach jam.

We take our time as it is a beautiful day and a spectacular view. There is cloth draped here and there over-head for shade, and in places open to the sky and the pretty court-yard trees. We can see and hear the cooking, clanking of dishes, birds singing, church bells gonging and clanging, and the hushed conversations of the Mexican families who are having breakfast with their very well behaved children and beloved grandparents.

We walk more before returning home. I help Raulito for a long time to get ready for his test on English subject pronouns and direct and indirect object pronouns. He is happy, and excited, and fun. He gives me a photo he has taken of all of the kittens in their basket into which he had somehow corralled them, and which he then had artfully posed upon the top edge of the courtyard fountain, snapping quickly before they all escaped.

We try to get my email, but the internet won't let us in. Too crowded.

Conchita is not back yet from her cousin's house, so I cannot help her with her school work. Raulito demonstrates his mastery of the wooden top his parents bought for him yesterday in the giant market, and then he accompanies me up to my room to watch me paint.

After that, Richard and I dress up and go to the Jardín. Estela comes to the Jardín with her son, daughter, and friend. She is vivacious and so nice. She says she is inviting all of us to her house on Wed. Should be interesting and lovely. We invite her to come with us to the Posada San Francisco, a beautiful restaurant right on the square where we are. One side is completely open to the Jardín, except for a very low knee-high wall, so we love the fun of eating while watching and hearing all the doings in the street and the park. But they have already eaten and decline.

Across from where we are seated is a big display of some kind. We walk over to take a look. There are speeches which turn out to last all afternoon, we find out, until eight PM. There is a platform with a tent for shade. In the street are tall boards covered with announcements, photos, information. There are many Jesuit priests and nuns. At least, I guess that is what they are. They are all young and are dressed in brown robes like pictures I have seen of St Francis of Assisi. A sign says, "Vocational Fair". Maybe this is a tech school graduation or an awards ceremony. It does not interest us enough to stay or to find out.

We enter the restaurant at seven PM, and we enjoy a delicious comida. This hotel used to be the finest in San Miguel, and I dreamt about someday being grand enough to eat in this restaurant. Now here we are! The hotel is as wonderful as ever, entirely old San Miguel Mexican, lavish, without a trace of modernity or change. Except that no place can claim to be the very finest of all now because there are so many beautiful hotels and restaurants all over. To us though, this one will always be special.

We have hot, fresh bolillos with butter, guacamole, homemade tortilla chips, three kinds of sauces, two vino tintos each, and enchiladas suizas. We leave a twenty per cent tip, and still our whole bill only comes to nineteen dollars! At last, somewhere that is a great bargain.

In the Jardín, a wonderful band is playing cumbias. We walk the half block to Holandia ice cream parlor and get double dips. Then we stroll around and around the walk in the Jardín that encircles the band-stand, enjoying the Sunday evening crowds, listening to the music, and doing exactly what all the other Mexican families are doing.

32

DISASTER IN THE BIRD SANCTUARY, TAMALES! AND MY FAVORITE MOVIE IS NOW MY LIFE

Today my pants are tight. It must be the result of restaurant eating and not enough walking. My extra girth will dissipate as soon as we get back to eating with the family and doing our usual walking. We head for the French Park.

But something horrible has happened. This park is a bird sanctuary as well as a botanical display, and there are also a series of playgrounds for all ages—soccer fields, swings, basketball, climbing set, etc. It is the cool of the morning, and normally the only sounds are birds and whispery bits of overheard conversations. But today, Oh, Horrible! Scratchy, awful music is being squawked out everywhere from about fifty tin cans with microphones in them that have been strung up throughout the tree branches! We feel like we are in Mao's China or the Ayatollah's Iran where mind control messages are blasted out all day long from rooftops and street corners, penetrating into every spot that should be a quiet refuge. This is a disaster.

What can we do? We head for home, which leads us through the Jardín. Things are much better here. Some sort of ceremony is going on involving large numbers of school children of Junior High age. There are bands, microphones, speeches, drums, marching, and lots of flags and trumpets. The kids are every single one fresh in immaculate uniforms, perfectly combed black hair, and walking by them, one smells the just-showered, perfumed, and cologne smell of kids dressed up and growing up. There are many proud teachers standing around, marshalling their groups. We are hungry and head home.

Breakfast is a WOW! We buy a bag of oranges and a cluster of tiny bananas, intending that we will make the OJ for breakfast because the cook won't be back from her rancho until noon. On the way, I give the bananas and some coins to the woman who cooked the nopales and onions for me.

We enter the kitchen with the oranges, but Nita is already there. She has also bought oranges, and not only that, she is making a wonderful surprise. Atole! This is a drink I love which is almost never served anywhere except at huge Mexican parties or in the market. It is a thick drink of chocolate, cinnamon, milk, and some type of corn starch-like powder that thickens when cooked. Yum, yum.

Also super sweet yellow mangos are washed and served whole as a first course. There is a long two-tined fork shaped like Neptune's spear which is used for stabbing into the mango pit (called the bone). Fork secured, one peels the fruit and bites off the sweet juicy pulp. This is another of our favorite Mexican treats and is only served this way on the streets or in markets.

Now Raúl takes the top off of a large pot, and Richard and I say at the same time, "Ohhhhh, OOOOOO!" Tamales! We love, love, love tamales and so far have not had any. There are tamales stuffed with hot chiles, oh, we love them. And tamales filled with piloncillo, very sweet, which predictably Nita loves. After we had eaten our fill, Delfina offers me bread, pan dulces, tortillas, believing that we have not eaten enough. But we are stuffed. We linger at the table until 11:30 talking about so many interesting topics. Richard decides that he is now ready to start speaking Spanish. He has been understanding the conversations at meal times, and now he starts talking a little. He does fine, which makes all of us happy.

We intend to go walking and want to invite Nita. We enter the Botica to find her, and just as we do, Perla says, "Sonette, the telephone, it is for you". This is an amazing coincidence that you cannot appreciate unless you have lived in Mexico where it is almost impossible to receive a phone call for many lengthy reasons. So this is a surprise. It is Nita calling to tell us to hurry up to the plaza in front of the church, "La Salud", to see the wonderful regional dancers.

First presentation is "The Dance of the Old Men" from Pátzquaro. Kids dance it and do very well. It is very long and authentic in steps and costumes. I know, because this dance is famous. I have seen it countless times, including in its own habitat, its place of origin, Pátzquaro.

Next there is a dance by high school girls and boys. The girls wear, top-to-bottom, a colored, braided headband; white cambia blouses with embroidery; many colored leis; orange sashes; red and gold bandanas tied to the sashes; skirts woven of black with a few colored threads in tiny stripes; barefoot. Boys wear white cambia shirts; red and gold bandanas attached to the waist; white cambia pants; barefoot. The construction of the blouses and pants is like hospital orderlies or pajamas, just a simple fold-over with a v neck cut out; pants, just two legs and a drawstring waist.

After many dances, the boys and girls pick up very long cloths of either purple, or gold, or red. They hold the ends and dance in such a way as to weave the cloths into many patterns, dance them apart again, and dance them again into new patterns. Then enter a bride and groom, and there is a dance by them.

I kind of think that these shows will go on all day. We head out to buy a magazine for Richard, Southwest Art, and some pastels for his drawings and collages. This makes us forget about the dancers, but when we return at 2:30 to rest before comida, they are still dancing.

Nita is out with friends for comida. We have:

- Fruit water.
- Papaya.
- Soup of caldo de pollo with tiny macaronis in the shape of dots, to which one adds lime juice and cheese cubes.
- Hot tortillas.
- Tostadas with ham instead of chicken. (A tostada is a flat, fried tortilla, crispy, onto which has been spread mashed beans, and then the ham, and then shredded lettuce, and then sour cream. The moment you lift it up and take one bite, it snaps into lots of sharp pieces which fall all over the place. Inexplicably, they are served at parties and eaten while standing around and talking. This is always a disaster to my clothes.)
- These tostadas also have added to them chopped onions, crumbled goat cheese, avocado, and hot green chile sauce. Delicious! (But I use utensils.)
- Rice.

- Chamote. (A green vegetable shaped like a pear, boiled, sliced, and then put into the microwave to melt soft white cheese all over it.)

Lots of fun eating, and lots of fun talking.

I help Conchita for a couple of hours to get ready for a test tomorrow in English class. There is a movie that I love, titled "Danzón". There is a scene from this movie that takes place in hot Vera Cruz, in the patio of the posada where the heroine is staying, and poor women with their little children, who are living in the back part of the posada, are out in the patio doing their wash and showing the details of a timeless daily life. Today, with Conchita and me working together in the patio, this was such a day, the embodiment of everything I loved about the movie.

We are sitting at tables under the arches as we always do. There is an explosion of big thunder, and although it never rains, it is cozy to think about that it might. The darling doggies hear the thunder and crowd under the table to curl up on top of our feet. The parrots are screaming, the mommy cat comes over to say hi, the six little kittens romp around in the grass close to their basket under one of the benches. It is the bench where Abelardo's mother always sat, and I can visualize her now.

Raulito comes home carrying a plastic bag filled with water and two miniscule fish. When he announces that they are for feeding to his turtles, a horrified Conchita sets about to convince him of the cruelty involved in that plan. They settle for putting the fishes into the courtyard fountain. The instant the fish are released into their new watery home, the mommy cat smells the opportunity and jumps onto the wide stone ledge of the fountain to investigate. How she could smell those one eighth of an inch long little fishies from way over in the corner where she was nursing her brood is remarkable.

The cat gets shooed away, the fishies swim about, and I am called upon to reassure every one of the fish's probable safety and survival.

A friend drops by to leave her baby girl for Conchita and me to take care of while Mom does an errand. The baby is about one year old, and getting started at taking care of her involves lots of giggling, and hugging, and getting baby cookies from the kitchen, helping the baby walk around so she can look at the parrot, and such like. Raulito comes to join us and falls in love with the baby. This requires his getting positioned just right in a chair in order to be entrusted with holding the little curly-headed girl.

All the while, we are trying to work our way through Conchita's fifty words for tomorrow's test in spelling and definitions, plus she even has to make drawings to illustrate each vocabulary word. When we finally have mastered all but two words, Raúl comes to get the kids to take them to mass. Richard and I go walking, sit for a while in the Jardín, and at eight o'clock we are back home.

Larry calls and invites us to meet somewhere tonight for drinks. The place they mention is far away and requires a taxi. Also, they like places with really loud music, and we are not ones who like to scream out a conversation in order to make yourself heard over the music. So we say, "OK, but somewhere close enough to walk and quiet enough to talk". They say no to this. Too bad. We like them a lot, but our idea of what to do when you go out is very different from what they like.

Raúl comes home and says he and Delfina really want us to see the movie, "Callejón de los Milagros". They are making lots of arrangements for what to do with the kids so we can watch the movie tonight in their living room. We are looking forward to it. Delfina is also asking what Mexican foods we would like for our last two weeks. For some people, two weeks is a long trip, but for us, it seems like we have such a short time left.

On the plane ride here, I read my funny novel, and then I kept reading it during spare hours in the days or evenings. Then a mediocre novel, but only before falling asleep. Now I have time only to read my Bible Lesson in the morning, and nothing more, as there is so much to do each day. I love the unexpectedness as the days unfold. Like today with the kids, and pets, and someone else's baby.

We don't know if a merienda will be served during the movie, so we have eaten one half of a roll each. We are not sure what to do. The bakery will be closed, but still, in case something is served during the movie, we have to be hungry and enjoy it. My pants are not tight standing up, but they still are when sitting down, so it wouldn't hurt me to go to bed without a supper. But I know

Richard would not like to.

We watch the movie and really enjoy it. I had not seen it before, even though by the description I thought I might have. The movie is realistic, and very dark in subject matter and portrayal but not sensationalized. The main fun is all being together watching. Raúl makes it a cozy party by ordering a huge pizza. Chita brings it to us after the children fall asleep. Delfina and Raúl have a refrigerator tucked under the stairs in their living room, and Raúl gives us cokes. It is a very long movie, with English sub-titles for the sake of Richard.

33

IRRECOVERABLE THEFT STASHED ON RANCHO, ALLEY OF MIRACLES, AND RICHARD MEETS EL LOCO

Before I came here, my poor fingernails were all broken off, ripped, peeling, and dying. I think it was caused when I applied cuticle remover. Since being here the nails have healed, the ruined parts have grown out and are gone, and my nails are long and healthy again, almost normal looking. Goodie. Chita, although she probably spends four hours or more each day washing dishes, and all the hours not washing dishes she is working at housework, laundry, cooking, chopping (besides doing errands, ironing, and more). Even so, Chita's nails are long, strong, and attractive. Mexicans generally do not drink milk, so I don't know what the calcium source is, but it must be a great one.

I slept until 8:45 (off and on) and wanted to go for our usual pre-breakfast walk, but Richard is in the mood to stay here and drink coffee. It is now 10:00 AM, and I hope Raúl comes and calls us for breakfast pretty soon. Not that I am so hungry; I just want to start the day. The movie did not end until midnight. In the mornings, Raúl and Delfina have to get the children ready for school, and then I think they go back to sleep. So they appear to sleep late, but their sleep is in bits and pieces, I guess.

For sleeping they wear thick sweatshirts and sweatpants, whereas I am so hot at night that I have a large fan (which I take everywhere) blowing right on me. I wear the skimpiest gown that is decent (in case someone glimpses me through the window) and often at night I have to stick my arms and legs out from under the sheet to cool off.

On the topic of feeling the heat, also, all the school kids in town wear uniforms. One school's uniform is understandable—pleated plaid skirt, white shirt, and long white socks. But all the other schools' uniforms look unbearably hot. At mid-day it must be ninety degrees, and even when we awake in the morning, it must be about seventy-eight. One school has unisex uniforms of thick, heavy sweatpants, white shirts, and sweat-suit jackets! Another school has woolen skirts, or for boys, dress pants, and heavy, long-sleeved, white V necked sweaters, like tennis sweaters, with the school crest. How can anyone survive wearing such suffocating clothing when I can barely stand to wear a light T shirt and modest shorts? Even the runners in the French Park wear sweats and jackets.

Breakfast today starts pretty late, ten thirty, but that doesn't matter. Nita goes out with friends. Delfina, Raúl, and Richard and I are the only ones at the table. We have O J, papaya (our favorite fruit), huevos rancheros (again our favorite), and bolillos with butter, served hot. We could always have coffee, but we prefer to drink our coffee in our room when we are relaxing.

Delfina tells us about how one of their former maids robbed them over a long period of time of enormous quantities worth a great deal of money, including diamond rings, new expensive dresses and purses, new table cloths, which amounted to enough to fill Raúl's entire van, when Delfina and Raúl finally recovered part of what had been stolen. And that was only a part!

It is quite an involved story, culminating in their going with a lawyer to one of the maid's three houses. (Yes, the maid owned three houses.) They entered and found tons of their stolen property. Evidently the maid had enough nerve to wear Delfina's new black silk dress that her mother had bought for her to wear in the Good Friday procession and passed by right in front of the Botica, whereupon everyone recognized not only the dress, but also Delfina's accessories!

The same maid even stole Chita the cook's new dress, money, and things she had bought for a family event. One month of her salary was also gone, so that is when Raúl and Delfina said, "This is the last straw", hired a lawyer, and recovered their property.

The rest of their belongings were most likely out in the house the maid owned on a rancho, but the lawyer said not to go there because they might get into the house and find their stuff, but they would probably not leave the rancho alive. "The people on the ranchos are like that", Raúl and Delfina say.

They couldn't have the ex-maid put in jail, because she knew "all the habits of the house". The lawyer said she would tell the people on the rancho, and they would come and hurt or kill their children. This woman sold her own baby, so it wouldn't be hard to believe that she would hurt Raúl and Delfina's children. And all the while this woman was stealing and amassing possessions, and clothes, and money, her own mother, and brothers, and sisters on the rancho were hungry, and suffering, and going without food. The maid did not buy them food, but she did buy all new furniture for her house in town with the money she stole.

My, oh, my.

Last night part of the movie was about a pretty young woman who was tricked into being an expensive prostitute in a bordello in Mexico City. She was beaten and couldn't escape, etc. I say to Raúl and Delfina, "Sometimes women get trapped in those places and aren't allowed to leave". "Oh, yes", they say, "for sure. Each week there are more and more ads in the big city newspapers about "disappeared" children who are assumed to be kidnapped and sold, or their organs are taken out to be sold".

This has been common in third world countries for a long time. The fiends take the children's livers, eyes, and I don't know if anything else. Then instead of killing the children, these people drop them off six months or one year later in the same neighborhoods from which they were kidnapped, to be found and then to lead lives of horrible suffering because of their mutilations. I think this is even worse than murder. Who could come up with such diabolical plans, let alone carry them out?

We do our wash because Richard wants to kill time until it is the hour for us to pick up his watch at the repair place before we take our walk. It becomes 12:45, and still we have not been out of the house. But it is fun to do the wash. Our windows are open to the outside stairs, and we see dogs and people going up and down, and Chita's radio is playing as she finishes washing the breakfast dishes and then immediately starts preparing comida. I feel like I am living in an Italian movie. I love it.

We walk up the hill which is so steep it is hard to believe that cars and buses can make it. We are going to El Mirador. Richard starts talking to some Americans who have parked to look at the view. The man has a Ford truck just like Richard's, and they begin to chat. We get two tips: take extra sets of keys when you go to Mexico because you cannot get keys replaced anywhere in this country, not even at a Ford dealership. And: if you drive a camper, bring your own replacements for shocks and springs for when they get jiggled to death on the cobblestone streets and on the topes. "Topes" are big rocks buried to stick out pretty far in areas where you should slow down. Stop signs are ignored, but no one can ignore Los Topes.

This couple keeps on telling us things about camping in Mexico, all of it good, and Richard is interested. But for me, it gives me the creeps, so I back away. I love camping at home, but to come to Mexico, and live in your own camper, and cook your own food, and hang out with other American campers seems to entirely miss what being in Mexico means. It is like going on a trip and never leaving your hotel room, like bringing all your own same food, and ideas, and people with you—how insulated and sad. Oh, well, these people like it. Maybe somehow it is great.

I didn't tell about Gertrudis. She mops every "outside" floor, including the sidewalk, every day. She has to walk two hours each way each day just to get here and get home again. That does not include the bus ride! The two hour walk only gets her as far as the bus stop for taking the bus to San Miguel! To arrive here at nine AM, she has to get up at five. Her entire job, non-stop, every day, is to mop everything. That shows how big this house is. Rafaela mops the floors of the insides of the rooms and cleans everything. Chita does everything else. The gardener comes once per week. The workman, who at present is restoring the library, comes every day. He evidently will be here for years, has been here for years, because he is restoring everything, one room at a time.

Raúl had some of the one hundred and fifty year old columns replaced in the patio because the moisture from the ground underneath cannot escape through the tile that comprises the floors of the patio. So the damp creeps up through the walls and pillars instead, eventually causing them to crumble on the outside surfaces. Raúl doesn't like the new pillars because they are almost identical to the originals, but not quite. The old have a bulge at the bottom, and the new do not. The bulge was designed to fool the eye into making the pillars, arches, and ceilings look even higher than they are.

Rafaela is not washing floors or cleaning right now. She is sitting on the outside steps of the closed-for-lunch Botica, waiting for the kids who get dropped off on the corner after their uncle picks them up at school and drives them home. From the corner to their front door is only twenty feet, but they must be escorted by the maid.

When our children lived in Puebla with a Mexican family and attended private Mexican schools, they also had to be walked to and from school by the maid, even though Bobby was fourteen, and Mary was twelve. The mom, Rolita, promised me before I left Mary there (Bob flew down later), swore fervently, as if I might doubt her, that my children would never be out of her house alone for one second, and that she would take care of them, "Like my eyes, Señora, Como mis propios ojos!"

I guess reading about the disappeared children makes everyone cautious. Where dogs are kidnapped for ransom, where the family maid sold her own baby for money, I guess people with property and wealth must be ever vigilant.

We are still in our room upstairs, and I hear Rafaela's voice drift up from the kitchen. I catch the words, "chile rellenos", and the wonderful smells make me think I might be right. Delfina and Raúl just returned and are now in the kitchen too. I hear Delfina tell Chita, the cook, "I bought everything on both lists". This is in reference to our last days here, and making sure we eat all our favorite foods. All fresh foods are purchased by Chita daily, but dry staples, household supplies, and such like, Raúl and Delfina buy at some store on the edge of town, and going to that store requires the use of the van.

Someday we are sure that the family will come to our house. We will try to show them a wonderful time. I said, "Come in the summer so we can swim, and boat, and go to the Yacht Club". I will take them all the many places I know of in Milwaukee and Chicago, like I did with all of our exchange students. And as Richard and I did together with our own children, for many years. So we know that we can be super hosts to them, even though nothing could equal what they do for us.

We have a deluxe comida. Not chile rellenos, but still deluxe.

- Fruit water.

- Fruit plate.
- Puree of tomatoes, to which we add at the table, fried dried tortillas, cubes of white goat cheese, avocados, dried cut-up ancho chiles. The name is tortilla soup.
- A huge platter of fried bananas and fried mashed potatoes. Both have been first dipped into a batter of eggs and flour, and then deep fried. The bananas are very sweet. The potatoes are so rich that we have to add hot sauce to cut the "grasa", the grease.
- Rice.
- Tortillas. But for once I couldn't eat the tortillas. I was too stuffed.

I help Conchita with her English homework which is "sumamente largo", very very very extra is what "sumamente" means, and "largo" is long. The homework was long, long, long. She understands the work perfectly, and still it takes two hours. I am constantly astonished, being a teacher myself, by how much homework Mexican children are assigned, and it is complex advanced mastery. Usually Mexicans kids are about two years ahead of American kids. That is because we in the USA have to educate everyone, and in Mexico anyone who possibly can pays tuition for private schools, the public schools being so deplorably underfunded and under-equipped that explaining that could be a book in itself. You would understand a lot about Mexico's whole poor people system and immigration, and politics, and lots of stuff, if you had any inkling about education for the masses.

I leave with Richard to pick up his watch. Conchita has more left to do, but she knows how to do it. We more or less just do homework together to be pals. We pick up the watch. It needed a new crystal. In the States Richard was told it would be fifty dollars to do the replacement. Here we pay six. And the watch is perfect.

We walk more and meet three sun browned, wrinkly, old, very poor men with ancient instruments. A small accordion, a bass, and a guitar. We have wandered around and are now in the poor section of the poor market, by the stinky river. I say, "How much for one song?" Their spokesman says, "Twenty-five pesos." I say, "That is a lot for just one song".

This seems to insult their leader, and he menaces me by getting very close, glowering, etc. We feel that we are out of "our" territory, and something could go wrong here. Then I think, "Wait a minute, Sonette. Anyone can see that these men are really poor, they are old, it is very hot, and it is getting late. They are trying hard to make a living". So I say, "OK, one song. Anything ranchero".

They play "Allá en Rancho Grande", a song I truly love. It is not played everywhere because some of the verses are not exactly polite, but sort of funny, I guess. Anyway, I love it. They play and sing verse after verse; I didn't know there were so many verses. I can't understand it all, and Richard can't understand anything, so we are not offended. We are delighted. I feel ashamed, because they have given us way more than our money's worth. We were expecting just one verse of whatever when I said that twenty-five pesos is a lot of money for just one song.

They are so great, and now we all shake hands and thank each other. Then I think, "How can three men divide twenty-five pesos?" So I say, "One more ranchero". They sing a song about San Miguel, very long, and really wonderful. We shake hands again and say good-bye. But even though this has turned out to be great, Richard looks at me, and we think the same thing. Get out of here and go home. "No more walking here", he says, and he is right.

At home I set up my painting stuff in the patio and try to paint the patio scene as a remembrance. Conchita sets up her "art spot" next to mine, and she makes me an adorable pet collage of pictures cut from one issue of her darling pet magazine. This is what is so fun for me, Conchita, her sweet ideas and company, and entering into the world of little girls in Mexico. I would never know about Barbie magazines, or pet magazines, or the adventures of the fish, and the turtle, and the frog, and the kittens, and the cat without Conchita and Raulito.

Conchita and I work on our projects side-by-side until 8:10. I get so sleepy that I have to go upstairs and lie down. Soon I revive and get dressed up to go for a night out with Raúl and Delfina. It is the dinner that is our turn to treat. We all walk to the restaurant together, Nita having suggested La Posada de San Francisco, which is only around the corner, and a restaurant that is a favorite of everyone.

I am always saying that we have so much fun talking, and here is a sample of what that means. Tonight we talk about items of interest to all adults, one primary item being taxes, comparing here to there, Mexico to USA. Raúl pays a yearly car tax of over one thousand dollars. One of his friends pays twenty thousand dollars, yes, American money dollars, not twenty thousand pesos, twenty thousand dollars per year car tax because he has a Porsche. I forget what their house taxes are. Now even water is going to be taxed.

The problem, from Raúl and Delfina's point of view, is that all the taxes go into the pockets of whoever is in charge. That is the system of corruption all over Mexico, and I doubt if you could find anyone to dispute the truth of this. We Americans do pay high taxes, but we do get a lot of services. (On the local level.)

Nita tells us how she got a job in Canada, her home of many years. She didn't know anything, not even computers. So she said she would work for free. She arrived one hour early each day and taught herself. She worked for commissions only, and she must have been successful, because I think she still works there. Except she is not in Canada very much. I'm not sure. Then we talk about our own volunteer work, which we have done all of our married lives, and we tell of Richard's great success as an art teacher and giving all his free time to helping troubled students. Well, not exactly troubled, just standard issues that many kids have and want to talk about. In any case, his office and art classroom are always full, even while he eats his lunch.

Raúl takes Richard to see "El Loco", a trick that is played on everyone who comes to this restaurant. We are delighted to have an unsuspecting victim. It is hard to believe that Richard started coming to SMA when he was thirteen years old and doesn't know about El Loco. You get the person all primed to go to the back of the restaurant where there is a high window with wooden bars. "El Loco" means the crazy man. Everyone present has to convince the victim that there really is a crazy man back there, and he just must go take a look. Then we have to make Richard jump up to look in the window, as I said, it is high up. When he does so, it is a mirror, and he sees his own face. Then everyone laughs and says, "Oh, you must be crazy to fall for that". Ha, ha, or in Spanish, Ja, Ja.

The food and service are wonderful. Delfina, Richard, and I

have enchiladas verdes. Nita has "Enchiladas al Portal", which means prepared the way they used to be cooked and served on the sidewalk under the arched overhang of the buildings on both sides of this very Jardín. There used to be fires of charcoal burning on the sidewalks, with huge black iron cauldrons, like witches' cauldrons depicted in Halloween pictures. The cauldrons were filled with boiling oil, into which were thrown large hunks of pig, to be retrieved with a gigantic meat hook, whenever a customer wanted to buy a slice or a chunk to eat there or take home. Many other tiny bits of savory foods were prepared under the arches, and we all fondly remember how good they tasted. An American stomach prohibited me from sampling everything I would have liked, since sanitation was almost non-existent in those circumstances. Now to have a few of the dishes replicated here in this beautiful restaurant delights us.

Raúl is more cosmopolitan when ordering in restaurants. He selects points of beef, chicken broth, and other side dishes. We have a great visit and a great dinner.

34

TUXEDOS FOR BREAKFAST, A SHOCKING HERESY, AND NITA PACKS FOR CANADA

It is wonderful to wake up hearing the clanging and banging of the morning church bells calling everyone to mass. We awake about seven AM. Sometimes these loud, joyous bells lull me back to sleep. One wouldn't think so, but the sounds are so comforting and beautiful that no matter how loud they are, to me they are a lullaby.

One of the luxuries of being retired is that I almost never have to hurry in the morning. Instead of dragging myself out of sleep and far enough towards consciousness to grope my way into the shower, to stand under it with my eyes still closed until the water brings me farther and farther towards the surface, so I can call myself awake.

But now I can read my Bible lesson while drinking a couple of cups of coffee, which I do while still in bed, gazing out at the clouds, which are either pink or white, depending on how late it is. I can just sit and contemplate, as I wish. Except today is a little different. The family has just returned from 6:30 AM mass for some special occasion, and we hear a great deal of family chatter going on from the kitchen through to the patio as the children prepare for their ride to school.

Richard finishes his shower, which entails first taking down our many hangers full of now dry clothes from where they were hanging on the shower rod and piling them all on our respective beds. And now it is my turn. The shower is ready for me, and I am ready for it.

We go walking and just happen to return twenty-five minutes before we usually do. We have barely returned when Raúl and Delfina call us for breakfast, but what they mean is to go out to breakfast, and to meet Estela! We are not dressed up. We didn't know about this. I have on a white T shirt, and kacki bush shorts, and tennis shoes. The only thing nice about me is that my nails are still manicured from last night.

Raúl and Delfina say that, no, we are just fine, come on, let's go, so we do. Raúl drives us to an enchanting hotel restaurant high up on a hill. There are about twenty-five different levels of rooms, each more beautiful than the next, porches, balconies, terraces, pools, plants, flowers, vines, trees, gardens, paintings, birds, everything! The waiters are wearing tuxedos. The clientele is gentile. It is super.

Estela is already there and says, "Oh, good, Sonette. I thought you would come all elegant, and I would look like Cinderella". "Never happen", I answer. Estela is very athletic, and even now, wearing her bathing suit with shorts over it, hair in a ponytail, she looks glamorous. Delfina, as always, is beautifully tailored in classic pants, a silk shirt, high-heeled sandals, and wonderful hair and make-up.

We sit on a beautiful balcony outside. The day is already hot, but we are airy, shaded, and cool, with an entrancing view of the terraced gardens falling all the way down the side of a steep gully.

Breakfast is beautifully served and delicious. We hear opinions and facts from Estela based on her being married to a Mid-eastern man of position and power. We agree with all of her observations and opinions. She tells us that on purpose she gave birth to her two children in the United States so that they have the safety of being US citizens. Otherwise her husband's relatives could claim her children if her husband died. She and her husband live part of each year in Lebanon at present. Maybe the majority of the year.

Estela says she will not step one toe into Saudi Arabia with her children because the laws and customs there are severely against women. In fact, your children can even be claimed if male relatives decide that the husband is not strict enough with the wife, letting her get away with something. Like talking back? Or driving a car? I will ask her more later.

We pay for everything in order to thank Estela for her party and to take another turn in favor of Raúl and Delfina. Estela says she wants to get together again before we leave. We all agree. I suggest that we could go walking which is a fun way to visit. We shall see.

Raulito told Estela's son, who is his friend, that if he didn't know the Lord's Prayer, he didn't know anything. So Raulito taught Kairy the Lord's Prayer. Delfina is shocked to hear this and doesn't want Estela to feel insulted. I say that I think Raulito meant well because he is very kind and courteous, and probably he had never met anyone who didn't know the Lord's Prayer and decided to teach his friend, just like here in Mexico all boys know how to play soccer, and a boy would teach a friend if he found out that the boy didn't know the game.

Estela replies that here we can share and discuss any ideas we want, but in her husband's country that would be heresy and would be dealt with severely. We continue with our very interesting conversations about differences regarding living in the Mid-East.

The breakfast is long and delightful, but finally we each must move on. Richard and I go for a walk. When we return, I paint, and next we proceed to the dining room for another delicious comida. Fruit water, fruit plate of banana, kiwi, cantaloupe, and papaya. Tacos made of squash blossoms with melted cheese. Tacos of cactus leaves fried with onions and tomatoes. Soup. Plates of fresh radishes with limes squeezed over them and then sprinkled with chili powder.

For dessert, something rare and wonderful, "zapopotes". These are hard to get and very expensive. The fruit looks like a purple avocado. Inside there is purple flesh. It is yummy and tastes a lot like prune whip, which I have not seen in the States for many years, but which used to be very popular. I accept two bowls.

Are you seeing why I list all the foods? For those who have never lived in a Great House in Mexico, I want to give you an inkling into the world of food as beauty, food as exotic, food as a gift that life has at the ready, if only you will claim it. For those whose lives have included these delights at some point in the past, just the mere words of it, written or spoken, will bring a beautiful explosion of memories, of, "Ah, yes, I can see it now, I can smell it all again, I can taste, and I hear the voices of family and friends, I can sit in my mind's eye at tables from the past, I can feel the heat of the day, or the cool of the garden, or the comfort of believing that this life, and these meals, and these days will go on forever".

In the evening, Nita returns. She asks if I will help her pack, but what she really means is for me to bring to her room all the dresses which I brought for her and which have been hanging in the wardrobe in the downstairs of our suite. I enter her sala, and the

Botica employee, Perla, has been commandeered to do the actual packing while Nita directs and at the same time talks on the phone with Ignacio. Ignacio does not ask her to come over and say good-bye. She is going back to Canada, so she thought he would want to see her and has already invited me to go over to his house with her. Ignacio is her only living sibling, out of eight children, yet during her visit he has never invited her to dinner or lunch, nor has he come here. But Nita is completely loving and excuses and forgives anything and everything, and she and I love Ignacio no matter what. But we think that he is missing out on a lot of fun. However, Ignacio is a hermit, and hermits do not seek fun, as far as I can tell.

While I am helping Nita, the baby comes to visit again, but of course I do not know this because I am in another part of the house with Nita. The mom of the baby brings the baby with her, naturally, but we just say that "the baby has come to visit", because for us the baby is the main event. The little brother has come too, to skate-board around the patio with Raulito. This patio is so big that Raulito can skate-board or roller skate around and around, and the little doggies can run behind him, yipping, and yapping, and sliding, and careening, toenails scratching helplessly for purchase.

By now I have come out of Nita's room to be delighted by the kind of hubbub I enjoy. The little black kittens, tails straight up, have gotten all brave and come running across the patio towards us. The mommy cat is trying to keep an eye on them. One keeps climbing a tree and getting stuck, some run around under our feet, and what with the parrots screeching, me with the baby now in my arms, and Conchita doing her reviews while I help-- Goodie! This is my kind of day!

I had, before I got the call to help Nita, been trying to continue on my painting of the patio. But now the mom of the baby and Delfina come out to sit on a near-by bench and visit, exactly as Nita's mom used to sit with her friends. This is Delfina's house, and she is entitled to some alone time with her friends without me around every minute, so I pack up my painting stuff and head upstairs where I always have plenty to do to keep me entertained. Delfina is generous about sharing her family and friends with us at all times, so it is up to me to make sure I give her some privacy once in a while.

After a while, Conchita, Delfina, the baby, and the baby's mom go out. Raulito stays behind, and pretty soon I hear his voice from under my window. "Sonette, would you like to play cards?" "Sure", I call down, and we play Fish. It is windy, and the cards keep blowing away. Raulito regards this as a fun part of the game—blow away, retrieve, set up; blow away, retrieve, set up. Delfina and Conchita return. Conchita joins our game. Raulito asks the cook to bring him oatmeal and milk. This drives all the cats wild. The cats come running, the cards keep blowing, and our game of Fish seems more like putting worms back into an open cup.

Richard and I go to the Jardín to hear the Mariachis, enjoy the breeze, and soak up the atmosphere. When we come back, Nita is still gone but soon returns with Perla. They have been out shopping. We have a lovely "final" family merienda. It seems like we should do something special, or find something to say beyond thank you, and we love you, and how wonderful it has been. How can one express enough that tells how grateful we are? Nita is leaving. Part of our hearts will go with her. We can't express it, but she already knows. She feels the same.

Earlier, I had offered to help take care of Conchita and Raulito in case Delfina wants to accompany Raúl and Vito to Acapulco. Delfina thanks me but feels her place is with the children. So Raúl and Vito will leave tonight at 4:00 AM (to avoid the traffic), drop off Nita at her aunt's house in Mexico City, and continue on to Acapulco to the pharmacists' convention. Nita will stay for a few days with The Aunt, visit with her Mexico City relatives, and then fly back to Canada.

But that is not how it goes. After a few hours into the journey, Nita remembers that she has forgotten her insulin. They turn around, come back, and set out again. When they finally do reach Mexico City, it is peak traffic time, and the final fourteen miles takes two hours. Raúl had planned to arrive in Acapulco at ten AM but doesn't get there until 2:30. This sounds maddening, but remember, this is Mexico. I also remember times when I have made worse mistakes, and maybe so has everyone, because no one complains that Nita's mistake has delayed them so much. I also remember that Nita spent hours waiting for Richard and me to arrive at the Mexico City airport so that she could buy our bus tickets to Querétaro in advance, or we would have been stuck at the airport overnight. So everyone helps everyone else, and slowing someone down from an original plan is not regarded harshly at all. The person is always more valuable than the plan.

Who is Vito? Vito has lived here in an apartment on the roof for the past two years. He is not going to school, and he does not have a job. He is young and handsome and is very nice. We don't know how he passes his days and don't think about him very much, just as we barely ever think about anyone who is not in the immediate family. Vito has become a friend, I guess, and Raúl thought he would enjoy the trip.

Anyway, what with all the leaving and returning, Conchita didn't have much of a sleep before her big test at school, but she feels well prepared and confident that she will do fine. And no doubt she will.

35

ALONE TIME, SEÑOR SANCHEZ'S RANCH CONFISCATED, AND WAKE UP FOR REFRIED BEANS

Now that Raúl, Vito, and Nita are gone, we think it will be kind of cozy and quiet around here, and we feel nestled into our snug apartment. We go down to breakfast thinking that the big table will seem empty, but Delfina has invited a friend. I like her, and after enduring a great deal of girl-talk, Richard excuses himself retreats to our suite.

I am not exactly sure of the friend's name. It is not "Goo goo", like baby-talk: it is not "Gau gau", the Mexican way of writing for a dog bark. It is something like GG, a nick-name because she talks so much. Delfina and I talk a lot too, especially me, so we all get along fine. GG is very pretty and fun. Richard says he could hear us laughing all the way upstairs.

I stay upstairs to paint, even though I want to work on the painting of the patio, but I don't want to go downstairs and interrupt the visit of Delfina and GG because they have now moved to the "visiting bench" under the arches of the patio. So I finish my third still-life, and I like it. The first few paintings cannot have much in the way of expectations, because they are mostly a way of warming up. To have one that I finally like feels good.

Richard has washed six of his shirts and two pairs of Levis. They are hanging on the roof to dry. We set out on our second walk of the day.

All of a sudden it is the hour when we hear children's voices, home from school, we smell cooking and hear chopping, and before we know it, it is time to eat again. This time Delfina has invited her father, Señor Sanchez. He is an exceptionally gentle man, very dignified, has been everywhere in the States, speaks English very well, and does so for Richard's sake. He has so much to tell. He used to own I don't know how many thousands of acres of farm land here outside of town. He had eleven tractors, a couple of hundred farm workers, fifty acres of peach trees, and lots, lots more that I can't remember.

All of his acres were confiscated by the government, supposedly to give to the peasants as communal land, El Ejido. He received in return only a worthless IOU called a Bono. He was on a tractor in the fields working when the government man approached him and gave him the news and the Bono. Señor Sanchez was so disgusted that he said he just walked away, even left the tractor running. He left all the animals, all the imported sheep, the orchards and vegetables, the eleven tractors— everything, and just walked away.

I am in favor of El Ejido (the returning of the land to the poor) but only if the poor actually get it, and only if the government pays the owner the full value for everything that has been taken. Mexico started out with communal land, called the system of El Ejido, long before the Spaniards arrived, and long before Mexico was given its name. But you can by yourself read all the history and understand what happened and how that system disappeared.

Fortunately Delfina's family still owned property and their own Great House just one half of a block from the Jardín. Now Señor Sanchez says that he lives in a tiny apartment, which really is not tiny, but after living all his life in a Great House, the apartment is very hard to get used to. Their home had Napoleonic era Venetian mirrors, twelve foot high armoires, massive vanity sets, expansive dining room furniture, Venetian chandeliers, Italian black marble on table-tops and bureau dressers, and on and on. You can't fit furniture on that scale into a new apartment.

Comida always starts at 3:30 and ends at 5:30. I help Conchita prepare for another test, this time in math. The test will be tomorrow, it is now 7:30, and after two hours of preparation (for just one subject), she feels fully prepared. Conchita says she wants to walk with us to the French Park, show us her favorite video store, show us her favorite videos, and rent for us a video about American cheerleaders (in English). Then she wants to take us to an ice cream shop and buy us ice cream. Richard says, "Come back for me for the ice cream part".

Meanwhile Delfina has been distraught, thinking that Raulito has appendicitis. He finally falls asleep, awakens at 9:30 PM feeling better, and wants an apple. Everyone is greatly relieved, and we rejoice together. (This is why, when friends back home say to me, "Six whole weeks in Mexico? What do you do?" I have to laugh. They would never understand what I do, nor what it is that happens. To everyone I know, a trip to Mexico is a week on the beach at a resort with other American tourists who are also there for a week on the beach at an American resort. Oh, well.)

Conchita wants to teach me how to make burritos the true Mexican way, so even though I am so sleepy, I say OK. I have never seen a burrito in Mexico. I think they have been a new idea imported from Taco Bell in the US. Conchita shows me her "true way", and we have fun. Except that the cook has already gone to bed, and Conchita wakes her up just to open the cupboard when Conchita calls out, "Where is the can of refried beans?" Being a mother myself, I already know that kids don't look very hard before shouting for Mom, and I try to stop Conchita, saying that I will find it. Too late. The cook comes to the kitchen with sleepy eyes, opens the cupboard door, and there it is. And I feel so bad because Chita must have been truly exhausted to go to sleep before everyone else. Plus she took a while to come out of her room, and usually she jumps quickly to any call.

At least, I think, I will clean the kitchen and wash the dishes so no one will get her up again. Quickly I get the kitchen all washed. But Chita does get up anyway. I suppose it is her duty.

36

TIME IS RUNNING OUT, MEAN LITTLE GIRL TYRANT, AND STRANGERS LIVING HERE

Only one week left! Time has gone so fast. Richard and I are recounting our money. We put it aside in piles by categories. Room and board, and tips to Chita, Rafaela, and Gertrudis. Should we also tip Silvia? We decide upon two dollars per day to Chita, One per day to Rafaela, and fifty cents for a daily rate to Gertrudis. That means for Chita, eighty-four dollars; for Rafaela, forty-two; for Gertrudis, twenty-one. We then convert it all to pesos and raise the amounts to round it off in one hundred peso notes. Now we have to get the exact number of one hundred peso notes at the bank, and some envelopes. Maybe I will make little paintings for the cards and the thank-you tips.

Breakfast includes chilaquiles, which we love. I paint all morning, no walks at all until after lunch. The light is just right, and I can't stop, even though the sun gets brighter and hotter every minute. It is worth it. The painting captures just what I want of the patio in blinding hot sun on the courtyard, fountain, tile and plants, and the deep cool shade all around the edges, under the arches.

Comida is delicious, featuring deep purple chiles stuffed with ground beef, but I won't tell it all because Conchita is so sad. Something terrible happened to her at school with some mean little girl tyrant. We all try to console her, and I give her some tips from my teacher experience with bullies. I ask her if she'd like to paint with me after she finishes her homework.

I say that Richard and I will have coffee in our room, then take a walk while she does homework, and then we will paint. But while we are still in our room drinking the coffee, we see her standing alone on the terrace across from our window. She has never done this, so I call out to her, "Would you like to paint right now?" She brightens considerably. I hurry down, and we set up for painting.

Richard brings to her five sheets of heavy water color paper. Conchita gets out her own set of tempera paints and brushes. We use two little patio tables for our painting spots. Conchita, at my insistence, wears a smock, although this precaution still does not prevent two orange paint disasters on the plaid skirt of her school uniform and the school white blouse. We get started on our respective paintings, and this interests Raulito, who decides he would like to paint too. This requires our finding and bringing a third table, getting something protective for him to wear, then a trip by Chita the cook who is sent downtown to buy more brushes and a little jar of white tempera paint, one of the missing elements for their projects.

Conchita's painting idea is to make an anniversary card for her grandparents. Raulito's painting is of a door. I keep on with my own painting of the patio and almost finish.

All of a sudden it is already 7:15 PM. Richard and I dress up and go to Posada San Francisco for dinner. I don't need to eat anything, yet I order enchiladas, thinking to just taste a little, but they are delicious, so I eat the whole of it. I am stuffed. Never-the-less, we go to the corner ice cream parlor and get cones to eat while sitting in the Jardín and enjoying the Mariachis.

By ten o'clock I am so exhausted that I say, "Let's go home", and Richard agrees. Tomorrow night we have been told that there is a program, maybe from Cuba, of Salsas and Cumbias. I'd love to hear it, but I just don't especially feel like going out so late at night. And it costs one hundred pesos each. That is just to enter. Maybe too it will be somewhere where drinks are served—that would add up to too much for us to spend at the end of the trip like this. Is it dancing? Is it listening? I suppose we could find out.

Maybe going out tomorrow night doesn't hold much appeal because I got extra hot and tired by standing in the sun all morning painting. I got so tired on our walk after lunch that I had to stand in the shade while Richard went to a little tienda and bought me a Coke light, just to get enough energy to make it home.

I do have the energy left though, before I go to sleep, to tell about the people who live in apartments on the second roof. (Not the top roof.) You can barely notice that there are such apartments unless you go up there and look, so cleverly were they built. But I like the thought of it, all those people living their separate lives, playing out individual novels, as we all do.

Besides Vito, there is an old single man, ruddy face, white skinned, blue eyes, and curly white hair. He always, always wears a yachting cap and carries a large woven plastic plaid shopping bag.

There is a pair of newly-weds. He looks like a sophisticated forty-five year old handsome Latin. She looks like a very young American blond. She just got a darling lab puppy which she carries around everywhere, and I would too, because they are so loveable.

There is a square-ish older lady with thick short black hair, looks like a Mexican secretary. Smart enough, but not sophisticated, not much of a dresser.

Then there is the newest couple who are apparently rude and complainers. He is nineteen and an actor. She is seventeen and studies ceramics. One of the dads pays the rent and is also rude. Apparently they do not attend school, or work, or read, don't have a TV, and only go out in the late afternoon or evenings.

One of the couples (I can't figure out which) gives very noisy crowded parties, and some other tenant complains. (I don't know who that is either.) But what is funny to me is that "we of the family" are barely aware of any of them at all, we don't notice a thing, we always think we have the whole house to ourselves, and in fact, even though there is only one door to the outside, we don't even see them go in or out, except if we are in our bedroom or bathroom and looking out the window while one of them is passing by on the outside stairs.

37

RAULITO TAKES COMMAND OF COMIDA, SWIMMING AND DINNER AT ESTELA'S VILLA, AND WHY THE GUNS?

This turns out to be a swell day, as all days are actually. Full of surprises.

We have our morning walk and paint because breakfast has not been called and we need something to do. At eleven o'clock, it is finally ready. It turns out that Delfina is at her Junta. (Mexican women have breakfast clubs, whereas American women meet for lunch.) Raúl is still in Acapulco with Vito, and Nita is en route to Canada after having spent a few days at her aunt's house in Mexico City. This is an amusing breakfast because even though it is just Richard and me and the two little kids, we are still served course after course, plate after plate, in the usual formal and grand style. And since Raúl is not here, eight year old Raulito sits at the head of the table in Dad's giant chair and calls out all the orders to the cooks, just like Dad.

It is funny, like being in a children's movie, to sit at that giant table and be served so obediently and efficiently by the cook and her helper, with the whole drama of breakfast being conducted, like an orchestra leader, by a little kid. It is even funnier because Raulito adopts all the mannerisms and nuances of his father, exactly like a miniature version of the Master of the House. No one questions his authority for even a minute. Interestingly, Conchita does not try in any way to copy her mother. Probably because the mother has no directive role in the commanding of the dining room process.

Finally all the courses have been served and cleared. The formal breakfast has ended. The children jump up and run to the kitchen where they fix themselves bowls of cereal, becoming children once again.

I paint more in the patio, accompanied by Conchita, who is still working on the anniversary card for her grand-parents. Raúl finished his painting of a door last night, so he plays at boy things, racing around happily.

A hubbub starts in the patio because Graciela, who washes all the outside floors, needs to leave now, her work-week ending Saturday before comida is served, which is always at 3:30. She has to catch a certain bus to make it back to her rancho. The problem is that she is supposed to take home two of the kittens, and this necessitates calling to Delfina to come out of where she is working in the Botica, to catch the kittens. One is easily caught, but the others escape many times until they all hide behinds a cluster of garden plants. They have to be lured out with a bowl of milk.

Finally both kittens are in Gertrudis's possession, ready to leave on the bus with their new "mom". Conchita cries, and I almost do too, because it is so sad to think of the mama cat endlessly searching for her two kittens, which she will never find. Thank heavens that pretty soon I get so busy that I forget to be sad all day.

Richard and I go walking to a faraway little store and buy instant coffee, and bleach for washing our socks. When we return, Conchita wants to do more on the card for her grandparent's anniversary, which is tomorrow. I don't believe in touching or changing other people's art work or poetry, or even making suggestions that could hurt the feelings of the artist. So all I really do is stay by her as she painstakingly finishes the card. She has made a bride and groom standing in front of La Paróquia with hearts all around the edges. It is sweet, and everyone will love it. They might be mystified by Raulito's door, which looks pretty much like a large dark rectangle, but the effort and the cuteness of the idea will be very pleasing.

Now it is 4:40. No comida today because we are all invited to Estela's villa, and we are supposed to arrive at 5:00 for swimming. No one seems to have done anything towards getting ready, but Richard and I rush around to dress up, and still Richard will have to go to the Jardín and find a taxi. It takes a long time because all streets are one-way, so even though this house is not even one full block from the Jardín, it is quite a long and complicated route that must be taken by the taxi in order to come here for us. It is obvious that we are going to be late. Then Conchita tells me, "Sonette, remember that you are in Mexico!"

Delfina has to stay behind to keep the Botica open, so Raulito, Conchita, their cousin Carl, and Richard and I, all set out together. We arrive and have a wonderful visit, that is Estela, Richard, and I sit on one of her balconies enjoying the spectacular view of all of San Miguel and the surrounding hills and mountains. The children jump around in the swimming pool and play with Estela's children, Clarita and Kairy.

After a while we all get into Estela's hot tub, which is actually another granite sided swimming pool, a long rectangle, which is just under the main pool. Usually a waterfall spills over the edge of the main pool into this other pool, but when the heater is turned on, the lower one becomes a hot tub. And it is really hot. Plus, the so-called tub is just as long as the swimming pool, and fairly wide too.

The view from the "tub" is also spectacular, and we are getting really relaxed. Estela has invited another couple, Americans, and they are in the pool with us. The husband is a major executive of one of the big oil companies, and the wife is an artist. They regale us with tales of the outstanding accomplishments of their grand-children, but one of my faults is not liking to hear too much about how great other people's children and grand-children are. I am sorry to say that once in a while I do not just love everybody, and I drop from friendly, to polite, to barely civil, and to even maintain civil is about the most I can do.

Conchita and Clarita get hungry, so the girls cook dinner for Raulito, Kairy, and Carl. Delfina arrives, so Estela gathers us into her beautiful pool-side kitchen, scrambles eggs and prepares sausages, and we help to cut and slice a watermelon. All drink wine or fruit juice, heat tortillas, and last, we eat pie and drink coffee. Everything tastes good, and we have fun because of Estela's enlisting us all to help. I really like her. She is amazingly talented and bold in following her heart and being so successful in all that she does.

We return home after mid-night, and Delfina herds the kids into their apartment, their private family quarters. Richard goes to bed the minute we get back, and by the time I get there, he is snoring to beat the band. I hope I can get him to stop so I can sleep too. But I decide to write in my diary instead, and here is what I write:

Let's see if I can tell why it was so fun and exotic at Estela's. I already told all about the beauty of the gardens and property which we saw at our first visit. The last time, we arrived at the front gate. This time we entered by Estela's front door and were ushered in by a uniformed guard, and another guard was also visible. Both were nice healthy looking well-groomed young men. Their uniforms were crisp black, and they were constantly on patrol. I supposed that this was for various reasons.

One. Since Estela's husband seems to be a very important man, and Mexico has the custom of guarding the children of important families very carefully, that could be one reason. Another logical reason could be that when renting luxury houses by the month, or several months at a time, or in the case of the main villa, by the year, it would make sense to give out keys only to each individual's home, although not for general coming and going into the compound. There probably are many visitors to the renters, lots of workmen and servants, and therefore having the gates staffed makes sense.

Nevertheless, I have not been accustomed to relaxing in a huge hot pool, under the palms and the starlight, with the children splashing happily in the pool just above our heads, while black uniformed security guards patrol around us, crossing through gardens, and keeping us in sight. I think they had guns, but maybe that is only my too vivid imagination. They were keeping us not only in sight, but were they also keeping us safe? It made me wonder who would storm the gates and what would they do if it weren't for the guards?

I have been at large parties at home in Wisconsin where security guards are present, with guns very much in evidence, but the guards are generally there to make sure party crashers or fake caterers don't sneak into the private rooms for the purpose of theft, and I suppose to protect the guests' jewelry as well, since at those parties most of the diamonds are real, and guests often bring along one or two of their own friends. But that always felt very different to me. On those occasions, the guards were guarding stuff. Tonight the guards were guarding us.

The pools seem to be made of large black rectangular stones which are lava? Or granite? The main front entrance, the formal entrance, has a circular drive with a fountain in the center, also of stone. There is are exotic plants within the fountain, as well as all around the edges of the high stone-walled enclosure. Nothing at all is visible from the road. There are flat-stoned walks and terraces weaving throughout the gardens and surrounding the pools.

Clarita and Kairy led us from the pool patio into their kitchen which is large, beautiful, and exotic. Still, it has a family feeling. Every bit of the décor has been purchased by Estela from the local artisans and craftsmen. All is of the finest qualjity, from the carved furniture to the painted tiles that cover almost every surface, to the beautiful scenes of landscapes painted on the walls, to the plates and rugs and pots and ornaments and, and, and!

Each room opens into another, and the twenty feet high ceilings, together with the large open screenless windows that lead to balconies or terraces, made me feel that we were in a luxurious tree house in the midst of a tropical paradise.

The walls of the main dining room are Arabic arches so wide and tall that they reach all the way to the second story. Mostly made of granite, faux painting has made the granite work seem to be in other places as well, where it would have provided a structurally impossible, but visually pleasing, continuity of form. There is a glass topped table apparently resting on an organ pipe cactus garden. The chairs are black wrought iron of an open floral design, further complementing the illusion of living in a dream-like tree house.

On one of the balconies, we sat visiting and admiring the view below through foliage that had been shaped to form a frame, but not the stiff clipped topiary kind of frame. This was cleverly done so that the plants and trees seemed to have made a frame just by fortuitous happenstance. The bottom of the "frame" were the gently moving top leaves of trees below, not even all close together in reality, but none the less forming a "frame", when seen from exactly this location.

When we arrived at 5:30, it was brilliantly hot, and that is when Estela took us to the balcony to enjoy the cool shade and the breeze, as well as the view. I was wearing a bright blue dress with little straps, buttons down the front, and a slightly gathered skirt. Also high heeled white sandals, and some jewelry. Thinking that I would need a sweater later, I brought one, but it never became necessary, and that is why I forgot it.

38

NAUGHTY KITTENS WREAK HAVOC,
AN IRRITATING WOMAN,
THE AMERICAN GRANDMA

It is 9:30 AM, and we are dressed and sitting on the bench in the patio, waiting for our ten o'clock date to go out to breakfast with Delfina and the kids. Richard said, when we were invited, that we really should leave Sunday for personal family time, but Delfina said, "Oh, no, the children want you to come because it will be our last breakfast all together". So of course we agree. (The kids will be back in school, and they have grown to enjoy our big celebratory breakfasts. On school days they do not come to the dining room because the cook brings pancakes or cereal to their private quarters, very, very early.)

I have already taken a short hurried walk. I wanted to be back and dressed by ten o'clock. Cousin Carl stayed here for the night, and I guess getting three cousins, who were up until who knows how late, all corralled, and showered, and dressed must not be easy. Especially since today is the day off for all the maids.

I think that when we return from breakfast, I will really need to paint. If not, I won't finish the second patio painting. The children were fascinated by the first one, because it is of their house, so I said they could have it. Anyway, I always need to paint the same thing several times before learning about the light, how my paints handle, the colors, my brushwork, and application. Even getting the proportions right takes a long time of practicing. So far I am not satisfied that it even is a painting; it is more just telling a visual story of what I see. Much must be left out too, in order to show what you think you see, or want to see, rather than all that you actually do see. Choices, choices.

We are still waiting, so I get my diary. I record not just events, but thoughts to myself. This time I write of my puzzlement of why

Estela has taken to me so strongly. It is easy to see why I like her so much, but she doesn't know much about me. Or maybe she does. Maybe, as friends do, and because this is a small town, maybe Delfina has talked about Richard and me somewhat.

I immediately feel at ease and especially happy in the company of some people. I particularly like intelligent, active, creative, action people. I bristle in the company of the self-centered or the braggarts. For example, the other woman in the pool with us last night, the American, in her stubby, short, chopped-off, nothing haircut, was the bragging, clothes-appearance-unconscious, tough type of woman who instantly repels me. She didn't like me either and answered scornfully to whatever I tried to ask her about her art, not caring really, but at least I was trying to be polite, to show some interest in her as a courtesy, since she was Estela's guest. The guest assumed that I knew nothing about art, and she didn't interest me enough to tell her otherwise.

She and her husband also couldn't understand why everyone doesn't talk on the telephone every day to each grandchild and adult child. It didn't occur to them that this could be very expensive for some of us, impossibly expensive maybe, and also that in order to love and care about my children, I don't feel any need to call them and know who is going out to eat with whom, and for instance what tap-dancing competition their eight year old granddaughter is winning now. The "Who Is Best" and "How Many Others Can You Beat" philosophy finds no spot in my thinking other than for me to struggle constantly to be free of such thinking.

I do know that instead of being irritated by bragging, I need to work on being more grateful for the successes of others. This is surprisingly hard to do, and I think I know why. I used to easily be grateful for every success of every person, feeling that I too had accomplished, or would accomplish, the goals on my own life list. But I am getting older, have already retired, and it seems that some opportunities and hopes have passed away and are over. How could that have happened? Do others feel as I do? Am I believing that the bad things that have happened to me in life have some sort of power to discourage me away from my own nature, which is sunny and thrilled by being alive? Am I letting myself be that ugly, evil thing, envious? No, no, no. Fight it, Sonette! Fight it!

I put down my pen because Conchita is finally calling for us, ready to go. Conchita and Delfina look lovely and fresh, but guess what happened. The kids had let the kittens into Raúl and Delfina's sitting room, and they pooh-poohed and wet all over the chairs, new carpet, sofa, and into the bedrooms and on the bedspreads. All that time that we were sitting and waiting, Delfina was cleaning up and trying to get out the smells and stains because the Rodriguez family are all immaculately clean, and spotless, and careful, and everything they have is new or a precious antiquity. All of the clean-up, plus getting three playful children cleaned and ready, what a task!

All the awful clean-up has been finished, everyone bounces around cheerfully, Delfina is surprisingly calm, and is ready to leave for the breakfast outing. We go to Puebla Vieja, where Nita had once taken us. It is better this time because the screechy flute music and amplifiers are gone, and the jazz band is nowhere to be seen. Instead, accompanied by children on a sunny Sunday morning, the Old West décor looks cute and pleasing, just right for breakfast with kids.

Raulito and Carl abandon our table to watch the giant movie-sized TV screen in another room. This is because in Carl's life with Grandmother, he eats all alone in front of the TV every night, while his grandparents eat in the kitchen. Grandmother, who is American, is so regimented that each day of the week is designated for a specific American junk food, and that is IT. Thursday- pizza. Wednesday- hamburgers. Tuesday- hot dogs. Monday is spaghetti. And so forth. The exact same each week on the exact same day, every month, all year long. Therefore, Carl only likes those foods, and it is rare that he will even take one bite of Mexican food, or any other food, but sometimes he does. He is a great kid though, smart, good-looking, fun, polite, and a wonderful pal to his cousins. When at home, the children "talk" all day long by computer which is set up to somehow ding or ring to signal a message.

Richard, Delfina, Conchita, and I have a wonderful time, enjoying each other and the super food. Richard orders chilaquiles with green sauce. Delfina has crispy hot cakes with chocolate chips and potato chips over the top of that. Conchita has Eggs Benedict. I have enchiladas with mole, and an extra bowl of mole on the side, and beans. Great! Unfortunately the tortillas are flour instead of corn, but after all, this is a restaurant frequented by tourists. We have orange juice and coffee, and the waiter brings two baskets of home-made breads and butter and jam. How can an intelligent person (me) stuff herself to the point of pain just because the food is there and is so delicious? I don't know. But that is what I do.

Delfina has noticed the graffiti which has started to appear around the town. I tell her that it is gang signs and explain what that means. She hadn't known anything about what the scribbles meant. We talk about gangs and how terrible they are. I relay what we learned at my high school when local police presented a program to the faculty, what to look for, the causes, and how serious a problem it is to have gangs come to your community. I advise her to tell her friends to urge the police to get started ridding San Miguel of gangs right away before they get too strong. We talk more about local issues, and of course there is a great deal that I am unaware of, being insulated from the cares and troubles outside of the walls of our house.

Richard and I take a walk until three thirty. Then we paint. Conchita finishes the card for her grandparents just in time. The grandparents arrive, and they all go out. We are invited, but we believe we would be intruding on family time since this is their anniversary celebration.

I call Estela, who invites us, but I say, "Anytime starting tomorrow. We have already declined one invitation, and therefore we would not feel right about accepting another". I tell her that the best way to reach me is to call the Botica. "We could go for a walk-talk", I suggest. I hope she calls tomorrow.

Richard and I take another walk. When we return, I put on a strapless, backless, flowered dress, stockings, white high heels, and earrings. We settle in at the Jardín to listen to a fifteen piece band. The men are dressed in bright yellow shirts and black pants. I am thinking that they sound like Vera Cruz. Delfina later affirms that I am correct. We both love the music of Vera Cruz and stay quite a while. Finally we are hungry but don't want to leave the music, so we sit down at an open air restaurant 'pegado al parque', which means 'stuck to the park', slammed right onto the park, but which in less dramatic English we should say as "adjacent to the park". First we have crispy tortillas, guacamole, and hot rolls with butter.

Richard orders spaghetti with cream, and I get a house salad which means lettuce, ham, goat cheese, tomatoes and onions. Yummy.

We must head for home because I promised Delfina I would help Raulito learn the times tables. Raúl phones and says he is staying in Acapulco for one or two days more. That means Delfina has to man the Botica, and that leaves me to help Raulito. Today is Sunday, the test is Tuesday, and he only knows the threes! Caramba! I will make flash cards.

Thinking that I am almost finished with the second painting of the patio, I prop the two up side-by-side. Shocked! Yes, I am shocked! The colors in each one do not resemble each other at all, nothing alike, because of the time of day. One seems all cool blues, the colors of feeling refreshed under the arches and in the shade. The other is all reds, the colors of late afternoon glowing hotly. In each, the patio itself shows a gloriously hot bright center of the courtyard, yellows and golds, and shimmers of white as accents glinting, even from the gray granite fountain as bits of sparkly rock catch the sun.

We go to bed to the music of a Cumbia band drifting in from somewhere. I like Cumbia, so it is pleasant. I drink my evening tea, turn on the fan, and prepare to sleep, lulled by the serenade, dreaming of the way my friend, Mary Keeling, andf "My Mary" (meaning my daughter), and Mary Keeling's children went to sleep in Puerto Vallarta, hearing the ocean, moonlight pouring into our suite, the dance band by the pool below so pretty. But alas, instead, Richard snores in my ear like a loudspeaker until finally at four AM, an hour's worth of fireworks out in the street awakens him too. We probably both fell asleep at last around five thirty. It is easy to tell the hour. All night long I could hear what time it was, every quarter of the hour, by the gonging of the church bells.

39

I DO ANOTHER BAD THING, SOMEONE, (ESTELA) UNDERSTANDS ME! DADDY RETURNS FROM ACAPULCO

I awaken at 7:45. It takes me a long groggy time to get out of bed. I go for a fast walk by myself because Richard doesn't want to come.

We start breakfast late. Delfina and I have such fun talking that Richard takes his leave, and all of a sudden it is one o'clock. Finishing breakfast at one o'clock? "Oh, no", I think," it must be five to eleven, I am reading the clock wrong, it can't be one o'clock". But it is. No wonder Richard left.

Now Richard feels like walking, so we do, for a short while, and then I work on my painting until comida. Comida is delicious, and Conchita claims the pit of the avocado we have just eaten. She wants to draw onto it a face and hair to make a doll. Raulito wants it to plant, so Delfina says he gets the next one. Delfina tells us that you can plant one hundred avocado pits, and none will grow. It is a very difficult plant to get started. She and her sisters tried all the time. The pit has to be very dry and unscarred. I wonder how many tries it took to start the fine huge tree that grows in this patio and supplies us with eight or more each day. They do not ripen all at once like an apple tree. Every day there are some on the patio floor. Here the pit is called the bone.

I help Raulito with the "times fours" for over an hour. We work hard, and I think he needs a break, so I let him go, which he does gladly. He has other math reviews to do also, besides learning the rest of the tables for tomorrow's test. Poor guy. And he is only in second grade!

But, uh, oh. I do something that isn't right, and pretty soon I know it isn't right, and then naturally I am sorry, and soon I will have to go and apologize. Darn. Why can't I just slow down and do things right in the first place? Here is what it is.

Estela comes to the Botica to see if I can go for a walk just as I happen to enter the Botica myself. It seems like such a perfect opportunity and such a perfect coincidence. So I say, "Great, let's go, first I have to tell Richard". Here is the part why I am badly wrong. Richard has been in our room waiting for me to finish practicing math with Raulito. Just a few minutes ago I had already gone up to our room and told Richard, "OK, let's go for one hour. Then I will come back and practice with Raulito again". So when I saw Estela, I should have asked Richard to come along and all go for the walk together. He likes Estela, and Estela likes him. Instead I holler up to him that Estela is here, and I am going walking with her.

Estela and I walk around and around the Jardín, fast walking, talking, and having fun. I have only recently met her, yet Estela gives me a gift. The gift of approbation.

I have never been able to act smartly jaded, with the frosty attitude so popular of, "I can't be pleased by anything, I am too important to care much about something so trivial as…" Oh, not at all. I am obviously and hopelessly in love with the world, and always raving about everything, to me everything is wonderful, and darling, and great, and terrific and…

I have become used to my delighted praises being received as weaker than water and dismissed with the scornful, "Oh, yes, but Sonette, you love everything." As if loving everything is moronic. So when Estela counters with, "But that is the most wonderful achievement, Sonette, to love everything. To see life and love all of it. That is what everyone needs and rarely attains."

What! What! Estela understands me! She does not see my looking at the good side of everything as a mark of imbecility. She who has money, and power, and success, and recognized achievement, she sees why I can be content with or without all that, and she still respects me! She still likes me! Wow, she is truly my friend. She gets who I am. Wow! Wow, wow, wow, wow.

Her kids are only one half block away, at drama lessons, and we pick them up. Estela invites me to come with them to her house, but I explain about Richard waiting, and also I have to help Raulito. She invites Delfina and me for breakfast at her house tomorrow at ten thirty, and I think, "Goodie!"

Delfina says she wants to go with me, but the plumber is supposed to come. "I will tell you at ten o'clock tomorrow morning if I can go", she says. If Delfina comes, we will take a taxi. If I go alone, I will walk.

Back at the house, I discover that Richard has already left, as he should, giving up on me and taking a walk by himself. I feel selfish and mean. I wanted Richard to be here so I could apologize and be nicer. But... I guess all I can do is learn a lesson. Maybe it was all meant to be, though, because it was important to me to hear what Estela said.

I help Raulito who has been working on math reviews by himself. Conchita asks me if I will help her, even though she knows more answers than I do. I can, though, check her answers with the calculator.

Richard returns and has not been at all upset. He says, "Let's take the kids for ice cream". We buy sundaes to take home for Chita and Perla. We tell them to order "the biggest and the best", and they seem pleased. Now the kids want to go to the pet store, so we go for looks at fish and mice.

We are back at the house when we hear a great banging and clanging from the front "doorbell" The door bell is not a little buzzer or electronic ding-dong like we have back home. Instead it is an actual bell, an eighteen inch, heavy, cast bronze bell hung on a large iron hook in the entryway, to which a cord has been tied. The cord goes through a hole drilled in the heavy wooden entry door and hangs down just enough to grab, and yank, and make your presence known, except that the cord ends high up so that passing children cannot reach that far to give it a mischievous yank.

Hearing the bell, everyone runs to the doors and into the arms of Raúl. He and Vito are back from Acapulco. The children leap at Raúl and cling to him. It is a delightful exhibition of total unrestricted love. Happily, Richard and I have just gotten ready to go out for dinner, so the family gets some private time for their reuniting.

We walk the two blocks to Casa Sautto to dine in their patio restaurant. It is a wonderful feeling to eat outside surrounded by the gardens, trees, arches, with everything unchanged since I lived there for six months as a student forty years ago. I feel so close to

Abelardo. It is as if he not only gifted me with his language, his country (and thus my career), and also his family and home. I feel a great sense of "husbanding" from him. It is a strange and wonderful feeling that I have not expected, except here it is, tangibly so, and I love it.

40

BREAKFAST FRAMED BY TREES, THE STREET MADE OF STEPS, AND CHITA'S RANCHO STORIES

The time is going so fast because we now have friends, activities, and some chores, so we can't really fit everything in.

For my ten thirty breakfast with Estela, as soon as I awaken, I use all my time getting ready. I walk up, up, up the steep, steep street, over and across El Mirador, and then down through the crooked narrow streets that look like the back alleys of nowhere. Even though this dusty, rock-strewn passageway hardly qualifies as a street, every so far there is a brand new house, from the street-side looking like a large blank wall, while the majority of dwellings still are old, humble, or terrible, sometimes just tumbles and patches of house, gardens, and drives, all stuck together. Still, each part of this lane does qualify as picturesque, charming.

Arriving at Estela's gate, I see two men waiting. They ask if I live there as they would like to be admitted to see the houses. One is old, and one is youngish. I say that no, I do not live here, I am a guest. When I am admitted, it is by Estela herself, who comes to the door, speaks to them, and says that she is having a party (me), so she will have someone else show them around. She says they may look at the gardens, and then they should make an appointment.

There is another guest. She is Felipa, a very nice Mexican woman whom I like immediately. Delfina couldn't come because of the plumber. A fantastic breakfast is served to us on the little balcony terrace. I say fantastic as in fantasy or dream. Estela's maids all wear very pretty pink maid's dresses, like you see in old movies of Fred Astaire where he is vacationing at some posh-posh hotel on the French Riviera back in the thirties, when money equaled style and flair. The uniforms are trimmed with the whitest of white little aprons, and maybe white caps. The maids are tiny, dark skinned women who look like campesinas, from the country. They look shy and pretty. The food is not like anything I have ever seen or heard of in the United States. Course follows course, and although we are three slender women, we eat lavishly and with slow savory delight.

We are sitting above the swaying tree tops, and Estela has given me the best seat, the one with the most spectaular view of San Miguel far below. Down there is hot hustle and bustle. Here we are shady, and lazy, and cool.

The pretty little women bring our food on beautiful hand painted dishes made in Dolores Hidalgo, the ceramic top-of-the-line for this state. Our glasses are hand blown glass, probably made right here in the center of San Miguel. First, orange juice, coffee, then dishes of mangos and apples topped by sour cream whipped together with cottage cheese. Our empty plates are removed, and now we are given chilaquiles with thick cream, crumbled goat cheese, and diced onions. That would be enough, but here come irresistible chicken breasts with green mole, the sauce made by Estela herself from a very complicated recipe. Next, yes, still more to come, next more chicken, this time with nopales and sauce. To finish with a flourish, a dessert! It is croissants stuffed with dark chocolate. And more coffee. And as I already said, we eat it all, every bite, and with great appreciation and delight. It has taken us two hours to consume this food.

Now we can really talk. We talk women-talk, mom-talk, girl-talk. Finally Felipa has to leave because she must pick up her children. Estela and I visit more and then tour her gardens. We talk to the many laborers and gardeners until two o'clock. Estela offers to drive me home, but I want exercise.

"I will drive you to the best spot for a walk", she says, and she does. It is a marvelous walk, as in one marvel unfolding to the next. This tiny "street" consists mostly of steps. It is sometimes so narrow that you can almost touch both sides. The steps are all winding, twisting, irregular, hundreds of years old, flanked by doorways and balconies very high up, cascades of flowers, arches, and you have a view of San Miguel all the way down at the bottom during every step of the walk. I don't want it to end, but eventually I am led to "Casa de la Cultura", The House of Culture. Here all the fine arts of Mexico (and therefore of international importance) are taught and preserved. If you come at the right moment, you will see on one of the many terraces or platforms young people dancing the historic national dances, see swirling of the skirts, hear clapping, or clicking, or stomping of heels. You will hear music from every region of Mexico. You may hear a sort of military band which is a part of some local school.

Casa de la Cultura is built like a red adobe waterfall on the side of the mountain, level after level irregularly clinging to the side of the rocky slope. In fact, this point actually is the location of the real "El Chorro", the town's waterfall and maybe a major source of its water. El Chorro provides water also for another red adobe structure, the wash tubs for all the women who wish to lug their clothes here to scrub them in the large crimson cement tubs which rim the edges of a spacious flat space above the French Park. The side of each tub has been slanted and indented in rows to be a wash-board scrubbing surface, and the women rub their clothes up and down to get them clean.

Children play while the moms do the wash. Sometimes the children get into the tubs too and get a washing themselves. Women chat and visit, there are large trees over-head for shade, the water is clean and clear, so it is a pleasant place to be. However, the moms have to carry home all of the now even heavier laundry, because it is wet, and it still remains to hang and dry and iron upon reaching home. That part is not so idyllic, and someone who has to do this much hard work each week probably does not have a large space at home for dealing with all these clothes jobs. It must be exhausting.

But for me, all I have to do is admire and enjoy the beauty, the breeze, and the exotic feeling of being in someone else's world. I walk through the French Park, continue through the side streets, through the busy Jardín, and home.

Richard is waiting for me. I change out of my dress and high heels and jewelry into shorts, and I am glad to take another walk. I need to take a hundred walks now. We return by three thirty, and it is comida already! A mountain of walking, and a mountain of breakfast eating, and it is time to eat again!

The table has been set under the arches of the patio, "en el aire libre", in the free air. This was Raúl's idea. Delfina has spread a pretty tablecloth. Chita serves, as usual, a giant delicious meal.

Dessert is sweet fresh strawberries with sweetened yogurt.

I help Raulito again with his multiplication tables, the fours, which he learns perfectly. Conchita invites me to walk to Cousin Carl's house to see their completed school project. It is a super-duper model of a jungle. To get to Carl's house we took what I call "the school bus route", a zigging zagging route in order to pass the maximum number of houses of friends. It is fun.

The grandmother, and her son Carl, Cousin Carl's father, gave up their American citizenship so that son Carl could go to medical school here for free and become a doctor. They own about half this city block, which is a lot of property. The grandmother and her husband, Carl and his wife, and another couple (the parents of the recently baptized baby girls) all live here in their own separate but interconnecting houses, along with also Carl's doctor office, a computer business , and lots of parking space, all within these walls. So much parking space is a real luxury.

Carl's wife is Delfina's sister. She is really nice and interesting, just like all of Delfina's family.

To return home, I am alone, so I walk back the quick direct way. See how it is so much fun to be friends with kids? They never care about quick and direct. They care about adventure, and playing at everything, and having fun. They make me play, which otherwise I would never do, and they make me have fun. All I ever have to do is say, "OK, sure, of course, Yes".

Richard has changed our return flights to make them better. Yea! We have to call Mary and Bob so that Bob will meet us at O'Hare at nine thirty PM instead of close to midnight. So much better. We still have to get our bus tickets tomorrow, cash some travelers checks, buy postcards, and buy a brightly decorated ceramic plate for Mary, maybe.

When we get back to the house, Raulito wants me to paint his model boat. I am all done with painting my good-bye cards, which we will stuff with money, the tips. The boat doesn't take long to finish, and Richard and I can sit in the cool of the patio as dusk falls. I haven't told much about Chita, but she is with us in the dusk and has time to talk a little. I have become friends with her, and talking while I watch her cook has been important to me. Now she tells me, because I am always asking her questions and being delighted by her answers, even though they are not all rosy pictures, a little more about her life. It has been like coming across a delightful treasure chest of stories, tidbits about her family, her rancho knowledge, her out-in-the-country rancho experiences.

She had to work in the broccoli fields for years before getting this job. In the hot sun, in the pouring cold rain, even sometimes in water up to the knees, they had to keep working. Chita's rancho at least has water, but Gertrudis' does not. After her long work day, and long, long bus ride, and the long, long walk to her house, Gertrudis has to walk even more, carrying an empty bucket or bottle, to another rancho to get the water for her family. And home again, carrying the heavy water, which then must be carefully parceled out to her children and the rest of the family. And the next day the same, and the next, and the next.

One of the gifts I gave to Gertrudis, and to the others, were umbrellas. I thought they would be for the rainy season. "Oh, yes", she said, "but also for right now, to keep off the sun". I hadn't even thought about that.

I have been in San Miguel at Christmas time, and in January, and I know how cold it gets. Inside it feels even colder because of being in shade instead of sunshine, and because of drafts. So I give Gertrudis my coat. I am sorry to let it go. It is a London Fog, lined, excellent against the rain, stylish, and it has helped me enjoy many a rainy day in London and Paris. My raincoat is my treasured friend, but I am American. I can buy more. I give it to Gertrudis.

Tonight Chita wants to cook us a merienda, but she looks exhausted. I want her to rest. But just as she is going to her room at nine o'clock, Raulito wants a hot dog and some yogurt. I heat up left-overs for Richard (a tamal, some beef with green chili sauce, and soufflé). For myself, lettuce salad, a bolillo, and half of a "pan de leche", bread made with milk. Delfina joins us. She too is exhausted, from helping Raulito prepare for his tests. Sixty pages of review! For a second grader! Besides all of whatever else she did all day- working in the Botica, dealing with the plumber, and more, more, more. Yet she never loses her temper, never complains. She is a wonderful person.

41

TICKETS FOR HOME, THE FOREVER POOR AND BROKEN STRANGER, AND GIFTS FOR THE MAIDS

I see Estela again by coincidence this morning. So many coincidences are very interesting. Just as Richard and I are going out the door to do something we had not planned on doing, there is Estela coming out of the bakery on her way to pick up Delfina in the Botica to go to a "Junta", the ladies' breakfast club. It is a real coincidence because she was not looking for me, nor I for her. We have a nice visit about yesterday's breakfast at her house. Estela says that I had touched something special in Felipa's heart because she shed some tears at what I was telling.

Richard and I go to the travel agency to buy bus tickets from Querétaro to the D.F. airport. D.F. means "Distrito Federal", Federal District, which Americans call Mexico City. Mexicans call it simply, México. Bus seats, just like an airplane, are sold by numbered seats and therefore might be sold out, so Richard wants to be at the agency at nine sharp, which is when they open. Supposed to open, I should say. As I expected, it is not open. I was pretty sure that no one would be there on time, but oh, well, it gives us an opportunity to take a walk and return at ten. Finally the agency opens.

We buy tickets for a departure of seven thirty AM, which should get us to the airport at ten thirty for Richard's flight, three thirty for mine. But American Airlines says that we have to arrive three hours early because they unpack you and inspect every little thing. Oh, brother. What a giant farce is all this checking. It is like going down to the ocean with a teaspoon and trying to take out all the pollution. A huge, stupid, waste of time and money, and everyone pretending that there is any point to it. Bah.

We walk home for breakfast with Raúl. Vito drops in with an

enormous, unappetizing box of store cookies to share, yet the thought behind it is very kind. I sound mean, but I do not like cookies, and especially from the store. Vito has a generous heart and also brought us special hot pepper candy and gooey brown squishy candy, both home-made in the market of Acapulco. He is carrying two large folders of pictures of Raúl and himself at the convention. It was not a pharmacists' convention after all. Vito almost drowned in the huge surf. For some reason Raúl gave up his room at Fiesta American and stayed at La Princesa, still on the beach, but smaller and less posh. Anyway, Vito lived through the near death calamity and is tan and happy.

Our breakfast is huge and great and nice. And now I will tell why I was going out this morning when I ran into Estela.

On my first walk of the morning, I took a pretty red and white dress to the lady who sits by our door and sells nopales. She is the one to whom I always give some money, the one who cooked nopales for me one day. She had asked me to give her a dress, so I found one that she might look fine wearing (not too fancy or too American) and gave it to her. In the bag with the dress I also put two fresh bolillos, candy, gum, and some coins.

She asked for my address. I said not to write because it is so expensive, eight pesos just for one postcard stamp. She says it is because please, will I lend her one hundred pesos, and she will pay it back little by little. It is for medicine, etc., blah blah, blah. I doubt about the medicine, but of course she could use the money. I think, "Look at her poor broken teeth, the few she has. Her nails like claws. Her "job" of sitting in a doorway all day trying to sell a few cactus leaves. Her work of getting the leaves each morning, coming to town—it all sounds very hard and hopeless".

So I think, "What does it matter to give her eleven dollars compared to me not being able to sleep and worrying about it for years to come?" (which I would do). And that is why I was going out the door for the second time. I came back into the house, went up to my room, got the one hundred pesos, and was setting out to give it to her. (Which after seeing Estela and talking, I did.) I told the lady, "Don't pay me back, but don't use it for medicine. Buy yourself some good food, and that will do you more good than medicine". She wanted to know what time I was leaving for Mexico City so she could cook me some nopales, come early, and give them to me for my going-away breakfast. Can you imagine the humility of her offer? She knows that she is too poor, and broken, and a stranger, to ever be invited inside this house. And yet, she is offering to get up extra early, cook something for me, and wait outside the door, sitting on the curb or the sidewalk in the dark, and wait for me to come out and eat her little gift. I had to say, "No, it will be too early, but how nice of you. I thank you greatly".

Again comida is served outside. Delfina's parents are here, and I really like them. Conversation is great fun, and we start our wonderful meal, which includes flowers batter-fried, and also purple flower water. I have gifts for the parents which I hope they will like: a fine men's cologne, and a dress. For Delfina a very good quality shirt and sweater which seems to please her very much. And a swimming suit that she likes a lot too.

After she cleans the kitchen, Chita helps me to divide the remaining things I have brought. Clothes, shoes, umbrellas, sweaters, and other items. I am also giving her my fan and an extension cord. She is delighted because her room has no windows, except for a skylight, and a small high up window in her bathroom that opens into the boiling hot laundry room. She loves her room though, and it is very pretty and surprisingly full of light because of the overhead square blocks of glass that function as waterproof skylights. Naturally it is also a great joy to her to have her own bathroom with a shower and limitless heated water for washing her beautiful, long black hair. I let Chita pick out all the clothes she wants to keep. She is very happy. Some will be for herself. There are enough for her father, and mother, and sisters, and cousins too.

For Rafaela the maid, I give a package of new socks and new underwear. A pretty blouse, a skirt, a warm soft robe, a sweater, shoes to match, a new back-pack and toys for her children, a tote bag, jewelry, and all of our left-over toiletries. Plus Band-Aids, cotton balls, feminine pads, soap, and rubber gloves. She is thrilled with everything, especially the rubber gloves, because she must wash all of her children's clothes by hand. (As a matter of fact, rubber gloves are a very popular gift in Latin America, at least where I have gone.) Also lotions, shampoo, wash cloths, everything.

For Gabriella, dresses, a jacket, shoes, heavy sweater, (umbrella and raincoat I already gave her), and a few other things. I will give the maids their cards and tips tomorrow.

Richard and I go out and cash one more check for twenty dollars and buy gifts in the market. We are now down to zero pesos. We shouldn't need to buy anything more. We always keep some American one dollar bills for last minute tips, baggage handlers, etc. We like to give everything away and go home with nothing. Well, almost nothing. I gave away most of the paintings, but I will take a few home.

At five o'clock I meet Estela in the Jardín. We walk until six. She will come to visit us on June 21 and stay for two or three days. I have to give her my mailing address. She already has my email address. She will be dropping off her son in Cleveland and then will fly to O'Hare where I will pick her up. Then she will fly all over the US. She is excited because her husband will be arriving here soon, April 29. It is nice to see such love.

I arrive back at "our" The Great House, which we have been calling home, to the exact kind of scene that I love. Under the arches, Conchita is sprawled in a chair while a woman gives her an elaborate, lengthy pedicure. Raulito has everything ready for me to show him how to paint his pirate ship. Delfina asks if I will paint flowers on one of the many huge wooden crosses that hang high over each door of the patio. Then it is Delfina's turn for a pedicure. Conchita wants me to draw something for her to paint, and I draw the hundred year old parrot. She paints it beautifully, from memory, because the parrot doesn't like so much attention, and so he retreats into his cage and won't come out.

It is all so much fun—Conchita painting, dressed in her cute turquoise underwear (remember when I was mad about that?) and a smock. She wears the underwear because of the heat, and because it was from me, and after all, the underwear is the same as a bathing suit. Raulito, all excited about his ship model. Chita, bringing things and helping. Lots of girl-talk about make-up, and manicures, and pedicures.

Finally, at about eight forty-five, we clean up from all our projects, and for the final time, Richard packs up all our paints. Richard plays bouncing ball with Chita the cook, and I go with Conchita and Raulito who say they want to go for a walk. At the end of the block we stop, and it is evident that the children's real purpose of our walk is to get ice cream.

The inside of the ice cream parlor is as it has been almost forever, dark, shadowed, a few light bulbs on cords dangling down for needed light. Uniformed girls scooping up delicious flavors. Wide doors open to the street like windows. Views of the Jardín and all the passers-by. Tiny ice cream tables and chairs, some occupied. A woman comes in to use the pay phone, and even though she is poor enough to not have a phone, I wish I could be her, just a sort of wish, because she will stay here, here in San Miguel, with so much that I love and must leave, but which will still surround her every day. She will stay, and I will not. I memorize the scene for later, for forever, for pulling out and re-living whenever I want to remember this day.

The kids enjoy their ice creams, and we walk back home. At last Raúl and Delfina have locked up the Botica for the night and are ready for Richard and me to take them out to dinner for a thank-you and a good-bye. It is late though, and all the restaurants are closed. We find one little restaurant on the square that is still open. It is so small and crowded that it is boiling hot. It is a very popular place, apparently. Raúl and Delfina tell us about their volunteer work. I had no idea that Delfina does just as much of the volunteer work as Raúl. That is why they are late sometimes. They help any troubled, desperate person who phones, often in the middle of the night, and often in order to help, they have to drive way out of town. They listen endlessly to anyone in trouble and devote themselves to helping others.

We already packed for home early this morning. Tomorrow we will lay out airport clothes and finish the last bits of packing. What a relief. I am always nervous about packing.

I hear the bells strike twelve forty- five, then one AM, and then I don't hear any more.

42

EVERY PRECIOUS MINUTE OF OUR LAST DAY

This is my last "real" morning in San Miguel. Tomorrow we have to leave here by six thirty AM, arise at five thirty?

I feel glad that I have awakened early enough today to hear the clanging and banging bells greet the morning. How I will miss the comfort of those bells welcoming everyone in town to come to church, to start the day surrounded by the indescribable beauty of the arts that fill the churches, art as expressions of glorifying God, and man's tribute to the ultimate art, the splendor of Soul.

It is tempting to think we could keep on here, but although we could afford to buy or rent a house, that kind of privacy is not what I would like. What I love is the wonderful acceptance we have had into the heart and soul of this family which made out trip develop from a bud into a blossom. Now the blossom is at full flower, and from the full-blown rose, petals will begin to fall. The season of sweet perfume, with us as the rose in the loveliest of gardens, has flourished, and next would begin to pass. Trying to keep the blossom beyond its time never works. Attempts to do so only result in dry, dead parodies of the freshness and the life which endears any garden.

So with great gratitude, I open my hands to let this visit go, in its season, and to wait for whatever will appear, around the next corner of my life.

With my mind now clear, my heart can freely enjoy this last day, these few remaining precious hours, all fun, no regrets. We walk before breakfast, and Richard and I return to eat with just Raúl. Raúl sits with us for a long time, talking. He invites us to his private "sala" (his family's private living room) to hear him read excerpts from his very well kept travel diary and to see pictures of his and Delfina's three month trip to Europe. Three months! When he brings out his next album, which is of their family's travels through Australia, I have to leave and do last minute things, plus I get jumpy from sitting too long. But it is all very interesting, and Richard is enjoying the visit, so he stays.

I need to give the maids their gifts before comida as I will be busy after, and then they will be gone, except for Chita. First Graciela. I bring her into the downstairs room of our apartment where I already have her things laid out for her. Each item she really loves! Very thick, fine, Pendleton sweater, almost a jacket. White high heeled shoes. Lots of clothes and hangers. Earrings. Plastic zip-lock bags. Last I give her the card with the cash. She gets so happy that her hands are shaking.

Then I go to find Rafaela, the maid. She is upstairs cleaning, and I bring her into our apartment. She also loves everything. Clothes for her, a carry-all, more new socks for her daughter, zip-lock bags. Pretty high-heeled shoes that delight her. She puts them right on. Christian Science magazines written in Spanish, which I have been giving her all along, and which she says both her children enjoy reading. I bring her into our upstairs rooms and give her hangers, clothes pins, detergent, and rubber gloves. She shows me her hands and short cracked fingernails, all rough from the washing she has to do. She is thrilled to have rubber gloves.

I show her all the toiletries we have left, some new. A new un-opened toothbrush in its box, toothpaste, shampoo, razor. She asks if we are leaving our extension cord here. I say, "Yes, for you if you like. Be sure to come here and get it the minute you arrive tomorrow morning because we will already be gone." I give her the card and money. I am sure it has to be hard for her not to count the money right then and there. She thanks me again for the things I gave her yesterday. She says they are so wonderful and that the new toys, backpack, and socks will make presents that she can give to her children on April 30, Children's Day. Usually she can't give them anything. Gift giving is so much fun!

I have already given all of Chita's gifts to her. All that is left is to give her now is the card, which is a painting of the patio, and the cash. She is surprised and doesn't think she should take it. I tell her about all that she has done for us and how much we appreciate it. I say that all of us who work have to get money. She is pleased. I just love Chita. She has become such a special friend.

I have saved Dakar-Noir men's cologne, two beautiful dresses, and a smart blazer for Delfina's mother and father. Delfina says they will like everything.

Raúl wants me to hear excerpts from his Australian diary. I have finished all that I needed to do, so I am delighted to hear him read aloud about the opening night of the Olympics. Also about going up on the magical sacred rock, and some other parts of the diary. It is touching how much he shares with us.

It is only one forty-five. We have time to walk to El Mirador for one final look at San Miguel. Who should drive by and honk, but Estela! We must be star-crossed. She invites us to come to her house, but she is headed downtown, and a big line of cars instantly piles up behind her as she talks to us. I have to holler, "Thank you", but shake my head "No".

We walk back home via the tiny callejón, which means alley-way, the steep route which is all ancient narrow steps, irregular, ziggy-zaggy, beautiful. We arrive at the women's public clothes washing spot where two sweet children are having a shampoo by an older girl using a plastic bowl to pour water over their heads as they sit in a wash tub. The weary mother has finished her washing, has spread it out to dry over the red cement railings and benches, and she is resting while everything dries. It is a tranquil scene, a lovely portrait of a family together.

We continue to the French Park, rest in the shade of palms, savor the soft breeze, the sounds of birds, and families, and lovers, and friends. Soon we are greeted back at the house, greeted by wonderful rattles and smells as we head past the kitchen to go up to our room. The children have just arrived home from school. Raulito runs to me and gives me a kiss. He tells me, with delight, that today he will finish his model ship. Conchita comes over and kisses me too, then heads off to do something else. I go upstairs to Richard, who is resting on the bed, fan on.

After our last big family comida, the family is spending every possible minute with us. Tomorrow, so early that it will still be dark, we will all arise so that Raúl can drive us to Querétaro for our bus journey to the Mexico City airport. Therefore today is important, and we are enjoying every bit of it while we can.

The children are always wonderful, and for me, to sit in the patio with them for homework or games is indescribably tender. Delfina is helping Raulito with his math practice. I suggest to

Conchita that we play a game because there is not enough time to set out her paints, clean up, etc. We look through all of her games, and she selects one that is a lot of fun. Raulito joins us for the game, after I check his math practice, and after Conchita recites to me her speech that she is practicing for Friday, the one in which she and Carl will show their model of the tropical jungle.

Delfina is really wonderful about making sure that the kids always do their homework, know the material for tests, and understand everything. For me it is just pure fun to practice with them because I don't really have any responsibilities, and it is a nice way to enjoy the children.

Raúl says he is going to drive us to an ice cream parlor to say hi to his dad. His dad is usually there about this time each day, I guess, playing chess with his friends. "Raúl Padre", the grandfather, (we would say, Raúl Senior) is eighty-two but looks unwrinkled, content, and healthy. He looks just as he did all those years ago, but I don't think he particularly remembers me from before.

After the visit, Raúl drives us past the super-deluxe house that his dad used to own. It is so big that his dad had his own bowling alley! Now he has married again and has a son and daughter. On the way to the ice cream parlor, by coincidence, we saw the son careening down a steep cobblestone street on his bicycle at a fast clip, weaving in and out of the traffic like an expert. I only saw him from the back. He looked about eighteen or twenty years old.

When we get back, Conchita wants us to walk to the Jardín. She always has a cute kid idea about something to do that I never would have thought of. I like that freshness. We have to walk all the way without stepping on any cracks, which is much different on irregular, not quite flat stones, than at home on sidewalks.

We walk around the park in a circle for a couple of times. Conchita tries to buy another little cardboard box of sugar and chili powder as a gift for me to take to Mary, the same kind I had told her that Mary liked here in Mexico when she was a child. Isn't that thoughtful?

We go home, dress up, and Raúl and Delfina say they are taking us out to dinner, wherever we want. We chose the outside dining room of Hotel Posada San Francisco, where the walls between the sidewalk of the Jardín and the restaurant are almost non- existent, and you have huge expanses of open nothing between you at your table and the liveliness of the park and people in it. The interior patio restaurant is far more beautiful, but we want to be with the life of the town as much as possible tonight.

Raúl calls through the window and hires a whole Mariachi band to come over and serenade us, and this is not cheap! Conchita, Richard, Delfina, Raúl, and I can each chose a song. All the songs are beautiful and long. The men are handsome and gallant in their beautiful black Mariachi suits with white blousy bow ties covered with white sequins.

We order more than we really need because it is our last chance to eat Mexican food. Raúl says we should order full meals because we had such a light comida. Everyone laughs because our comida today was enormous and of everything we could possibly call our favorites.

The restaurant table is soon loaded with beautiful dinners. Our conversations are sweet and fun, and salted by Conchita's tears. She doesn't want us to leave. Even Richard starts to cry as the Mariachis play the farewell song. While we are trying to comfort Conchita to stopping sobbing for long enough to eat dinner, Raúl asks Raulito if he too feels bad about our leaving. We all explode in laughter as he answers, "Sí, Pero lo aguanto". Yes, but I can stand it! Ha, ha. It was so funny.

You can imagine the rest, going back to the house, the hugs, the promises, the tears, thank you, I love you, we will be back, we will come to your house too, and finally, sleep.

Then wake up, and off we go, "Home again, home again, jiggity-jog", as I end this bed-time story, the San Miguel story, my story.

I do not realize, not until much later, that "My Mexican Life", "My Abelardo Life", started with his Mariachi serenade, and tonight a different serenade has closed my current episode. I think it means that, just as Abelardo's death did not finish him, neither does leaving tomorrow end Mexico's love affair with me.

End of Trip One

Trip Two

Four Years Later,
Mexico City, Midnight Arrival
August 20, 2005

CONTENTS

1

CONFUSED, EXHAUSTED, SCARED AND RESCUED

Safe! "Oh, thank you, God, oh, thank you, thank you, thank you." At last, I am where I want to be, with Nita once again, where we are expected, where we will be welcomed, sheltered, and pampered. And where we are safe.

Before I left the States, newspapers and TV had been full of dreadful stories about vicious kidnappings in Mexico City, horrifying tales of what happened to Americans who left the airport, even for a journey of only a few blocks to a hotel. Don't go! Too much danger! Wait until some other year!

And indeed, my nice, safe, non-stop flight transformed itself into a long and frighteningly uncertain journey, full of dire warnings, of things going wrong, of me unable to contact Nita to alert her to my travel changes, not knowing what bad and scary thing might come to pass, but in spite of it all, in the end, at last we have arrived at the apartment building of The Aunt. Nita will press the buzzer of the intercom, someone inside will hear it and will admit us to the lobby, we will take the elevator, the doors will part, and there we will be, and we will relax at last, in the shelter of the apartment of The Aunt. Yes, yes, yes. Not kidnapped on a midnight ride down the wrong streets of Mexico City, not tricked into a taxi that is not a taxi at all. Not somewhere with a cut-off finger, or ear in a little box on its way to a relative as incentive to pay my ransom.

Not any of the terrible things that the newspapers, and television news, and the United States State Department have been warning about, should you find yourself needing to leave the safety of the airport in Mexico City, needing to trust someone you don't know. Not at the mercy of whatever could happen to you when you arrive nine hours later than scheduled, and all the buses leaving directly from the airport have been shut down for the night, when you don't have a hotel reservation, or don't know what to do because you have been through so many delayed flights, transfers, arriving in cities where you did not expect to be, answering confusing questions, filling out forms while exhausted, and worrying that the only friend who knows where you are could have given up waiting for your arrival, and could have given up on you, and could have left.

No, none of the terrible maybes happened. Instead, here we are together at last, me rescued once again by Nita, and now I am greeted with hugs, and kisses, and smiles of delight by people I don't even know, people I have never met, and all because of Nita.

We step into the apartment of The Aunt. As expected, she is not available to greet us. And I think once again, those wonderful and beautiful words, "We are all right".

I am introduced to Belinda, the care-giver of The Aunt, who ushers us into a bedroom, so simple, and clean, and breezy, and calm. We have our own bath, our own blankets, and our own open windows, and although we are in the heart of Mexico City, we are listening to the silence of the night on the beautiful tree-lined street of The Aunt. We are far enough away from the busiest of streets to muffle any sounds of traffic, still filled with cars at this hour. In fact, I do not even know at this moment where this apartment is located, I do not care. I do not care about anything except that I am in the company and care of my dearest Nita, and nothing bad can happen to me now. We go to sleep.

2

THE PUFFY DOLL, AND A WILD TAXI

Nita and I awaken at the same time. We ready ourselves for having breakfast, for explaining to The Aunt's caregiver all the details of why we arrived so late last night. We proceed to the kitchen. There sits the caregiver, Belinda, with her beautiful young daughter, ready to hug and kiss us, and ready to serve us anything we would like for breakfast. But all we want is papaya and coffee. All our time is spent in talking instead of in eating.

I explain how my non-stop from O'Hare, Chicago, was changed to a journey that lasted from five AM to nine PM. How I had no way to find Nita who was planning to meet me at the airport here in Mexico City at noon. I didn't know where Nita was staying, I had not expected to need to know. I had not brought Raúl's phone number, never imagining that I would need it either.

All I could do was to call my friends in Lake Geneva from the Dallas airport, explain how my flight had been rerouted, my whole schedule of careful plans for being met were useless now, so my friends all pitched in by telephoning everyone they knew who maybe might have the phone number of Raúl in San Miguel (saved from four years ago when I last stayed at Raúl's house), and if Raúl might know where Nita was, and if he could find someone in Mexico City who might be able to catch Nita before she left for the airport, and warn her, and if maybe she would finally be able to find me, and rescue me. Everything worked! My friends made a huge, complicated phone chain, got the important numbers, and reached the right people!

When the last of my flights finally set me down at the airport in Mexico City, I expected to collect my luggage and go looking for Nita. Instead, the airport officials held back my suitcase and giant duffel bag, kept me filling out forms, and made me answer the same questions over and over, while all the other passengers breezed along and out of the airport. I didn't know what to do, but I did know that by then the bus for Querétaro, and from there to San Miguel, would have already left, and although I was never given my luggage, at least finally the officials let me go, which by then felt like an escape from a nightmare.

And then came my great relief, when right in front of the doors that let me out of the confinement that the airport had become for me, when those doors swung open, there was Nita!

She had found out my flight arrival time, planted herself, standing, where she knew she could not miss seeing me, and there she had stood, patiently waiting for four long hours. Four hours without taking a break for the bathroom, without finding a chair for resting for even a minute, without even taking her insulin. Nothing was going to make Nita abandon my arrival.

I consider continuing my explanation to Belinda and her daughter, of how also, knowing that the next step of leaving this city once she finally found me would be impossible until the next day, Nita had even arrived at the airport extra early to stand outside the entrance in the long, long line to purchase our taxi tickets, shortening our wait once she could finally emerge with me in tow. How when I was finally released, and Nita found me, it was far past the time she should have taken her insulin. And that when she told me this, I was emboldened to ignore the two-people-wide and one-block-long queue of those passengers who, having already endured the wait for the purchase of a taxi ticket, and now had been directed to take their places at the end of another even longer line, dragging their luggage (unlike me who had none) and inching along to the secure zone of taxis whose licenses and plates were being checked by guards in an attempt to stop the kidnappings and hold-ups.

Ignoring all courtesy (remember, this is Mexico, so naturally the only people in line were Americans, the only ones to be so obedient as to politely and tiredly wait their proper turns), I decided to act as "Mexican-style" as I could. I headed for the front of the line, spied an amiable and well-dressed man, pushed Nita towards him and said, "She needs to take her insulin right away. My plane was very late, and we must get home". Kindly he slipped us to the first of all the taxis, opened its door, told us, "Get in quickly before anyone can object", and he resumed his place in line, willing to take the brunt of any complaints for the sake of us, two women in need.

I have been long in my telling in the kitchen. I have talked enough. All that matters now is that "Airport Day" is over. We are here, we are safe, we are fine. It is time to greet The Aunt.

I have heard about The Aunt for years, but I have never seen her. Belinda leads us to her room. Belinda has already dressed her, arranged her wispy white hair, applied powder, lipstick, rouge, and even perfume. The Aunt has been propped up on her bed, in a semblance of a sitting position, but she does not look alive. Not at all. Neither does she look dead. She looks like a puffy doll, she has slits where she should have eyes, she does not take note of us in any apparent way, and yet Belinda, and the daughter, and Nita love her. All kiss her, including me, on both cheeks. Belinda and Nita hold her hands, sit beside her, pet her and pat her, and everyone talks. Except, of course, The Aunt.

On the wall of the bedroom are photographs of long ago days. They show a younger, vital aunt, beautifully dressed, in night clubs, at parties, in gardens, always with her handsome husband, animated, having fun. Those who love her must see her this way still. Everyone explains to her who I am, she is fed broth, Jello, and yogurt, and the TV is turned on for her, just in case, I suppose. We go back to the living room.

We have been proceeding with the morning at a languid pace, when all of a sudden Nita asks what time it is. I tell her, and she says, "Sonette, why you don't tell me? It is too late. Our bus will leave!" Yesterday, after finding out about my delay, Nita had gone to a different bus station and purchased new tickets for today. Our new tickets from the different bus station are direct and non-stop to San Miguel, which is better than what we had previously planned to do, which was:

- Nita would meet me at the airport.
- We would right away take a bus from the bus station that is within the airport to Querétaro.
- Nita would have previously purchased our tickets to Querétaro to correspond with my arrival and would have telephoned the Botica, letting Raúl know the time of our arrival.

- Raúl and Delfina would be waiting for us in Querétaro to drive us the one hour from there to San Miguel.
- Everyone would be happy, and we would be comfortably inside The Great House by mid- afternoon.

The reason for not taking a direct bus to our ultimate destination in the first place was to avoid stepping for an instant outside of the airport because all over the USA were dire warnings about the terrible things that were happening in the city, especially when taking taxis. There were no buses going to San Miguel leaving from the airport. Therefore one had to journey to some other town in the proximity of our goal and then proceed from there. Nita, naturally, did not take any of the scary warnings seriously, but understanding my unaccustomed caution on this issue, had kindly offered to come all the way to Mexico City in advance of my arrival, to spend a couple of days at The Aunt's and visit friends, and then to meet me at the airport so we could hop right onto the bus, with an airport worker who would be glad to earn a few pesos helping us by wheeling my luggage from baggage claim to the hold of the bus. And then we would settle in for a pretty ride and lots of catch-up talking. At least, that was the idea we had in mind. It was to be so smooth and so easy.

Not so. Here we are, still in Mexico City, and at the apartment with a new plan, different tickets already purchased for some other station, and it is time to go. But we are not ready! How can we do this? What happened? And now Nita is telling me that we are late, late in getting a taxi, late in leaving here, too late to make it to the bus station, and I already know that bus tickets are sold well in advance, so there will be no more possibilities of getting tickets for a later ride today.

"Nita", I answer, "I don't know what time our bus departs! I don't know what time we are supposed to leave here!" "But, Sonette", she answers "You have a watch. I already tell you yesterday that I am not wearing a watch. Why you don't tell me what time it is? You know how far away is the station with busses for San Miguel." "I have no idea", I counter, "I don't even know where we are now. You never mentioned what time our bus leaves." "You know Mexico!", she replies, as if I have a map in my head of all the many bus stations in Mexico City, as if I have the slightest clue about this neighborhood, or street, or its proximity to or distance from anything. "There are clocks here in the apartment", I add. Nita answers with an explanation, "But you know that I am talking, and I forget. You should tell me." I think that this line of logic is highly unreasonable, but what can I do? "Hurry", Nita urges," you must go and get a taxi. But don't look on this street, because there aren't taxis on this street."

Where should I look then? I don't have any clue to where we are. But in the need of the moment, I head out the door to do as instructed. I grab my little carry-on which has functioned as a purse. At least there is nothing else for me to gather up since I was never given my luggage at the airport. Nita hasn't even started to pack, and this does not bode well, because she always has a servant pack for her. Is there time for this? Is, or is not, I try anyway.

Finally, after a frantic search and much waving, I jump into a taxi, and even though all the streets seem to be one-way, so that I barely know how to get back to The Aunt's building, somehow I direct the driver to the right block, and we wait. We wait more. And a little more. At last, here is Nita.

"Hurry", she says to the driver. She tells him the time of our bus's departure. He knows the location of the station and declares that it is impossible. "Señora, it is way across the city. It is too far. There is too much traffic. There is not enough time." "Go", she commands. "You go, you hurry!" And he does.

We enter a narrow overpass, and all the cars are stopped, side-by-side, not an inch anywhere. "Hurry", Nita urges, "Go around! Pass!" This is impossible, why even suggest it, but somehow he does. We creep along another crowded street. "Honk", she demands, "Honk more. Go faster." Again, how? And again, he succeeds. We speed whenever others speed, we crawl when they crawl, but Nita is relentless. "Hurry, faster, you must get us there, we cannot miss our bus!" How is this possible?

The man is a genius. He has gotten us to our station with two minutes to spare. Nita is prepared with the money in her hand, thrusts it at him, and we jump out, thanking him all the while. He is beaming as he hands our luggage to a waiting porter. Not because of the tip, which I consider modest, but because of his triumph. He has won the race. He is a champion. He is a rescuer with a perfect success.

Our luggage is loaded as we board, and just as we find our assigned seats, the door closes, the bus backs out, and we are on our way. On our way to San Miguel!

The bus is second class, but to me it seems like luxury. The seats are wide, soft, recline, and even have foot rests. There is a working bathroom in the back (an important feature for me since the trip takes three hours), the windows are huge so I can see all the sights of the city and let it sink in that I am really here, really in my beloved Mexico, right now. It is not a future dream any more, and we have been served a soda and a bag lunch. I am content. I am hungry.

Our lunches are good, and we dive right in. Croissants filled with cheese, ham, and slices of onion, a bag of chips (ugh), and a cookie, which I don't want, but eventually I get so hungry that I eat it. We get to choose our own soft drinks, and I get Coca Light, a version of diet Coke, so I am happy. Included in the bag, whereas we in Wisconsin would be given mayonnaise, here there is a packet of hot, green, chile sauce. Goodie, we are in Mexico for sure.

Nita wants to nap. So does everyone else on the bus, because everyone closes their curtains except me. Fine, no more talking for a while, because all I want to do is gaze out the window, first at the enormity of Mexico City, and its energy, and activity, its buildings, and houses, and shops, and restaurants, and stores, roof tops alive with washing hung up to dry, and then to the tumble of poorer houses, dwellings stuck together with a few bricks, some sheets of metal, cactus plugging up the empty spaces of what are meant to be fences, dogs wandering, chickens and burros mingling with the people, and finally to the purity of the countryside.

Today is Friday, August 21, 2005. This is summer, crop season, all is green, lush. Valleys have been planted. Men are tilling, or weeding, sometimes by hand, sometimes following an ox, but rarely by tractor. Children play in the streams we pass while their mothers pound clothes on rocks, rubbing a bar of soap over the wet laundry, rinsing in the flowing water, and spreading pants and shirts over bushes to dry in the heat of the day.

Even the mountains are green. This is the rainy season, and we pass through rain for a while. We do not care. It makes our bus feel even more cozy. Finally it is four o'clock, and we arrive in San Miguel, San Miguel de Allende, "Mexican Hill Town". "Wake up, Nita, we are here."

In an echo of Trip One, this day seems endless, and once again that is because our time is so filled with good things. The first is being welcomed into San Miguel when we see Perla and her husband waiting for us with their pick-up truck. Because of the changing of our entire schedule, Raúl has stayed to work at the Botica and has sent Perla for us. Much hugging and kissing, and the husband, with only Nita's suitcases to heave into the truck, quickly settles us into the cab. We pass through the ancient cobble-stoned streets, and my four year's absence melts away. I am back, back in my San Miguel, back with my friends, my family, and at last, back in The Great House.

It is now four o'clock. The cooks offer us a complete and lavish comida, but we are too excited to eat, and after all, we had croissants and cookies on the bus. We accept papaya and coffee, and the family enters the dining room to greet us. Raúl is exactly the same, Delfina is even more beautiful and slender, Conchita is fifteen, and Raulito is twelve. In fact, today is his birthday, and after the Botica closes for the day, we will all go out and celebrate with a fancy dinner at a gourmet restaurant that has all the exotic treats that Raúl and Raulito enjoy.

Everyone has things to do, and Nita and I head out to a Cambio to change my traveler's checks into pesos, and then to buy birthday cards. We walk to the Jardín, turn left, and enter a papelería, a paper store, which is in this case a stationery store, selling also school supplies, pens, little paint sets, ledgers, diaries, anything that has to do with writing. We are bent on our task, but more than caring about purchases, I am flooded with memories. The owner is also the clerk, the same tiny, old, old lady who waited on everyone in town all those years ago when Abelardo brought me here.

Abelardo and I were on some errand, but at the time I was greatly interested in paper flowers, much more so than in pens and note papers. Here and there in the town I had started to purchase a great many of these flowers- large, bright, exotic, fanciful. Now, in the papelería, hanging from the dim reaches of the dusty ceiling were brilliant orange marigolds, of a type I had not seen in other stores. "Oh, Abelardo", I said, "Look how pretty! I will get some."

"No, no, Sonette, you must not! You can't! They are not for you to buy!" He was terribly upset. "What do you mean?" I asked, "They must be for sale. Everything in here is for sale". "No, no, if you buy those, someone will die. You must not buy those. Those are for the grave, for the cemetery, for a death".

I shrugged off his obvious concern. Was it fear of some odd superstition? I had heard interesting and mournful tales for months now, about moaning and crying that could be heard on certain streets late at night, as a long-dead mother searched for her children. About other such macabre legends, and I didn't give Abelardo's plea the consideration that simple, common courtesy demanded. All I could think of was, "How interesting. Another primitive superstition." I didn't even care that the owner of the shop herself cautioned me not to buy them, agreeing and supporting Abelardo's claim with a downcast look and head shaking as I insisted on purchasing those bright flowers to add to my collection. "What a funny story this will be" I thought, thinking of who among my friends and relatives would get a kick out of such an odd belief.

But Abelardo did die. Granted, not during my first trip, which was when I bought the dangerous flowers. Not during the several times I returned for Christmas vacations and Easter breaks, sometimes with my mother and brother, sometimes just Mom and me. But while I was still in college, not that long after my flower purchase, if you count time in terms of years and not of visits, his death was not so long in coming.

I still remember where I was standing when I opened the black bordered letter on heavy cream colored paper, the foreign handwriting of my name and address, the Mexican stamps. I was in my dorm room at Beloit College, dressed in a pleated woolen plaid skirt, wearing a fine matching lamb's wool sweater, standing by my dresser, next to the window to catch the light as I pulled out the printed card from its envelope. Behind me the window expanded into a view of the friendly campus I so loved. I had been preparing to join my friends in the Commons for lunch, as curiously I read the black-bordered, heavy card.

In a stiff and very formal way, the engraved black script informed me of the death of Abelardo. My Abelardo.

I don't remember any details other than that it stated the date of the death, which I did not understand to be by murder. It probably listed his date of birth. There was nothing else that meant anything to me. What could this announcement possibly mean? How could this be?

Did I tell anyone? Did I telephone my mother? I don't recall what I did. I have no idea at all. In my mind, I stay frozen, frozen in my skirt and sweater, frozen by the window, frozen with that letter in my hand.

It is not a new memory, which I have just described, that has come to me while Nita chatters about which birthday cards we should buy for Raulito. I am used to the memory, whenever I enter this store, but neither is the experience sad. I feel closer to Abelardo, here doing an ordinary errand, in the company of Nita, on an ordinary day. Would you think that I would feel guilty? Did my purchase of the flowers cause his death? Did Abelardo have a premonition of what was to come? I have the answer to all those questions. It is an answer that has come to me more and more of late, in the recent years. It is an answer that greatly comforts me. It is an answer that makes me relax, that takes away worries, that even absolves blame. The answer, and I like this answer, is "I don't know".

We select our birthday cards, and before we pay, I look for some little token gift for Raulito. I won't be here for Conchita's birthday, so all I want is something to mark the occasion, not a real gift. I brought gifts for everyone, but of course I have no luggage, so that is of no help. I decide that in honor of all the fun the kids and I had during my last visit, I will buy a deck of cards.

The only deck for sale is "Bicycle". We have the exact same kind at Wall-mart in Lake Geneva for sixty-nine cents. Here they cost three dollars and fifty cents American. I suppose they are imported? All paper of any kind costs more in Mexico than at home, so I am not surprised. We pay and go out to stroll.

That night Nita and I offer that dinner will be our treat. We will split the bill as our contribution to the birthday festivities. Raulito wants Mama Mía, the hugely noisy and crowded pizza restaurant downtown. Raúl says, "No, we will go somewhere more elegant".

Raúl drives us. The elegant restaurant is Vietnamese. Strange that for my first night in San Miguel, my second day in Mexico, I still have not had any of what I would call Mexican food. There is nothing on the menu that is at all different from any restaurant in the USA, just steak-and-potatoes-and rolls type stuff, so I select from what they offer of Vietnamese. It is good, and the main thing is that we are together, we are laughing, and we are having fun. I don't tell about anything. I am unusually quiet because this is really the event of their own family. I listen and enjoy.

3

WHEN A SERVANT IS YOUR FRIEND,
AND SOMEONE IS DIGGING
A TUNNEL UNDER THIS HOUSE!

We had gone to sleep last night in what are and always have been, Nita's private quarters, her apartment inside of Raúl's Great House. On the last trip, Nita had lent it to Richard and me. I am no longer married to Richard, so from now on, when I say "our room", or "our apartment", I will mean Nita's and mine. I have also started calling Nita "Nita" more and more. Therefore the maid named Nita will have to be called Rafaela, as she is also known here, although in reality, both women are often called Nita, and you just have to figure it out by the conversation.

Nita has "Richard's bed", if I am thinking about my last trip here, and I have "my bed", the one by the window, same as always. It is sad to be here without Richard, but I am used to a lot of things being different now. It is comforting to be here again with just Nita and me together. Jackson has stayed behind in Canada, as he often does, so we are two gals on the loose, except we are somewhat old, I guess, in a way. I never think that I am old, though, and probably never will, except for when it is funny.

Nita has loaned me a nightgown. She says she brought it as a gift for me anyway, so I guess it is wrong to call it a loan. Before we left Mexico City, Belinda gave me a gift of new socks. I had extra underpants, a sweater, and a toothbrush in my carry-on-purse, so I am fine. So far. I slept only a little last night, and I have just drifted into an early morning sleep when at seven thirty, someone is beneath our window, hollering, and I finally recognize my name.

There is a man from the airport! He has brought my luggage! I am so grateful and groggy that in groping around for a tip, which I intend to be two dollars per bag, I mistakenly give him twenty each. USA dollars! Oh, no, by the time I come to my senses and mentally re-calculate the peso to dollar rate, I am appalled, but he has already gone. Still, I am delighted to have my things at last and console myself that maybe I did only give him four dollars and not forty, then I think maybe I didn't, and finally I give up.

Nita and I are thoroughly awake now, so we go downstairs to the kitchen where Chita makes us coffee. Chita! I am so happy to see my friend again. One is not supposed to become friends with a servant, and for a very good reason. You can really like each other, even love each other, and you should always treat each other with the greatest politeness and respect.

But being friends is not a good idea. The job of a servant is to take orders. A friend does not issue orders to a friend. A person who has agreed to take orders and fulfill certain conditions of work is a worker, and a worker in whatever capacity is not to supposed to pick and choose which orders to obey. "Please" is a good idea, "Thank you", also, but not, "If you feel like it".

A worker has a job to do. Chita's job is big and occupies all of her time. There are many demands that send her to go here and there, do this and that, as the moment requires. She cannot possibly be expected to get all of her jobs done if someone is always hanging around in the kitchen, talking and laughing, and that someone would be me.

I am not a boss of anything. I never give orders. It is rare for me even to make a request. So Chita and I can be friends, but her position still requires her to address me as Señora, and not call me by my first name. It is delicate, but it is not that different than a secretary of a company. Employees should not hang around the secretary's desk telling jokes and just in general hanging out. One has to let her do her work. And not force the employee to think, "I am so busy. I wish she would just go away". I don't want Chita to think that about me.

But there is a bond between us, and while she is chopping, or stirring, or dish washing, there are periods when we can have some fun talking, sharing adventures, or philosophy, or telling our family tales, all the things that friends do. I am glad to be back to this kitchen and to my friend.

Now I have clothes, so Nita and I go back upstairs to shower and dress. At eleven o'clock we are served a big breakfast. Chita has remembered and served all of my favorites. I give the gifts I brought to the family, and I think they like them all, not like the last visit when I didn't know anyone and made a lot of gift mistakes. Also I have brought a large, deluxe box of Anderson's Home-made Candies, chocolates, from right near where I live, from Richmond, Illinois. I see that this gift is a total crowd pleaser.

Unpacking will take much longer than just today. I have finished enough before comida and can leave the rest for later. Downstairs I have my own dresser, and upstairs I hang my dresses behind Nita's. It is one of these awkward closets that is only one hanger wide but very deep. It works, though. Nita and I divide up all the other spaces, and we are each satisfied. Sisters once again!

Raúl invites us to go to a restaurant for comida. Chita will go home to her family's house, out in the country to the little rancho which is what tiny towns like hers are called, as soon as she can get the breakfast things all cleaned up. She leaves at one thirty, and we all wish her a happy time with her family. When she comes back, she will tell me all about it, which I really enjoy. It is as if I have two living soap operas going on at one time, the drama of Chita's village, and the events of this house.

Nita and I primp and get all dressed up for the restaurant. Which is funny, because when we get there, we find that it is just a little, tiny, humble taquería, a place where you order at the counter and carry your food to the table yourself. There are only a few choices, such as a platter of tacos of goat, or tacos of chorizo, or tacos of a couple of other things. They don't even give out silverware, just tiny, thin napkins.

But the food is very Mexican and very good. In fact, it is delicious. Mexican at last.

Delfina and the family are wearing the new clothes that I brought for them as gifts. Delfina's mother, who is also named Delfina, has come too. Delfina's dad slipped on the soap in the shower and didn't feel like coming. It doesn't feel like I have been away for as long as I have. We are all, once again, a comfortable fit.

I get so, so tired that when we return, I put on my robe and lie on my bed while Nita and Conchita go shopping. Nita buys lots of jewelry. I have just fallen asleep when they return. It is a good thing that this wakes me up, because I probably would sleep for too long. Nita leaves to visit Ignacio, so I put on shorts to take a walk.

But I quickly discover that I look awful. What was good four years ago now looks out of place and wrong altogether. When Richard and I walked everywhere together, we were both tourists and looked it, two Norte Americanos on vacation. Now, as a woman alone, downtown on a Saturday night, the contrast in my clothes and the way everyone else is dressed is embarrassing.

There is a very elegant wedding taking place at La Paróquia across from the Jardín. Everyone in the group is beautifully dressed, made-up, adorned. I feel foolishly out of place, shabby, and alone. I feel embarrassed and left out. At home, left behind and not packed, I have all the clothes that would be perfect, I see that now. But it is too late. Here I am, outdated, dumb looking, and lonely.

I haven't felt lonely for a long time. If I looked ok, or if this weren't Saturday night, or if I had something specific to do, I would be fine. So I take myself in hand and think, "Do what you can do". I walk back to the house, put on Levis, a white tank top, sandals, gold earrings, gold bracelet, re-do my hair, and now I feel better. Now I am dressed like other people here. I feel like I fit in. I go for a long walk and feel twenty years better looking and twenty years younger. That is step one.

Step two is a plan for the future. Next trip, instead of bringing only clothes that I can leave here for the maids, I will pack a few of my own nice things that make me look good. That is my long-term plan. Short term is: if Nita comes home from Ignacio's early enough, we will get dressed up and go out for a copa. If not, I will get in bed with an excellent novel for cozy night.

Something nice happens though. Even though it is a Saturday night, Raúl and the family are staying home. Raúl calls me for merienda, and what a tale I am told!

Someone is digging under this house! In fact, tunnels have been made under all the houses in this block. Someone is searching for gold which was hidden by the inhabitants of all the Great Houses, it is believed, centuries ago, or maybe as recently as the Revolution of 1910. Families at that time kept all their money in gold. They did not trust banks, and houses were built like fortresses anyway, with only one door to the street, and with heavy iron bars over every window. Servants were always at home, and usually so were the women. Houses were never left empty, and one's own home was considered the safest of places.

In the back of each house there were latrines, and also stables for the family horses, and for the carriage which every Great House would naturally have had in the Colonial era. Colonial means that Mexico was a colony of Spain, and the highest officials of that government built their residences in concentric circles around the Jardín. The pattern always went like this: A park, the Jardín, one block square for the center of the town, for the seat of power. On one side, the most magnificent of the churches, for the church ruled as much as the governors and officials did. Opposite the church, the police station and other government buildings. On the two remaining sides of the Jardín, the largest and most prominent residences, with balconies and highly decorative facades. Underneath the residences were arcades of archways, of stone or adobe, with stores or restaurants at street level.

Radiating outward, comprising the next blocks in concentric rings, were the next most important houses, being built also in the same style. Raúl's house is one of these.

In times of danger, and certainly here in San Miguel, the family gold was likely thrown into the latrine or hidden under the horse manure in the stable, if there was only the shortest of warnings about bands of soldiers approaching the town, and immediate flight was required to save your lives. I already knew all of this from my teacher, Miguel Malo, who in 1963, and I think he was about sixty years old then, told me about his own family's flight from the Great House where his teensy- weensy elderly mother still lived. In fact I had stayed for a week as a resident of that house, hoping to make it my home in order to speak Spanish day and night, instead of hearing English from my college friends since we were all lodged together at Casa Sautto.

The Malo house is known to everyone as "La Casa de Los Perros", The House of The dogs. The name is because each of the stone downspouts that spew overloads of water from the flat roof is the chiseled face of a dog. Naturally the water shoots out from the dogs' mouths. Many of the oldest of the Great Houses have animal adornments; some decorating the corners of the roof top walls, others as water spouts, and all are carved of stone.

Living at Señora Malo's house was like entering a time capsule.

Not one thing appeared to have been changed since its inception. I did not even dare to touch the heavy red velvet curtains that darkened the street-side windows, nor the thin white organdy or silk which had almost turned to gauze beneath the velvet massive draperies, for fear that they would crumble into dust. My room, enormous, with a floor so old that it had valleys where feet repeated centuries of travel from bed, to face-washing stand, to door, to window, was on the main floor, great shuttered window facing the street, my little self inside, protected by the window's iron bars.

The location of my bedroom was far from enviable as not only was I the only downstairs dweller, but also late at night unidentified men repeatedly crept into the entrance hallway, yelling and speaking to each other loudly, banging on my paper-thin, two hundred year old door, so thin that in some places you could see through it. As I trudged up the limestone staircase each morning for breakfast, a staircase so massive and mysterious that I always thought of the entrance to Cinderella's castle, I placed my feet in the deep hollows worn there by how many feet? How many times does it take how many people, ascending and descending, in order to rub away hard stones into a scooped out smoothness, like what would have been an erosion of endless, gentle water, flowing how fast? For how long?

Dear, tiny, brilliant Miguel Malo, former dueño (owner, possessor) of lands and gold, a person who could command others, now reduced to becoming a school teacher. Although much taller than his tiny mother, Señor Malo's black haired, balding head reached no higher than mine, possibly not even that much, and remember, I am five feet two. Yet what a towering, aristocratic persona, humbled by circumstances, but in no way diminished in the regard of his town, nor in the eyes of the great archeologists and museum officials of El Museo de Antrolopología in Mexico City. When Señor Malo told his family tales, the stories of Old San Miguel, the stories of his discoveries under the ground on his family's rancho, of the servants thinking they had uncovered Hell and running away terrified when an ox-pulled plow unearthed an idol made of clay by a long forgotten tribe, no one in our advanced Spanish literature class showed any interest at all, except for me. So when he met me occasionally while he visited his mother, or when I stayed late after our classes, he told me many of his stories, and one was of the day when men ran from the countryside into town screaming that everyone should run for their lives, soldiers were coming.

Señor Malo's father, like all fathers who had any money at all, kept his life worth (the part not invested in land and business) in the form of gold coins, in a bag, under the bed. Señor Malo, as a little boy, was used to seeing his father, when he wanted to spend money, go to the bag and take out what he needed. When the cry came to flee, you definitely would not want to take your gold. It would surely be stolen by someone as you wandered defenselessly out of town, searching desperately for somewhere to hide in the mountains until the soldiers finished their rampage and you could finally return to whatever was left of your house and your town. All you wanted to take with you would be to get your family on a cart, if you had one, to be pulled by your horse, and take along some bags of beans and flour to sustain you for who knew? Weeks, or maybe months? In the case of the Malo family, he said it was months.

And your gold? Naturally everyone hoped and prayed to survive, and you would assuredly need and want your gold, so most of the panicked people threw their gold down the deep, deep hole of the latrine. Having already heard this history from Señor Malo, having lived in the Malo house with his mother, and seeing what their ancient courtyard looked like, I could well visualize the occurrence and the truth of what Raúl was telling me now, about his own house, and about all the other houses on his block.

Raúl's story is long, with Delfina backing up every statement with details and telling of their fears. After our divorce, Richard came to Raúl's and rented an apartment on the roof for a few months. I knew that one whole section of the upper story had collapsed because Richard was there then, and thankfully neither he nor anyone else was standing in that area when it happened. He easily could have been, because the fall took away the roof, which was Richard's terrace, I guess you could call it, the large walkway underneath which were the arches of Raúl's patio, the place where the children always played, the place where we customarily sat for coffee and visiting, the place where the children and I played games and did homework.

Richard and I had settled into friendly terms, and he called to tell me about the event. He also, on the day of the disaster, generously and immediately made out a check for one thousand dollars which he gave to Raúl for the immediate expenses, whether as a loan or as a gift, I was not quite sure. No matter what, it was a kind and helpful gesture. Little did anyone know that it would cost two hundred thousand dollars to totally repair the damage and reconstruct.

So now that Delfina and Raúl have found out what caused the collapse, naturally they are more than concerned, their children are terrified, and anyone would see the need of having this digging stopped. But it has not been the easy and obvious thing that one would suppose, just go to the police, report everything, and let the lawyers and the courts take over from there. Oh, no, not at all. Remember, "This is Mexico", says Raúl.

Delfina and Raúl believe that their entire house may cave in, and with good reason. I can already see where the walls connecting their house to the one next door are crumbling at the base. The floor is all lumpy. It is soft underneath.

There were tunnels under all of the central area of the town, connecting the churches to certain of the Great Houses, tunnels large enough for a horse and carriage. This network was in use at the time of the revolution. Later, all of those tunnels had presumably been filled in. Perhaps the diggers are excavating these same tunnels now in an attempt to burrow from house to house. Perhaps they have old maps. Nobody knows.

Delfina says that if a tunnel has been excavated, then when it rains, the tunnels fill with water. This loosens the soil, the water drains away, and the underpinnings of the house, which is just built on dirt and rocks, fall away, leaving the huge, heavy house undermined and ready to shift and collapse. Houses like this one, begun in 1640, were built directly on the ground. The base of the central patio was just dirt, being a garden area. Much of the patio is still dirt so that the trees and all the flowers can grow. Ceramic tile was only added under the arches recently. And that is all there is for a foundation, so naturally the family is very much afraid.

Unbelievably, the police already know, everyone on the block knows, and this digger-man has a long criminal record. Raúl and Delfina have photos and have filed complaints, but nothing can stop the digger and his crew, because there is reason to believe that the digger has help. I say, "Oh, yes, there is something that will stop it, and that is prayer". Delfina and Raúl agree, and we all plan to pray and are convinced of good results. What we expect is to figure out what methods will yield practical results in protecting this home. Wow, this is a lot to think about.

4

MEAN MAN CALLS AN ANCIANA A DEVIL-FACED OLD WOMAN, AND ESTELA IS IN TOWN

Nita and I try to go to mass, but we arrive late, and that is a good thing. Where we want to go this time is not to the large churches that had all of the Semana Santa productions of my last visit four years ago. This time we are headed for a little chapel that is in the back of one of the side-wings of the huge El Oratorio. To reach it, one goes towards the entrance of El Oratorio, but not up the final stone steps and in through the tall three-hundred year old wooden doors. Instead, just before the entrance stairs, there is a smaller door (although still very big compared to ordinary doors), dark and wooden, almost always closed and locked, but at the times of special services, like right now, the door stands open, rolled aside on the curved rails that are imbedded in the interior stone floor.

We enter and are under an archway that surrounds a beautiful little courtyard filled with tiny flowering trees, flowering vines, pretty benches, a small fountain, lots of religious stone statues, and is generally airy, sunny, and friendly. We have to turn to the left, continuing under the arches, past a row of old wooden benches, before entering the dark, and gloomy, and clammy, and musty hallway, then up cement stairs, and down a long and narrow corridor, and then—but wait. We only get as far as almost to the dark stairway when Nita is stopped by another of San Miguel's "ancianas", ancient ladies, old in years, old in customs, old in ideas. Everything about her is not only old, but also poor.

Let me call her humble, not poor, because it is clear that although she has very little in the way of worldly goods, especially money, she definitely considers herself rich in spirit and is a proud, independent, and respected woman. Her clothes are handmade, clearly by using a large needle with white thread to have stitched her long skirt, several blouses, and a sort of man's shirt which she wears as a jacket, and over this, an apron that she has also made herself. Her feet, tiny, lumpy, calloused, are bare inside of leather "huraches" that have, by their constant use, molded themselves long ago to fit her feet.

Nita, of course, knows this lady, and Nita, of course, is never in a hurry and always has time to talk to anyone who wishes to do so. The anciana takes Nita's hand and asks us to sit down with her on a bench facing the garden.

The anciana is extremely troubled. A mean man has hurt her feelings. He got very angry with her because she told him he could not enter some part of the giant church complex to wherever he wanted to go, whereupon he told her that she had the face of a devil.

This has hurt her on many counts. One, her job is to sweep the garden paths and under the arches, where we are right now. She has done this job for who knows how many decades. This gives her dignity, a sense of worth, a position, and a place. Secondly, any woman would be hurt by an insult to her face. Thirdly, she probably believes in the Devil as an actual being. Even though Nita and her family are Catholic, and I am a Christian Scientist, everyone seems to really like all the ideas from Christian Science, and although we believe that there are evil beliefs and evil behaviors, Christian Scientists do not believe that there is a terrible man in a red suit orchestrating bad things and calamities. Still, I do like a great deal about the Catholic Church, on a personal level, although I am not in agreement with the Catholic position regarding the Devil. But this little lady, so very old, probably does believe, as many do, that the Devil is a real person, and she has strong convictions and fears. So to be told that she has the face of a devil is a terrible thing for her.

She lives in one room somewhere, I am not sure if it is here in the complex of the church or near-by, but she lives alone, doesn't seem to be part of a family, and in any case, this church and her church job are the most important part of her life. So she needs to confide her hurt and shock to someone, and Nita is exactly the right person. We are so glad that we came along just when we did.

Mass is forgotten, even though the chapel where we were headed is only open twice a week and is very special for many reasons, but naturally none of that matters compared to sitting with the little woman. We let her tell her tale again and again, we pat her, hold hands, assure her that the man should not have treated her that way, she has the face of an angel, she is important, she is good. And we can say all these things because they are all true.

Finally she feels better, we give her some money, my contribution being a one hundred peso bill, hug and kiss good-bye, and promise that we will come back many times over the weeks we will be in town. She accepts the money and puts the coins and bills into her apron pocket, but not as charity. She has a job, and it is proper to donate to the upkeep of this garden. We have restored to her her position of respect.

We return to the house, take off our church dresses, and I put on my one good outfit, the white tank top, tight jeans, sandals, and gold jewelry. Actually, I guess I have figured things out to be able to say that I now can think of three acceptable combinations. I have a tan, and a new haircut, so I think I look fine, which makes me feel very good.

In fact, I feel so good that I think I will call Estela. Maybe we can go see her. Estela picks up the phone! She is not in Lebanon, she is here! Yippee. She says that she has not received any of my letters, so she didn't know that I was coming. However, she is already talking to Lebanon on the phone, and she will have to call me back. This is almost impossible, so I say, "When you can, call me at the Botica. But the Botica phone is broken, so I will try to reach you some other way." "OK", she agrees, and we have to hang up.

The family says we are all going up the hill to eat tacos and enchiladas. Nita, Conchita, and I walk up. The others drive. The restaurant is so tiny that they only have one long table, and everyone sits together, "everyone" consisting of just our family and one other family, a mamá and papá and children. The kitchen is within this little dining space as well, giving a cave-like, cozy atmosphere. On the walls are clusters of red plastic roses, pictures of saints and of Jesus, and there are crude attempts at landscape paintings, friendly in their obvious sincerity although lacking much ability. The front wall is not any wall at all, just open air. Outside, about two feet from our table, many, many cars struggle up the hill, and a great number of trucks also use this route, the only one out of town in this direction, and right in front of this restaurant is where the trucks gear up, because the hill is only called a hill. In actuality it is the side of a mountain. The noise is magnified because the narrow road, hemmed in between stone houses all the way to the top, is like a tunnel, so we can't hear anyone talk, and we don't even try. The food is good, and we all have fun, especially because Raulito is a funny kid and loves to make us laugh.

Instead of going home with everyone else, Conchita and I continue walking to Estela's house. We buzz the intercom at her gate, and she answers, but she is not answering from inside the house. Her cell phone is connected to the intercom. She says that she has gone out of town and will call me when she gets back.

By the time we walk back down the hill and arrive at home, it is already 7:45. Nita has to wait at the house for Belinda to arrive from Mexico City. Belinda is the caregiver of The Aunt. After that we will go walking around the center of town because it is Sunday night. Sunday night is a big deal. People come from everywhere to the Jardín with their families.

In Mexico, Saturday night is for the Americans, and Sunday is Family Day for the Mexicans. Americans go Saturday nights to the bars and restaurants in couples. In beach towns all the young drunks fill the streets and give our country a bad name. Here in San Miguel, the Americans act fine. It is just their normal custom to go to bars and restaurants for a date, so to speak.

But Sunday for Mexicans is Family Day, all day. It starts with church. Then every family member gathers at someone's house, or in a park if no one in the extended family has much of a house, for example, in the case of poor people, or should I say people with very little extra cash. It doesn't matter too much where the families meet, just that they do, and everyone thinks this is a great way to spend the day. I think this too.

If you are in a house, most of the afternoon is spent eating a wonderful comida and talking for hours, the children eventually escaping into the patio to play, or into wherever there is a computer to do whatever kids like, such as games, I suppose.

Lots of times the whole family gathers in lovely restaurants, tables set up out of doors when possible, always with endless courses, and fruit drinks, and laughing, all ages included. If a park is what works better, everyone can bring something to share, even if it is only traveling by bus with your kettle of beans or rice. Once at the park and locating your giant group of grandparents, and cousins, and aunts, and everyone's children and babies, then blankets are spread out, and basically the same thing happens everywhere, a day of eating, or cooking on a grill, and running around playing, with the oldies sitting, watching, and talking. After all the endless dinners have been eaten, and everyone is finally caught up on jokes, and news, and filled with love, and with full stomachs that just can't accept one thing more, then it is time to go home.

If your family gathering was at a park, of course you go home and do not return to another park! But if your family eating all took place in a house or a restaurant, you are very likely to proceed to a different kind of park, not a park at all really, called El Jardín.

The Jardín means the central plaza of your town or "barrio", neighborhood. The Jardíns fill up with parents and grandparents on benches. If you are alone and lonely, just go and sit by anyone, and they will be nice to you. Kids run everywhere, but happily, not crying or fussing, and always in sight of the parents. Vendors sell balloons, squeaky toys, toys on sticks, toys that jiggle or make noises, or anything that would make a kid think, "I want that!" Parents are indulgent and often buy something.

Food vendors line the fringes selling corn-on-the-cob held in giant black pots of boiling water, fires burning directly on the stones underneath. The "elotes", corn ears, are fished out, stabbed onto a stick, smeared with mayonnaise, given a good shaking of parmesan cheese, and red chile powder is thrown over the whole thing for good measure. Some vendors have little carts full of "paletas", sort of like popsicles but which are made of milk, sugar, and fresh fruit juices or fruit chunks. Hot dogs and hamburgers are grilled on stands and in little tents in the street. Candy and junk food is available at miniscule sized portable kiosks. Fresh fruits and vegetables are cut to look like flowers, placed on sticks, limes are squeezed over, and chile powder is added. Every single thing sold is good, looks good, tastes good, and has great appeal and selling power. Except that I get so much magnificent dining at home and in the restaurants that I can never manage to eat any of these snacks, except for sometimes an ice cream cone.

The bandstand in the center of El Jardín will always have great live music on Sunday afternoons and Sunday nights. People stand, sit, roam, dance, stroll. It is people, people, people. And this is what Nita and I plan to do tonight.

We guess that this time the kids will not join us. Tomorrow is the first day of the school year. A great flurry of activity has taken place at home. Being Mexico, although school supply shopping has already been done, there remains much left to do, at the last possible minute, meaning now, late, today. Every item in the long list of school requirements must have the student's name on it. Even pencils! I have helped by using a ruler to mark the obligatory red line margins on every sheet of paper in every notebook. The notebooks for Mexican school are not like students use in the USA. The paper is all graph paper, the tiny boxes being used for uniformity of letter placement in writing assignments, and it must be a good system, because the children's printing (they do not seem to use cursive) is highly (and mercifully, for the teachers) legible.

Our day of family, our evening of the Jardín, and last minute helping of the children, still at their tasks in the dining room, ends for me, because I am tired and go upstairs. I lie contentedly on my bed, window open, fan on, listen to the clanging of the bells, and wait for sleep.

5

I HEAR THE DIGGING! AND
DOGGIE HELPS WITH HOMEWORK

How do you count your days? Usually I start from when I get up in the morning. But "today" is different. This Monday starts around 3:30 AM. I always know what time it is by the bells that mark each quarter hour. Well, I hear the bells for 3:30, and then 3:45, and then I hear something else. When the bells finish four o'clock, I hear, or maybe I feel, no I hear, a slight pounding, pulsing. This could be digging the tunnel!

Nita's bedroom is next to the house that we consider to be the source of the excavations. Her apartment is also built over what at one time probably were the latrines or stables. In fact, the next-door house was built on the stable yard that used to belong to Raúl's house, in whatever long-ago year that this house did not use horses any more, or else used fewer. Anyway, the land was sold, and another house was built next door. We can look down upon it from the roof of our house, if we stand just right, up on the edge. Their patio is right next to Nita's quarters.

I stand up next to my bed, but standing I don't hear a thing. I lie down again, head on pillow, and there it is. I must be hearing and feeling the vibrations of a hydraulic pounder of some sort being conveyed through the ground, up the walls, through this floor, and through my bed. It is like when you put your ear to a wall to hear someone talking on the other side. Or if you are really snoopy, you place a drinking glass open end to the wall, and press your ear to the solid bottom. Somehow that amplifies the sound. Is this what is happening now? Am I really hearing the digging?

I will not awaken Nita. What could she do? I may be wrong anyway, but should I disturb Raúl? If I tell him at breakfast, will he say, "Sonette, you should have come and got me"?

I creep down our apartment stairs, open our rattley door, pad on

271

cold feet across the stone floor, cross the icy tiles of the patio, and reach the door of Raúl's family's private apartment. I bang on the glass paned door (there are no buzzers or bells), and I finally hear him coming, but it takes a long time, because he puts on pants, a jacket, and shoes.

I think the shoes are a mistake, because they are loud, but anyway he comes. I whisper and he says yes, I did the right thing. We enter the downstairs door of Nita's apartment, and next to the wall, where the tiled floor is getting loose and where the wall has started to crumble, he lies down and puts his ear. He says he hears something.

We go up to the bedroom, but he doesn't hear it from there. Nita wakes up. "Who is that?" she asks, startled. We have not turned on any lights and are still whispering. I say, "It is Raúl". "Why is he here? What is happening?" We are sorry that we scared her, but I thought she would either sleep through or else recognize Raúl, and after all, she too had heard all the talk about the digging.

Raúl says that he thinks the diggers only work at night, and when they know that Chita has gone to her rancho. Plus, Chita's room is not directly over the supposed digging spot, which we are pretty sure we have identified by the loose flooring and crumbling wall of Nita's downstairs.

Why don't we just go up to the roof and look down and catch them? For one thing, Raúl and Delfina had already done that, so the government knows all about the whole story, and the action that the government took was to order the neighbors to erect a huge tarp that covers the neighbor's whole patio! So now when you look down from the roof, all you see is a big, blue, giant, wrinkly plastic. Therefore it is no longer possible to take pictures or to ask anyone to be a witness. Whatever there was to see is hidden now.

There is nothing we can do. We all go back to our beds and go to sleep. I sleep until 8:30, and then Nita and I wake up together. So should I say we continue with our Monday? Or was this early episode a part of last night, of Sunday night?

What does the naming of the day matter? We have to continue as usual anyway, the sunshine of morning is beautiful, and it is time for breakfast. Nita and I cook our own since no servants are here yet. We do errands and chores, all of which are pleasant, and all of a sudden it is time for comida. Chita returned while we were out, and it is comforting to start a new week. In the midst of troubles and uncertainty, one falls back upon a routine.

At comida the children tell about their first day of school. Conchita likes it, and as we are eating, several school friends come over to do homework, all thrilled to be back together again, excited to talk over the new day of the new school year. Conchita kisses us all, is excused, and disappears happily with her friends.

But Raulito doesn't like school at all and comes home with a stomach ache. He is very sad and tired. I understand kids who feel like this, and I believe that I can help, having had a string of such experiences as a teacher, mostly resulting in success. So I say, "Would you like to have your English practice hour with me every day, and I can help you with your homework?" He brightens up considerably and says. "Yes". I say, "What time?", and he says, "In about forty minutes". This is a good sign, or he would answer something like, "Oh, later", or "I don't know, maybe before bed". I am happy, because he wants to get at it!

When we meet, we sit in the patio, under the balcony, at the family's huge outside dining room table. We set up for our work and begin. Every little while, Raulito leaps up, races around the patio, or runs with the dog. Then he is ready to work again, sits down, and we take up where we left off. The dog gets into the fountain, which delights Raulito, because now he can show me how funny it is to make the dog chase him as she slips at every corner on her wet feet and skids over the now wet and slippery tiles.

Since I love this dog, and probably every dog, and I am glad that this little fun makes Raulito in a mood of optimism over his school work, I think all this dog playing is helpful towards our project. On the other hand, this is a different dog from the last time I was here, and the current dog jumps up on people. Her paws are muddy, of course, because after all, the patio is a garden. I don't want to be jumped on and muddied, and Raulito is now ready to get down to more serious work, so I suggest locking the dog in the laundry room. "We will let her out as soon as you finish all of your homework", I offer. "OK", he readily agrees, and picks huge leaves from a tree in the garden.

Why? To lure the dog to her confinement. The leaves are from the fig tree and are one of her favorite foods. This new dog is bigger than the doggies which lived here during my last trip. She is friendly and sweet. Raulito faces her, holding the leaf just out of reach, even when she leaps, and backs towards the temporary prison of the laundry room. As she enters, he gives her the leaf and a push. She loves figs even more than the leaves, and Raulito withdraws one from his pocket, puts it in her mouth, and closes the iron door with an echoing bang. Then he turns the key and locks her in, as if she could somehow get out otherwise.

Back to work, with no more distractions, we finish the work in this way. I say, "Do you want to finish your homework quickly, or shall we go slowly?" "No, let's do it fast", says Raulito. "OK", I say, and he concentrates. I say, "Let's look at the clock. What time do you want to be finished?" He sets a time and puts all his effort into making his deadline. It works! No more dallying, he is on a mission.

In the evening, when I am already in bed, Nita returns from play practice. She has a part in a local theatrical production, and she has been at rehearsal. The drama is about Ignacio Allende. She will be a dancer, and maybe a singer also, if they have a chorus.

When I first heard that a historical drama was to be presented in the local theater, I had no interest in attending. But now that I know that Nita will be in it, of course I want to go. Also, a drama about Ignacio Allende, for whom this town was named, will be a drama about the Mexican Revolution. Allende was a key figure, starting the whole revolution formally right from his balcony two blocks from here, his balcony and house still just as they were, facing the Jardín and across the street from La Paróquia, the massive main church that occupies an entire block.

A drama about the Mexican Revolution will also be a drama about one of the key points of Mexican history. Mexican Independence day is celebrated on September 16, and the drama will be presented on September 12. The recently restored theater is only two blocks from here, and probably was in use at the time that Allende lived and would have attended. Wow! Not only that, but the townspeople who will take part as actors will, in many cases, be actual descendants of those whom they portray. And, if that isn't historically intriguing enough, these are all people who have been friends of Nita and her family forever, and, as another fun, some of them are people whom I know. Oh, boy, now I am getting excited.

Here is another "and"—the drama was written by someone local, will be directed and produced by locals, and most of the places where all the action took place are still standing and in use!

Nita and I are wide awake now, and Nita is still on a high from play practice. We talk and talk, the way roommates do, and here is the source of our loud and long laughter. She starts to tell me about when she was taken to emergency surgery in Canada. She was put into a ward with the oldest of the old, and their questions to her, and their antics, were hilarious as she acted out each of the characters in her hospital stay, which she makes so funny that it sounds more like an escapade than any painful trauma drama, which is what most hospital survivors usually want to tell. Evidently the ladies in her hospital ward have never seen a Mexican and give her the name of "Strange Girl". They cannot figure out why she is there. Her accent baffles them too.

Nita, being Mexican in nature and upbringing, is very gentle and patient with all of the old ladies, no matter what. They soon like her and grow to depend on her. She sets their hair, and after her release, she continues to visit them to keep up with their hair-dos and just generally to be a friend. I wish I could describe how believable and funny are all the exaggerated facial expressions, hobbly walking, forgetting, and starting over, as she depicts the hospital events. Everything is done in a sense of "laughing with", not "laughing at". I don't know how she does it, but she has me convinced that she could go onto the stage as a career any day.

6

I AM HERE TO RECOVER, AND
THE TIRED, POOR, DUSTY, RUMPLED FAMILY

Nita has decided to get up every morning at exactly seven-thirty AM to take her insulin, even though in Mexico she usually sleeps much later. I say, "But everything you do here is hours later than you do in Canada. Can't you adjust your times for the shots to your Mexican schedule?" No, absolutely not, she cannot. It doesn't do any good to argue, so I will just have to get awakened too, so, oh, well.

Today, though, she would be getting up anyway because she is going walking with her friends. When she returns, I ask her about it. The friends always walk through the French Park, and when I was there a couple of days ago, I was very disappointed to see that every bit of walkway had been dug up and was pure dust, except for piles of bricks and tools, and the entire park looked completely out of service. This will obviously be a long project, and I will only be here for a six week stay, so I thought, "Darn. Where will I walk now?" That is why I question Nita when she returns.

"You walked in the French Park?" I am incredulous but delighted. "What part? Where are the paths ok?" "Everywhere", she answers. "No, I was just there", I say, "and the walkways were all ripped up. Did you really find paths? Where? Which ones?" I am hopeful but doubtful. After more of the same questions, with more of the same answers, during which I have noticed that Nita's shoes have not even the slightest trace of dust, she admits that they don't actually enter the park on their walks, they merely walk around the outside of it. Darn, again.

We move on to another topic. Sometimes we are like this, having coffee in our room, chit-chatting. Nita has more news. She will be going to Cabo San Lucas for a while, and I am invited. What a great invitation, but I want to stay right here. I like being with the family, isolated when I want to be, or included in the doings of the family, and I also plan to seriously paint.

There will be another trip as well. Nita will accompany Ignacio and Fernanda to Monterrey, the home of Fernanda's parents. This is the only way that Nita can really visit with her only remaining brother. No one knows why, but here in San Miguel, Ignacio and Fernanda are hermits. Fernanda is plump and soft. Ignacio is skinny and has a long, long, narrow white beard. Both are intellectuals, and I love their company. But their policy is to never answer the doorbell or phone, except for rare times for the sake of Nita.

"But in Monterrey", Nita says, "they are lots of fun and go everywhere. So I have to go there to be with them". Why don't they just move to Monterrey, I wonder, but maybe San Miguel is where they rest up from whatever social life they allow themselves in Monterrey? I guess ordinary people do not understand hermits, and I suppose hermits have no interest in being understood.

Nita leaves for somewhere, and I have an eleven o'clock breakfast with Delfina and Raúl. We finish at noon, which is pretty quick, for us. I set out to buy heavy plastic sheets for under the long patio table so I can paint out there when I am ready. For right now, though, I plan to paint in our bedroom, exactly the same as when Richard and I were here together. Sometimes doing everything the same, except without Richard, makes me feel nostalgic, sometimes a little lonely.

Right after Richard announced he wanted a divorce, just barely before Estela and her children came to my house for a week's visit, I entered, foolishly, disastrously, into a romance, definitely on the rebound. What seemed so thrilling, and had the hearty approval of all of my friends, turned out to be not at all what I thought. I proceeded to spend three years of ups and downs with this wrong, wrong, wrong boyfriend. Everyone I knew, for many reasons, insisted that my suspicions were wrong (my suspicions were not wrong), and I let myself keep on, so that when the end finally came, relief was mixed with a lot of anger and a couple of weeks of tears. Relief prevailed, that the awfulness of the deception was finally over, and next came my anger at being so tricked, and with that, my own role, in hindsight, of letting myself be victimized.

But as far as the relationship with Richard, he and I settled what we needed to settle and have continued to support the policy that our children and friends should keep their love and relationships with both of us. I came to agree that the divorce and all that it entailed turned out to be fair to both of us, except, of course, that a divorce makes you pretty much think that your life is ruined. You know that the break has to be half your fault, and naturally you can see the other person's responsibility in every sorrow or disaster, but you cannot figure out what you yourself did that was so bad. So I have come to San Miguel full of good memories of the best parts of the marriage, and I am giving assurances to this family to please continue their friendship with Richard, and to forget about whatever his faults may be, which I don't consider right to discuss, and no one wants to hear blames and criticisms anyway.

But the bad love-affair, that is another matter. I have described to Raúl's family, and even to Chita, the cook, how stupid I was, and that I am here to heal from anger, blame, and all the other emotions that you can guess for yourself. Also, physically, I seem to have ruined my feet by ignorantly wearing the wrong type of shoes for my new love, ball-room dancing. I can hardly walk, at times, and have spent the last year, almost, wearing tennis shoes, huge loose ones, or bedroom slippers. So I am here to heal from that too.

This is my Mexico time, my time to leave everything serious or troubling behind me, and I plan to do just that. I have to come to Mexico as always with a blank slate, and that is another reason why I will not be going with Nita to Cabo San Lucas. One thing I do know for sure, though, is that I am finished with men, in any capacity that could be called a date. I do not even accept phone calls at home, nor will I join a group for ice cream, not have a coffee, not even car-pool to dances, not anything, not anything.

This is not a decision that I have made. Something inside me has become free and happy, like escaping from terrible restrictions, like getting out of jail, the prison of trying to please another person, or caring if they get mad, and all such-like, that I do not want any part of any of that any more. So it just is not in me to say yes to anything at all that involves more than family, friends, my dog at home, and my solitary, contented life. I am happy, I know that I will heal, and I don't want more.

The sheet of plastic that I buy is four meters long and twelve feet wide. Oops, when I get it to the house, it sure looks bigger than what I need, than what I will ever need, in fact. I suppose I can cut off a little piece. Then I set out again to go shopping for a stopper for my bathroom sink.

Who would want to read about that in a book! You think anyone wants to read about buying a stopper for a sink? Yes, if I can explain that this is another odd-ball adventure, for me, because I notice everything so much, yes it is interesting to read about shopping for a stopper for a sink. I do not know which one of the hundreds of tiny, little, two hundred year old shops in San Miguel would sell stoppers for sinks, so I just have to guess and go exploring.

I don't know why, but among families that are so immaculately clean that it is almost fanatical, families, and restaurants, and everywhere one goes, I never see stoppers for sinks. It is even hard to find any store that sells them. Instead a rag is used to stuff into the drain hole. Some sinks are the standard factory produced porcelain, but many are hand-crafted, maybe roughly made of cement, as for washing laundry on the roof, and others are beautiful made of expensive brass. Some are molded of ceramic by hand, painted with fanciful and beautiful glazes. Some are covered with tiles, or I don't know what-all, but few are of an industrial, identical product type that has an accompanying stopper that fits a variety of sinks. Maybe this is part of the answer. But I intend to wash my own laundry in my own little bathroom sink, which looks like a nice ordinary one that should easily have a matching stopper, but where?

I prowl the streets. Not in tourist shops. Not in restaurants. Not in schools, churches, theaters, not in shops that sell cloth, that sell tires, that sell clothes, or shoes, or anywhere that I look. Finally I remember, from years ago, that if I go downhill, on one of those streets I will finally come to a little, dark, dusty shop that I remember as selling keys and locks, and that has rows and rows of little brownish boxes on shelves going way, way back into the dimness . This could be a likely spot.

My search is in the area nearest the poorest of the markets, through little twisty streets that don't connect, except by what appear to be alleyways, or entrances to a driveway, or by some means that I don't wish to explore. There are tortillerías, the little ovens hot and open while clanky conveyer belts slide freshly patted corn masa over the flames to be toasted, and then to fall out into piles for the ladies who wait with woven baskets lined with clean cloths, wait to take tortillas home for another meal, a meal that could not be complete without tortillas.

There are ice cream shops, with magazines and books hung from strings outside on the sidewalk, running parallel to the street to tempt children to buy a comic, if not to enter for a scoop on a cone. There are notions stores selling a few baby clothes, a little of this and that, potato chips, barrettes, rubber bands, cards and ribbons. There is every kind of little store and shop, even restaurants that only accommodate two tables and eight chairs. There must be a place that sells stoppers for sinks!

After trying several streets, which means descending and therefore ascending again each time, I find it. It is just as I remembered, and yes, they have sink stoppers. Why didn't I measure the opening before going to all this trouble? So after having fun waiting my turn, and seeing all the interesting customers come and go, practicing my Spanish by hearing vocabulary words for things I don't know how to say, like wrench, or screw eye, or door knob, I finally select two stoppers, one a little bigger than the other. They only sell three sizes, and the third is way too big, so one of those I purchase must surely fit. Right?

Finished with my big deal errand, I have enough time left to buy an apron. I want the kind the maids and cooks wear, one that slips over the head and covers all of you, even in back. The front has pockets, and I need one for painting. This is just right, that I am near the poor people's market. This is probably where the cooks buy their aprons, so I'm sure I'll find one.

Not only I find one, I find a whole row of apron sellers. The lucky lady who finally has a customer, me, is overjoyed when I buy two, one for painting, and one for home for cooking back in the states. The price is so good that I decide to buy several. They will be perfect gifts for my American friends who must not have very good aprons, because I never see them wear any. (I don't realize until I notice that no one ever uses my gifts, that aprons are passé. Maybe gardening is passé too? Everyone has displaced Mexicans, cruelly described as illegal aliens, who do all the yard work in the area where I live, I finally understand, when I at last awaken to how out of date I am.) But at this moment I am enthused about the aprons. The seller is now doubly happy and offers me a still lower price, even after I have already agreed to make the purchases. She is trying to be generous, so I pay what she asks, thank her, and then give her some extra pesos (to bring it up to what a fair price would have been), saying that it is a tip for being so helpful and nice.

I am on a roll now. I remember from the last visit where to buy cloth as a backdrop to a still-life. It is a walk of a little distance from here, which I enjoy. Finally I am back at home and set up everything in order to start painting. This involves a lot of furniture rearranging, just like a few years ago, and luckily Nita does not care at all that I tuck the TV out of our way. She is far too busy socializing to care about sitting around watching the box.

I forgot to bring pliers with my art supplies, and I can't get the tops off of some of the paints. Why? They were fine when I left my house in the US. I will have to walk all the way back to where I bought the sink stoppers, (which don't fit.) But I'm sure they will have pliers. Pliers are heavy, and I do not need more back in the States, so this will make one more gift for one of the maids. The price of pliers equals about two days' wages, or more, for a servant, so someone's dad will be happy. Probably I will give them to Chita. She is so honest; she will tell me if her dad already has some, or even one.

Yesterday I passed out lots of the clothes I brought to each person, new for Raúl's family, good quality used ones for the maids. I think Nita took all of the shoes. They fit her perfectly. I saved out what I will wear during the trip, and when I leave, I can give all of my "trip shoes" to the maids.

Finally I start my painting. It is horrible and clunky. I knew it would be, because I haven't kept up enough, so I expected to be rusty. I will force myself to finish it anyway, and keep on with new paintings until I get my skill back. It is like being an acrobat. If you don't keep limber, you lose your flexibility and have to work really hard to get it back. When I don't paint, the flow from eye to hand to fingers and to the visions I store in my mind's eye stiffens up. The only cure is to paint, paint, paint, until finally you can stop throwing away the junk you have created. Until finally your whole being creates the painting. Until finally the act of painting means that you are just you being you. It is lovely when it finally happens.

After comida I go to my room to write postcards, and on my way to mail them at the post office, I have another adventure. The post office is closed, so I walk up the hill to the mask store. If I had a camera, which I do not even own, on purpose, I could have taken so many pictures and painted the plethora of startling, funny, fanciful masks which cover every inch of the walls. I love these masks, and it is so hard not to buy some. I have to remember that I already gave away the masks that I had all over my house when we hired a decorator to switch us from Southwestern to Old English Cottage style in order to once again use all of the beautiful mahogany antiques my mother had given to me. What is so enticing here in San Miguel looks out of place, garish, and overwhelms the usual decorating colors and styles in Wisconsin, usually, not always. I restrain myself for now, and walk on.

I am walking past a very tired, poor, rumpled little family who are trying to sell squash flowers and some kind of wild fruit that they have gathered out in the country. My adventure with them starts the moment I notice that they are carrying a tiny baby. The mother says that it is nine months old, although it is far smaller than my own grandson, whom I have left behind, and little Bryson is only two and one half months! Imagine carrying a baby all day in your arms while walking around in the country finding fruit and flowers to sell. I figure that even if they sell everything they are carrying, their day's income will not amount to more than five dollars.

At first I answer, no, I don't have a kitchen for cooking the blossoms (which are meant to be fried). Then I say, "But here is something for you", and I give them ten pesos, which only equals one dollar. As I walk away, I am still thinking about them, and I go back and buy the flowers for their asking price, ten pesos. I feel so stingy about their desperation that I go back again, yes, a third time. I have to search a little for them, and finally, there they are. They are not beggars, but I want to help.

I am trying to come up with a plan. To keep them here while I think, I start a conversation. I intend to say, "Did you come into town by bus, or on foot?" But accidently I ask, "Did you come by bus or in the mail?" There is a pause, and I realize what I have said. We all start to laugh, they turning their faces slightly aside so as not to offend me by guffawing right in my face. Since I laugh just as hard as they do, it is a good moment, and everyone feels friendly.

Aha! I think of something. "I am very interested in squash flowers", I tell them. "Can you tell me all about how they are grown, and picked, and used in cooking? I will pay you, because this information will help me" I suppose they think this is odd, but after all, I am willing to pay, and this is a service that they will be doing for me. I end up giving them another five dollars. Now they have something, and I have something.

I take the flowers to Chita, tell my tale, and she quietly and with her soft smiles assures me that indeed, times are hard out on the ranchos. It is very dry, and there is hunger. She and I chop up onions, and tomatoes, and the flowers. We fry them with a clove of squeezed garlic. These will fill tortillas, which then will be called quesadillas, even though they have no cheese. (Quesadillas = queso y tortillas, queso meaning cheese. Cheese is melted inside of tortillas.) Oh, well, what does the name matter? These will be my first taste of squash blossom quesadillas.

It is time to help Raulito with his homework, which means it is way past seven PM. Nita has gone to play practice. I am scheduled to help Conchita with her homework next, but she is fifteen now and doesn't really need me. I help for as long as Raulito needs me, and when I finally finish, I am very tired. Conchita is nowhere around, so I decide to go to my room, lie on my bed, and fall asleep reading my novel. (Her name really being Chita, sometimes I call her Conchita, and other times I Americanize the sound, which written in Spanish is spelled Conchi.)

7

MY OWN CHILDREN AT HOME,
MY NOTHING PLAN, AND SHAMELESS
LAUGHING AT AN INJURED MAN

I have a long list for today. It all involves calling home. My adult son lives at home, so he is there to take care of everything for me. We have an easy and relaxed life. He works all day, we have a dinner together whenever one of us is not going somewhere, and then he goes out around seven o'clock for practice with his rock band, for a show they are giving, coffee with friends, away for the week-end to Chicago, whatever strikes his fancy.

Right now I plan to ask, "How is Puffy?" (Bob and I rescued her together, terribly abused, she finally trusts us, but she still has traumatic hair loss at times.) I will say, "Please vacuum a lot, extra, under my bed, or under your bed if that is where she sleeps now." I will further request, "Please cover the couches." (Puffy likes to sleep there, sheds, scratches, and worst of all, nibbles away at the fabric.)

"Please drive the boat or the battery will die, the engine will clog and get sticky." "Water all the plants in front of the house on the bench and in the hanging baskets" "Be sure there is water in the ground birdbath as well as in the pedestal birdbath too. Clean them. The birds will drink poopy water and die. That is vile. Don't let it happen."

And I will call Mary, "How is Bryson?" "What did the surgeon say?" "Please return my keys to the high school." I will end my trip and be back home to be a three days each week grandmother caregiver before Mary's maternity leave ends. The other grandma will get two days a week with the baby. A perfect plan.

I am making lots of requests. I am thinking lots about home. I am not homesick, just still connected to my responsibilities and loves there. Will everything be fine without me? Of course, of course.

Other than concerns about "My Home Without Me In It", I am feeling very peaceful right where I am, doing basically nothing as I await whatever the wind will blow my way, whatever will step forward to shape my life, to the unexpected, which tickles and delights my curiosity about the gift of life that I have been given.

When Richard first announced that he wanted a divorce, just a few days after returning from here on "Trip One", I was terrified. I was not surprised, in that of course I knew we had problems. But everything had gone so well during our stay here in San Miguel. And Richard did make one last offer, that if we could move to San Miguel, he thought we would be happy again. I had to say no, because selling everything in Wisconsin, leaving my two children, and Mary's husband, leaving my new baby grandson, leaving all of my friends, my brother and his family, everything that I love, that was not possible. And moving to Mexico, no matter how beautiful a house we could buy, no matter how fine a cook we could hire, it would not be anything like living here with this family. Why Richard and I were happy here is because we were living not just in Mexico. We were living with and in The Great House of Raúl Rodríguez.

So the divorce papers were filed. I was panicked by what I saw as the ripping apart of my life. What would happen to me now? One night when I couldn't sleep, I awakened Bob, even though I knew that he had to get up for work the next day. I was crying. I said, "Please, Bob, please help me. I am so scared. I don't know how to think. What will happen to me?"

By now we were sitting in the living room. Bob was silent for a minute, and then he said, "Remember how they burned the big field across the street this spring? It looked like everything was gone. But they burned it to get rid of all the weeds that were clogging it, and to make room for new growth. That is your life right now, Mom."

With those few, simple words, Bob gave me hope. He cleared up every question with the answer, as I understood it, of "Take 'I don't know' as your answer. Take a clean blank page as the ok next day, and next year, and forever of your life. Let go. Let Life come to you."

That is why I say now, here in San Miguel, I have arrived on

"The Nothing Plan". That is why I don't want to go on quick tourist trips, or start anything like a social life, or have any plan of action at all. That is why I feel so free, so not needing or wanting anything to "happen". The "Nothing Plan" is my "Right Now Plan", and I am sticking to it! Yes, sir! It is so relaxing, so far away from stress. Nothing can go wrong, when there isn't a so-called "Right".

My days are quiet, comprised of long, rambling walks. Today I wander through a poor district, through streets I have not visited before, or at least not lately. I think I am gone for a very long time and am surprised to find I have only been walking for one hour. Probably this is because it is so hot.

If I could, I would be wearing shorts instead of heavy, tight jeans. But even though tourists can get away with a lot, shorts are a definite no. Not only would I be the only one in town dressed in what are called "beach suits", meaning a shorts set, a "playera", but also I would attract way too much attention, from men who would wonder what I was after by being so scantily clad in public, but also I would be an embarrassment to my family. And I personally would feel burning shame at the stares I would get.

But at least no one seems to care if I wear a tank top. Although tank tops are worn by a number of younger women, most people here seem perpetually cold. Babies are dressed in knitted leggings and sweaters and then bundled in a blanket or in mamá's reboso, a long shawl. Children wear the sweltering uniforms of their various schools, thick woolen sweaters or blazers, knee high stockings, or as one "casual" school uniform has it, heavy matching sweatshirt jackets and sweat pants. Adults wear sweaters over everything, and as soon as late afternoon begins, on go the jackets that we would wear in the winter: fleece lined, or leather, or woolen plaids, anything to guard off the falling temperatures that may go way down to seventy-five degrees. Maybe that explains a little more about why I would make a spectacle of myself if I walked around in shorts! But I am so hot, I sure would like to.

There is always one shady side and one full-sunned glaring side to every street. Instead of using sun screen or sun glasses, everyone crowds along the narrow sidewalks on the shady side, wherever they go. I do too because, one, I am always hot, and two, I don't like wearing glasses or hats. There is so much foot-traffic that no one walks in a straight line. Yielding your spot on the sidewalk is a constant, with everyone having an idea of courteous deference in favor of old age, or being a woman, or carrying a baby, or a heavy bundle, or being old, or letting the very slow walkers keep their places. I am quite agile, so I am almost always the one who hops out of the way.

Today starts more officially when after my walk Delfina calls me to breakfast at eleven AM. She and Nita and I prepare breakfast. Before I left the house alone early this morning, Chita gave me a huge glass of orange juice which she had squeezed and was keeping ready for me. Chita therefore must have known that this would be a very late start day, and she knew that I would need some tiding over. I love Chita! (Even if she didn't take care of me like this, I would still love her. But it is so great to be mothered, even though she is exactly the same age as my son.)

Since we have to fix our own breakfasts for some reason, we have hard boiled eggs and left-over green chiles sauce. And tortillas. I don't know why Chita isn't cooking. Maybe she is shopping for comida. It turns out that Delfina was up until two AM drawing red lines at the top of every page of every notebook for the first day of school. Mexican school rules are very strict, and Mexican ideas about when to do everything tend greatly towards the absolute last minute.

I tell Delfina, "I have nothing to do. Tell me when I can help the kids to do projects like that." I really do enjoy working or playing with them, so Delfina says a relieved "OK" because she knows I am sincere.

After breakfast I am allowed to set the table. There will be nine people for comida. Delfina's parents maybe are coming? Yes, eventually it is time for comida, and it is they who help fill up the big happy table. I tell about the two brand new fans I brought with me. One is mostly ok, the pedestal fan, but the table-top other one didn't make the journey intact. One of the plastic blades is split near the base. Señor Sanchez can fix anything and takes the fan home.

After we leave the dining room, Nita tells me about problems with her houses here, regarding rents and repairs, the usual landlord situations. I think I am helping her by the ideas I offer, because she listens intently, discusses everything I have suggested, and then we set out to buy account books to implement what I think she has decided to do. But when we actually arrive at the store that sells all such business forms, instead she buys only one very elementary receipt book. Hmm. I don't think she is very serious. Maybe she was just venting and only buys this one little item to make me feel that I have helped.

Nita goes out to visit friends, and I retreat to my room to wash my khaki pants. In the sink, of course, the sink with one too big stopper and one too little stopper. I solve this problem with a wonderful invention of my own. I cut up a Wall-mart plastic bag (from home), fold it into a pad of squares, put the squares in the drain hole, and force the too small stopper into place. "Exito"! That means, Success! I triumphantly wash my pants. I have to repeat my stopper solution a couple of times for the rinse, and then I hang the pants over the showerhead using the blue plastic ring with dangling blue plastic clothespins that I bought during another shopping spectacular. With it I also bought powdered clothes washing soap and a couple of other exciting items.

This calming bit of domesticity sets me to making a long gratitude list, which I love to do, because with every word I write, I feel as if I am opening a present. And I am! Skip the next paragraph if you don't want to know what it is.

Within these rooms, Nita and I have everything we need. Downstairs, a couch and two easy chairs. A trunk for a coffee table. A dresser with a mirror for my clothes and accessories combinations decision making. Upstairs, where I am writing, another living room, a closet for our hang-ups, two couches, and two stands with shelves and drawers. A separate painting table, and the big window ledge for setting up a still-life. Another huge ledge in the bathroom large enough for both our toiletries. A mirror over the sink, and an outlet for our appliances. Two TV sets in the living room (although we have faced them to the wall, thank God). A full length mirror for passing our own inspections before going anywhere special. A new clothes hamper. (We throw everything in until it is time to wash. Nita's washables go to the maids. My dirty clothes go to the bathroom sink.)

We have rugs, a night table with a drawer and a cupboard, and a crooked necked lamp. I am delighted because the lamp being askew allows the light to shine on my book, and not in Nita's face, when I awaken in the night and cannot sleep.

I have postcards to write, novels and Christian Science magazines to read. We have huge windows that are always open, although this year Nita has hung large, gauzy curtains to keep out the mosquitoes and moths, which here are called "palomitas", little doves. Nita hates moths because they will chew up everything, except we don't have anything woolen- oops, I guess she does. Nita is always cold and has heavy woolen shawls to go over her layers of blouses and sweaters.

We have my brand new upright pedestal fan, the one that survived. This, however, has to be aimed so that the air only blows on me. It is a measure of Nita's friendship that she allows it to be on at all, because even on the hottest of nights, she sleeps with her layers of blankets pulled up over her head, as she says she is freezing.

That was more than one paragraph, wasn't it? That is because although I was only getting started in the gratitude category, I was getting squirmy to move, or my list would have run for pages until this wasn't even a book about the telling of my tale anymore.

When it is late afternoon, I go downstairs. There in the kitchen, at the teeny-weenie table, sits Señor Sanchez. He has brought my fan, the one he intended to fix. Chita is doing the cooking and washing up kitchen things, and Señor Sanchez, now having an audience, begins to relate what went wrong. Just as he thought he had the ripped fan blade safely glued together, he decided to test it. Unwisely, he did not put the cover back on before starting it up. And in another obvious mistake, from the perspective of hindsight, he was watching the fan to see how it performed. He illustrates with dramatic gestures and sounds how at first everything was all right. Whrr, whrr went the fan. "How nice", he just had time to start to think, when WHAM, the broken "wing" (here they are called "alas") flew at him. Still whirling, and with terrific force, the wing flew right into his astonished face! He points to the several cuts on his forehead and cheeks. However, nothing gets Señor Sanchez down, and he has made this story so funny that Chita and I are doubled over with laughter. I am going to wet my pants any minute.

At first Chita is respectfully doing her duties at the sink and trying not to listen. During the telling of the tale, her shoulders start to shake. Soon she cannot hide her laughter, and hearing my loud guffaws, until I am almost screaming with laughter, she turns around and joins in.

We both look at Señor Sanchez's cuts and try to twist our faces into expressions of sympathy. But we can't even talk. Every time we try, there is our hilarious laughter just squirting out from us again. It should be so sad, poor guy, just look at him! This is a terrible sight, isn't it, after all?

However, our laughter seems to delight the señor, and he starts to tell his story again. He embellishes by using the fan and its broken wing as props. We laugh just as hard again, anticipation and Señor Sanchez's heightened sense of story making it even funnier in this second telling. He gives several repeat performances, until we have no laughter left in us. We are not tired of the story, but we have squeezed ourselves dry. Señor Sanchez is very satisfied.

After a while I decide to go up to my room. We ate comida really late, 4:30 instead of 3:00. That makes me think that merienda will be extra late too. It is 8:45 right now, so I make myself a sandwich and get into bed to read. Nita is still out. Soon I hear Delfina calling the children to come to the kitchen, so I guess merienda will be soon after all, but I would rather stay right here, so I do. Eating a sandwich in bed while reading a good novel, what a luxury! I am glad I am so easily pleased.

8

A STEAMING SULK, TAMALES AND TEQUILA, AND I FORGET ABOUT THE GOOD SAMARITAN

Morning is the same agreeable routine, but everything gets very lively the minute Nita and I step out the door to go along as her guest to Card Club. That means it must be Thursday.

We are to walk across town to the house of yet another of Nita's friends. We are dressed up for the party. As we walk, we get into a terrible argument. It is about how I do not like people to give me gifts. This causes Nita to scold me. "You have to know how to receive as well as to give, Sonette. You like to give gifts. So does everyone else." I try to explain that I already have way too much and feel burdened by more stuff. I want fewer possessions. I give to people who really are in need. That is what I say. Naturally I do not see that this is not strictly true. I gave new hospitality gifts to Raúl, Delfina, Raulito, Conchi, and to Nita. But I have over-looked that in order to make my point.

"Sonette, it is selfish to only give and not receive", continues Nita, and more such chastisement. I am insulted. I am mad. "I am not selfish", I defend. "I am very generous and always have been. Everybody says so", and blah, blah, blah. I can't believe that she is making such unjustified accusations. We walk faster and faster as our argument heats up. We arrive at the party house door steaming mad.

The maid answers the bell and ushers us upstairs. Each of us lets go of our anger in an instant as we are embraced by our hostess and the other guests, each beautiful and of just the age I like, MY age. All of us are dressed up. Mexican style, all are wearing beautifully applied, heavy eye make-up. They could all walk right into the set for the swankiest of Mexican soap operas, called telenovelas (TV novels) in which all the main characters are rich and glamorous. Except me. I don't look good in eye make-up, and

I am vain enough to think I don't need any. Therefore I don't even know how to put it on. But everyone else here looks terrific.

The house is magnificent too. All of the living spaces that one would think belong on the ground floor are on the second floor here. The rooms of the house conform to the floor plan of a squirmy snake, one room leading to the next in a decidedly non-linear plan. From within the house, one looks down from each room into gardens below. Street-side are windows with the expected iron balconies and heavy shutters that can be closed from the inside.

Most unusual is the fact that the entire interior is made of wood, a dark mahogany, brightened by bowls of flowers everywhere and by the surprising number of interior views of the gardens. Wood in Mexico is extremely expensive and is not even used for doors or window frames unless the owners are paying dearly for the sake of maintaining the traditions of the town's heritage, or because someone is just plain willing to pay a lot of money because he darn well wants to. Our hostess' house is in a different, gracious category of "Beauty costs money, and beauty is worth it". At least that is my assessment, because this definitely is not a show-off house. It is a lovingly cared for and lived in home with a relaxing feel of graceful living.

We are led to a table that is round and beautifully set. I try to remember the names of the ladies present, thinking that because they are Nita's life-long friends, I will see them again.

First we are served a cheese that Pilar has made herself. It is just like a large, white, round lump of gum. It is delicious! The lump is surrounded by black, chopped, fried mushrooms with green olives in them. The name of this is "Huitlacoche". (If you want to try to pronounce it, say, Wheat La Co Chee.) Other tiny white balls also surround the big lump, but these are made of vegetables. Everything tastes great. To put on crackers, there is a pink sauce made of tuna, and obviously other ingredients to make it pink and saucy, but I don't know what. Yum.

The only place I am used to seeing people drink tequila is in movies where drunken South-of-the-Border rancheros swill it down in big gulps. Or on the awful ocean resort day cruises filled with youngish Americans who are there for the open bar and picking somebody up. But I am to learn that tequila drinking is really something entirely different.

Tiny, cut-glass, stemmed, and delicate, are the glasses set by each woman's plate. Tequila is poured by the servant, and "Ahhs" of appreciation swirl around the table. This tequila is savored, apparently just a few drops at a time, resting on the tongue. One could ask for more, but a single serving must be considered sufficient, because no one does. I have a set of four glasses very like these, inherited from my grandmother, and we never had an idea of what they were. (A gift? Alcohol was never served in my grandmother's house, I am sure, because my mother's stories include the men disappearing down into the old cellar that once hid run-away slaves, when the men wanted a nip of something frowned upon by the ladies.) But here, a fine brand of tequila is revered as a great delicacy.

The main course is pure heaven. Again, Pilar made these herself, or the cook used Pilar's own recipe. We are given delicious hot tamales with a rich mole sauce that adds bananas to the traditional complicated mix of chocolate, cinnamon, chicken broth, dried crushed pumpkin seeds, crushed, old, dried out tortillas, ground nuts, and many other spices. This mole is perfection.

Wait, I thought that tamales were the main course. Next we receive new, clean plates for the huge platter of chicken that is brought out. The chicken has been stewed with oranges, bananas, pears, nutmeg, cinnamon, and fruits unfamiliar to me. The fruit is dished out over our portions of chicken with some of the slightly thickened fruit sauce. Eating is leisurely, with delicate expressions of appreciation from everyone, and the same kind of ladies talk that accompanies any fancy party.

This group is sort of like a Bridge club, except that their games are Old Maid, or Poker, or Dominos, or Bingo. One of the women is from Germany. She just loves Dominos, and that is how she got in with these ladies.

Well, this day everyone has forgotten to bring Dominos, so they decide to play Old Maid. Or maybe Poker, because everyone forgot to bring Bingo either. However the German says, "No!" The only reason she came was to play Dominos, and if they don't play Dominos, she will go home. (Not very tactful, I am thinking.) Finally she says that she is going to drive home in her car and get

Dominos. So she does.

While she is gone, everyone tells horrible, true, local stories about accidents and beatings. They go from that to monstrous recent births, and that leads to more grisly stories, until finally I am glad to see the German return with her dominos. We play, and I enjoy it, but the game is so simple that it is hard to see why she is so devoted. But I suppose the point is to have fun with a very easy game that will not distract from what is always even more fun, that is to say, gossip and stories.

At six o'clock, although that is considered very early, I leave. After all, we arrived at one. Everyone else will stay until the regular hour, nine thirty, except Nita will leave at eight for play practice. I need exercise, walk home (about a mile), planning to change clothes, and to set out again at dusk.

But when I approach El Jardín, on the very crowded sidewalk right across from the giant church, La Paróquia, I see a very old, very poor lady, lying on the sidewalk. One tattered, terrible, broken, black plastic shoe has come off, exposing her calloused and tired, ancient foot. Of course the scene is horrible and pathetic. She has her old rebozo covering her face, and she is crying.

Her ancient friend stands near-by, kind of guarding, not knowing what to do, but she will not abandon her friend. I ask her what happened, and she says the woman on the sidewalk is drunk. She begs until she gets enough pesos to get drunk, and this has happened before. People keep on streaming by.

I don't know what to do. I am not carrying a purse, I have no coins, and I start to leave. But I can't. I stop a Mexican man who looks prosperous and smart, and I ask him what to do. He says that he already called an ambulance on his cell phone.

So I kneel down and talk to her. I pat her and rub her back and tell her that the ambulance will soon be here to help her. I am there for a long time while she sobs about her life, which is probably much worse than she could ever tell. I don't know what else to do except to keep patting her and talking to her soothingly, like "There, there".

I think about somehow getting a pillow and a blanket, but the authorities wouldn't let her stay here all night long. Another poor old man stops and talks to the lady who is standing guard, helplessly, like a good dog that will not desert its fallen master.

This man doesn't know what to do either. The friend tells the man that this woman's husband is at the movies.

No ambulance ever comes, but all of a sudden, walking down the street towards us, is Nita!

"What are you doing, Sonette?" she asks me. It must look a strange sight. I tell her, and she says, "The ambulance will never come. We will go to the police, and they will come for her". From what I know of Mexican police, this seems an awful prospect, but Nita assures me, "It will be fine". So that is what we do.

All night long I keep waking up until finally I think of what I should have done.

- Gone home and gotten my purse.
- Gotten a taxi and taken them to a cheap hotel.
- Paid for their room, and supper, and breakfast.
- Come back the next morning and bought them shoes and socks at the market.

Why didn't I think of that? For all my reading of the Bible, why didn't I think of The Good Samaritan? I just can't imagine.

9

THREE DAYS IN JAIL,
PORTRAIT OF THE SECOND WIFE

At seven AM I go down to the kitchen and tell Chita all about it. And I tell her I am so ashamed. Chita says, "Don't worry, everyone is the same. We think of the right thing too late. The old lady will be in jail for three days, and then she will be let out free." So it is not as bad as I thought.

Nita says, "No, we did the right thing. Being drunk is a matter for the police, and they will not hurt her." But still, I wish I had done more.

I am invited to a breakfast party at Estela's villa. Wow, it is so much fun. We are seated at the big, glass-topped table in the dining room. The glass floats upon clusters of cactus plants, looking real, but which are actually hand sculpted and painted. We overlook the pool and the view of San Miguel way down the mountainside. The room is dominated, not by the view, as breath-taking and spectacular as it is, but by the huge life-sized portrait that hangs on the opposite wall. It is a painting of Estela and her husband in the dress of his native country. They are both wearing the robes and head coverings, with bands, that are usually shown being worn by Jesus and his followers. I am not informed enough to give a better description, but it is a commanding presence. Estela says she loves her husband's ways because she loves her husband. And she sure does!

Estela always calls him "Daddy", to the kids, so that is how I think of his name too. I haven't seen much of him, but I am impressed as well. He is most pleasant, very intelligent, a highly successful business man, and devoted to Estela and their children.

Estela freely tells everyone that she is his "Second Wife". You might think, "Oh, the first wife died? Or there was a divorce?" No, she is his second wife as in he can have as many wives as he wants, according to the laws of his country, and how many he wants is two, Estela being the second.

A man's first marriage is arranged, I guess, according to custom. From the first wife there are several children, and Estela's husband is steadfastly loyal to the first family, even though Estela is his "Love wife". Estela is willing to share, and in fact she admires that her husband will not abandon his first family or his responsibilities, especially since he has given Estela another villa of her own in Lebanon, and houses in Orlando, and in London. Sharing the same house with the other wife would never be an option. The two wives treat each other respectfully, from a distance, I think is how it works. All of that is way beyond what I could stand, but I guess it is fine when you are as happy as Estela.

The guests at the breakfast are all interesting people. Each is well informed, well-traveled, and of some profession or avocation that contributes to the conversation. The conversations are of the type I like, which means, no ailments, no movie or TV talk, no bragging, no personal gossip. I don't consider it safe to talk about politics either, just in case their house is bugged by misguided American spies who seem to be monitoring the most innocent of friends just because of their nationalities. Estela's husband called me one summer inviting me to spend one month with them as their guest at their villa in Lebanon. American TV and radio has told us that all communications to the Mid-East are monitored, and "key words" set off some kind of alarm that puts you on the United States "Watch List". I suppose just getting a call from the Mid-East makes a big flurry for the phone spies to fret about.

While Estela was in Lebanon, and I was in the States, every time she called, there was so much clicking on the line. Then all of my long-distance calls started to click. Finally my emails couldn't go through to Estela either. Even my letters were returned with "Undeliverable" stamped on them. At last our friendship was just about stopped cold. American TV and radio have stories about this same thing happening to lots of people. Bah, I think all this fear is a stupid bunch of bunk, and since all of my friends agree, why even talk about it?

So we don't talk about stuff I don't like, and we do talk about stuff I do like, such as art, poetry, things amusing and light-hearted. And the food! At Estela's house all of the maids wear the prettiest pink dress uniforms with little white aprons and caps. They silently serve the many courses, except to softly whisper about what we might like or request. The food is always the specialties of the "Indios", the indigenous people of the region. Except there is more presented to us than a typical family would ever serve at once, a huge variety, with exquisite preparation and presentation. Estela has lived all over the world, but she is always very happy about her own Mexican culture. Nothing is "show-off". Everything said and done is gentle and relaxed.

When I return from Estela's, it is almost time for comida. I don't do much today. Having begun with such a flourish, I am content to stick around my rooms for a while. Having such a feast of fun and food requires a digestion of more than just the food.

Comida is served, as usual, and as usual, it is so good that I eat it and enjoy everything. Then I wander around doing a tiny bit of shopping, come back, and try to paint. I say, try, because the results are so discouraging that I stop. I haven't painted much since the last trip here, and I am stiff and stymied.

When I was in the middle of the bad romance, I got the thought to write down what my heart would really enjoy, what I would really like to do, forgetting about any reasons why not to. I wrote five, and two were: "Go to Mexico" (which means to me to come here to this house for six weeks), and another was "Paint". The minute the awful break-up happened (as I said, half awful, and half a big "Whew!"), I called Nita. We arranged that I would come here as soon as Mary's baby was born, and that I would stay until Mary's maternity leave ended. And naturally I brought my paints.

Years ago, when my attempts to return to doing art were frustrating, ghastly, pinched, and ugly, I had the blessing of unintentionally enrolling in a children's summer art class. I signed up because of a tiny ad in a local paper and after arriving found out that I was the only one over nine years old. Even though I had been an art teacher myself for eight years, I thought, "Why not? I could learn a lot from the sweet expectancy of good in these little children." I did the assignments that they did, starting from zero, I guess you could say, and it didn't hurt me a bit.

Here is what helped me the most, and I have applied to many things since. My dear and wise teacher, Marita Magnuson, said, "Sonette, get the largest size pad of newsprint and a pencil, and bring them to the next class." I did. She said, "Put your hand under the top paper, and draw by only looking at the object. Throw every drawing away until you get your love back. Don't even look at the drawings. Get back your love of the paper, your love of the pencil in your hand, your love of gliding your pencil while your eye drinks in the object of your drawing."

In other words, forget the product, and get the love of the process. Therefore I know that eventually my painting "arm-eye-brush-paint" will start to roll out of me again. But not today.

My stomach is still too full to be interested in much food tonight or in a late merienda with the family. I hang out with Chita in the kitchen, and we talk and laugh as I boil orange leaves for my sleepy tea. I make a sandwich to eat in bed and look forward to reading my novel.

10

MY SATURDAY NIGHT DATE
WITH THE IRONING BOARD

I am about to start painting again. The start I had made was worse than worse, so I put everything away, thinking, "Why torture myself with this? Something will happen, and I can start again."

Something indeed did happen. I figured out that one of the yellow paints must be bad. The brushes were getting glued together, and nothing went onto the paper in the ways that I wanted. So I tested each yellow. Both were like glue. I also had a large tube of white, and that was also bad.

Bob had bought me another large, new tube of white in Milwaukee, a different brand, and some new brushes. The tube he bought is ok. As soon as it gets to be four o'clock, I will go walking to search for the artists' paint store, "El Colibri", The Hummingbird, on Calle Solano and buy two new yellows. I am hoping that they will be open on Saturday afternoon. The rest of the painting maybe I could do without yellows, if El Colibri does not open, since now that I have my courage back and have figured out why I could not control the paint, and why everything made such a mess.

Nita leaves to go out to comida with friends. Chita already left at one o'clock to take the bus to her village to be with her family until Monday afternoon. Raúl and his family will probably go out somewhere for comida and will also probably invite me, but I won't go. They need alone time together, and also I am getting fatter- so much party food. I'd better stay behind and walk, and paint, and write, and read. I can go get an ice cream cone later and also make myself a large glass of water with fresh lime juice. That cures the thirst.

I walk around feeling homesick and lonely. Of course I think about Richard and all the times we were here together, and got dressed up, and went out, which was almost every single night. Except at times we took drinks and sandwiches up to the rooftop and watched the day dim, the sun set, and all the little lights of the town turn on.

I could go up to the roof again any night, but I haven't yet. I am reminded of being a little girl. Every time I walked by the North End Bakery, I thought, "If only I had a nickel, I could buy a bismark." (That means a jelly donut.) "I would buy one every day, if I had a nickel every day." Finally I always had plenty of nickels and could have purchased anything I wanted, but I still could not buy a bismark because now I would get too fat.

That is how I feel now that I am here in San Miguel. I have the time and the money, but I can't go to any one of the thousand beautiful restaurants because I have no one to go with. Sometime I will invite the family. I already did invite Estela (family of four) and Raúl (family of six). With the cost of drinks, appetizers, dinners, and desserts, I can do this sometimes, but not every Saturday night, even though it would be lots of fun.

I am walking around, thinking about all this, and it is hard seeing all the couples and families. They are everywhere, in the park, in all the restaurants, in the churches, everyone dressed up, and walking on their way to somewhere. But on the other hand, I remind myself, I too have a family, a home, and friends, both here and back at my real home.

Finally El Colibri opens up. I remember paint as being enormously expensive here. I have brought peso bills in various denominations. I spread these out on the counter in front of the distinguished looking salesman, who is also the owner.

"How many tubes of paint can I buy with this money?" I ask. "All of them" he answers, as he waves his hands towards the rows of colors in boxes on display. It only costs $1.75 per tube (American)! I buy three different yellows. What happened? Do I have so much money now, compared to when Richard and I were here back when we had just recently married, so that paint seems that much cheaper today?

On my way back from El Colibri, I start to get hungry. I find a tortillería open, right at the entrance of the market. I buy a huge stack with my last coins, five pesos. I must have given out ten dollars today to poor old ladies, if this is all I have left. I could have given a lot more, too, if I had chased them down by crossing the street. If I go out again tonight, there will be ten or twenty more, just as needy, and just as old.

I go home and make a dinner of six tortillas, Chita's delicious left-over salsa, sliced tomatoes, and half of an avocado from the tree in the garden. Also I have a glass of water with lime, and a half cup of coffee. What a banquet! Ja, ja.

I decide to iron my pleated khaki pants because Rafaela washed today, and somehow she washed mine along with the family's clothing. I climb up to the washing roof and wash my own Levis by hand in the big cement laundry tub (still with no stopper, just a rag to stuff into the hole). I open the screeching metal door that leads from the washing roof up the stairs to the drying roof and hang the heavy, dripping pants to dry on the roof. I had previously hand-washed my one white tank top, so it is dry, and I decide to go down to the family's private laundry room and iron the top as well. I, being considered family, am allowed free access to this part of the house also.

I struggle with the ironing board, which I have never mastered. How in the heck can you make this thing stay up? I sort of get it in an ironing position, hold it in place with one foot, and iron the tank top. But I must have had paint somewhere on me, because with the final sweep of the iron, two blue streaks appear. Oh, no! Right in front. Fooey. I had thought I would wear this when I am invited to Estela's next week. That is, she invited me, but hasn't decided which date yet.

When one is a working mother caring for a complete home and family (used to be me), all the chores seem hard to get done. But all alone (me now), it helps to have some homey chores to do when you are divorced and alone on a Saturday night. I guess I am really homesick.

Well, I will take a look at my painting, and now that I have the paints, maybe I can figure out what is wrong with it and fix it. I've got it! The basket is overpowered by the background because the flowers that fill it are tiny, insignificant, dull. I can brighten the picture with larger flowers in yellow, and more green and black in the background.

My back is hurting. Time to do exercises. That takes up a few more minutes, and I feel better, but it is still only seven PM. I have nothing left that I can think of to do. I put on my nightgown, walk down the stairs, go out and sit in the patio, and I write postcards.

I have to get over "the blues". This is not a serious case. I am just getting empty, I tell myself, empty to be ready for something new to happen. One of the reasons I came here was for exactly this. At home I was going to parties, and Garden Club, and the Yacht Club, and boating, and swimming, and, and, and. I could still be there, doing exactly that. No, I chose to come here, to Mexico, to Nita, to this house, for exactly what is happening to me now. Getting ready for another new beginning.

11

LAWYERS, GEOLOGISTS, ARCHEOLOGISTS AND THE DEEP PIT, AND THE TALL DIRT PILE IN OUR BEDROOM

Nita and I awaken at seven o'clock. We drink coffee in our room, and at eight thirty finally mosey down to the kitchen, where Nita prepares her oatmeal. We take our time getting ready for mass, which starts on Sundays at eleven o'clock. It is going to be a lazy day. This is a good time for me to tell about the tunnels.

I don't know why I haven't been telling about the digging as I describe each day's events. Maybe that is the key, "The Day's Events", I see now, have meant what is happening to me, and I have neglected to tell of "The Day's Events" concerning Raúl.

Whenever Delfina has a friend visiting, unless it is for a meal, they sit on the benches under the arches that surround the beautiful, flowering patio. But when Raúl has something to talk over, it is always with other men, and they shut themselves into the dining room. That is Raúl's room for having a conference.

I have been present for conferences with the lawyers, regarding the digging going on under this house, and I have seen the men all sitting at the big table and talking seriously as I walk past the dining room on my way to do something else, my mind on my own affairs. Here is what has happened.

Guanajuato is the name both of this state and of the capitol city. The town of Guanajuato is about two hours away from here, driving the serpentine highway over sharp curves, next to steep drop-offs through the mountains. Guanajuato is also a colonial town, like San Miguel, which means that the whole town is a national, historical landmark. Everything within designated boundaries has to be preserved to look exactly like when Mexico was still a colony of Spain.

Within this city is one of the oldest universities, The University of Guanajuato. The university has a branch here in San Miguel, The Instituto Allende, from which I obtained my Masters of Fine Arts degree in portrait painting and in Spanish. The U of G in the city of Guanajuato is the "serious" branch, specializing in engineering, law, and I don't know what else is serious enough to be taught there, maybe medicine? It is the geological and engineering department that is of use to Raúl at this moment.

Raúl has had an architect here several times to access the danger: of collapse, of cracking, of whatever dangers there could be. The architect needs to know exactly what is going on under the house before he can make predictions and decide upon remedial or preventative action. And the only way to know what is going on underground is to dig.

There are many men in San Miguel who would be glad to earn some money by digging or by any other kind of labor. But what good would that do? To make excavations from inside of this house, the ones removing the dirt must have an expertise in both removal of dirt and rock, but also in understanding every level of what they uncover in order to determine if this is the original, undisturbed dirt and rock upon which the house was built, or are there identifiable tunnels filled with a different replacement dirt? Therefore the geological and archeological skills for "reading dirt" must be employed.

A team of such professionals was hired, and here is what I watched them do.

Part of Nita's suite is our downstairs "living room", I guess you could call it, but Nita and I have always used it for clothes storage. So it has a large chiffonier and a free-standing, huge, antique wardrobe, a trunk, and other odds and ends. All of this has to be shifted around to make room for the first exploratory excavation, which will be directly under Nita's bed, at the foot of our stairs, almost exactly where I first heard the digging when I ran and got Raúl. If nothing is found, either we are mistaken, or the excavation will have to be broadened along the edge of the house until something is found. But this is the most believable of the spots to start, given all that we know at this point.

The workmen pull up the ceramic floor tiles. One ordinary laborer has been hired to do the heavy work, and the other two experts must oversee each shovel full and each exposed side of what will become a pit. It is surprising to me to see that the tiles rest on no foundation at all, just the hard-packed ground that has not seen the light of day for a century. (Remember that this part of the house was the latrine or stable until Nita's apartment was added to the back of the house.)

The tiles are stacked to the side, and the digging commences. I had supposed that great care would be taken with the excavated dirt, but instead it is thrown in the front corner of the room, by the glass paned wooden door, in a heap, raw dirt tossed right onto the floor. Although astonished, I say nothing and just watch. I am lucky to be in on this at all.

The removal of the earth has to be slow because of the examination being made and because of the detailed notes the experts are making. These are qualified, licensed people whose testimony, written and oral, will be presented in court. I am not always there to observe and hear everything, but since I have to pass the hole, the dirt pile, and the people (during the hours that they are there), I am kept abreast. And of course the day's findings are discussed at mealtimes, but delicately, because the children are already scared enough, which means they have been so frightened that often they cannot sleep, ever since the collapse of the upper balcony floor, which took place before I got here.

As the dirt pile grows all the way to the ceiling, the hole becomes proportionately deeper and wider also. It is always something to bear in mind when coming home in the dark, because the hole is not covered over in any way. The only way not to fall in is just to be careful and not fall in! You are thinking, why don't you turn on a light? Because one, the overhead fixture (the only one in the room) does not have bulbs in it. And because two, the only switch is by the door, so the light could not be turned out after reaching the stairway. Therefore, we rely on the "Be Careful!" method and feel our way along the other edge of the wall, across from the hole, reach the slope of the staircase, and keep touching it until we feel the iron rail that indicates we can stretch one foot onto the bottom stair and start up. I don't mind at all because it is kind of fun, even in high heels which we wear whenever we are really "going somewhere".

Definitely there is evidence that soil has been removed and replaced. Every so often Raúl is called to look at the findings, and when Nita and I are around, we look too. There is much cautionary, "Don't fall in!" while we lean over to peer at the flashlight beam illuminating rocks and dirt that offer conclusive proof.

But the pit must stay open, in case others might be called in as witnesses, I suppose. Good thing we never cared about using this room as a real living room, because it is definitely uninhabitable. Another precaution that must be taken is the tracking of dirt and mud. Besides Nita and me, Rafaela the maid cleans our room. Raulito sometimes comes to visit. If the door is open a crack, the jolly, bouncy dog makes her way in in a flash, and she is big enough and curious enough to mean real trouble when let loose near a tempting pile of dirt, and even more trouble should she succumb to the tantalizing prospect of leaping into the pit and doing a little recreational digging herself.

Since we know that tunneling has happened, for sure, and that it is likely continuing, more pits must be dug. The men start in the corner of the patio right next to Raúl and Delfina's entrance to their private apartment. The mound of dirt grows huge, findings are made and recorded, and another search commences, on the other side of the patio. Now there are two outside dirt piles that are irresistible to Turis, the dog. If not digging, she runs to the top and down again, just for fun. But it must not be in any way fun for Rafaela, or for Gertrudis, whose job it is to keep all the floors clean. This dirt from underground is moist, it sticks to the paws, and it is dragged all over at each doggie romp.

One night there is thunder, and I am thinking, "Oh, no. The dirt is safely under the arches, but the entire floor of the exposed patio will become wet, and doggie play on dirt piles combined with wet floors....Uh, oh!"

I get my huge, folded up, plastic sheet that I unwisely bought when I first arrived, the one that was supposed to protect the floor while I paint. I bought so way too much that I have never used it. I offer it to Raúl to cover up the piles. He is glad to take it, cuts it in two, and there is plenty. We spread out the plastic and weight it down with whatever is handy. There! I am relieved.

Rain never does come, but everyone is happy to have the piles covered anyway, because now they are too slippery for the dog to want anything to do with them.

On a more serious note, the findings of the research team need to help the architect answer several questions.

- Have the tunnels already caused damage?
- Can an open tunnel be found to show to the police?
- The under foundation is damp and uncertain. Will the house collapse? One section already did utterly cave in and fall, as I have described, so will this happen again?
- Can further collapses be prevented?

There is something else to consider too. Raúl and his family have been students of astronomy, and geological, and historical phenomena for generations. Raúl has read that the recent tsunami was concurrent with a one degree shift in the earth's axis. And certain scientists predict that within seven years, the earth's axis will again shift, and this time by even more degrees. How will that affect this house?

To most listeners this might sound absurd. But Raúl has an interested audience for these theories. Me. When I was a teen, in the 1950s, my mother subscribed to Fate magazine. It was filled with oddities, but some really odd-ball theories, or "secret scientific facts that the newspapers refuse to publish and the government doesn't want you to know because it would create a panic" actually did have large groups of followers, and in some cases eventually gained respect as being worthy of consideration. Among them was continental drift, which when first published in Fate magazine was considered just as zany and stupid as any other weird idea. My mother regularly attended The Flying Saucer Club, as my brother and I laughingly called it, although the group named itself something more scientific. So we were comfortable with ideas that did not fit the standards of "group thought" of our times, and our town, and our nation.

Anyway, Fate magazine predicted exactly such a shift in the world's axis. Those who wanted to save themselves from the flooding and earthquakes that would result should hang a large bell from the center of the living room ceiling, and my mother contemplated doing this. My brother and I contemplated it too, except with a lot of derision and hoots of laughter.

Further advice was to have sufficient cash on hand to rent an airplane to take you up as soon as your living room bell started to ring so that you could circle the globe until you found a safe mountain, not one that was collapsing before your eyes, like the rest of the planet would be doing. Simply land your plane there and await the stabilization of the globe. Eventually, although the face of your planet would be greatly changed, at least you would be alive, and you could figure out the rest of your plan for staying alive from there.

Mother thought the airplane flight would be wise also, but she was too busy with her luncheon clubs, and the D.A.R. Club, and the Mayflower Club, and her Delta Gamma sorority luncheons, and her dance troupe performances, and her Vegetarian Club pot-luck dinners, and her new husband's circus friends who stayed at our house during breaks from performing. So she never got around to it. But Mother's expectation of the earth's axis jumping around was not the kind of prediction that you forget, even if only to trot her ideas out once in a while for my brother and me to make fun of, the way we often made fun of Mom, who never got mad about anything.

In addition to old 1950s memories, I have attended a few classes at Harvard University while being my aunt and uncle's guest in Boston from time to time. My uncle was a member of the faculty and told me that visitors are allowed to sit in on three days of classes, if the professors agree. So naturally I did exactly that. In one of the science courses, the lesson for that day included the fact that the earth's magnetic pole has changed thirteen times during the existence of our planet, from north to south and back and forth again. So, since I never knew this before, and I don't know anyone else who ever mentioned that fact, maybe such a theory as the one contemplated by Raúl could also be true. That is the way I am thinking about all of this.

Raúl is thinking that as long as we have to deal with the concern for the stability of the house, should we try to figure a way also of making the house stable in an earthquake? So I suppose the architect can access the advisability and possibility of that too.

Just in case, Raúl may also build another house, all on one level and earthquake resistant, a little way out of town on land he owns. But how terrible it would be to lose this Great House after, how many years? Hmm, 2005 minus 1640 equals... Oh, my gosh! It equals exactly three hundred and sixty-five years! One year of the house for every one day of the year! We should have some kind of a celebration!

12

MY DEGREE FROM A MONASTERY, AND SPOTS OF COLOR

Meanwhile, back to my own life, which this morning is the usual. The great new happening though, is that now I am successfully painting. I struggled along with the wretched old still-life until I diagnosed what was so wrong, and then I improved it to the maximum. My dear painting teacher, Marita, also taught me that when you get to a terrible part in a painting so that you just want to give up and start again, do not do so. You must solve that problem before you can move on. Otherwise you will never learn the difficult lesson that you would rather not face. After you have solved whatever was impossible for you, then you can throw the ugly painting away and start anew, because, remember? Process, not product.

My next step is to select a painting teacher right here in SMA, and here is how I do it. San Miguel is filled with art galleries, both for selling to tourists, and also because San Miguel is filled with artists. Many people came her originally just as I did, to experience exotic Mexico by enrolling in the Instituto Allende, which was renowned for its atmosphere, beauty, and excellent teachers. These students kept coming back, as I did, and got hooked with the way of life. Houses were purchased, word spread, and now there are thousands of Americans who paint. Naturally they want to exhibit and to sell.

The Instituto was originally a monastery. It is all made of stone, has a grand, central courtyard with the typical patio, fountain, gardens, and surrounding arched walkways. It has many rooms that branch off of the main section, some being up narrow winding stairs, some being in back of others, and recently added are new, large, spacious, light filled studios for learning many types of art, principally painting. Spanish, History of Mexico, History of

Cultures in Mexico, photography, creative writing, and other "artsy" classes were all taught, and the degrees granted were accredited and acceptable in the United States, so it was a great place for many reasons.

On one of the first days of my first visit, our college group was taken to the home of the owner, founder, and director of the school, Sterling Dickenson. Now, as I tell this, remember that I am not giving an official history of anything. Do your own fact checking if you are that kind of a nit-picker fuss budget, which I obviously am not. I am telling the truth as I know it. Just remember that I was eighteen years old then and had a lot of other things on my mind. So what I say is what I think is true, and that is the best I can offer.

Sterling's house was built in the remains of an old leather tannery, high up on the side of a mountain overlooking San Miguel. The vestiges of the old tannery pools and work spots had been filled with flowers, principally with orchids collected from all over Mexico by Sterling himself. I know that he loved orchids, and I would guess that the search for a variety of the plants was a good reason to roam all over the country, which is something that always appealed to me, even though I had no yen for a flower quest.

I still feel, and always will, a connection to the Instituto, although it is not as strictly academic at present, from the little that I know. For a long time some of the art teachers and their spouses have resided more or less permanently in San Miguel, with some opening galleries, and others exhibiting. It is to these galleries that I turn in my search for a painting teacher today.

But my teacher will not be a person. In all my walking and strolling, I have passed the window displays of many galleries. Now I will enter, look carefully at works that interest me, and select the paintings of one artist to begin my lessons. My lessons will be this: I will stare and ponder and fill my eyes and soul with what I see on the canvases. I will analyze. I will look for technique, color, and the motive and message of the painting. I will try to discern the how and the why. I will absorb everything I can.

There will be no need to guard against my copying someone else's work, or subjects, or style. That is not what I am after. Everything I do will become my own. This I already know.

After having begun with my plan, I return to the house to be on time for comida. Nita, and Rafaela, and I are upstairs in the bedroom. Nita goes shopping every day, and today she is showing me the dress she just bought. It is short. Nita has an enviable figure and pretty legs, but you would never know it because she favors long skirts or very loose pants, and she is always so cold that she is covered with layers of clothes, often topped by a thick woolen shawl.

We try to convince Nita that she looks twenty years younger in the becoming, simple dress, but to no avail. "Sonette, I am not eighteen", she says. We have to give up, and Nita moves on to giving me a very pretty blue tank top that she bought for me while on her dress buying expedition. Her estimate of my shape is far more tiny than I actually am though, and it is with great difficulty that I squeeze into it. No matter, Nita says it is great. She is so happy with her gift to me that I feel I must wear it for a while, even though it is almost impossible to breathe. I think that I will wear it a couple of times and later give it to one of the maids for a child of this tiny size. Nita won't care because although she buys an article of clothing or jewelry every day, I only see the items once or twice. Sometimes she gives them away, and the rest, I don't know.

But there in our room, still cleaning, stands Rafaela, never expecting or receiving anything, while we can buy, and Nita does buy, anything and everything. I decide to give Rafaela one of my best sweaters, making this a "girl's party", not two rich friends showing off more new stuff while the servant cleans the sink and the toilet in the background.

I get the sweater. It is a beautiful, thick, soft, pale yellow cardigan. "Rafaela", I say, "I brought this for you. Do you think it will fit?" Rafaela's whole face lights up in a radiant smile. "Ay, señora", she says, "Are you sure?" "Sí, Sí, It is for you. Let's see how it looks". Rafaela puts it on and looks in the full length mirror I have removed from hanging sideways on the wall and propped up lengthwise so we can see ourselves as a whole picture. "Mira, mira, mira", she can't stop saying. "Look, look, look". She rubs her hands over her arms, feeling the cuddly softness, admiring how she looks in the beautiful sweater. Now I feel right. Now I feel happy. Even if you are a maid, and even if you are grateful and delighted to work in a house like this for as nice a family as this, even so, you are still a woman, like everyone else.

After comida I go walking, looking for the right gallery with the right paintings for me to select as my teacher. I find one. The art is beautiful and conveys just what interests me. I will return again and again. I study the paintings intensely. I am looking for "spots of color". Richard also was a painter and an art teacher. So was his father, at the U. of AZ in flagstaff. So was my grandmother, at the Art Institute in Chicago.

Richard's father taught him, and Richard taught me, to look for "spots of color" to paint. People do not always understand this way of painting. Instead they draw outlines, with brush or pencil, and color them in with paint. But if instead you can see the shape of each color, and put that color-shape just where it fits in relation to each other color-shape, then you really have a painting.

After a while I have studied enough for today, thank you, teacher, and I leave the gallery to walk more and locate something that I want to paint. I find it. It is a street section. I stare and stare at this little piece of wall and road. I try to think, "What color is the road?" If you don't look and think, look and think, you would answer, grey, the color of dust. But if you really, truly try as hard as you can with your eye and your powers of discernment and observation, that is when you finally start to see.

And finally I do see. I see lavenders, and hints of dusty pinks, a wash of golden sunlight, a deeper green, or a purple, here and there in the cracks between the stones that make the pavement. I look at the wall of one house, and finally I see the almost black of shadows thrown by the plants that cascade down from someone's balcony. Marita also taught me that the shadow is the opposite on the color wheel, so on the green wall I look for yellows. It is hard to find, must not give up. The bright color from the wall of the next house reflects, to a degree, on the stones of the sidewalk. What colors do I see? The scene needs to be within my eye, not in notes, or sketches, or in the brain. I have to remain here, standing still for as long as I can and drink it in.

When I think I am ready, I go home. I tape a fresh paper to the plastic covered table top. I squeeze colors out onto the piece of broken glass that I use as a pallet. With a fat brush dipped in black I delineate the composition. It is a small paper, my limit being the size of a pad I can lay flat in my suitcase. The scene is simple, two houses (differentiated only by a tiny jog in a flat wall, and by their colors), an ordinary street, and a fountain made of stone at the corner. I paint and paint, smearing one color into another, I become excited, this is working. It is finished, and I prop it up on the sofa for study.

Nita and Rafaela come to look. They are rooting for me. Although the painting looks nothing like a photograph, they instantly recognize the spot and proclaim that they like the painting very much. I do too. Yippee!

Many nice things happen today. Conchita will start going to a dance class tonight, jazz. Dancing is so good for a girl. She is also going to a special mass with Cousin Carl. Carl' grandfather died on this date. Plus it is his father's birthday. So, first they will go for comida in a restaurant to celebrate the birthday. After that will be a mass in honor of the grandfather.

Raulito asks me to help him with homework tonight at seven forty-five, "But not outside", he says, "because the dog will dig in all the dirt and jump all over us". Yes, indeed the dog would do exactly that. I have time to walk down to the Instituto first and look at a certain wall with trees along it. That will be good for a painting which I can start next week.

I help Raulito with his homework as soon as I get back. When we let the dog out of her confinement, we find that there is no dog food left in the house. Raulito and I think she deserves a reward for being so good, even though she had no choice. Plus we think that she must be hungry, so we feed her what we believe are great doggie treats.

I give her two bananas and a slice of bread. Raulito feeds her two tortillas, but just in little ripped up pieces, one at a time, to make her show me all the tricks Raulito has taught her all by himself. I give her a fig leaf. We know that she has also eaten all the avocados and figs that have fallen today because there aren't any anywhere. We decide that we have done a good job on doggie dinner-time.

By nine thirty I am in bed, not sleepy, just comfy and done with the day. I am happy and decide to write more in my Good Things List. One was visiting Ignacio and Fernanda. They are so easy to talk to, and when they hear that I am here to heal from the bad boyfriend and my tight-shoes-smashed-feet they say, "Stop praying and start listening. You have done enough praying, and also, Be Quiet." (Oh, no, I am hardly ever quiet.) "Be still". (I am even less still than I am quiet.) "Listen". (Ok.) "Be a Blank Page". (At least I had already figured this out for myself. But they are right and helpful on all counts.)

Fernanda says not to blame anyone else for treating me badly.

    a) Take it as a life lesson to listen to my own judgment more, to trust myself.

    b) Think of the other person's life and what made that person do what he/she did.

This is most interesting because right before I went to Ignacio's I had been thinking, "God is taking away my material dependencies in order to get me ready for something better, and to make me look around and be more aware and grateful for all that I do have." And that fit so well with what Fernanda and Ignacio pointed out to me!

Here is an example I was thinking of. The first time a certain couple, Richard's relatives, came to our house to spend a week, they announced that one of their two daughters would only eat cake and hot dogs. They had talked to their doctor, and he said that was fine and would not hurt her. So the only things they fed her were cake and hot dogs.

I did not respond. Instead I cooked every meal, breakfast, lunch, and dinner, as a beautiful meal to be eaten all together on the patio at our picnic table. I tried to make a huge and delicious variety, especially serving different, colorful vegetables at every meal, and every food fresh, nothing from a box or bag. The two items I did not buy, did not serve, did not have in the house, were cake and hot dogs.

No mention was ever made of their absence, by anyone, and the little girl ate everything that was served and asked for more. UNTIL... After a few days, the mother noticed and said, "What are you doing? You know that you hate vegetables!" The child dropped her fork and refused to eat whatever that meal was and demanded cake and hot dogs, which the parents then supplied.

Well, I think God is very kindly taking away from me cake and hot dogs. And without knowing this story, Fernanda and Ignacio summed it all up very well in what they told me. And it is working! Already I am enjoying my better life without cake and hot dogs. And once I learn to be more quiet, it is possible that other people will enjoy that too! Except I really think that they meant to be quiet in my heart. It is something to think about though.

So besides Ignacio and Fernanda, here are more things for my list:

Two. Painting is going great. I have started another painting and plan to finish it tomorrow.

Three. Raulito is enjoying doing his homework and is doing it very fast without interrupting himself. We got to this point by me always asking him at comida what time he wants to start. Then when we start, I have always asked, "What time do you want to be finished?" He then makes it a race against himself, betting on himself to win.

Four. The architect and diggers are continuing to discover and document that the dirt has been tunneled and replaced, and they will take their findings to be analyzed in Guanajuato and will file a full legal report.

Five. Nita is going to ask the priest to say a special mass for the man in charge of the digging, to ask all evil to get out of him and to leave him alone. I think that is a great idea and is a very loving thought. Instead of resentment and fear, she is turning to Love.

I have finished my list and feel ready to sleep. Nita is at play practice. The dog is locked in the laundry room where she has her bed. Chita is relaxing in her room. Raúl is not here. He ran as fast as he could right out the door the minute Nita told him that the whole family had gone to his favorite restaurant, Mama Mía's, and that they were waiting for him to come as soon as he finished his homework. This is a happy night.

13

AN AWFUL SLEEPING BEAUTY, AND LITA'S LOVELY LUNCHEON

Nita and I are invited to go for comida today at her friend Lita's house. Here is how she invited us. On Sunday Nita and I made it to the eleven o'clock mass. It is in a special tiny little chapel that is very, very tall and every inch covered with deep relief, ultra-baroque carvings covered with gold. There are many small statues of saints, centuries old hand-painted tiles on the floor, lumpy and worn from all the feet taking the devoted to mass, and there are beautiful, fancy crystal chandeliers. It is inspiring just to be there, and I love everything about it.

There is only one creepy feature. In a glass coffin, like Sleeping Beauty, behind the priest's podium/table, in (or is it on) the altar, is a life-sized figure of some dead saint. The fellow is in languorous repose, but clearly this is death, that is, I guess the saint died a graceful and elegant death. He is fairly young and looks quite healthy, otherwise. However, this is a real passed on individual. Evidently his corpse had never changed a bit and this was considered a good sign, and therefore a good reason to cover him in wax. And here he still is.

Usually I would call a corpse "it", but this figure obviously is important to the church in some way, so I try to show respect, if not comprehension. "He" has a number of holy medals pinned to his outer garments, and as I understand it, each medal represents a prayer answered (a prayer for him to intercede with God? I suppose?), such as a little silver foot means a healed foot? Or a request to heal a foot?

Anyway, keeping the dead people does not match my beliefs, but everything else about the service does. The masses are almost completely about Love and forgiveness and are giving me good ideas. As mass ends, Nita starts talking to her friend, Lita. We all continue talking outside, and Nita says, "Let's all go out for breakfast." I say, "I will treat at Mesones del Parque", or maybe the name is "Mesones de San Francisco", because it is near the church of that name, and it fronts the park also. Anyway it is Mesones something, Nita and Lita love this restaurant, and so do I. I used to go there with Richard every Sunday for a breakfast or lunch.

The restaurant is an old inn, which is what "Mesones" means. The tables are all in the patio, absolutely beautiful. I also like their menu. It is what is called "all inclusive" which does not mean a buffet. It means that each breakfast or lunch is complete. For example, I will describe mine. I order fried eggs on tortillas covered with mole, the great quantity of extra mole being at my request. We are also served either a fresh fruit or an orange juice, which I always want. Also endless, dark, delicious coffee. And a basket of home-made bread, a whole loaf, and a pot of fruit preserves, and another tub of sweet fresh butter. The price for all of this, as I say, it is a package deal, is six dollars. Everything else on the menu is similarly priced, and each person's plate looks so good that you always think, "I must come back here and try what the other people ordered the next time."

I really like Lita. She is older than I, with an attractive way of dressing and an ample female figure. She has a pretty face, well done make-up highlighting her eyes, and a wonderful smile. She is enthusiastic, and I feel like I have known her for a long while.

The days pass, as I have described, and finally it is time to go to Lita's house, today, Wednesday. Naturally Nita and I walk there, because we walk everywhere, so getting there is half the fun, as the saying goes. Getting anywhere is always fun, around here.

We ring the doorbell. Doorbells are really buzzers and are discreetly placed high enough up not to be easily accessible to kids sauntering along the street, who would gladly ring every bell along the way, in lieu of running a stick along the rails of a fence. Bells are as hidden from view as possible too, sometimes behind climbing vines, for the same reason. And sometimes there are no bells or buzzers at all. You just pound, and sometimes you lean way back, aim your voice at an upstairs window, and call the person's name. We do all, and soon there is Lita, all smiles, opening the door and ushering us in. Lita does have a maid, but the maid is busy in the kitchen, and anyway she is a cook and housecleaner, not a "real" maid, not someone who would wear a uniform and open the door. She is just a good hard worker about the same age as Lita, and she has probably been helping here for most of both of their lives.

We walk up the couple of stairs to Lita's living room. We all hug and kiss and exclaim over how happy we are to be here, and how happy Lita is that we could come, and how pretty her house is, and soon we sit down. Lita serves us lemon aid, except in Mexico there are no yellow lemons like in the U.S.A. There are little, juicy key limes, and so we are served fresh, tangy lime aid. With the drinks we are also passed a tray of cucumbers and jicama. Both have been peeled and sliced and are sprinkled with ground red pepper.

Next to arrive are Lita's granddaughter with two of her children, a seven year old boy, and a fourteen year old girl. They have come directly from school, as they do every day, and are still in uniform. Naturally they are very nice children, and I like the granddaughter instantly too. They have their own home somewhere else, but they come here every day for comida, and since school sessions are either mornings or afternoons, their school is now over for the day. The kids stay with Lita, their great-grandmother, for the afternoons, while mamá goes back to work.

We move to the dining table, which is set to one side of the good-sized living room. We have chile rellenos, (Mmmm, heaven) and rice, re-fried beans, chayote (green, sliced, boiled, a delicious vegetable) and hot, fresh tortillas. I am full because I have eaten a lot of everything since it is so good. But now I am urged to have more.

The reason I am told that I must eat the next food is because the name is so funny, "Calzones del Indio", which means The Indian's Underpants. They are tortillas filled with cheese, dipped in egg batter, and fried in hot oil. And they too are delicious.

The final triumph is tapioca pudding, which, later in our friendship, Lita will tell me is her signature dessert. Our bowls are heaped, and on top are Lita's own homemade plum preserves and, again homemade, orange marmalade. I could do without the jams on top of a dessert that I already like as is, but I have to admit that Lita really knows her stuff.

Now Lita and Nita move to the couch. Nita has brought her photo album. I like Nita's album because she brought it to show photos of her daughter's wedding, and it includes shots of her house. But I have already seen it a few days ago. Ordinarily, I am not a fan of photos, even to the point that I have almost never taken any of my own. I feel like it means missing the actual moment in order to later see just a little piece of what took place. But in this case, I skip the album activity only because I have already seen it.

Instead I pass the time agreeably by talking to the fourteen year old great-granddaughter. We talk about her school, which interests me, because Mexican schools are different from American schools. Naturally these children, and the children of all of Nita's friends, attend private schools. Well, wait a minute. The mom, Lita's granddaughter, is divorced and single, so maybe in this case there is a good enough public school somewhere around here? Having seen the public schools from the inside, though, I doubt it.

A child has been asleep on the other end of the couch during our whole visit. She is the youngest great-granddaughter, too young to go to school, and now she wakes up. To my astonishment, I am told that this beautiful child is only two years old. She has the face of an angel, of a cherub carved for a cathedral, her proportions are perfect, she looks exactly as an ideal two year old should. Except she is so big! She is as tall as a four year old, or even five, or possibly six!. I do not mean the body and proportions of an older child. She is clearly two, but I have never seen a child of her age so big!

In future years, I will come to see many very large children, and eventually my own grandchildren who are extra in size as the whole race seems to grow larger and taller right before my eyes. But this little girl is the first, and I am startled.

It has clearly been a day of starting new friendships. Lita and I plan to see each other again soon. Nita and I walk home, talking about our day, and as soon as we arrive, Raulito greets me by telling me what time he wants to start his homework. I say, "Ok, I will be ready". I have only one hour until time to start, so I change to walking clothes (we always dress up to go to anyone's house or out to a restaurant), I scoot out the door and take as much of a walk as time allows.

Raulito's homework tonight is to read a long story about Jackie

Robinson and Pee Wee Herman. In English, of course, because that is what I am supposed to be doing as his helper, although what I am really doing is opening the door of his thought to liking homework and figuring out for himself how to focus and accomplish tasks without interrupting, dawdling, and daydreaming. His assigned story, for such a young boy, I consider very advanced. He reads it aloud as fast as he can, and mostly he does not have to enlist my help with pronunciation. He races through answering the questions because I have already shown him that it helps to read the questions before reading the story.

I have always loved awakening self confidence in kids, as their teacher or otherwise, (especially since my own son finally got teachers who did that for him and taught me that sometimes the mom should just be a mom and not a constant tutor). Both Raulito and I take delight in his passage from school-induced stomach aches to the thrill of knowing that he can do anything, and do it quickly, and well.

I am happy about the whole day as I pick my orange leaves and go to the kitchen to wash them and make my boiled leaf tea. Nita stops in the kitchen to tell me she is going to play practice. I make a sandwich of a sliced-in-half bolillo with a filling of sliced plum tomatoes, the kind that are always on hand for Chita's daily inclusion of them in so many of her preparations.

Up the stairs, into my nightgown, and at last, it is just my sandwich, my novel and me, a perfect end to another perfect day.

14

THIS ANGER IS NOT ABOUT TEETH

I finally thought of a good way to pay Raúl for staying here. Earlier, when I suggested paying my share at the same rate as when Richard and I stayed here, Raúl said no, and he is so quick witted that he said, "If I accept that, then when we come to visit you at your house, I will have to pay you four times that much per day!"

However, although I am treated as if I were family, in reality I am not family, and I eat a lot, and it must be expensive to have me because of that, and something about me not paying just does not seem fair and right. So I just waited for God to show me what to say or do.

Here is what came to me: I calculated how many days here in total, and I wrote out travelers checks to cover twenty days, and I signed them all payable to Raúl. I told him that I owed him the rest, and that I could pay it now or just before I leave. That is, I wrote this all in a note and put it in an envelope with the signed checks. I put in a quote from "Science and Health", "The right way wins the right of way, even the way of Truth and Love, whereby all our debts are paid, mankind blessed, and God glorified".

"He can't reject that!" I thought. He and Delfina really liked the quote and the good intentions on my part, but still they said, "No, do not pay". But I said, "Yes, I must. Look at that quotation. It is right for me to pay, so it will bless me as well as you for me to do what is right". They couldn't argue with that, so they said "Ok". And now I feel relaxed, and satisfied, and not a freeloader, or a burden. The amount will probably only cover my food anyway, I would guess. You would be amazed how much food costs.

And was I not right? Here is what we are served for comida:

- Papaya.
- Red noodle chicken broth soup.

- Hollowed out zucchinis filled with ground beef.
- Sauces, chopped zucchinis, onions, tomatoes, potatoes, and garlic, covered with cheese, and melted in the broiler oven.
- Rice.
- Flower blossom quesadillas.
- Hot tortillas.
- Three kinds of homemade sauces.
- A separate huge bowl of cooked nopales with raw chopped tomatoes and onions as a topping.
- A platter of fried onions.

That is not all!

- Flat steaks with pico de gallo.
- Gaspacho topped with chopped hard-boiled eggs.
- Coffee.
- From a package that Nita bought, whole wheat crackers.

!!!!!!

And this is not a "company" dinner, it is just us, and it is not a holiday, this is just the wonderful way we live! So, yes, I suppose that what I am paying is just a token, but as we say, "It shows good intentions".

Delfina and Nita and I sit and talk until six o'clock. We especially talk about Raulito and school, and his great progress from his former extreme dislike. Now he is a happy fellow about school too. Life does not have to wait to start for him until after school ends.

All morning, except for going to early mass with Nita, I stayed inside because between breakfast and comida I was painting. The painting went so well that I just stayed and stayed. The only other thing I did was to give a lot of clothes to Chita and to Rafaela.

Therefore, I had planned to go walking now, after comida is finished. But it is raining.

I brought an umbrella with me, so I decide to go upstairs, get it, and take a walk anyway. But after half an hour only, my sandals are so wet that I think, "They may get too soggy and rip, and then, no more walks. Uh, oh". So I come home. I don't care. I like rain. I need the umbrella inside the house too, because as I explained, all rooms are not connected, as they are in the states, so I need the umbrella to go to the kitchen, where I make my bollilo with tomato and mustard sandwich, the usual tea, and then I need the umbrella again to reach our downstairs door. Or I can just scamper and get wet.

Once inside, I am glad to have another "cozy night". I put on my nightgown and robe and get into bed, same book, same sandwich, same me.

Oh, was today supposed to be cards and dominos? Did no one remember to arrange it? Did they not meet? Maybe next week? "Oh, well", I think, "tomorrow we will find out".

Except that before I fall asleep, thinking of the nice day, Nita suddenly comes up the stairs. I have started leaving the downstairs light on for her because of the deep dirt pit and the even larger pile of dirt right by the door. And I have also taken to leaving the light on in our bathroom, so she has a mild light to see for undressing when she comes home from play practice at ten thirty. I even move all of her stuff off of her bed and put it on the couch so she can just crawl right in.

"Nita", I say, "It is still early. What happened to play practice?" "I didn't go", she answers. "It is raining, so I was sending my emails instead. Raúl and Delfina just left to take Raulito to the dentist", she tells me. "He has a terrible pain in his wisdom tooth."

I say, "It must be a molar. You don't get wisdom teeth until you are eighteen or twenty, and Raulito is only eleven."

"Twelve", she says, but angrily. "Here" (she emphasizes "here") "one gets wisdom teeth at age twelve or younger."

I should just have said, "Ok". But Nita said the tooth was loose, and the dentist was going to pull it out. I try to lighten things up by telling her that when Mary had a loose baby tooth in front, and it was just dangling, we have a funny photograph of Richard pulling it out with needle-nose pliers. Now she seems even more mad and says "No, Here" (again emphasizing "here") "not the father pulls the teeth, the dentist!"

Now Nita tells me that here children are often born with teeth because the diet contains so much calcium. "Didn't you know that?" ("That" being said exasperated and loud) "Then why do you think the Indians have such wonderful teeth?" she demands. I say that I don't know anything about the Indians' teeth, and that I have never thought about the Indians' teeth. I ask, "How it is that they get so much calcium in their diets?" "Because Indians are in the sunshine and fresh air all day! Didn't you know that? Also they eat tortillas. You know that!"

Somehow she thinks I am arguing with her, and she gets even madder.

"Is something wrong?" I ask. "You seem so angry. Why are you angry?" She says, "I am shouting because you never hear me, and you have this fan on, and anyway, you don't understand Spanish!" There are many replies I could make to the last part, such as that everywhere I go in Latin countries, people tell me they have seldom heard an American speak Spanish so well, and with such a good accent. I even translate for businesses, and once for a hospital. Or I could say, "Of course I do not understand every word and don't pretend to", or I could make many defensive or hurt responses, but these barely flicker to my mind because this is all so sudden and strange.

"You don't even know about the babies' teeth, and I do because I worked in the Botica and saw the babies." She continues. "Nita", I say, "I told you that I don't know anything about newborn Mexican babies' teeth, and I agreed with you about all of your experiences. Why are you so mad?" Now it is getting worse, and she is fuming.

I don't know what to do. I feel sort of sick and frightened. I do know that I cannot turn off the light and go to sleep, so I put on my robe, take my "Heraldo de la Ciencia Cristiana", Spanish edition, and go to find a place to read. But everyone else must be asleep or gone, and I wouldn't go knock on Raúl's door anyway.

I can't sit in our living room because the floor is entirely pit or dirt, and the light is way too dim anyway. The kitchen is locked, the dining room is locked, of course the Botica has long since been closed and locked, and the grand salon, library, and little personal miscellaneous rooms are always locked. I pick a bench in the patio under the lantern which serves as a night-light, a light so soft that I can barely make out the print of my magazine. I cannot concentrate anyway. I cannot go back upstairs and get dressed and go for a walk because not only is it too late, but I have not been given a key to the front entrance, so I could not get back in. All I can do is go to the shadows and sit.

Now my only recourse is to ask God to help me. I say, "God, what should I do?" Then it comes to me. This anger is not about teeth, or babies, or Indians, or tortillas. This is about our relationship. Maybe Nita feels that I am with her too much, although we are only together for mass, meals, and every few days I accompany her to something with her friends. Most of the days and evenings she is out with her friends without me.

I think about changing my ticket and going back to the States. Maybe I really don't belong here. What am I doing here anyway?

I consider spending my days in the town's public library until Nita leaves on her trip. But I could hardly stand that for one whole day, let alone a lot of days.

The only other person I know here is Estela, and she did not return my call yet, so she is busy or else not back from her trip yet. I give up.

Raúl was not asleep after all, and as he walks in from somewhere towards his private quarters, he sees me. "Sonette, what is wrong? What are you doing?" I tell him, and he listens with great concern as I say, "I think I should go back to the States." "No, no", he says, "you must not. We want you here. We want you to stay even longer. We have noticed that Nita gets very angry lately, and for diabetics, sometimes it is their medications and their eating. You have not done anything wrong. I will talk it over with Delfina, and we will figure out what to do."

This gives me hope because Nita's true nature is so sweet and happy. And I have thought that she is eating far too much sugar, but I am really not here to be a judge over someone's eating, and certainly Nita does not want my opinion.

I go upstairs. Nita has left the bedside light on for me. I try to read.

Then it occurs to me that Nita said late this afternoon that she found out that her Thursday Club did meet today, but they did not invite her. I realize that it might be because of me. Perhaps they think that I will always come along, and they want to be by themselves, to talk or gossip as friends do, without a stranger, even a nice stranger. That could hurt Nita very much, to be excluded, and she would naturally be reluctant to tell me that now she wasn't being invited, and all because of me. At first I am puzzled, because they all seemed to enjoy my company. Then I realize that perhaps they did, but only as a one-time guest, not as a new unasked for member of their own club.

I can't sleep, even after turning off the light. I come up with another thing, that I probably talk way too much to Delfina and Raúl during and after meals. I think they really do enjoy talking with me, but that is not the point. Nita probably has no interest in the topics we find so entertaining, scientific discoveries, obscure theories, history, conspiracy theories like the Masons, and Knights Templar, intellectual pursuits, God, the nature of the universe, and such like. Most people dislike this type of conversation, and that is why Raúl and Delfina and I are sort of starved for this kind of talk, but others find it boring. Maybe that is it.

Or, maybe by my talking too much to her family, Nita feels squeezed out of her own house and shared time. I resolve: One, to be more quiet. Two, at meals to ask Nita to tell us more about her childhood in this house. Her stories are so interesting, and the whole family would enjoy them.

Also Nita has said tonight that I have a very loud voice. Unfortunately, that is true, because of me being a teacher for so many years, and from being a performer and having a stage voice. I really try to speak more softly, but although usually I do, sometimes I no doubt forget and put out too much volume altogether. I don't like hearing loud voices either, so I will have to try harder about this.

Now that I am thinking about it, I am not particularly delicate about anything. I am blunt, shake hands with a strong grip, and am extra healthy and energetic. I must be very far from the Mexican idea of feminine. And maybe also, for that reason, very far from being a model of polite, reticent deportment. Oh, my, now I am getting even more wondering how I must seem to others. Oh, dearie me, again. It can be so hard to understand someone else's culture and how our own behavior affects others.

Finally I think I have things figured out, I feel a little better, and I fall asleep.

15

WE MAKE UP, AND HOW ABELARDO DIED

Oh, today is Friday! So yesterday was Thursday, not Wednesday as I had thought. That explains why Nita was upset about not being invited to her Thursday card club, and since I thought it was Wednesday, that explains why I didn't pay enough attention when Nita told me she hadn't been told where the club was to be held, which meant that she was not invited. That explains my confusion about her card club, and why I was still attempting to figure things out about what was really wrong.

This morning I discover that one of the women of the card club stopped by the Botica to ask if the American always accompanied Nita everywhere. Perla said, "No, she doesn't". But the club was scheduled to meet at the German's house, and maybe the German didn't want to take a chance that I might come along and therefore did not tell Nita where they were going to meet.

I have been staying in our bedroom a lot since my painting is going so well, and that is the only place where I do my painting, so I also wonder if Nita feels that she can't even be in her own room without me there too. Boy, oh, boy, what shall I do? "Do what you can do, even if it is only one very little thing", I have told my children and students. Now I plan to take my own advice.

At breakfast I ask Nita questions about her childhood and then just listen. Good results! She is fascinating, and all of us are entranced by her stories. So far, so good.

At lunch, I get her started again and then am quiet. The children are back from school and at the table. They too love hearing her tell of childhood. So do I. She is a very good teller, and her tales are of an old, far away time, but all the events are easy to picture because they took place right here, in this very room, and right out in this patio. Plus Nita can be really funny.

Our enormous, fabulous comida includes both soy sausages and flat beef steaks. I don't take the steak because a few months ago I decided to be a vegetarian again, as I once was, more or less, for a period of five years. Later, after comida, I am in the kitchen chatting with Chita, and it dawns on me that she has been making all of my meals separately! Whenever everyone else has beef as a stuffing or filling, she has made my portions with soy substitute! What a lot of extra work to do this for me. She is so considerate and modest that she would have done all this without ever telling me, except that she wanted to reassure me that I could eat whatever she serves to me.

I am not as dedicated as all that, eating anything and everything when at Estela's house, or at a party, and I didn't dream of making such a request for special treatment here. I think at the beginning of my visit I only said something like, "When you take the count of how much meat to buy for a meal, I will be skipping that part and eating more of the rest". What a loving gesture on Chita's part. I wonder if this is another of those things about my own life where everyone else is aware of it except for me?

I have been painting all of this morning, and now I will go back to my room to paint again. But first, I want to invite Nita to go out to dinner with me tomorrow night, Saturday. The family is leaving right now to drive the kids to parties, one for Raulito, and one for Conchita. (That is how I learned that today is Friday, because the children do not have to do homework tonight, they tell me, since tomorrow is Saturday.)

Tomorrow the family will not be here in the afternoon or evening because they are all going to another baptism at two o'clock at Atotinilco, and after that to a fancy party at the Atascadero, a lavish resort high at the top of San Miguel. Rafaela and Chita will return to their villages right after cleaning up from serving breakfast, which means they can leave about one PM. That means Nita and I will be on our own.

Nita loves the idea of going to the restaurant La Posada de San Francisco because on Saturday nights they have La Tuna playing, and Nita is crazy about La Tuna, so she immediately says, "Yes". Of course, she really says, "Sí, Sonette", since we have been speaking all Spanish on this visit, and so has everyone else. That has been wonderful. And since I have been so happy, that is another reason why I don't want to be the person who spoils this time for Nita. This is her visit too, not just mine.

I think things are getting better between us already, because she gets out her old photo album of Abelardo. Wow, this is unexpected and wonderful. To see pictures of Abelardo, taken during my years of being back and forth on visits here, this is wonderful. I seem to be in only one of the snapshots; we can't tell for sure because they are not especially clear. But Nita is included and looks just as I remember her, and so is one of Abelardo's friends.

We spend a long time reminiscing. This is a time when Nita talks a little more about the circumstances of Abelardo's murder.

First I will tell what I remember being told the first time I returned to Mexico after his death. Things were very different then. Mail from Mexico to the States, or vice versa, took sometimes weeks to arrive, and sometimes did not arrive at all. More than occasionally, having arrived, a servant set a letter aside and forgot to deliver it. Some went to the wrong address because the Mexican way of addresses is different from our way. Numbers are not written the same. For example, the USA numeral "one" looks like the letter l (lower case of L) in Spanish. The Mexican "one" looks like the American numeral "seven". The Mexican number "seven" has a slash or dash through the center, making it look like the American letter "Z". Handwriting is different too, letters of the alphabet not being read as they were intended. Both Mexican and American postmen could not always decipher foreign handwriting, and who could blame them? I once received, while here in Mexico, a very important life-changing letter two years after it had been posted, too late for going back and changing what had happened in the meantime.

Therefore, combining those facts with the Mexican habit of not writing letters very often anyway, there was almost no written correspondence between us, other than the formal death notice (received much later than the event), and my letter of sorrow and sympathy in return.

Phone calls? Making a call to Mexico, or from Mexico to the States, was so rare that there was only one place in town that could place such calls. In San Miguel you had to go to a certain restaurant that had a desk and a phone booth way in the back, make a request, sign a form, and wait to see if your call would go through that night, starting at eleven PM, although you had to arrive hours before that to get on the hopeful list. Many times, after all the waiting, I got turned away with, "So sorry, but all the international lines are busy tonight. Would you like to try again some other day?"

My poor mother tried so many times to talk to me during my first visit to Mexico. She could get an operator to reach Casa Sautto, where we all were living, but I was seldom there when a call came. Maids were sent to search for me, knocking on my door, looking for me in the swimming pools, checking all of the gardens, calling my name and asking about my whereabouts to anyone who knew me, and sometimes even going out to the street to see if I could be sighted walking back from the Instituto. All those months that I was gone, maybe my mom reached me twice. That had to be hard for a mother.

So I did not hear anything about Abelardo directly from the family, by way of explanations. I doubt if they had any idea of my phone number. Certainly Abelardo and I had never called each other. They probably had to locate an old letter from me to him to even find my address.

So it was not the family but Abelardo's close friend, Eddy, who told me the following account. Abelardo was at El Patio, the town's finest restaurant, the one where he took me for dinner and dancing so many nights after picking me up at the Bellas Artes at nine o'clock, the time I finished my private Flamenco dance lessons with the fiery Fernanda. Abelardo was at El Patio with a friend, and they had been drinking until very late. Somehow Abelardo offended a waiter who followed Abelardo, who was by then alone, out to the street at three AM. The waiter stabbed Abelardo in the leg, by the groin, cutting an artery.

Only a short two blocks from home, Abelardo staggered to his house before passing out on the sidewalk by his front door. The few people who saw him thought he was drunk and didn't do anything to help.

When Abelardo and I had been going out almost every night, there were occasional times when Nita wasn't with us. I don't remember how it came about, but one night when it was just the two of us, we stayed out very late. Abelardo escorted me back to Casa Sautto, but the entrance doors were locked, as they always were by that time. After much pounding and hollering, someone woke up and, clad in pajamas, came to admit me, but I was made to understand that once the doors were locked, it was time to already be inside.

The next day, Abelardo told me that his father had sternly said to him, "I won't try to make you come home at a certain hour, but once the doors are locked for the night, you will have to find somewhere outside to sleep." So it wasn't too hard for me to believe that Abelardo bled to death on his own doorstep, because Abelardo's father was not the only one to have such a policy, and seeing a young man sleeping on the cold lumpy stones outside his own house, and therefore thinking better about staying out that late the next time, might not have been such a rare thing as to arouse the worry or concern of a passerby.

I don't think I ever asked the family for the details of that tragic night, believing that I already knew them, and I think all I really learned from the family was that there was a fight of some kind, Abelardo was cut, and he bled to death.

What Nita explains to me now is different from what I have believed. Abelardo's mother was told that it was the friend who insisted that tired, drunken Abelardo must wait outside the restaurant and give the rude waiter a good punch. Abelardo would have just gone on home if not for that. Seeing the two young men waiting for him, the waiter apparently took out his knife to defend himself. I have to admit that I have never really understood the correct details of the terrible circumstances.

Nita says that her mother was such a God devoted, kind-hearted woman that she cared enough to learn about the man who had killed her son and was in jail. She found out that he had a family of a wife and two little children. He was not a murderous type. Not wanting the children to live the terrible life of poor orphans, Abelardo's bereaved mother went to the jail, or maybe it was to the judge, and asked for mercy for this man. I believe because of her intervention, the death was ruled an accident. The waiter has been eternally grateful and has led a good life, I think is what I am being told. Again, so much time had passed, and I have believed the wrong story for so long, that sometimes old "facts" linger and get mixed up with the true version.

When Nita was so angry Thursday night and said that I didn't understand Spanish, I think she was mostly just mad, but she must have been referring to more than vocabulary, because of course I cannot possibly know every word and expression. I think she must have meant that in certain situations I do not have the cultural or situational background to put everything together correctly. Even in English I find some stories and explanations too tangled to figure out, let alone remember correctly. There will always be times when a foreigner, or even a stranger who was raised speaking the language, simply does not have enough background to understand, not the words, but the whole picture of what is being explained. All I know is: Abelardo was at El Patio. Abelardo got stabbed and bled to death. Abelardo's mother interceded and obtained mercy for the waiter.

It is so comforting to sit here in the library among the shelves that contain generations' worth of books, looking at this old album. We reminisce, Nita tells more stories about the other friends in the album, and it is a sweet time together.

Next Nita brings out the photo album of her marriage to Jackson. This one does contain photos of me, and of Richard too, because I was bride's maid in her beautiful wedding at the giant cathedral, La Paróquia. I will tell about the wedding, but not now. Now I am full in my heart of our making up, with words unsaid, but we both feel it.

This is still Friday, so I tell her that tomorrow night we will go out together, but on some other nights I will make my torta and eat in bed with my sandwich and book, as I have been doing. "I do that because you need time alone with your family, your friends, your play practice, and you should be able to have merienda without anyone else sometimes", I tell her. "No, no, Sonette, nobody feels that way. We want you with us", she responds, and she is completely sincere. "Thank you", I say, "But I enjoy my little habit, I truly believe that you should have some time to yourselves, and it is ok, I am happy." She accepts this, and I think things are better again.

16

RUBBER BANDS FOR BREAKFAST, RAFAELA BRINGS HER DAUGHTER, AND NOSTALGIC FOR MY CIRCUS ACT

Nita and I go to early mass. It is in another of the El Oratorio's labyrinth of rooms, a tiny chapel, and only lasts one half hour. It is all singing and Bible reading, plus a sermon of just three or four minutes, usually one I like, almost always about forgiveness, which is good for me. The Lord's Prayer, (which I am trying to learn in Spanish, although it is recited at break-neck speed), the collection, which is tiny because normally everyone in attendance is very old and very poor, except for Nita and me, and taking communion. It is really friendly, and I like it.

Afterwards we stop to chat on the corner with two of Nita's friends who also attended today. I hear all of the town gossip, which is of an interesting nature, even though I don't know the people involved. Then we come home for Nita's oatmeal.

I start a new painting before breakfast. Then today I am served scrambled eggs, tortillas and bananas, but for Raúl and Raulito it is menudo. Menudo is the only food I find disgusting in the extreme. It is cow's stomach cut up. The pieces are big, tough, wrinkly, white strips. It feels exactly like chewing the thickest of rubber bands, and you will not make any more progress in chewing than what you would on the rubber bands. The texture is awful, and the taste is worse.

I guess there are some cooks who can cook it enough for you to swallow, but usually it has to be ground up. Strangely, it is one of the most loved foods, and I have never met a Mexican who doesn't get all happy about menudo. Many years ago, here in San Miguel, a party was given, although at first I did not realize that the party was for me, in my honor. I was told that it would be a barbeque, so you can imagine what I expected. Instead it was a very dress-up garden party, and a table was brought forth, with only one chair, where I was to sit while all the guests circled around me to watch my delight as I was served the first portion of- guess what! This time it was a goat's stomach, all wrinkly and repulsive, stuffed with big, white strips of pieces cut from another goat's stomach.

This treat had been grilled outside, although the cooking did not make it look any different from when it left the goat, and the big awful thing was placed proudly on the table in front of me. The papá of the family cut me a generous slice. I was given nothing else but a fork. No tortillas, no drink, nothing on my plate except the accursed stomach. Being a proper type of person, I would never have offended my lovely friends by saying that I didn't want any. I had to desperately struggle not to offend by throwing up as I gagged through swallowing the loathsome chunks. Sweat broke out on my forehead, and I twisted my uncontrollable look of revulsion into a closed mouth smile, nodding and doing my best to gulp it down.

"More?" smiled the delighted host. "No, no, that was a very generous portion, thank you" I managed.

The horror of having to eat menudo has never left me, and Chita somehow, God bless her, must have guessed that I would rather have anything but that. Or maybe I have been saved because menudo is not vegetarian? In Raúl's house I am so comfortable that I could easily say, "No, gracias" and no one would be offended, thank goodness. I don't even like to think about menudo.

Chita has so much to do in order to be ready to leave for her rancho on time to catch the bus, that today she has served orange juice from a box. Except she serves me last, and mine is squeezed! After breakfast I thank her, and she smiles. "Nobody will know except you and me, señora". Isn't she sweet?

I had washed and dried some clothes, which I have barely put on when the dog pounces on me with muddy feet. Nita says she has some dirty clothes too, so we can do a load in the washing machine, and soon the clothes are finished and hung on the roof where they will dry in no time.

Raúl gets me aside privately and says that he and Delfina feel very bad about what happened with Nita. "We do not want you to go, Sonette. You can stay in our apartment until Nita leaves for her trip if you think that would help. Remember that with the problems of the diabetes sometimes she is not herself." Then he tells me that Delfina would like me to stay even longer, and so would he, because of the great change in Raulito, and besides, they enjoy having me here.

Naturally I am very grateful to hear this. I tell him that I think things are getting back to normal with Nita and me, that I have thought a lot about how to be a better sister and friend to her, etc. "And" I say, "Raulito will be fine by the time I leave. He is probably fine already. We just do homework together now because we like to." Also I explain that I must leave on my scheduled date because my daughter's maternity leave will be over, and I will be a care-giver grandma.

Raúl accept this and says, "That is excellent, Sonette, but do not go home early, and if you need to, you can stay with us, remember."

I telephone Estela from the Botica, and to my delight, I reach her. She has been in Mexico City meeting her husband at the airport, and then they went to Taboada (where the hot springs pool party was), and they had not returned until last night. Not surprisingly, she had not received the message that I had called.

Estela says that tomorrow she is giving a party in honor of her husband, so she wants Nita and me to come to it, and bring clothes, because we are invited to stay overnight in one of her casitas. Oh, boy, this will be fun.

The next thing is great too. I reach Bob on the phone, and he is fine, plus Puffy is better. Puffy is my darling long, long haired, white doggie. I foolishly had her hair clipped short for our hot summer, and her tender pink skin sort of dissolved. The vet could not figure out why, and she has suffered terribly while I spent a fortune doing everything the vet suggested, but she only grew worse. Finally I decided that she needed all of her natural fur, and Bob says she is better since we have let it grow back.

This is Labor Day week-end, back in the States, and Bob's rock band is going to play a show for a large outside party. This is great. Also he is the one doing the majority of the work on the Tiffany windows that his stained glass company is restoring. Bob has interesting details to tell me about that. He also says Mary and Jason had a nice vacation in Door County. So I am filled with happiness that things are so nice at home with my family.

I go upstairs and paint. The time flies by.

Rafaela, the maid, stops by my room to tell me that today she has brought her thirteen year old daughter to help her in her duties. Rafaela wants me to meet her daughter, who is very pretty and sweet. The young lady wants to thank me for all that I have sent home with her mother for her, both on this trip and the last. It is more happiness for this day.

I talk to Rafaela often, and I like her. Rafaela has read the "El Heraldo de La Ciencia Cristana" editions that I have brought each visit. I bring as many copies as I can because here is how it goes. First Chita reads them, one at a time. Then they are passed to Rafaela. Next the daughter reads them, and then her son. (I forgot to say that I read them first because I do not want them back. Maids have very little time to read, so they must be allowed to keep the magazines for as long as they wish, and then pass them on.)

Chita reads some aloud to her mother. Her mother wants to read them all, but she needs glasses and can't see well enough.

Rafaela is the sole source of income for her family. They live on a little rancho, which means a little village outside of town. Her faithless, cruel husband lives there too, with his second wife (no divorce), and he never speaks to Rafaela or his own children by her. I tell her that this is a blessing because it means that he leaves her alone and she doesn't have to put up with anything from him. She says that she never thought of it like that, because it makes her children sad, but I tell her that he could be making trouble about them all the time, and she agrees.

Rafaela has a son, age eleven, and the three of them live with her parents. Her father cultivates corn and beans, which he plants by hand and harvests once per year. They save their tiny crop right inside of their house, as most poor people do, and parcel out the food in tiny amounts to make it last. The rest of their food, and all other expenses, come from Rafaela's income. She has to pay her bus fare each day, the children's uniforms and school supplies, all the rest of their food, and the electricity. It is impossible to imagine how she does it. I'll bet that the only meal she eats is comida here each day, giving the rest of the tortillas and small amounts of whatever other food she can afford to her family.

Rafaela's job is to sweep and mop all the floors of this house every day, also daily to clean out the fountain, to help cook the comida, and to help clean-up after. She also checks each apartment inside once a week to be sure that everything is working and that nothing is broken. Delfina likes to have everything fixed right away, which is an excellent policy.

I think that Rafaela also cleans the kitchen, bathroom, and floors of each apartment once per week. Maybe the people who live in the apartments pay her for that service themselves? Probably. Delfina and Raúl are very good to their help, and I know that what people earn from this generous family is more than most can expect. A job in this household would be greatly appreciated.

There are no bugs pestering us in this season, but there can be mosquitoes and flies in some locations, so I brought fly swatters for the maids and one for myself, just in case. Rafaela was so happy to have one. My plan also was to give her my electric fan, after I leave, because on my last trip I gave my fan to Chita, and it is still going strong. But because of the terrible experience I had arriving this time, with both brand-new fans getting broken on the way, I am not so sure. I think fleetingly of giving the fan that still works, sort of, to Rafaela with the condition that when I return, I can use it again during my stay. Then I am ashamed and think, "Give her the fan! What are you thinking of!" So when I leave, I tell Rafaela that she will get my fan. She is delighted. A fan here costs seventy-five dollars, the same fan that costs fourteen at home. That is how all appliances cost in Mexico, and they are not even as sturdy as whatever is from the USA. Thinner metal, thinner wiring, smaller scale.

If you ever give anything electrical to a relatively poor person in Mexico, or shall we say, a person in humble circumstances, give them also an extension cord and an outlet plug adapter that accommodates our type of prongs, the one side larger than the other. A person with very little money may only have one light bulb and one outlet in the entire house, or at least not much more than that. Electricity here is terribly expensive, so most people of Rafaela's income have little more than a radio and a small gas stove, if that. A canister of propane gas for the stove is also expensive.

Since I am thinking about this, and since Rafaela is finally going to have a little time with her children, because she gets

Saturday afternoon and all day Sunday off, I give her one hundred and twenty pesos, "Para el fin de semana", (For the week-end), I say. I am thinking that she can maybe buy a little extra food, or something required by the children's school. She is very grateful. It is only twelve dollars.

I finish my painting which is of a fountain on the street. When Abelardo was still alive, street fountains provided clear, clean water for the people in the surrounding blocks. Also, burros were still in use to haul in things from the country-side, and the animals needed their drinks of water too. Today the old fountains are still there, too beautiful to even think of removing, but not as many have water. I think this is because the problem of littering is world-wide, and sometimes snack wrappers or plastic cups are carelessly tossed into a pristine fountain. Probably all the downtown houses and businesses have their own water now, and burros are rare. I like my painting of this particular fountain, and I am already thinking of walking around to locate another paintable scene.

My first walk though, will be back to the little dusky store with its rows on rows of brown cardboard boxes lined up on shelves, contents being small parts for every repair possibility, and sundry other items. Once again, I am seeking a sink stopper.

I buy two, one larger than the other, to leave on the edge of the roof-top cement laundry tubs. Whoever does the wash up there next will be delighted. Chita was so pleased when I brought her one for the downstairs sink in the laundry room where she does a lot of scrubbing by hand. She had been using a foul, stinky rag as a stopper, so she was happy with my surprise. Except that after she only used it once, the dog found it, chewed it to bits, and swallowed all the pieces, except the part with the metal ring.

Finally it is six thirty, and Nita and I get dressed up to go out to dinner. Nita says that Raúl didn't go with his family because he slipped and hurt his back. She asks if he can come with us. "Oh, of course!" I am delighted. I say, "I thought he was sleeping off pain pills", but Nita says, "No, he can come."

We all walk to the restaurant in time to get a perfect table, right next to the sidewalk, facing the Jardín across the street. Barriers against auto traffic are put up on week-ends, so the street is filled with families, children, couples, all having a cheery late afternoon. La Tuna plays just like Trío Los Panchos, the same as was always played for Abelardo and me to dance to under the stars after a wonderful late, late dinner at El Patio.

We are in the perfect position to watch the parade that now comes by in honor of The Queen of San Miguel. Soon clowns on stilts pause right in front of us to do the hypnotic stilt-dancing that is shown in "Teatro Bellas Artes" in the beautiful marble palace in downtown Mexico City. They are dressed Vera Cruz style, and their dancing is about the magnificent fish in the ocean, slow, languid, dreamy, with beautifully colored streamers and paper-mache giant fish creations held on long poles and waved around to imitate swimming. It is entrancing.

We all order my favorite of the specialties of this restaurant, red enchiladas. We have a wonderful time laughing, eating, and talking. Raúl goes home because of his back, and Nita and I decide to stroll through the park. On the other side of the park we see the platform for the crowning of The Queen of San Miguel, and we watch the ceremony.

Like all such pageants, the contestants are dressed in their absolute best, groomed and made-up to be beautiful, and each one is cheered on by her excited family and friends.

Now there are more clowns, and next a fine trapeze act. The poles for the trapeze rigging have been pounded and anchored right into the cobblestone street. The act takes me back to my own circus days, when I too performed as an aerialist. I long to climb up on own my rigging, gone these many years. I still have dreams that somehow, somewhere, I discover a place with the right rigging, all set up, which someone allows me to use.

This did happen to me once, in southern Mexico, when my college abroad group was on an expedition to explore remote, little known pyramids. We arrived in a tiny town at night and saw banners for a small circus. I immediately found the circus tent and asked to see the Ringmaster. Wherever I mentioned the name of my step-father, in those days, every circus person of any standing knew of him because he had been advance man (business end, not performer) for Ringling Bros. for twenty years. And if they didn't know Joe Taggart, then they knew of my mother because of her calliope music which she played and had recorded to sell to circuses, carnivals, and Merry-Go-Rounds. And if the ringmasters didn't know about my mom, (many circuses had her music right with them to use daily), then they knew of my friend and mentor, Terryl Jacobs, who with his twin sister, Carol, taught me my aerial act. Terryl made me my riggings for Spanish Web, Swinging Ladder, juggling hoops, and a platform with wide diameter pipe for Rolla Bolla. He also taught me Rolling Globe, but a rolling globe is huge and made of cement, so I did not want my own. The twins were better known in the circus world as Punch and Judy.

When I explained to the Mexican Ringmaster who I was, and that I would like to practice my old act, immediately I was warmly welcomed and told what time to show up in the morning. Someone in the show would lend me practice clothes. Oh, it was so fun.

You see? Adventures always come to me, because I am open to them.

While I am standing by Nita in the Jardín, nostalgic for my act, the next performers do the exact same dance as I used to do when our dance troupe, directed by my mother, was giving an "Islands Show" featuring Hawaiian, Polynesian, and Tahitian dancing. Right here in San Miguel, dressed just like my dance troupe used to, are dancers twirling poi balls, although theirs are on fire. We usually performed indoors, and we never used fire. But our own poi ball act always brought down the house with applause because it is so hard to do, and it looks it. I am sure I could still do this too, so tonight is an exciting night for getting my blood pumping! I can't help it.

Nita and I are hungry for ice cream cones. We walk around the Jardín more, sit on a bench, surrounded by many, many people, and we enjoy the ever present Mariachis. Finally we come home.

17

ESTELA'S PARTY, ESTELA'S POOL-SIZED HOT TUB, AND ESTELA'S CASITA FOR THE NIGHT

Nita sleeps late, we go to the beautiful eleven o'clock mass in the gold encrusted chapel, and then she and Lita invite me to go out for coffee. I have to say no because I need to go home and pack for Estela's party. The party starts at one thirty, and it is twelve o'clock now. I am taking one of my paintings as a gift.

The party is fabulous. There are ten round tables set up in the outside dining room by the pool. It has its own bar and bartender to serve us, and we are seated at linen covered tables. The tablecloths and napkins are red, white, and green, the colors of Mexico, for a welcome party for Estela's husband. Everything is catered, fancy, and abundant. The waiters are attentive, I get acquainted with some of the guests, and we enjoy ourselves greatly.

It looks like about one third of the guests did not show up, or are invitations here kind of casual, and you just take a guess at how many might come? I am used to formal RSVPs for such a grand occasion, but Estela does not seem bothered by anything, so I suppose, once again, different country, different culture, different expectations.

Around six PM most of the guests leave. Now we are: Estela's mamá, four aunts, three brothers, one with a wife and children, Estela's children, Estela's husband, Nita, and me. And of course, beautiful, vivacious, talented Estela, the one so devoted to everyone's happiness.

The mom and aunts have been assigned to one casita, the single brothers to their own, the married brother and family to another, Nita and I to a casita just for us, and Estela's family in their own home, which is the main villa. We all go to the casita of the aunts and talk agreeably for quite a while. Then a few of us move to the hot tub, which is really a large, shallow pool made of blocks of lava which overlooks the cascading gardens, and far below are the twinkling of lights coming on in the streets of San Miguel. In the hot lava block pool we have reduced numbers to Estela and her husband, Anselmo (Estela's handsome brother), another of Estela's brothers, and his children, and me.

Someone brings floating lounge chairs for the women (Estela and I are the only women), and the dad of the children serves us beautiful little glasses containing port wine, which tastes like syrup of Bing cherries. This is to just sip a drop at a time onto your tongue and savor all evening long. Except since we linger in the pool, drifting around idly, until long after mid-night, some of us opt for refills.

I think Anselmo likes me, because he has stayed right by my side ever since I got here. He is so good-looking and interesting that I am tempted to like him too. Except that I am so off of dates or romances, or even going for a twosome walk, with no matter how charming the man may be, that although I am really pleased by Anselmo, I do not have it in me to encourage anyone. Maybe he feels the same way, because he is divorced too.

In any case, he is way too young. I am frequently mistaken for forty, and he is forty-five, someone has said. I don't want him to be horrified or repulsed by finding out that I am actually, let me think, how old am I anyway? I never have been good at keeping track of that. Maybe I am sixty? Around that, anyway. So I slip this information to him subtly by telling him about how old my children are, and something about my new grandson.

As soon as he figures out my real age, I sense a difference, but who knows, I have not been very good at understanding people lately, maybe. He is still fun and nice though, and the evening is all-around wonderful.

Nita didn't want to be in the pool, so she has been in the guest house assigned to us. There is only one bedroom, because although our casita contains a large bath, a living room, kitchen, dining area, and balcony, this is really a vacation house meant for a couple, maybe for a honey-moon. The bed is a king size, and there is a fan overhead. Nita has closed every window and will not allow the fan to be turned on. There are heavy, woven, woolen blankets covering the bed, she is wearing a T shirt and robe, she is in the bed under the pile of blankets, and still she is cold.

I am way too hot to sleep like that, so I go to the balcony, put down a cushion from the sofa (although it is only long enough for my head and torso). There are no blankets left, so I take pillows from a chair, and cover myself with a beach towel. Oh, well, at least I am outside in the air, the view from the balcony is beautiful, and it is pleasant to hear the roosters first thing in the morning, except morning for roosters is five o'clock, and once started, they do not stop.

18

THOROUGHLY BEFUDDLED, AND MAD AGAIN

When I realize that my rooster serenade is going to continue forever, I decide to enjoy it. I have brought a bit of instant coffee in a plastic bag. I boil water and sit on the balcony. It is great. There is a bowl of fruit on the counter, and there probably is coffee in a cupboard, but making instant is easier. I can't get to the shower or to my clothes without awakening Nita, but there are plenty of the irresistible, page-turner, vacation type paper-backs on a table. I am on vacation, right? So I settle down for a delicious read.

At ten o'clock, we all meet in the villa for a breakfast. All the family is there, the food is lavish, beautiful, and delicious, and we have wonderful conversations, in Spanish and English, because Estela's husband does not speak Spanish. He knows other languages besides Arabic, called Farsi, which I guess is understood all over the Mid-east, and he speaks English. But some of Estela's family members do not speak English. So we try to translate for everyone into whichever language they need, and several conversations can get going at once.

When breakfast ends, I say good-bye and thank you. The guests say, "Why are you going so early? Why don't you stay?" I say, "This was a wonderful invitation, for the party, the night, and the breakfast, but a good guest departs before everyone starts wishing she would leave." They all laugh. (I don't say, "Because I am not sure how long the invitation is for, and I don't want to embarrass myself or anyone else by asking.")

Estela asks Anselmo to be the one to let us out and bid us good-bye because she will be busy with her manager. Anselmo sits in the patio of the casita with me to wait for Nita to pack her things so we can leave together. We wait and wait, but no Nita.

Finally I go into the casita, and she is sitting reading magazines! She says she doesn't want to go, what is the hurry, and she wants to read more magazines. I have to relay this to Arturo, and he very courteously invites us to stay for another night. I am embarrassed, but Nita is happy, and of course it would be great to stay, but I feel awkward about it. "No, no" says Anselmo, "This is fine. You should stay."

Nita says to Anselmo, "First we have to go back home because I have to get something, and then we will come right back". Anselmo therefore has to give us two keys to the outside gate, because he does not know Estela's plans for the afternoon, and Nita has not given a time-frame for "right back".

As soon as we get back to our own house, Nita remembers that she has promised someone else to go somewhere, plus she had forgotten a breakfast date with another person the next morning, and she has errands, and there is play practice tonight, so "Sonette, you go back. I will stay here".

Now, whether I stay at Estela's overnight or not, I have to return to get my stuff. And I have to return the keys, and explain to Anselmo, and to Estela if she is there. I go inside the villa gates to find that everyone in Estela's family has gone somewhere, and of course the maids do not know when anyone will be back, and I feel so embarrassed and stupid. Nita has not left anything at the casita, I now see, so did she know all along that she was not coming back? I am thoroughly confused and befuddled. Should I gather up my things and go? What if Estela comes back for my sake and I am gone? What to do?

I think about Mary. Mary and I took many trips together, to Mexico, Latin America, and Europe. Here was our philosophy. "Nothing ever goes wrong. We just have unexpected adventures."

For my first adventure, all I can think of is to take a lime from the fruit bowl, add juice to water, and sit on the balcony. It is beautiful, and I enjoy it, but there is no one else anywhere in the compound, so after one and a half hours, I think, "Better just go back to Raúl's".

Nita is not at home. Early in the evening I make my sandwich as usual, eat and read in bed, and fall asleep. But I do not stay asleep. When Nita returns from play practice, she turns off the fan, which wakes me up. She is very angry.

"I have had a sore throat from that fan ever since we got here" she says. (I have the fan positioned so it blows right on me and then out the window and not in her direction at all.) She is also angry about the window being open, even though for quite some time now she has kept all of the windows closed except one half of the one by my bed. She goes on and on, really mad, and I have no idea what to say, so I don't say anything.

"I will go and sleep with Conchita", she says, madder still. "No, no, this is your room. We won't have the fan on", I say.

I go downstairs where I know the family has not gone to sleep yet because they stay up very late. I find Delfina and tell her that I'd better go home, and will Raúl please help me to change my reservation? "I am too much of a strain on Nita, and my being here is ruining her visit" I say. "No, no, don't go", Delfina says, just like Raúl. "It is only a few days until she goes to Monterrey with Ignacio and Fernanda. As soon as she comes back here, she goes to Guadalajara and from there flies to Cabo San Lucas."

No matter what I decide to do, all that is left for right now is to go to bed and go to sleep. Nita has left the lamp on, so I read Heraldo magazines until, finally, I fall asleep.

19

UGLY EL GIGANTE, PANORAMA PAINTING, AND SCARY WAR RUINS MY INVITATION

I sleep until eight o'clock and wake up with an inspiration. I can gather all of my painting stuff and take a taxi back up to Estela's. I will make a painting of this view for Estela. While I was sitting on the balcony yesterday with my lime water, I was looking intently at the panorama below. From there the view is, as I said, of San Miguel, tiny, at the foot of these hills. Behind the town there are other hills covered with crop land, or pasture, all in different soft colors, with rocky outcroppings here and there. In the distance one sees a series of high mountains in varying shades of purples and blues. Above is the huge and glorious sky.

I will sit on the balcony (spreading plastic everywhere, to be cautious), and I will paint all of this as a gift to Estela. This will get me out of Nita's way, and I will forget all troubles while I paint.

I arrive at Estela's, and she says I am just in time for breakfast. It is all of her family, just like before, and again, the food and the conversations are unparalleled. Members of her family have been all over the world, they have fascinating ideas to share, and I am in heaven.

Estela announces that we are all going to the house of the artist, Fawn, to see her paintings. Estela is supportive of every art. It is worthwhile to describe Fawn's house and her art, but later.

Everyone else is staying down below in San Miguel for the day because they have something to do, so I walk from Fawn's house by myself, up, up the high steep sidewalk to Estela's villa. I am admitted, deposit what I have been carrying into "my" casita, and leave the compound to continue walking higher up to find the store I have heard so much about, El Gigante. "El Gigante" means The Giant. It will be a big-box store, and I am confident that it will be impossible to miss.

After a while of trudging upward towards El Gigante, during which everything on both sides of the road begins to look dustier and less ancient, I arrive at the barren, desolate, bulldozer scraped land that contains ugly types of "modern" businesses and restaurants. There is a big highway, with no way to cross except run for it in between speeding cars, and finally I see, unmistakably, perched on a dirt blowing flat of what used to be a beautiful flower and cactus covered hill, a huge intersection, and on the other side, is El Gigante. If you walk on past this mega-store, presuming you make it across the road from the other direction alive, there is a high pedestrian overpass which I can use to cross an even busier street, since I am on the right-hand side, and El Gigante is on the left.

I climb the many stairs, cross the ugly metal structure, although I have to admit that I am glad the stairs are here, and descend safely on the other side, and Here I Am! I enter El Gigante.

After looking all around, as much as I can stand to, because I do not like big box stores anywhere, and least of all, here in the paradise of Old San Miguel, I find the wine section. I am thinking that when Estela returns, I can invite all of Estela's family to my casita, serve them wine or lime aid, and present to Estela the painting that I hope to have completed. Also, I need to buy something to eat for myself for later today.

I cannot bear to buy food in this awful store, with the hideous fluorescent lights of all such monster stores, knowing that "real" food is available almost everywhere else, so I settle for just the wine. I lug it back to the villa, stopping on the way at a miniscule tienda. There are a couple of dogs relaxing in the dusty entrance, kids hanging around the cookie and chips rack, and a tubby señora with a good, wide apron ready to sell me what I need. This is more like it. I buy one bolillo, a mango, and a slice of cheese.

But Estela's family does not come back. I paint and paint. I eat my little meal on the balcony. I paint as long as I have light. I put on my nightgown. There is always that entertaining paperback that I can read. And I can enjoy more time on the balcony watching the lights come on below.

Just then the phone rings. It is Estela. She says they have arrived back at the villa this minute, and they have decided to pack tonight and leave tomorrow. She invites me to have breakfast with them in the morning before they leave. Soon the children arrive at my door.

I already know the children, Clarita and Kairy, from when Estela brought them to my house, right after Richard filed for divorce and moved out. Kairy was enrolled in an American military camp for the summer. They all stayed with me for a few days of swimming and boating before I drove everyone (in my big, new Lincoln) to another state and to the camp. We stayed overnight in a lovely near-by hotel to be sure that Kairy liked camp, that camp was a good place, and waited for him to go through the orientation period. Everything was wonderful.

Later in the summer, Estela came again, I drove us all to see Kairy's graduation ceremonies, and then we repeated the whole thing- hotel, drive, swim, and boat at my house, and finally away they flew. Estela had invited me to come to Lebanon and stay with them, but I felt it would be such an imposition, and I was afraid that our government's curent war would reach over into Lebanon somehow, so I did not go. That is why

Estela's husband phoned me from their Lebanese villa, to assure me that I was indeed welcome, that the invitation was to be their guest at the villa for one month, and that the country was free and safe, perfectly at peace with the USA. Oh, how wonderful it would have been, but I was afraid of the war spilling over into Lebanon, so I did not go. That is another reason why I have been so happy to see Estela here. I have missed her. Years have passed between our visits until at last, here we are together.

Kairy is now twelve, and Clarita is eleven. The kids are enjoying being with me in the casita, and they stay for a long super-duper visit. They love the painting I just completed as a gift for their mom and are excited about it. Naturally with their mother's great support of the arts, they share the same interest. The children ask me to stay until Thursday, but I say that I have to see what their parents' plans are. I don't think the parents expect me to stay that long. I would like to make another painting of the same scene, but I may have to do it from memory back at the house.

Which makes me think of Nita, and that it must be a relief for her to have me gone for a little while. In fact, maybe that is why she got so mad after play practice. She must have thought that I had stayed at Estela's, that she had gotten rid of me for at least one night, that she could be alone in her own room. But when she returned to her house, I was not still at Estela's after all. No, here I was, back in bed in her room again, with the fan that she dislikes so much blowing away. I hadn't even thought about that. Sometimes people really need a break from each other. I guess it is natural.

Nita is, by nature, so dear and loving. She must be under a terrible strain by having me live in her room. Although we think of ourselves as sisters, even sisters of our ages, as much as I talk about everything being the same, the one thing that has changed is we ourselves. We have lived many years apart, and our life experiences have been very different. Usually when Nita returns to San Miguel, which is about twice per year, she comes by herself. So she has built a "San Miguel Life" that is now having to be re-adjusted to include me. Who knows what this makes her miss, even if it is just the solitude of her own room, her old childhood-memory-filled apartment?

And I have to give her credit that she invited me to come along to Cabo. Thank heaven I did not accept and purchase tickets to go with her, because now she really needs the time alone, and it would be so awkward for me to back out. Well, everything will work for the best, I have faith.

Before Kairy leaves me in the casita, he says that the family will be going out for breakfast, and I am to accompany them. He says, "Don't eat anything, because if you go very hungry to breakfast, then everything tastes delicious. Where we are going for tortas, you will love them. They are wonderful."

Tonight I can sleep in the casita's big bed, without blankets, and have the fan on, and have the windows to the balcony open. It is airy and cool. I fall asleep like a baby.

20

RUMPLED, SCRUFFY, AND BAD HAIR AT
THE PARTY, AND A GENEROUS OFFER

I sleep until nine o'clock and have awakened relaxed and happy. I brought extra instant coffee, so I can have that right away. I have no idea when the call for breakfast will come. There are oranges in the basket on the table, but what if I eat one, and just then Estela calls? Coffee will have to do. Naturally I drink it on the balcony.

Last night I had asked Kairy if he knew what time we would be leaving. "Oh, it will be very early, because they finish at one o'clock", he said. I don't know what he means by "early", but already it is not early any more to me.

I will read more of the paperback I began. I would rather start another painting, but I can't, because although the children are begging me to stay another night (and I am glad that they like me so well), I do not think that is in Estela's plans. Otherwise why would they have packed last night?

The children say they are dying to come back to my house in Lake Geneva next summer, and indeed I would love that, but Estela has said that it is not likely. However she has invited me to come to their house in Orlando. I won't, though, because I never want to be gone from Lake Geneva during the summertime. That is "The Season", and everything I love happens then. I only like to be gone in March, the Wisconsin mud month.

I have plenty of time to think over how awful I look today, and insufficient time to go back to Raúl's and get the fresh, clean clothes that I need. I didn't bring fresh clothes for breakfast because I was not expecting another invitation.

To look even worse, I had foolishly cut my own bangs not long ago, thinking that they looked perfect at the time, and therefore at the end of all the weeks in Mexico, the bangs would be way too long. My self-cut looked awful, so I had to trim the rest to try for harmony, and that cut off all the curl. Here I am with nothing for styling it since I did not bring my curling iron or anything else. My khaki pants that looked so crisp and smart yesterday are a wrinkled, embarrassing mess today. Naturally I did not bring an iron. I have all the right everything to fix myself up back in Nita's room at Raul's house, if only I could get at it, but I can't. And once Estela's family leaves for wherever they are going, I may not see them again for years! They will remember me forever as an old frump.

To stop thinking about my rumpled and scruffy appearance, I decide to set up my painting table on the balcony and at least make a start at another landscape. I don't want to squeeze out all the colors, the way one always should, because then I will paint in morning colors, and what if I am still here to finish it in the afternoon? Everything will look different. But I can get in all the shapes.

By ten thirty I give in and eat an orange. Anselmo comes by, and we have a wonderful visit. I wish men and women could just be friends, because I would really like him to be my friend. But he will soon go back to Mexico City where he lives and owns some business? A bookstore? A restaurant? Both? So I couldn't see him more anyway.

Then Kairy arrives and tells us to go up to the house. We are not going out to a restaurant after all. I am much happier to eat another wonderland, fairy-tale breakfast right here than to go out. (Except wonderlands and fairy-tales that I have read are always kind of mean and gloomy and are German, and today's fairy-tale is entirely and authentically Mexican, in foods, in people, and definitely in gaiety.) I don't know how else to describe Estela's phenomenal breakfasts though, except as so special that they can only be compared to fantasies.

Anselmo asks for my phone number, which I don't know, and it would be highly unlikely that he could reach me anyway. Being Raulito's best friend, Kairy tells Anselmo, "I know it. I will give it to you." But I think it is like a shipboard romance, great at the time, but forgotten after you reach home again. Anyway, whoever heard of a shipboard friendship? However nice, it is not all that lasting.

We all hug good-bye, I thank Estela and her husband, and

Estela says she will give me a ride downtown. They are leaving, so the villa will be closed, except for the manager, the guards, the gardeners, and the servants. Guests are booked to come shortly, and the manager will be in charge. Anselmo accompanies me to the casita and helps me gather my things. We all jump in the car, and off we go.

It is two o'clock when I get back to Raúl's. I go into the kitchen and tell Chita everything I can remember about Estela's villa, casitas, gardens, relatives, foods, servants and their uniforms, the children, even about Anselmo. Chita shares with me every Monday afternoon her week-end adventures on her rancho, and I feel like I know the place and all the people. I in turn share everything I can with Chita. (Although I never relay anything personal about the Rodríguez's family. Since Conchita lives here, she knows more than I do anyway.) Maybe I seldom take photos because I paint all of my adventures with words.

Before comida Raúl comes for me and asks me to come to the library to talk privately. We talk for a long wonderful time. He says that he and Delfina are offering me their own bedroom. Raúl will sleep with Raulito, and Delfina will sleep with Conchita. Such generosity and kindness, and all so that I will feel comfortable and not leave!

I thank him very much, very, very much. But I decline, saying that I will leave the fan off, the windows however Nita wants them, and I will be as quiet and nice as I can around Nita. It is just a few days until she leaves, and I don't want things to be bad between us.

Years later I will marry a diabetic, and he will explain to me that high blood sugar can cause what is called "internal aggravation". The person who has it is excessively angry for no apparent cause, and my husband says the person not only can't control it, but he cannot be convinced that it is not the people around him that are causing it. The diabetic who is suffering from this gets madder and madder the more you try to reason, or even to placate. In fact, my new husband tells me, the only thing to do is to leave that person entirely alone and don't even expect to speak or interact because you will not like the results. No matter what you do, it will be bad.

From this perspective, I will see that this is exactly what happened to Nita. But I had never heard of such a thing while I was on this trip, here in San Miguel, years before I met my second husband and had it all explained to me. I guess instinctively friends and family finally distance themselves until the other returns to his or her normal character, but that only works if there is somewhere you can go, or if the other person stays away.

Raúl and Delfina and I are living in the "now" without this knowledge, they have not heard of "internal aggravation" either, but they love Nita, and they know that this is not her true self that we are seeing. And they know and love me, and they understand that I am not the cause, really. (Although I still plan to make the changes in my behavior that I have contemplated and have begun.)

We go into comida, and it is cheerful because Delfina's sister, Margarita, has come to visit. Margarita tells us all about the terrible flood in New Orleans. I have not heard a word about it until now, having been engrossed in our own dramas, and never watching TV. Margarita's house and possessions are entirely gone. They were lucky to escape with their lives. Fortunately for her, Margarita's home was rented because she and her husband own a beautiful home here in San Miguel. Her husband was only working for a few years in the United States, or some period that made it too short to buy a house, and everything was great until the flood. We are all so grateful that nothing was lost except all their possessions (that puts possessions into perspective, does it not?), that the telling of this tale seems happy. That is because the destruction was so terrible that even if the only thing you have left is that you and your family are alive and together, you are rejoicing.

Delfina's father joins us, and he brings cheer wherever he goes too. He says he will fix my suitcase handle, which was ripped half-way off in transit. I was too asleep when it was delivered to notice, and by the time I did notice, maybe it was too late to file a report? Or maybe I didn't know how? Anyway, Señor Sanchez says he will fix it.

As I pass through the Botica on my way somewhere, Perla says that Estela and the whole family stopped by to say good-bye to me. Perla says that she could not leave the Botica to come and get me, and Nita said she would tell me. But I guess she forgot or thought she would tell me later. There is no way that Estela's family could have been able to wait for more than one minute, and even that would be long because of holding up traffic on the crowded, narrow, one-way streets.

I start to help Conchita with her homework. Her sweet, pretty girlfriends come over, so she takes a break to be with them. I use the time to finish the painting of the view from Estela's balcony. There is still a little left to finish tomorrow.

The view is still fresh in my eyes, and I think I will be able to make a successful painting. The first one is the hardest because I have to look and look to figure out, what is the shape? Where does it go? What color? What other colors are within the main color block? How can I paint details without picking at it with a too tiny brush, which loses the flavor of the over-all impact? Once I have figured this out, to the best degree I can, then in the next looking I can see even better, and finally I can try to put what I see onto paper with the paint.

I am ready to help Conchita again, her friends have left, and we settle down to finish her homework. Everything goes fine. All of a sudden, I am so tired. I make my torta and go up to bed. Before I am asleep, Nita enters. She has been gone all day with friends, and now she rushes to get ready for play practice. In a minute she is out the door and gone. I go to sleep.

21

ANGELS DELIVER THE VIRGIN MARY'S HOUSE TO SAN MIGUEL, THE GARBAGE RACE, AND DUSTY EXCITEMENT AT LA TUMBLA

This morning we go to seven thirty mass, and it is very special. I have said that on Sundays we go to the little chapel, the one covered in carvings and gold, the one with the tremendously high ceiling (in comparison with the very small floor space and so few pews), the one with the dead saint. All other days, if we go, we walk all the way through the main entrance of El Oratorio, down the long aisles, past the many rows of benches, past all the stone altars with their offerings of oranges, and trays of growing wheat that looks like grass, gladioli of all colors, past the giant oil paintings of the saints, or whoever they are, past the beautiful main altar, around the corner, and through the giant, wooden, carved doors that are not solid. The doors are made of ornate wooden bars, carved to twist, and mounted on iron tracks so the doors, huge and heavy, can be rolled aside, parting in the middle, to swing open in two arcs, admitting us to the small, small chapel, which today I learn is named, "La Virgin de Loretto".

Today is The Day of The Virgin of Loretto, and since this chapel is dedicated to her, there is to be a celebratory ceremony. There is a different priest than usual. He is a very clear speaker, so it is ok that he is not the one we have become used to. Extra lights have been turned on in the highest parts of the nave asp. I had not realized how many exquisite crystal chandeliers there are. Forty? More? It is so shadowed way up there, on every day until today, that I hadn't cast too sharp an eye on what might be way, way overhead. Now each chandelier is glowing with many, many lights, and the effect is breathtaking.

Festooned everywhere are fan style displays of the biggest pink carnations and white asters I have ever seen. There have to be forty, or at least thirty, of these lavish bouquets. In addition, there are blankets of flowers, three feet wide, and twelve feet long, hanging on pillars. This is a very small space, and although almost every inch of wall is covered by these splendid floral displays, there are still more flowers! Urns have been generously filled with the same flowers in the same colors, and the urns have been placed on parapets and balconies way up high! Everyone in town should come to see this.

So far I have not described this chapel of The Virgin of Loretto which is the one where we attend Mondays through Saturdays. "Our" chapel is not like any I have ever seen anywhere. We sit on old wooden pews facing a rectangular room. I don't understand why this chapel looks as it does, but eventually I find out that this is an exact replica of the house of the Virgin Mary (and Joseph, one would think, but I am not told that, so I don't know). Here is the story. Mary's house looked just like what we are facing, a rectangular room (with one of the small walls missing so we can look in from our benches). To give the idea of the missing wall, we are separated from the house by iron bars that depict the mortar without the bricks so we can look in. The central part of this "wall" is open so we can freely observe Mass. Today even the "open bricks" are festooned with flowers.

Inside the "house" are the altar, at the other small end, directly facing us, and on the wall above the altar, in the midst of carvings and pillars, there is a statue of Mary, not in the usual robe, but in a very elaborate dress made of layers of ruffled fabric, stiff, covered with gold edging on the white fabric. She wears a crown. Her face and hands are porcelain. Surrounding her are beautiful lights, flowers, the pillars, and fancy work.

On the side-walls are balconies, each directly across from the other, and on, or in, the balconies are a man and a woman, very elegantly clad, except they are made of painted, carved wood, and their dress is that of rich people in Spain a few hundred years ago. These depict the husband and wife who paid for this chapel, and I am not sure if they lived here in San Miguel, but I think they did. Why else would they donate this chapel?

(My eye for proportion is severely offended by these statues, because they do not have feet. In fact, they do not have long enough legs under their carved wooden garments. I have been coming here for months before I figure out that the devout man and his wife are meant to be kneeling, and the observer must forget that in that case, their legs and feet would be poking through the walls. It is not that I am so picky. I can't help trying to solve visual puzzles.)

At the front of the "house" are the various tables that the priest needs to use for mass, a podium from which he and members of the congregation read from the Bible, or lead the singing, or read from a Catholic book. At the other end, in front of Mary, are more tables and the little wooden double-door box on a pedestal that holds, I think it is called, a chalice.

There are a couple of chairs against the side walls. The walls go up only about twelve or fifteen feet, I am guessing at the height. The rest is open where the roof would have been, so we can see all the way to the top of the vaulted ceiling of this side-bar area of El Oratorio. The walls are painted pink, and black lines have been drawn free-hand to look like blocks of stone. (The lines are not exact, and I can't help but mentally correcting and straightening them each time I sit here looking at them during mass.)

Evidently the real house of Mary was somewhere around where the Biblical accounts took place. For some reason the angels lifted up the house, I don't know if Mary was in it, and set it down in Spain. The pious couple we see depicted as statues on the balconies paid for this exact replica to be reproduced here. There is a lot more to this story, but I can only relay what I remember, and at the time of today's service I had not been told even this much yet. It doesn't matter. The ceremony is beautiful, sincere, and so gentle.

Nita and Delfina are in a procession that passes in from the main church to this little chapel. All are singing, with very sweet voices, all are women, and they are carrying a velvet banner as you would carry a flag. The banner has been attached to a pole with a crossbar to keep the banner spread out. It is a painting of The Virgin Mary.

The masses are almost always about love. This one is about birth. Is this Mary's birthday? Christmas is the birthday of Jesus, so it can't be that.

Usually there are about fifteen of us in attendance at the seven-thirty mass we like to attend. Today there are more, so people not only fill the benches, but some are standing at the back of this little chapel, which means they are overflowing into the big side-wing of the main church part of El Oratorio, Still, there can't be more than fifty here. If they knew what this spectacle is like, I would think everyone in the world would want to come, except of course I am wrong. Very few people get as excited about beauty and sweetness as I do.

I don't have a chance to ask about any of my many questions about what all of this means. Nita and Delfina have to do other things and then come back here again because at twelve thirty there is another mass. Once again I feel glad, heart singing, and privileged to be in such a spot at such a moment, to be part of an "open secret", where everyone in the world is invited, but few have an inkling of the invitation. Wow! I feel that I am taking part in the most lavish of operas, even to trump the opera Aida, except there are no elephants in ours. We don't need any though, because what is presented to us is over the top.

Mariachis are playing down in front of the altar as we enter. The special chairs that have been set up in front have already been filled, except for a few in the very front row, so we walk right up there and sit in them. These are the best seats.

Some very important seeming priest dressed all in white and gold gives the mass and the sermon. While I am watching and listening, I am thinking that the priests must not get any exercise as they are all very fat and have a terrible time getting around, huffing, and puffing, and heaving just to get down into and up out of a chair. They probably get very little sleep and try to recoup strength by eating. That is very common.

There is a beautiful chorus way up in the old creaky, splintery, balcony at the back of the church. It sounds like the weight of the chorus could cause a collapse at any minute, and you can hear the whole thing groan and sway as they enter and exit. But the muffled noises only add to the lilting, ethereal, far-away strains of what seem like songs so sweet from a great distance in time as well as space.

The rest of the mass is singing (there are no hymn books. A leader sings a line, and we repeat it.) There is praying, and kneeling, and standing, and reciting. Then communion and some tail-end stuff. At our little morning masses you can go up front afterwards to have the priest swing a little ball on a chain or shake a ball on a stick to make holy water come out, and sprinkle you, and bless you. "Our" priest always gives me extra, and I like that. I don't know if this is done for the whole big group today because we don't stay.

That is, Delfina and I don't stay, but Nita does. There is to be a comida for all the women who participated.

I go back home and go for a walk. When I return to the house, Conchita says that Nita phoned for me to say I can come right over to the church and be included in the comida. This is a very special invitation because, first of all, Nita must want my company again, and this is so considerate of her. She knows how much I like experiences such as these, where you see the church from the inside out, and where I can be with other like-minded women, and I would really like to go. But I decline. Here is the reason. Nita has told us that this afternoon there will be "La Tumbla" in front of El Oratorio, outside in the churchyard. When I asked her, "What is La Tumbla?" she said, "You know, La Tumbla, La Tumbla." She explains, mostly by telling that it is a fair of some sort, a fund-raiser for the church, with lots of food being sold, and with prizes, "Wonderful prizes! It costs just a couple of pesos each!"

I decide that Chita should get to have some fun. Raulito will be going, so as his former nanny, I am guessing that it could be within her duties to accompany him. Especially if I help her with the mountain of dishes after comida so that she will have one extra hour for going to the wonderful fun of "La Tumbla".

I am very excited and tell Chita about this opportunity, practically once-in-a-lifetime, really, and she just must go. I insist that I will help her with the dishes, if fact, I insist on cleaning the entire kitchen because I do it three times a day at home in Wisconsin, and I am looking forward to doing some dishwashing. I can't wait to wash some dishes. I miss it. (At least, this is what I want her to believe about my love for dishwashing.) She must, must, must go with Raulito to "La Tumbla".

Raulito joins me, "Yes, Chita, you come too." "See", I say, "He has no one to go with. How can a boy have any fun at a fair if he has to go all alone?" We are starting to weaken her, but she has her job, I am a guest, and it would be a terrible disgrace to let a guest wash the dishes. (I already have, lots of times, but always while she was on an errand, or doing the wash, or asleep at night, and she didn't know it or couldn't stop me.)

I have already given her twenty pesos, thinking at five pesos a shot, doing whatever La Tumbla is, she should have a good time. Raulito has a little money of his own from his allowance.

"Go", I say, "Go!" But she doesn't go. I take a dish towel from the hook on the wall. I roll it up and snap it at her. She is laughing. "Fuera!" I say, "Fuera!", because that is what everyone says to the dog when she gets into the kitchen. It means "Get out!" I snap her and shout her towards the kitchen door, hold the door open with my foot, the way we do for the dog, and finally she and Raulito go out together. "Ahhh", I sigh.

Just as I am basking in my success and starting on the dishes (which aren't quite as many because Raúl and Delfina have gone somewhere for comida, and Nita is not here either), Chita returns at a run. "Basura!" "Garbage!" No one ever knows when the garbage man is coming. There is barely an inch to spare on the sidewalks for pedestrians, and no space either in the streets except for one car at a time. Garbage cans would never fit on sidewalks or in the street, and besides, this is charming, beautiful, fairy-tale San Miguel. Garbage cans lined up along the picturesque streets? No way.

Garbage is collected whenever, which means that there is no schedule of any kind, except you know the garbage collector is coming by the loud ringing of his very distinctive bell, which really is not a bell. It is a hanging bar of metal, like for use in an orchestra. At the beginning of every block, he strikes his melodic metal bar a few times, and everyone knows exactly what it means. It means, "Here I come to get your garbage, ready or not. Run, run, run as fast as you can, or your garbage will overflow for maybe several days, and what will you do then?"

Chita has heard the bell, and all the cans, one at a time, must be dragged from under the stairs where they are kept outside of the kitchen, across the patio, up the step to the entry way, over the threshold of the people door (there is no time to open the entire, grand, swinging doors on their tracks), and out to the street for the garbage man. Go back inside, lock the door, speed back to the other cans, drag them quickly to the outside, hurry back, drag, hurry, slam, open, until finally all the garbage has been safely placed where the garbage man is just barely arriving.

Stand there and watch, be sure nothing falls to the ground as ugly litter, drag all the cans back, nestle them under the stairs again, shut the clanging, clanking metal door that obscures them from sight, and turn the key that keeps the dog from overturning them and spreading rubbish everywhere.

Done at last. "Now! Go, Chita, go on!"

I can't know if she is truly gone, but she is not to be seen, so I hope so. I finish the dishes and sit in the patio to be on doorbell duty, since hopefully no one is at home except me. What I am really doing though, is thinking up a reason to keep sitting here, watching to see if Chita has really gone, and this way I can pretend that I am not spying, being a busybody.

Good heavens, here she is again. I guess I have got it all wrong. So I give up meddling, for a while at least. Wait a minute. I hear Raulito in the library having his drum lesson. No wonder they didn't go to La Tumbla.

In case you ever go to Mexico and want to buy a battery, the word is not "batería". Sometimes you can just "Mexicanize" an English word into Spanish, and you will be right. When you are not right, it is called a "false cognate", and this is a perfect example. The big elaborate drum set that Raulito has is called a "batería", so don't think you can go buy one in a drugstore for your camera. (I may as well tell you that a small battery is called a "pila", as long as I have brought it up.)

Raulito loves his batería and practices loudly and often. This is great by me because I love racket and clamor, of certain sorts. I am the one who always buys whistles and cymbals for children and encourages them to march through the house having a parade. So I frequently invite myself to Raulito's drum practice sessions. He is delighted that anyone wants to be an audience.

After Raulito's lesson, I will help him with his homework, if he has any. If not, I am going to paint. Painting is going very well, and I am painting whenever I can. I have been told that at seven thirty this evening we women will be going to another mass because of this being "The Day of The Virgin of Loretto". It will be one half hour of just pure singing by women. What will they sing? The rosary? I never know exactly what will happen until it does happen, and sometimes even then I still don't. I don't care, it will be beautiful. The vast edifice of the church and all of its chapels make voices echo and drift, they become softer, more other-worldly.

"El Oratorio" means The Prayer Place. Orar means to pray from your heart. Rezar means to recite the official prayers that one has to memorize. When first Abelardo asked his mother if he could bring me to church with his family, she asked him, "Sabe rezar?" I thought that a strange question because I didn't know that there were two verbs and two meanings for "to pray". I thought she was asking, "Does she know how to pray?" I may not have been Catholic, but who doesn't know how to pray? I thought. It is like asking, does she know how to breathe? If you know how to talk, then you know how to pray. You are talking to God, that's all. Later I understood that she meant, did I know the formalities, the ritual. I did accompany the family, but other than Abelardo's mother's puzzling question, I do not remember anything else, and I don't think I ever went again. I am sure making up for it now!

Raúl and the family appear from the Botica, and he and Delfina want to go out again, so he gives me the money to pay the drum teacher because Raulito will stay behind and finish his lesson. After I pay him, I tell Chita that I will come too to La Tumbla, and Raulito is excited to go. Ok, finally, this time we really leave.

After all of this effort to get to the church fair, I am startled to see…nothing. This is not a fair. There are a few food tables, of donated desserts, and a couple of tables for eating. And there is one lonely table next to the wall of the church, containing La Tumbla.

On the table are the most tired, dusty prizes that I have ever seen. There is not one prize that I would want for free. It turns out that "La Tumbla" means a drawing when you put numbers in something that tumbles them around, and then you pick a number that matches a number stuck to an item on the table. Except there is not even a tumbler. The numbers are just hand written with ballpoint pen on scraps of paper and put into an open basket. There are four women staffing this table (no customers), and one of the staff is Nita.

Nita thinks the whole affair is wonderful, her eyes are dancing, and her face is radiant. This is good, but this is the only part of the event that I can call good. All of it is so much lower than my expectations that I can hardly describe it. On the table are prizes, so pathetic that Mary and I would have been hysterical with laughter and would have to pretend to fall over into coughing fits in order to get away before our laughter became screams, and we would offend everyone present.

Except there is one thing that someone could conceivably want. It is a huge red pitcher with six tall red glasses, all hand-blown, made right here in the center of San Miguel. Chita really, really likes it.

I have only given Chita twenty pesos, understanding that whatever was going to happen here today will cost about two pesos, maybe as high as five. But each chance at La Tumbla costs twenty pesos. It will take all that Chita has, yet she gives it a try. Naturally she does not get the red pitcher with six red glasses. She wins a ceramic picture frame which disappoints her considerably. I say, "Let's take a walk".

Everything is closed, it is too late in the day, so even window shopping or browsing is not an option to make up for her disappointment. I tell her that somewhere in the market, when it opens, I will find a pitcher like that for her and buy it. I buy her an ice cream cone, one dip chocolate and one dip vanilla to cheer everything up. She says she is too full and does not want it. Of course I eat it, in that case.

We wander back to the display. Raulito did not go strolling with us. He is spending all of his money at La Tumbla. He is the only customer. He has already won several horrible prizes.

- A very dirty pair of chartreuse pants that some store must have had on display since the seventies.
- A mirrored box with doves painted on top. (Raulito considers this the worst.)
- A set of six Tupperware sandwich boxes. (He likes this prize the best.)
- A huge box of powdered Gater-Aid.
- A coloring book with a small set of crayons.
- Another set of crayons accompanied by an empty box.
- A rosary. (Donated by Nita)
- A pair of huge chandelier earrings. (Donated by Nita)

We greet Raulito. There is no other customer in sight. In the open basket that holds the folded papers, you can kind of see the numbers, backwards, of course, because of having been doubled over. Raulito is starting to think, at last, about how this drawing hasn't gone very well so far. He starts fingering the little folded papers which are still in the open basket. The basket sits on the table forgotten.

The women in charge have gotten completely bored (except Nita), and they are not paying much attention to Raulito. In fact, they have all been there for three hours, we have been their only customers, and they do not care anymore what he is doing, just a kid fiddling around and touching things.

I stand next to him and quietly say, "I think Chita is hoping for number 39." I tell him that she has tried twice now (I paid for a second try), but she didn't like her prizes. "What she really wants is prize number 39."

Raúl pays the last of his money to one of the ladies and hands her the paper he has chosen for himself. "This one" he says. My goodness, it is number 39! We go home very happy. It was a good end to a terrible game, and I don't feel like a criminal at all. We were the only customers all night, except we watched as two other young couples bought one chance each. The second woman disliked her prize so much that she gave it back.

(I do feel a little guilty, though, about laughing so much. Chita has a good sense of humor too, just like my Mary, and during parts of all this, we didn't even dare to look at each other and tried to pretend that our laughing at the prizes, and the "wonderful fair", is about something else entirely. Do I sound so mean spirited to make fun of everything? Can't help it. To me, usually, the world is a very funny place.)

When Nita comes home, she is happy too. She says that it is too bad that I didn't come to the comida at El Oratorio. They had every wonderful and typical Mexican food, including tamales, pigs' feet, and ice cream. Not only that, but the comida was served upstairs, where no one is ever allowed. The guests got to look all around, or maybe it was just that no one stopped them from looking, I doubt if it was a tour. The upstairs is full of secret rooms that were used by the nuns when it was a convent. This would have been an extraordinary opportunity because for sure nothing would have been changed in any way. I wonder if anyone lives up there now?

Maybe the caretaker lady of the chapel patio, the one called "face of the devil" by the mean man, maybe she has a room up there? I know that she told Nita and me that she has "a room" where she lives alone, not "a house".

Speaking of a house, Raúl's house has had more than the usual workmen and the tunnel–excavation-geologist-archeologist crew here lately. The regular workman who is on lifetime employment as maintaining this house, moving from one room to the next, taking one or two years per room as he goes, has been busy plastering for the last two weeks. The tunnel examination crew comes by from time to time. And now, last week and this, holes are being drilled into the walls, low down, fairly near to the floor.

Into these holes are inserted metal pipes, and plastering is done around them to neaten up the look. The reason is to drain moisture out of the three hundred and sixty-five year old walls surrounding the courtyard, meaning the walls which are under the arches that surround the courtyard. Underneath the house is a great deal of moisture which must be dealt with. The damp seeps and creeps up the walls, constantly moving upward, and even seeping up inside the stone pillars.

The procedure of drain installations seems to be completed because painting of the walls has begun. The walls, all the way to the ceiling, are chalk-white, except for a band of brick-red painted from floor to chest high. The pillars and portals are of gray granite. The doors are wooden frames with glass panes, authentic and expensive. The horizontal parts of the arches are painted the same deep, brick-red as the bottoms of the walls, and the vertical parts of the arches are the same flat white as the walls. The two story high ceilings are dark, ancient, hand-hewn beams with dark red bricks laid on top

The floor under the arches and in the patio, wherever there is a floor, are clay tiles glazed with golden swirls of the same deep, rich red as the walls. It is the floor, which is relatively new, maybe only forty or fifty years old, that is the source of the moisture problems. Their ceramic glaze seals in the moisture underneath, so the damp travels up into the walls and the pillars instead. The original floor used to be made of porous, unglazed, red clay bricks. I don't know if there was a floor at all in the patio itself. Maybe there were just walkways?

The granite fountain in the center is of large concentric circles, small, hand glazed tiles lining the inside. On the stone edges of the fountain, and on the concentric rings at the base, like a full skirt spread out, are rows and rows of potted, flowering plants, principally geraniums. The rest of the patio is crowded with fruit trees- fig, avocado, bitter oranges, lime, and papaya. Bougainvilleas cling to walls, sending upward their thick vines laden with violent-violet colored blossoms, and fiery-orange colored blossoms, spilling a profusion of flower clusters up to the top of the patio walls, and then back down again. There are rose trees, and many huge-leaved plants, descriptively named "Big Leafed Plant", sprouting out from vines as thick as a man's arm. There are an uncountable number of potted plants, giant ferns (taller than a person), hundreds of clay jars too large to encircle with your arms, and all are filled with ferns and flowers. Pots are everywhere, on the ground, in black metal tall plant stands, next to benches, clustered at doorways, and on every conceivable surface. They are under the arches, they are on table tops, they surround benches, they are beautiful.

22

NITA SNORES, AND SONETTE SNORES

Last night I was awake for hours because of Nita's snoring. (Before you can think, my goodness, are you criticizing Nita again? I must say that it is essential for you to know about this because of later in the story.) Actually, Nita is normally the kind of sound sleeper that I envy. It is she who has to put up with me, because I am a terrible sleeper, and most people would consider me an awful nuisance. I would not enjoy it, if I had to put up with someone like me. I toss and turn. I go to the bathroom, squeezing as quietly as I can through the creaky, clanky metal door that sounds like explosive crashes each time I try to silently pad to the toilet and back to bed, but I never succeed in not making a racket. And of course I am flushing the toilet about five times a night. It is Nita who so kindly and patiently puts up with me. Luckily, she usually does not wake up. Also, she even tolerates me turning on the lamp, with its shade bent to not shine in her face, so I can read during many a sleepless hour. So, no, I am not criticizing Nita. I am telling about one thing that happened that will later lead to another thing that happens.

At five AM I think, "I just have to get some sleep", so I say to her, "Nita, will you turn over? You are snoring." She says, "Well, last night you were snoring, and I didn't say anything." Oops. She is undoubtedly right. She goes back to sleeping again, and sets into snoring. I, justly chastised, go back to lying wide awake. About six o'clock, I fall asleep. We sleep until eight fifteen, so we both feel ok. Everything always seems better in the morning.

23

THE SHOUTER TAKES A TRIP, LAWYERS & LEGAL FEES, AND REVOLUTION RELIVED

Although only separated by a few hours, my night has finally become my day. We both awaken, shower, and we feel very cheerful. Normally Nita and I get along great, and I am glad that we are back to being jolly friends again. I am delighted about something else happening here today too. The shouter is leaving for a trip that will last for two months!

The shouter is a very nice, intelligent, good-looking American who lives in one of the apartments on the roof where, as a child, Raúl lived with his mamá y papá, his mom being Nita's sister. There is nothing wrong with the shouter man, I assume. I don't know him at all, but Raúl seems to like him. It is just that every time he passes by our apartment on his way up the outside staircase, he yells in his loudest voice, friendly things that he says to the dog, like, "Good girl, good girl, good girl, good girl…." Get the picture? But it sounds more like, "GOOD GIRL, GOOD GIRL, GOOD GIRL, GOOD GIRL…" a lot more times than I have written. I guess any dog likes to hear "Good girl", and for the dog, there is probably no such thing as too many. But for someone who was sound asleep, there is definitely such a thing as too much of a good thing.

In the day I like hearing things like that, little pieces of friendliness and affection. It is cute. But in the night, and whatever the shouter does has him coming home very late at night, according to the fact that I have already gone to sleep, it is not at all cute. It is awful because he wakes me up, and I can't get back to sleep. I think he comes up the stairs, which means about three feet from my open window, between midnight and three AM, as a rule. The shouting doesn't happen if the dog is already locked in the laundry room for the night, but Raúl's family keep very late hours.

371

More fairly I should say, they keep normal Mexican hours, and I keep early American hours. It is hard to reprogram your body.

I know that I am the odd one, so I never say anything about it. After all, this man has lived up on the roof for years, I guess, and his shouting doesn't seem to bother anyone else. Now that he is leaving on a trip, I won't hear the two AM "GOOD GIRL, GOOD GIRL, GOOD...." ever again, and I did not have to be a complainer or a spoil sport! And he should be happy too, because he is going on a trip! Yea!

For our delicious breakfast today, Nita is not here. After eating her oatmeal she has gone to get her hair dyed. I don't know where Delfina went. The children are in school, naturally. Seated at the breakfast table are just Raúl, his two lawyers, and me. When we finish eating, I leave so that they can talk alone. I go for a walk.

I return quite a bit later, and now only Raúl and Delfina are in the dining room. They call for me and explain more of how their case is developing. Naturally the lawyers' fees are growing and will be enormous by the time the case finally comes to court and if something gets settled, if, if, if.

I think that maybe they can hire the lawyers on a contingency basis and explain how it is done in the U.S. The malefactors will have to pay for:

- Expenses past and future on house preservation due to damage caused by the digging.
- Ask for the same sum as the total of the repair expense as damages caused by time lost from working in the Botica due to having to supervise the geological searches and to conference with architects and repair and reconstruction workers.
- Ask for the same sum again to be paid to the lawyers as their contingency fee.

"This will give the lawyers provable grounds for amounts requested, and since their fee will depend on your reimbursements and damage awards, they will naturally work harder. After all, what you have already spent is substantial, and you have a lot more spending ahead", I suggest.

Delfina and Raúl are delighted with this idea and say they will approach their lawyers with it. I am hoping that I have been helpful in this awful situation.

Tonight is the performance of Nita's play. I will walk the one and a half blocks to the Teatro Juarez and buy the tickets. Delfina and I plan to go together, and Raúl will join us after closing the Botica at eight thirty.

I approach the ticket counter with my one hundred peso bill and ask for three tickets for tonight. The tickets cost fifteen pesos each (about a dollar fifty), so I need change of sixty-five pesos. But I with my giant bill (about ten dollars), I have presented an insurmountable challenge. They do not have that much change. I should please go find change myself and come back.

Getting change is an obstacle everywhere in Mexico, I have found. I cannot figure out why, so I don't get upset or try to understand, I just do as I am told. There is no other way. Except sometimes, if there are enough employees or friends around, someone will take your bill and go all over to other stores and shops just in case someone, somewhere might have change. I have never had anyone take my money and run away or pretend that it was a different amount. I am never worried. But sometimes you have to wait a very long time until whoever was sent comes back, huffing and puffing, and happy at victory, presents you with your change.

This time no one volunteers to go searching, so I have to do it myself. I have already been to the bank once today, standing in the long line, to get a roll of two peso coins (twenty cents) which I hand out to worthy beggar ladies, at least maybe they are worthy, maybe they are not, but I can't pass by and then sleep at night.

Oh, well, back to the bank. But it is closed. (I was going to go back anyway, because this morning even the teller at the bank told me, "No change, no change".

I return to the house because I want to look nice tonight. In my room I lay out my outfit. Dress- black crepe top with chiffon white skirt. Belt- red leather. Earrings- white hoops. Bracelet- red bangle. Purse- white washable weave. Shoes- Hey! These white leather high-heels were brand new when I packed them. What happened? The heels are all scraped, and rumply, and wrinkly. What the heck? I get out my paints and paint all the scratches and scars over with white, looks not bad, or almost not bad.

That done, I still have plenty of time. I know where the hand blown glass store is, just a few short blocks from here. I will go there (surely it is they who donated Chita's prize red pitcher with six red glasses), see what it would have cost, and tell Chita. Hopefully it will cost a lot of money, and she will feel even luckier that the wonderful set is hers.

When I arrive at the hand blown glass workshop and store, I find that they do the melting and blowing of the glass right here over the store, upstairs. Great, maybe someday I can take Raulito and Conchita, and maybe Chita can come too, and she can see for herself how her set was made. While I am congratulating myself on the fun plan, I overhear customers talking about swizzle sticks. I take a look. They are darling! Hand blown fanciful birds in tropical colors attached to hand blown twisted, clear glass swizzle sticks! Wouldn't that be the cutest gift for someone's patio drinks served in tall glasses on a hot summer day back in Wisconsin?

The asking price is a big ten pesos each (one dollar), and they even wrap in bubble wrap for tourist suitcase transport. Oh, boy. I will also buy ten topped with fish instead of birds. In fact, I have now bought all that they have. And thus I have change to use for buying the tickets. Caramba, things are going great.

I ask the shop owner about what the red pitcher might have cost. "Señora, it was twenty-six pesos each for the glasses, and one hundred pesos for the pitcher." When I get home, I tell Chita, and she is delighted. I suggest sometime we should go there. I have already asked at the store if we could watch, and they said, yes, if we first make an appointment.

At the theater, while buying the tickets, which is a slow process, I see on a poster that on Monday night there will be a free Mariachi concert in the theater. I suggest to Chita that we all go, the whole family, or else at least Chita and the kids and I. She is delighted and excited.

At last it is time to get dressed and go to the theater for the performance of "The History of the Mexican Revolution as Started Here in San Miguel de Allende". Raulito decides to come too. Goodie. We are planning to sit in the balcony, but Nita is waiting for us in the hall. She says the downstairs seats are much more comfortable, and she is right. Plus we get to see Nita much more close-up this way. She is very pretty in her make-up and costume, and she looks authentic.

The actors are very good and so is the script. What is of such interest to me is that the names of the characters in the drama are known to me because their homes, and many of the streets, still carry the names. And all the actors are local people, so what we are watching is a vivid, personal rendition of the history of this town.

The history of this town is the history of Mexico. This theater, and the house of Raúl, are only one block from where the original events took place, the birthplace of the second Mexican Revolution. It is an intimate experience, being surrounded by people sitting all around us in the audience, who are witnessing a vision of their own history via this drama. And the same for the actors in the production.

Of further interest, it was just this morning that the lawyers at Raúl's house explained to me that all of San Miguel is networked underground with large tunnels going from each of the Great Houses, connecting to the other Great Houses, and to the churches. The tunnels were built to be large enough to accommodate carriages!

The tunnels were built and used for the purposes of hiding from the Spaniards during the Revolution and during the 1920s and 1930s. Those of pure Spain blood were called Gachupines. They came raping and pillaging every so often, and the people needed places to hide. (Second generation were often a combination of Spanish and Mexican, called Crillollos. The third generation was called Meztizo.)

When the President of the Republic gave the order to close all the churches (church meant Catholic; there was nothing else) the tunnels were used to go to masses which had to be held in secret in someone's house. That is why Raúl's claim, confirmed by the experts, is so believable.

After the drama, which is excellent and makes me understand the events and the people better than I ever have before, I invite the family to go for desserts at Posada San Francisco, only two blocks from the theater. When we arrive, the owner says, "We are closed. We close at ten o'clock." "I say, "Three more minutes until ten o'clock. We only want desserts. Please, please, please." "No, we close at ten o'clock." I explain that we just came from the wonderful production about the wonderful history of his wonderful town in wonderful Mexico, and here we have one of the actresses, and we want to celebrate. I try one more "Please". He says, "Sí, muy bien, pasen." "Yes, ok, come on in." From our table we look through the open wall (there is no glass in the street-side windows), and we can gaze across the park and see exactly the building where the true drama took place. Imagine.

24

COMIDA IN A RESTAURANT, COMIDA STANDING IN THE KITCHEN, AND COMIDA IN PAILS

Nita tells me we are going to breakfast, a restaurant she has selected because she likes the bread and the coffee. We walk the two short blocks and enter through a door that I had never understood led to a restaurant, in all the many years of passing by. This is what is so fun, stepping into a secret when you thought there were no more surprises left. But you would be very foolish to think that about Nita, or about life with her in San Miguel.

There is a tiny patio, in the ancient style, with round cast-iron filigreed tables and chairs, each with a casual umbrella of manta cloth. Manta cloth is a whole story in itself. For now I will say that it resembles raw canvas, rough and cream colored. Trees, flowers, flowering vines are squeezed in everywhere. There are other small rooms farther back, and the farthest back of all is the kitchen. The smells are great, of coffee, of freshly baked bread, and of much more in the way of culinary promise.

We are lucky to get a table, and we chat happily until eleven thirty when Delfina, her sister Margarita, and Doña Delfina, their mother, arrive. I am happy to be all of us together, and all of us here.

Nita and I have the menus which were given to us when we entered (quite a while ago). Rita takes a look, does not approve of this menu, and calls for the owner. After a very long discussion, the first menus are removed and replaced with much better ones. What we have now are all-inclusive. The others were a la carte, substantially more expensive, and the new menus have choices much more to our liking.

I order OJ, chilaquiles with beans, and coffee. I add Carnation (which is what everyone uses for cream) and sugar because Nita was right. The coffee is delicious. While we were waiting we already have drunk several large cups, and I fear damage to my stomach or nerves if I do not temper the coffee with something at this point.

Presently we are brought a basket of hot, small, sliced bolillos, pats of butter, and a tub of fresh orange marmalade. Service is supposed to be slow. People who have magnificent cooks at home do not come to a restaurant to stuff down some food quickly and get out. A restaurant is a place of leisure and beauty, a setting for visiting with your friends, a party, an outing. Fast service, such as is expected in the U.S., is considered rude and money-grubbing. No one is waiting for your table. You and your happiness are all that matters for as many hours as you chose to stay. Nita and I arrived far before the rest, and even so we take a couple of more hours to eat, and then we linger for another two hours, talking. By Mexican time, this is considered just right, and I think so too.

All the while, although I did not suspect that there was a restaurant inside this block, a great number of peddlers are very familiar with it and have been coming in and out constantly. I consider this a nuisance, but all the women at our table are patient and gentle with each one. The women are taking turns buying a little something so that you can see a pattern to this. Each woman is carefully being sure that every peddler can make some kind of a sale. "They are working", is the reason given. So I buy too, even though I don't need the peach I am offered, and even though it is highly over-priced. The other women have not bargained the price down, so neither do I. As soon as I have done my good deed, the man tries to sell me his whole kilo! No, no more, enough is enough.

As we are leaving, the poor lady who used to sit outside of Raúl's house selling nopales, the one who cooked for me on my last visit here, comes in. We recognize each other. This time she is selling flowers that are used for boiling into a tea to cure stomach aches.

I give here five pesos. She looks a little healthier than a few years ago when I saw her last, but now she has only one tooth, right in front. She wants more money, some from everyone, but I don't like that and do not give her more. In fact, I really do not like being pestered constantly while I eat. I have to keep reminding myself that we are the ones with so much time and money to do what we are doing, and they are the ones with so little of either that I need to appreciate why they are doing what they are doing.

Every day I have been handing out anywhere between one dollar and twenty cents each to about ten or fifteen people. Sometimes more. So I am not stingy, and I am not adverse to giving. It is just that with these continuous interruptions while we are eating, I feel like... oh, well. More to the point, what do these peddlers feel like?

Yesterday I was down by the market when I saw a clean looking man in from the ranchos dressed in his best cowboy shirt and pants (trimmed with gold braid) selling mesquite honey. He had big plastic buckets of honey and was using a cup to dip out and fill take-home sized containers. He was standing on the edge of the sidewalk in front of the market, so I don't believe he had an actual rented, licensed spot.

I don't even like honey, but seeing his industry and attempts to present his product in the best way possible, I decided to support his efforts by buying some. I bought the size of a large mayonnaise jar for twenty-five pesos. It seemed too cheap for all the work involved, so I gave him a five peso tip. (In the States I found that fifteen dollars is more like it for such a home-grown product, at the least, and he was charging just two dollars and fifty cents.)

I think of all the hours and effort entailed in bringing his honey to the market, the danger of taking an unlicensed spot for vending, (police confiscate all unlicensed merchandise) and even what he had to pay for the bus fare, and the effort of getting his best outfit washed and ironed for his special day of selling. I think of his hopes, after all the work of gathering the honey, and getting his heavy and precious load here on the rattly, dusty bus that he would have had to take through the country. I think of how much he can possibly expect to earn, even if he has the good fortune of selling every drop. I think of his family back home, which undoubtedly helped with every stage of getting ready for market day. I think of the wife who will ask him, "How was it? How much did it bring?" I think of the children who will surely run to greet papá, and I wonder what he will tell them.

I take my jar of honey home and tell Chita to please divide it for herself and for Rafaela to take home? "Do you like honey?" I ask. Not only does she happily answer yes, but she also says that I got a very good price. Honey usually costs much more. I go back and buy a huge plastic carton full, for which I am charged fifty pesos, five dollars. At home, I tell Chita not to divide the honey after all. The big one is for her, and the smaller for Rafaela. Chita has lots of people living in her house. Rafaela has at least five.

Neither woman has ever in the slightest hinted about, or asked for, anything from me. I would give them much more if I could. It is not a question of how much I have to give though. I try hard to stay in balance of a friendship and as a guest of this family. I do not always know what is right for me to do.

Still, because I interrupted my own walk with buying honey, I set out again, and this time I buy squash flowers. (Although my intent was for Rafaela to take them home for her family's merienda, somehow they have been prepared for the family today, and we eat them ourselves, cooked into tacos and served for comida.)

All of this is by way of explaining that I am not averse to purchasing from vendors who need to earn a living just like everybody else. But somehow I am irritated by those who hover about my table in a restaurant. Yes, we are still sitting in the restaurant being pestered by poor, desperate people trying to sell whatever they can by going from table to table. Except there is an endless stream of them which to me is getting to be annoying.

In fact, right now, little girls selling chicles (Chiclet gum) will not leave us alone. They are trained to whine and plead and never give up until you give them five pesos for five little, white, sugar-covered tablets of gum. Rita buys several, more out of her own sweet nature than to get rid of the children. Don't I sound callous and mean? I sound mean to myself, but even I have limits.

These peddlers do not have formal jobs. Life is not as hard for those who do. Yet but even for servants, who work very hard, often far more than eight hours a day, five days a week, earning the week's pay is not easy either. Besides the daily bus and travel time, one must remember that workers and servants arrive home at what I would consider late in the day, and tired, and now must fetch water for preparing the evening meal for their own families. Therefore, it is the custom that whatever is cooked and served to the family for breakfast and comida should be prepared in a quantity sufficient for all the servants to eat after the family has been served.

Since portions are usually cooked and served one at a time, "preparing extra" does not mean making a bigger casserole, or a larger roast, or a bigger vat of stew. It is a laborious and time intensive procedure. Cooks and servants (not including the gardener, or the man who is constantly restoring and repairing the house) gather in the kitchen after comida, which in our case is always served at three thirty. Since we linger so long over our food and conversation, we often do not exit the dining room until five thirty. Then it is time to wash whatever dishes there are before they can leave.

The bus schedule is very important to follow in order for the servants to get back to their respective ranchos the same evening, which means that there is not time for them to sit down for a leisurely meal the way the family does, even though there is a little table provided in the kitchen. It is more likely that the women eat from their filled plates bite by bite as they serve, clear and clean up. The cooks would, of course, never ever dream of entering the dining room chewing, or with a morsel of food in the mouth, so I don't know how they do it. Raúl is generous in every way, and the food here is always magnificent. But in some families, I am guessing that this custom ensures that the cook will take extra care to make all the foods delicious.

When Richard and I were first married and rented an apartment on the roof of this house (which at that time belonged to Nita's father) we had a sweet little maid named Tecla. She usually brought her three tiny children with her, and they quietly sat on the steps whenever we were home, and they never moved or made a peep. Tecla was very close to having her fourth baby. She was twenty-seven years old, and her husband was nineteen or twenty. He was always in jail, and every week she had to spend her entire salary on bailing him out.

Anyway, Tecla brought all her children with her so they could have lunch, and probably there was no one else to care for them. I told her to make peanut butter and jelly sandwiches for them, and they ate as they remained sitting quietly on the steps. I considered this to be a nutritious children's lunch, and easy to serve, not knowing that Mexican children were not used to P B and J. But they were hungry, and they ate it.

We also instructed Tecla to cook sufficient comida for Richard, and me, and herself, and all of her children. For this purpose stores sold special blue and white speckled enameled pans. They stacked in several layers so that various courses could be packaged, topped with a lid, and carried home by one handle. Custom dictated that no left-overs were to be held back for the employer family (us). Everything went to the family of the cook, and there were many good reasons for this.

Tecla, as her job required, did all the shopping at the market each morning. I gave her the money, and she brought me the change. I could have dictated the menus, but I preferred to tell her that we liked her to cook anything she considered typical and liked herself. She was excellent. (I doubt that she would have had any way of knowing what was not typical, how could she?)

She washed all of our clothes in the roof-top laundry sink, ascended another stairway to the top-most roof, hung our clothes to dry, took them down, ironed them, and placed them in our closet. She scrubbed all the floors and cleaned the kitchen every day.

A maid, called a "criada" in those days, was expected to cook breakfast and a small evening meal as well as the big mid-day meal, the "comida". We told Tecla that the comida was sufficient for our needs. (We were only home from one o'clock to three each day because of our class schedules, and we didn't ask her to come in on Saturdays or Sundays.)

For breakfast Richard and I ate Rice Krispies every single day. There was no packaged cereal for sale in town except Rice Krispies and "Zucaritas" (Sugar Frosted flakes), which we would not consider. Richard came to loath Rice Krispies, almost with a fury, after a few months of nothing else. But we thought Tecla was doing too much work already without also making breakfast.

We considered her salary small, insufficient, but we were advised by the family that to pay more would throw the whole system out of balance. Normal Mexican families could not match the salaries of vacationing Americans, and problems were created in this way, such as resentment, and when the Americans go back to the States, then what about the criada? So our solution was to tell Tecla that she could leave each day as soon as she had cleaned the kitchen, and to arrive in time to do her work, but no earlier.

But for most criadas, after cooking and cleaning up from the evening meal, they arrived home very late, and many could not afford to have a stove or to buy the necessary propane gas, or even to have water in the little room they called their house.

I liked talking to Tecla, with her sweet nature and sunny disposition. She told me many stories, which in her eyes were true, such as that at her home, they did not have a front door. So, like many poor people, they hung a curtain over the entrance to their house. For this reason, a half-man, half-goat had been entering her house each night, during the late dark hours. "Señora, I have seen him. The bottom half is Christian, and the top half is a goat." (In a country where almost every person was Catholic, Christian was a synonym for Catholic, and Catholic was a synonym for human being.) "He comes in and drinks our soup." Tecla was too frightened to get out of bed and confront him. After a while he stopped coming.

Every night at three AM Tecla had to get up, take her water pail, and walk to the corner to get water. There were water spigots on most blocks, for the use of people who have no inside water, but like many public works, corruption reigned supreme. In the case of the water spigot, a man sat next to it, with the handle in his pocket, and you had to pay him to put it back on for the moments it took you to get water for your pail. Tecla did not have money for bribes, so she had to go to the faucet at the only time he was not on duty, between two and four AM.

So there was a very good reason why a criada should be allowed to take supper home after an exhausting long, long day. Maybe pay is better now, maybe systems have changed from years ago, but I have not seen anyone carrying these pails for years now. Certainly no one has ever taken food out of this house.

Back to today, after my reverie about Tecla.

Nita and I have finally left our restaurant breakfast. Do we go home? No, we cross the street to another restaurant! This time it is to meet Belinda and Tara Sautto in the magnificent garden patio of the "Bellas Artes", Palace of fine Arts. Belinda and Tara have coffee there every day at noon. It is far past noon, so Belinda has already left. Teresa remains with her gorgeous twenty-three year old adopted daughter.

Normally one does not say "adopted daughter". I think this is for my benefit because Tara never chose to marry. I'm sure she could have because she is pretty, smart, and funny. She is also sarcastic and can be intimidating, except if you understand her wit, which you then realize is interesting and clever. She probably was happy with her life as it was, but she did want a daughter, and it is evident that there is great love between them. I still feel close to Belinda and Tara because of staying at their hotel for months during my college abroad program. Belinda and Tara and all of their family were so nice to me. I loved Casa Sautto and later brought my own Spanish students to stay there at least twice for an extended Christmas break.

Today we have a great visit, as always. I enjoy Tara's wisecracks and breezy ways. By the time I get back to the house, I barely have time to dress for the discourse by the artist who was a guest at Estela's during one of the breakfast parties.

I arrive at the art lecture five minutes after start time, at seven oh five PM. This would still be early, by Mexican standards, because no one expects anything to start on time. But the artist is not Mexican, even though she owns a home and lives in San Miguel, and most in the audience are Americans or Canadians also. So it is likely that the program will start pretty close to the time announced.

I see the husband of a couple who were guests at Estela's, Juan Alfonso (whose wife is Camilia). I liked them from the first. They are tall, very good looking, and they have intelligent eyes. He waves me over to a seat next to him and tells me that Camilia had to attend something at her parents' house. There is a good crowd, almost all single women of my age, Americans or Canadians, intelligent looking, well dressed. There are fifteen rows of chairs, fifteen wide. All are filled. All the audience is attentive.

This is what it is like in San Miguel. There are far more single women than men in the ex-pat community. Probably most are divorced or widowed, have cash from their own savings or pensions, and here they are, all dressed up and having to be satisfied with the company of other women friends, going out often, and taking advantage of the endless and pleasant cultural events.

For married couples it is different. They are seen in bars and restaurants, laughing and having fun with other couples. They tend more to hosting and attending private parties. Couples have a different life-style altogether. I would be in the same category as the women in attendance here tonight, and although I probably could enjoy the friendship of many, I do not want to. It makes me feel lonely just to look at them. I like being single. I am happier than I have been for many years. I have no one to please or to get mad at me. But I do not want this life, the life of a single American woman in San Miguel.

I am glad that Juan Alfonso and I are seated in the front because I can see all the displays of paintings, and the talk is entirely about explaining the paintings. It is called "The Power of Symbols". I do not believe that there is power in symbols, but I am always interested in hearing other people's ideas and experiences.

There is not time for the artist to answer the many questions from the audience, so after the talk, I ask Juan Alfonso if he had any questions for the artist. Yes, he says, he did. And he starts to tell me many interesting things about his own life experiences. He believes in many of the theories just presented. One has to do with the arrangement of furniture in one's house, the orientation of the doors according to north or east, or something related to that. If everything is positioned wrong, your life will be all a mess. You can get an expert, a mystic? I don't know the title, to come and sense the bad vibes, rearrange everything. Do they have to knock out doors? And then you will all be happy in your family. I think that is the gist of it.

Juan Alfonso and Camilia would like to invite me to their house. I would like that too. They are such cultured and elegant people. They would like their children to be exchange students and want to know more about my own children's experience living with families in Mexico, France, Costa Rica, and Peru. They are beautifully devoted to each other and to their children, so I will enjoy a visit to their home.

I stay and help the artist with the clean-up of wine glasses and the cheese and appetizer trays. We put away the chairs.

It is already eight forty-five when I return. To enter the big front doors of the house, you pass by the Botica. The Botica doors are still open with Raúl, and Delfina, and Raulito all working. I feel so glad to be here with "my" family. I do not want to be one of the women I just saw who has to go out to dinner after the lecture, or else go home to an empty house. I invite Raulito to walk to the corner and get ice cream. He is delighted, and so am I.

Raulito and I sit in the ice cream parlor, enjoying our yummy scoops and watching the passers-by. There are no walls to the shop, just arches, so we can see everyone. I ask Raulito about life in San Miguel. He says he loves it because at age twelve, he can go out with perfect safety, and stay out as late as midnight, alone. It is true. The streets are always full, there are musicians playing in the Jardín, lights are everywhere, and it is very lively. Yes, he has freedom, has made a friend of every storekeeper, vendor, policeman, beggar, and all of the kids of other families. It is a good life.

I go to bed and read, waiting for Nita to come home from her last performance and cast party. Conchita accompanied her, and the show, the party, everything was great. Nita is justifiably happy and excited. Every part of the weeks of practicing, the performances, and the final celebration- all were a perfect success.

25

FORGOT TO MAKE THE BREAD, CHOCOLATE ON EGGS-OVER-EASY, AND LONELY SINGLES IN A BAR

Last night we had a wonderful and torrential rain. I love, love rain. First thunder and lightning as soon as I was cozily in bed with my book. Then came the crashing rain. Nita was still at the theater, which means it wasn't so wonderful for her two block walk home, but she was so happy that she didn't care.

At six thirty Nita has gotten up to leave on her trip. She is going to Monterrey with Ignacio and Fernanda. She will be gone for ten days.

I go to eleven o'clock mass by myself in the precious golden chapel. There is Doña Lita. "Doña" does not mean the American female name of Donna. "Doña" is a respectful title like the female equivalent of "Sir". "Ma'am" is not the same. We have no English terms as respectful as Don and Doña. It lets you call a person older than you by the first name until you become such close friends that you can drop the title.

I love today's mass topic. It is all about unconditional forgiveness and unconditional love. I have already read my Christian Science Bible Lesson this morning, as I love to do every morning, and after a life-time of Bible study, I have heard, and studied, and lived, and utilized the various Bible stories and teachings, so naturally I am familiar with everything read this morning. And the sermon's theme and message is familiar to every Christian, but today it is presented exactly appropriate for what I need to hear, it strikes me just right, and I feel happy, grateful, and uplifted. I still have much cleansing to do in my thought, hidden vestiges of resentment or self-blame for being tricked and deceived. I can't do this cleansing by myself. It is the beauty of today's mass, today's friendships, and today's yet to happen loving surprises that are washing away all the parts that are not really me, are not really part of my Sonetteness.

Doña Lita always comes to mass alone, and afterwards we visit outside in the churchyard. She says she waited all day for Nita and me to come and make bread, as we had planned, on Tuesday. (Nita had said we were not going to go, and that she would tell Lita.) I say that Nita told me that she tried to call all day, and that no one was home. Lita says, "But I was home all day". All I can say is, "I am so sorry. That is too bad." We agree to try again for this coming Tuesday, although it will just be me. I am to bring the ingredients, which are whole wheat flour and dry yeast.

I have invited Raúl's family to breakfast at "Mesón de San José", which means Saint Joseph's Inn. So now I finally know the name of the restaurant I have enjoyed so much, the one right across a large plaza from El Oratorio. I say good-bye to Lita and go to meet the family.

I get a kick out of our time-schedules around here. We sit down to breakfast after twelve o'clock, and we don't leave until two ten. Nobody is in a hurry. We are here to enjoy the beautiful, fresh day, the loveliness of our open patio surroundings, and our own excellent company.

We order the all-inclusive breakfasts which start with bowls of papaya, cantaloupe, and bananas. The open-walled kitchen lends charm to the intimacy of the cobblestoned patio where we are seated at a round table under a billowing, cream colored, cloth tarp which extends, on wires, between flowering trees, just gauzy enough to shade our table, and filmy enough to let in the light. We watch the cooks as they clank and clatter away at their tasks, so close to our gaze. There is only one waiter, a handsome, young, tall man, reserved but friendly. If there is enough demand for a spot of help from a second server, the owner's wife leaves her own table, where she and the whole family are enjoying their restaurant just as much as we.

Delfina and I order eggs sunny side up, except eggs are never hard fried in Mexico, so you do not have to specify sunny side up. Our eggs are served on top of corn tortillas that have been softened in hot corn oil, and then covered with rich, dark, sweet, chocolate mole sauce. I always order an extra bowl of mole because I love it so much. Raúl and the children make other selections. We are also brought, as usual, loaves of home-made bread, tubs of butter, and tubs of jam, and a tortillero filled with more hot, soft, corn tortillas. With this we are served endless large cups of excellent coffee.

Our conversations are always unusual, and today we touch upon the history of Mexico (because of the recent drama), ecology (because we all care and are filled with dread, so we need to encourage each other with advances made here and there in the world), Australia (because Raúl took his family there for the Olympics), and sharks. (Sharks because they abound around the beaches of Australia?)

It is three o'clock. Raúl has invited me to go out to another restaurant with the family at five thirty. Brunch was my treat, and he says the dinner is to be his treat. But I decline. I have nothing at all to do, no plan for occupying my time, but as ever, I believe that the family will keep on liking my company much better if they can get a break from me once in a while. And not only that, any family needs "alone together" time. So I thank them but say I am too full to eat again, which is true.

From so much breakfast, and from getting up early to say good-bye to Nita, I am tired. I sluggishly drag myself through town to the French Park for a walk. Its beauty and freshness always inspire me, calm me, cheer me up. Whatever I need, I find it in the French Park. It is my tonic.

Walking today is a struggle, hot, tired, alone, but things get better as soon as I arrive at the park. There are some paths open for walking now, which twist and wind through the semi-tropical foliage. The park occupies about two blocks of space, sloped as everything is in San Miguel, sort of sliding down the side of the mountain. Lovers like this leafy sanctuary, parents let their little ones run after each other, stir the fountains with sticks, and wander down to the play equipment at the bottomj part of the park. Teens and young men are playing basketball, and a charming little bandstand gets used occasionally.

I spend as much time as I can in the park and then meander further down the hill through little side streets to the Instituto. I stroll around and see everything the Instituto has to offer to a wanderer on a Sunday afternoon. I look at all the paintings in all the galleries. I glance at the giant photos with a lot of typed captions depicting something too serious for me to want to read.

I even mount the circular stairs leading to where Masters Theses are stored, just to see if mine is still there. It is. I read it and feel embarrassed for how well written I believed it to be at the time, yet I remind myself that a twenty-four year old girl wrote that, and keeping such in mind, I see that in it I laid the foundation for all I paint and bring into my awareness today.

I walk up and down through the crowded aisles of the Sunday Art Fair that can be counted on to always fill the central courtyard of the Instituto. I admire all the crafts on display by hopeful artists. I smile and compliment the creators of the beautiful art, but excuse myself from buying. "Just looking." "You are very talented." "This jewelry is lovely." "What beautiful weaving." "I admire your craftsmanship." "Whoever buys these will have a treasure."

I am sincere about each remark, but even for free I would not take anything because I am at a point in life that I do not want one more possession. I am an observer now, adding to my visual collection, not to physical acquisitions. Having less is so much more satisfying than having more. Naturally I know full well that no matter how much I eliminate, or do not buy, or give away, I will still have more than most people on this planet, and I will still live in comfort, and I can start replacing, and shopping, and bulging my house with stuff if I ever so incline. But I am not so inclined today, nor have I been for the last twenty years, or ten, or something like that.

The street that passes in front of the Instituto, if when you exit you go to the right, leads up the hill to the center of town. There are choices to be made, at a fork in the road, and I chose the branch which will lead to the church with a high, thick, thick wall, painted a golden orange, which at the top is scalloped by dips and points. Behind the wall is another Colonial church, the one belonging to what used to be the convent for San Miguel's nuns and is now The Bellas Artes. On my way up this road, I pass an open door.

Out of the doorway pours the live music of an American style blues band. I decide to go in. What else is there to do? I will investigate. Inside I am reminded of New Orleans because there are mostly Americans here, sitting in couples, or if single, at solitary tables. How sad. All are here for something to do on a time-dragging Sunday afternoon. All of the alone people are seeking company but don't know how to get together. I too sit down at a table by myself, order a lemon aid, and enjoy the blues, which sound very good.

Pretty soon I think, "I am not so shy as this. I will do what I always do, go and introduce myself." I see a woman who looks about my age, educated, interesting. I pick up my glass, walk to her table, and say, "Do you want company?" "Oh, yes" she says. She tells me that she is here in San Miguel for one year, alone, and that she always comes to this bar on Sunday afternoons because Sundays are very hard for singles, especially the late afternoons.

She has a daughter in high school. I think, "Left behind! How could you do that?" But I just say, "Oh". The woman looks too old for a daughter who is a teenager, but that doesn't mean that she is not attractive. She is a nice person. We talk all during intermission, and then the band starts again. I am ready to leave. I thank her for the company and go. As soon as I am partway down the street, I think, "How selfish I am. I should have stayed and helped her pass the time." But it would seem odd to return, and so I do not consider it an option.

I was not comfortable in the bar. I am not a bar person. I don't need to be here in Mexico listening to American music with an American audience. The people were not my type. Some looked cheap and tough. Men with long grey or white hair, old hippies, I guess. Women with too much make-up, several smokers. I know that if I made a few friends there, many would be nice to me. They are not bad people. They would soon include me in invitations to this and that. But I don't want any of that. I already have exactly what I do want.

I said that last night we had a torrential crashing rain. Perla in the Botica is delighted. I have not explained that for the last two weeks the entire one block of street in front of the House and the Botica was torn up by fifty workmen with pick axes, chisels, and spades. Every one of the beautiful, time-worn stones were removed, and great quantities of wind-swept dust billowed daily into the open doors of the Botica to thoroughly coat every single item on display, and the floor, and all of the counter tops and fronts, and even the walls and the ceilings.

Store-fronts in San Miguel may have a small display window in the front, or maybe not. Entrances to each shop are by floor-to-ceiling wooden doors. When open, the doors, which open in the middle, provide walk-in space, look-in views, fresh air, and sunlight. For the last two weeks, the open doors have also provided full access to all of the dust generated by fifty hard-working men bent to their tasks all day long, removing stones, digging up the dirt underneath, shoveling it into wheel-barrows, moving it from this spot to that spot, dumping it out again, and beating and raking the dirt into submission as a flat surface for a new road.

The new road would look pretty good if you were not familiar with the old road. The new is made of hand-cut flat stones, placed, spaced, and mortared by hand. But the old was better, had color, shine, a patina of two hundred years of feet on beautiful stones of a variety of only similar shapes, not identical gray rocks such as we see now. The old sidewalks were narrow, it is true, but the new, imperceptibly wider, give less room for cars and pedestrians to share the narrow street space, because two still cannot walk abreast comfortably, so stepping up and down to let another person pass is still going to take place constantly, no matter what. All of this looks too new and of little character and flavor to us. We are not only disappointed, but "we" are dusty.

I have not mentioned much about Perla, but she and I have always felt friendly to each other. Since so much of the family's life takes place in the Botica, I drift in and out of there almost every day. Usually no one in the family carries a key, and everybody uses the Botica as a short-cut into the house, whenever the Botica is open, which is almost always. Raúl and Delfina take turns working in the Botica with Perla, and Raulito is often there because papá is there. Raulito loves to learn by being just like papá, which is a very good thing. Conchita is there too, although being older, she has other things on her mind.

Now that Nita has gone, I need to occupy my time, and I am feeling that I would be of help to the family by offering to clean the Botica. How distressing it must be to face the monumental task of cleaning every single inch, and jar, and box, and counter, and all that stuff, stuff, stuff that comprises the stock. So I have volunteered to start tomorrow at nine thirty AM, which has Perla delighted. Understandably! I plan to report in full combat gear which means wearing my painting apron and the rubber gloves I brought along for washing out my clothes in the bathroom sink.

Our plan of attack involves using a tall and rickety ladder to reach the one hundred (or maybe only fifty?) antique, white, gilded, porcelain apothecary jars on the highest of the open-air display shelves. While Perla attends to customers as usual, I will wash them, in whatever ways as per how Perla will instruct.

As I have said, I feel better when I have made a little list of "To Do Today", if I am feeling a bit restless or a little blue. I am looking forward to being a cleaning lady tomorrow. But even acknowledging that I do feel adrift and a mite down in spirits, still I suppose I can say I feel ok.

It is only seven thirty, I have walked through the town to everywhere I can think of, and finally I am ready to call it a night and settle in. I could have painted all day long. This was the perfect opportunity. Why didn't I. Why didn't I want to?

I make my torta and sleepy-time tea. I carry them to my room, put on my nightgown, and get in bed to eat my bolillo and tomato sandwich while I read my novel. What luxury! I can now have all of the windows open. The fan is on. Music and street chatter drift into my room.

The siren of San Miguel's only ambulance screams, cutting through all the soft and sweet sounds of twilight. The siren indicates a dramatic urgency, "Everyone get out of the way, run for your lives before we race down the street and squash you flat, we must not be delayed!!!" At least, that is the siren's full volume message. In actuality every street is only one car wide. There is no room for anyone to pull over and let the ambulance pass, even if anyone felt like doing so. The ambulance is just as stuck in the crawling traffic as everyone else. Then why the siren? I guess it is just like owning and riding a motorcycle. Why would you have one if it couldn't be loud? Therefore, since the ambulance can't proceed to its destination, I get to enjoy the siren for a long, long time. And then I read, and read, and read. And finally I fall asleep.

26

ON THE LADDER IN THE BOTICA,
1848 SHIPMENT TO HERE FROM ITALY,
A SIX YEAR OLD MENACE

This is the big day! Cleaning time!

We started out, on this visit of mine, by having breakfast at nine-thirty. Lately the start time for breakfast has become unpredictable, drifting towards ten o'clock, and once in a while more like eleven. I am glad that Perla wants me to begin the cleaning project at nine-thirty. It gives me time to awake at leisure, attend seven-thirty mass, come back and drink cup after cup of coffee while I read my Christian Science Bible lesson, shower and dress, and all without haste.

Then just when I would otherwise begin waiting for breakfast with a rumbling stomach, instead I have somewhere fun to go, something new to do. Raúl will know where I am, I can off the rubber gloves and apron as soon as he sends for me, and I will be present at the table in a jiffy.

The Botica is a store of sorts, a drug store like others, selling Kleenex, cold cream, band-aids, perfume, candy, and a variety of patent medicines. In addition, Raúl fills prescriptions, and this particular Botica still has "ingredients", if that is what medicinal components can be called, that can no longer be found anywhere, or almost nowhere. This Botica was begun in 1848, I believe, and it must be unchanged except for the addition of Band-Aids (which are here called Curitas) and other such items. The jars I am to clean, starting with the oldest and most irreplaceable (and that is why they reside safely on the topmost shelves) have a long and interesting history.

The jars are called "frascos". Frascos are made of fine porcelain, hand painted with titles of their contents, and decorated with gold leaf. They were created and filled in Italy, crossed the oceans in ships, and trudged over the mountains from the port of Vera Cruz to San Miguel on the backs of burros, a journey taking six months. The frascos have stayed right where they are ever since. Many still hold bits of their original contents.

Each jar lid has to be handed down to Perla, from just one section of shelving at a time, which means ten lids, followed by ten jars. I am amazed to see the quantity of dust on each one, from only two weeks, blown in, dust carried by the tiniest breeze, each blow of the air lifting up dirt from the laborers' chipping and chopping.

Then climb down the ladder, trot each lid to the sink in the back room, individually wash it under the teensy trickle of water that threads its way out of the single, cold water tap. Then dry, and trot these on back to the counter, one at a time. The jars are not as dirty as the lids. We can wash them while they rest on the counter by using damp cloths which we keep cleaning out. Climb up the ladder again and clean the shelf. Now Perla can hand me one jar at a time, I space them perfectly to look evenly balanced, receive one lid at a time, replace, and finally we can start on the next section of shelves.

But this is not an uninterrupted process. Perla has a constant stream of customers. I must wait at the top of the ladder, unless I am in front of the sink cleaning lids and jars. It takes us hours to do just the top shelf, which we don't even finish. I am called to breakfast.

From two to three o'clock I paint. I am happy with my painting which is of a tall red house, fortified with thick clay buttresses to keep the house walls from toppling of their own weight. The house is high up the hill on the road to Querétaro. I think I have captured the look of the massive, strange, mysterious look of the red house which has only a few high up little windows, and a door opening to a tiny balcony, also very high up.

At comida, the family has quite a tale to tell. Little kids attacked Raulito at school! Some young troublemakers formed a gang which grabbed Raulito and held his hands behind his back while a six year old socked him in the eye and on the nose. Raulito could have beaten them all to a pulp, but luckily he had the good sense not to fight back.

The teacher said that the parents of those kids will have to pay the doctor's bills. Raulito is swollen and bruised, but we think he is ok, and the doctor thinks he is ok too, yet still the doctor wants to x-ray him when the swelling goes down.

Apparently the little kid has a history of attacking people. I am asked what my school would do. I say that good for Raulito that he did not fight, because then he would be punished too, even if he didn't start it. My school would start with a three day suspension and a parent conference with the School Board to know how they could be sure that other children in school would not also be attacked.

Raulito's doctor is mad because although the eye is ok, it could have been serious. Raulito is brave and smart, and he will not let this get him down. Everyone likes Raulito.

We eat our delicious comida, and then it starts to rain. I can't take my walk in the rain because of not having the right shoes, so I tell Raúl I will work more in the Botica. It is fun because I get to see what goes on there. No one notices me on the ladder. The Botica is a hub. There are regulars who come every day, tourists looking for Band-Aids, or for a few medicines like for diarrhea and colds, people needing prescriptions filled, a diabetic policeman who comes every day to get his insulin shot (given in privacy in a side room), little kids who buy a cookie or a candy from the big glass jar on the counter, and most interesting of all, the old, old ladies, the "ancianas".

The ancianas come first thing every morning, I will soon discover, to get their drink of tonic. They wear the long checkered skirts of the peasant "campesinos" (people who live in the fields), and "rebozos" (long narrow shawls), but the ancianas shuffle in wearing bedroom slippers, so they must live somewhere nearby. The tonic is a secret recipe, of course. To me it is mostly boiled, brown piloncillo in water. I don't know what else is in it, but a little glass-full gets them started for the morning. Vitamins and minerals maybe? Or just a sugar rush?

Pills, Band-Aids, cotton balls, anything that we in the States would buy in a package or a box-full, are sold singly here. Why buy a whole bag of cotton balls, or a vial of fifty pills, when all you need for today is one?

Raúl is a licensed pharmacist, so he makes up the prescriptions in the back room. I do not have any ideas about the laws today, but in Abelardo's time, the pharmacy was where you came for diagnosis and treatment, including medicines and shots. Doctors were more for surgery. Late one night a poor man from the country came banging on the door for someone to come and deliver his wife's baby. The only one who could go was Abelardo, who I believe was sixteen at the time. Abelardo knew no more than any kid his age, he told me later, but the man insisted that Abelardo must be a pharmacist because he worked in his parents' farmacia, and begged, "Come now! Come now! Come now!" So Abelardo did, and Abelardo delivered the baby. The grateful father paid him what he could, which was one egg.

"Farmacia" means pharmacy. There are other pharmacies in town, but a Botica is different. I think the difference is that pharmacies carry ready-made medicines and pills that they dispense. Raúl is qualified to make his own. There are other differences too, which make a Botica several steps above an ordinary pharmacy, but I don't know what is involved. Maybe it is because of the impressive collection in this Botica, of glass vials as well as frascos, many of which are labeled with a skull and crossbones. Raúl tells me not to sniff these when it comes time to clean the glass vials or take off the stoppers when cleaning them. As if I would! "No, Sonette", he clarifies, "Do not even breath when you pick those up." Well, ok then! I guess I won't!

When Abelardo helped in the Botica, you could sell poison over the counter. He said that Americans said you should not sell poison because it might make you die. Abelardo replied, "You have been cheated if you buy poison, and take it, and you do not die." Logical.

Since I have to remove the lids of the frascos, I naturally look inside. Some still contain medicinal ingredients which look to be leaves, sticks, crystals, and powders. The Glass vials hold the liquids and some powders as well. Since the names are inscribed in Latin, which is so similar to Spanish, I recognize the meaning of many, and you would too. I am startled to know what people take or took, but I guess all is fair in war and in medicine. I do not take medicine and never have, so maybe other people would not be surprised by what is new to me.

We continue cleaning just the same way as we did this morning. At six o'clock I stop to help Raulito with his homework. We work in the kitchen and finish in a jiffy. Chita does not want to go to the theater after all. That is, she says she does not want to, but I suspect that she has other duties which she must do tonight. Some things are private, and Chita never tells any of the family's business, which is a necessary trait for one who is trusted so much and loved so greatly.

That is ok. I go alone and do not mind at all. The performance is double wonderful. On stage is a complete band of Mariachis dressed in immaculate cream colored suits and with matching sombreros. The highly polished silver of the buttons and ornamentation on jackets, pants, and sombreros gleams. Their blousy bow ties are full and lavish. Their pointed cowboy boots are something to be proud of.

Almost the entire crowd consists of loyal Mexicans who, with wild enthusiasm, clap and shout requests. What a contrast to the dismal scene in the bar yesterday. Here I do not feel alone. Here I feel just like who I really am, Sonette having another beautiful adventure.

As I arrive home, and stop in the kitchen to say hi to Chita, she says she is leaving to go to the Jardín. She is being sent to buy elotes. Everyone has a craving for elotes, and she will buy one for me too. Elotes are large ears of white corn, cooked on the cob in a deep vat of boiling water at a popular stand on the street of the Jardín. There is usually a long line of customers.

Elotes are speared on a stick. A fresh lime is squeezed over the ear, and then it is slathered with mayonnaise. Next the corn gets a good shaking of parmesan cheese to stick all over the mayonnaise, and finally, a healthy dusting of red chili powder. Or, for the more fastidious, or those without strength or reliability in their teeth, the same mixture will be sliced from the cob into a cup, layered in the same order with the same ingredients, and served with a spoon.

I thank Chita but tell her I am making my usual torta of sliced tomatoes drenched with yellow mustard, which usually drips onto my nightgown while I eat and read in bed. Chita laughs. Before she leaves, she shows me a bag with a variety of breads (which means rolls from the bakery). She thinks I must get tired of the same thing repeated so often, and I agree to try another different something. "For you, señora", she proudly says as she points to the bag of breads.

I give the dog one half of the banana I am eating before I start making my "supper". This time I use the whole wheat roll from the bag and fill the sliced bun with salad left from lunch, add the usual overdose of mustard, and contentedly go upstairs.

It is a treat to me to lounge in bed with a sandwich and a book to read for as many hours as I wish. Tonight I am enjoying the clanking and smatters of conversations that float through my open window as the family eats merienda. From upstairs there is a lot of American laughter. Nancy must be having a party.

I know that I could go upstairs and say, "Can I join the party?", and they would say, "Sure, of course, come right in." Nancy is very nice and quite attractive, about my age, and she has had her apartment for years. It is beautifully decorated with Mexican crafts, arts, ceramics, and wonderful art. She has many ailments and is always in pain, so I am glad that she is having some fun.

I am all settled in, and now I get curious about what is happening to Claire and David. Clair and David are in the novel I am reading. They live in Ireland and just had a baby. It is a very good story.

27

PERLA'S MAMÁ ABANDONS HER FOREVER, THE GHASTLY PAMPLONADA, AND FAILURE AT BREADMAKING

After sleeping until the luxurious lateness of eight o'clock, I arrive at the Botica, ready to get started. Being women, while we work, we talk. When you try to talk to a man, tempers get short, questions are interrogations, and offering your own opinions brings a lot of sighing and head-shaking or groaning on the man's part. But to a woman, questions are fuel for a good fire.

I don't ask Perla much because she only needs slight prompting to launch into her interesting story. I ask how long she has worked here, and guess what is the answer? When she was twelve years old, her mother brought her to this Botica. Her mamá asked if Perla could work here, and not only that, if she could live here, and by the way, it would be forever. La Señora (Abelardo's mother), with eight children of her own, said, "Yes". Perla's mother left and never came back.

But that is all she offers. I have many questions now, but I consider it inappropriate to ask. Where did you sleep? Did you go to school with the rest of La Señora's children? Did you eat your meals with them? Were you a servant, or a member of the family? Why did your mother do this? Where did you come from? What was your life like before?

Instead I ask how old her three sons are now. I meet them here every once in a while. They are very nice, and Perla also has an excellent husband. Later I learn that La Señora bought, or gave, Perla her own house. When she got married? In the will? I don't ask.

Perla does tell me that her niece, who lives in San Francisco, left her two little boys, ages five and ten, with Perla and her family for five or six weeks this summer. Perla loved them, and they loved her. Perla treats them so much better than their own mother that they wanted to stay and never, ever leave. The mom pays five hundred dollars each week for day-care in the states, but she only gave Perla one hundred and fifty for the whole summer! Everyone is under the false impression that Mexico is so cheap to live in, but it is not. Groceries here cost the same as in the States, or more.

The boys want to come again next summer, and this will be fine, but Perla says she needs to get a reasonable amount for their food and costs in advance. When you love children, though, everyone knows that if parents want to, they can take advantage of you for the sake of the little ones.

Rafaela comes to call me for breakfast. Delfina and Raúl invite me to accompany them to Leon to a beautiful resort. We will go in order to escape the dreaded Pamplonada on September 24.

The "Pamplonada" is a copy of the Running of the Bulls in Pamplona, Spain. It is a horrid festival when drunks from all over the nation converge on San Miguel to mess up the town and blow money. The worst, really ghastly, is that all the men who think they're macho stab the bulls as they run terrified through the streets. It is a hideous, grizzly event, and the family considers it important for us to be gone while all of this takes place.

Also, with the current instability of the house, Raúl is afraid that the vibrations of the huge crowds running and pushing could make part of the house collapse, because part ofLa Pamplonada takes place right on their street, in front of this very house, as well as on the streets which circle the Jardín.

I work more with Perla, and then I get dressed up to go to Lita's house for comida. On the way I stop to buy whole wheat flour and dry yeast. At a breakfast together in Mesón San José, when they served the homemade bread, I had mentioned that for five years, while my children were in school, I had made all of the bread for our family, four loaves at a time, twice a week. Everyone considered this very hard, and I said, "No, it was easy". That is when Lita asked me to teach her.

I arrive at the house and am welcomed with a shot of tequila. Then before we settle down to eat, we make the dough, thinking that it can rise while we eat.

The comida is splendid, and what a lot of trouble she has taken. A salad of lettuce and tomatoes with her homemade vinaigrette, cucumbers, and onions. Little rolled-up chicken tacos, guacamole, cream, cheeses, homemade chilies in a jar, refried beans, tortillas, and lime aid.

Lita's kitchen is tiny, so she stores all of her pans in the small oven of her small stove. This means that every time you want to use a pan, which is several times each day, you must remove all of the pans, find the one, or ones, you want, put the rest back, and now cook in the pan. We find two pans for the bread, which should have risen, and now it is time to divide the dough and let it have the second rise. We place the pans in the sun on her patio for warmth because the first rising did not rise after all, but we hope that maybe in the sun, the yeast will get going and do its job.

Now we will eat "jamoncillo". Lita's son's refrigerator broke, and a whole carton of milk spoiled. He was going to throw it away, but Lita said, "I will use it to make jamoncillo". Here is what you do to make jamoncillo. Take equal parts of spoiled milk and sugar (that means, for every cup of milk, also one cup of sugar!). Mix this with cinnamon, which here is sold by the stick. Stir and boil until the whole mixture is as thick as stiff cottage cheese. It is unimaginably sweet.

To serve, spread it on cookies (more sugar, oh, my gosh) or on toast. I choose toast. The spreading is supposed to be as thick as frosting. With this we drink coffee, and finally we have to put the bread in the oven. Time is running out. It has not risen at all, but we bake it anyway.

When Lita hears that I went to the Mariachi concert last night, she is heart-broken that I didn't invite her. "Next time, please invite me." I say I will, and as soon as I see a suitable listing, I will call her. I tell her that I will bring her a gift of the same kind of apron that I wore today for our bread project, an apron that she greatly admires. This lifts her spirits a little.

I arrive home at seven PM, in time to start a new painting of a strange little hovel of a tiny, ruined, decaying house. It is in use as a shoe repair shop, as seen from the front, the only light entering the miniscule workshop coming from the sun. Evidently people still live in this house. San Miguel wasn't always fancy, elegant, clean, and perfect. This house is evidently one that the owner would never sell but could not afford to maintain. Or he doesn't like change. The house has thick, lumpy clay steps leading up to the open doorway where the old shoemaker sits partially covered by shadows. Except the stairs are no longer intact, and I think you would have to make quite a stretch from the top of what remains of the steps to actually enter that door.

The painting goes well, and before bedtime I think I have captured the spirit of the place in an ominous, mysterious painting. I am pleased.

Before I left for Lita's, Raúl and Delfina wanted to talk with me about the lawyers. I had written all my suggestions about contingency payments in English. I asked if I should write it in Spanish, and Raúl and Delfina said, "Sí, por favor, because the lawyers are coming today". Nothing can happen though until the soil results are returned. It has taken two weeks of delay so far. When the lawyers arrived, I excused myself. Tomorrow they will tell me what happened. I hope the lawyers accepted my ideas about their fees. But now, time to make my torta and go to bed.

28

KINDLY STORY, SCANDALOUS GOSSIP, FURIOUS RIDE FOR INDEPENDENCE

This morning the priest tells a little story during mass, and I think from his kind heart he is doing this for me. This is the same priest who always scatters lots of extra holy water over me, which I appreciate.

It has to be obvious that I am not Catholic and am ignorant of quite a bit that goes on here. He must have asked himself why I come. One of the things that I do not do with everybody else is make the Sign of the Cross. So he tells a little story about making The Sign.

He says that when someone gets sad, it is a devilish temptation. No good fruit comes from sadness. So to resist such evil, we are to slowly make the Sign of the Cross, saying, "In the name of the Father, and the Son, and the Holy Ghost". I can do that, I think. I believe in God and the Bible, and this does not violate any of my principles. I had always thought that the Sign of the Cross was a veneration of death, an over-emphasis on Jesus dying on the cross, when the whole point of the cross experience and the lesson for us should be the resurrection and the ascension, as a lesson about eternal life. But if this is what The Sign of the Cross means, a reminder to ourselves not to accept sadness, then I can do that. In fact, I need to do that.

Certainly everything this good man preaches sounds like gentle common sense to me, explained in such a helpful way, and I don't notice if there is dogma included. So I decide to participate when everyone else does. I consider this a great kindness on the priest's part. I believe that he senses why I am here and what I need.

I leave feeling light-hearted, and I walk more, looking for another scene to paint. I already have one in mind, a fountain and great huge wall behind La Paróquia. The wall is curved, slopes down the steep hill, and has tree tops just barely poking above the wall, indicating hidden gardens, an idea always intriguing to me. Yet I continue to walk anyway, looking around for more. I do find a new and interesting place to set into my eye for another painting. Good, it doesn't hurt to be one ahead.

When I return, it is time to start in the Botica. I work until eleven thirty when Rafaela comes to call me to breakfast. Oh, it is delicious. Papaya, chilaquiles, beans, special hot peppers in sauce, hot tortillas, orange juice, and coffee. Then I work in the Botica again until comida.

Delfina's family members are all wonderful. Today we are visited by Margarita, Delfina's sister. Felipina is Margarita's daughter, except they look the same age, and Margarita takes care of Felipina's daughters so much that I thought Margarita was their mother. They are all present, and a lot of fun. Also Benito is there, and I do not figure out until later that Benito is the father of the little girls, he is Felipina's husband, and these are the kids who were baptized at the big celebration I attended some time ago. We talk for hours, or I should say, for hours I mostly listen, and I enjoy it all.

The talk is about a prominent man. It is public knowledge that he beats his wife. Her parents insist that she stay with him because of his money, power, and prestige. And who knows if another husband would be any better anyway. This man is so mean that he even beats his own grandmother. There are other shocking things that he does, and if I describe them all, he will be too recognizable, so I will not say another word except it is like hearing of some outrageous soap opera.

Just like all juicy, scandalous gossip, it is so tempting to relate what I hear, but believe it or not, there are many things that I am too discrete to talk about! Even though I am definitely a blabbermouth deluxe, and I love captivating an audience with a good story, I try to keep away from saying anything bad, or hurtful, or truly personal. At least, I think that is what I do.

Here is something that is just fine for me to relate. I suppose that everyone knows that September 16 is Mexican Independence day, the day that began the revolution, starting right here in San Miguel. I told about the secret tunnels connecting the Great Houses. To advocate freeing Mexico from Spanish rule was just as dangerous for the Mexicans as it was for our patriots in the revolutionary war.

All of the history of the events that took place in this town will be reenacted in the streets, just one block from here in the streets surrounding the Jardín. Today the cowboys are supposed to ride into town at full gallop in authentic costume. I have tried to be present for this, but timing is not like a bus schedule. It will happen when all the men and horses are ready. The ride starts way out in the country. It is not like a quick gallop in front of a movie camera or in a parade. This will try to be the real thing.

The time we have been told they will arrive was one thirty. At two o'clock I give up the wait. At five forty-five, Conchita and I walk to the tienda Bonanza to buy a roll of paper towels. Raulito comes running, finds us, and says, "The horsemen are in town right now, already at the Jardín". We hurry to see them, and they are great.

"Caballo" means "horse", and "cabellero" means, "Horseman", which means "gentleman". One cannot be a gentleman without a horse, and owning these horses, which we see today, requires time and money. If you want to see a display of manliness, watch these young men in the prime of life ride at breakneck speed through the hot countryside and right into your little, dusty town, and stop precisely in front of you, horses jerking and dancing, men sweaty, and male, and tall, and high on their horses. There is the creaking and squeaking of leather clothes, leather saddles, and the click of hoofs on the cobblestones.

We are told that this group of solid, strong men, very much in command of their excited, nervous horses, started their ride in Querétaro, (one hour away by car), and they will ride on all the way to Delores Hidalgo, which I think is at least a half hour from here (by car). These men represent the Mexicans who started the fighting for their independence.

Of course, in actuality these are the rich and powerful men of the town, and they are very good looking. I see Lalia, the beautiful manageress of Estela's villa, riding behind her brother, so Conchita, Raulito, and I yell and wave. The brother draws near so that Lalia can talk to us, which makes us feel that we are taking part in the emotional and dramatic event. Everyone in town is here. We are of the favored few who "know somebody".

When the interlude of stopping in El Centro, the Jardin area, is over, the horsemen spur their horses for a gallop up the steep street towards their next destination. Quickly the clatter and dust and shouting die away, and we go back home.

I start a painting of a stone fountain, nestled under shaded trees by the French Park. I paint the semi-circle of carved stones that comprise the fountain in dusty purples, blues, lavender, and gray. It is an isolated fountain, away from most passers-by, with a few broken parts, a chip here and there. I think I give it a properly mysterious flavor.

The torta I make for myself tonight is more inspired than all the others. I put avocado on one side, sour goat cheese on the other, add a huge chile and lots of mustard, and pat down the lid, the top half of the torta. This time I use a plate large enough to add a slice of papaya. My tea tonight is manzanilla. Everything is just, just, just right, right, right.

29

THE DAY BEFORE THE BIG DAY, EL GRITO, AND LOCKED IN LIKE A DOG

This is a major day in San Miguel, the Eve of Independence Day. There is a major celebration tonight, or maybe there are events all day. Conchita and Chita went last year, and they said you get so pushed, and shoved, and squashed by the crowds that it was scary. They couldn't even move enough to get away. Chita will not go again, but Conchita has had a whole year to forget the scary feelings and to remember only the excitement. This year she hopes to go with friends. Being fifteen is just right for crowds, music, ice creams, fireworks, the whole shebang!

I have decided that it is too dangerous to invite Lita. She is older than I and has a hard time walking, even very slowly. There will not be enough chairs and benches. What if we have to stand for the ceremonies? This could over-power her, and what would I do if she got tired and couldn't make it for me to walk her home? I will try to find some coming event at the Teatro Juarez that she would like.

I go to mass as usual, and it is "Los Siete Dolores De La Virgen", The Seven sorrows of The Virgin. "Dolores" means pain, and I have always wondered why anyone would name a daughter that, although it is a pretty sounding name. It must be a name to honor The Virgin.

All of the sorrows are described, regarding Mary's witnessing the tortures of the crucifixion. This should sound horrible, but I am thinking that since we know of Jesus' triumph over death, and how his triumph over all he was made to suffer, his response was always love, he proved what he taught, that no matter what, Love is always the answer, and Love is always the victor. And it is of great encouragement that when it is the darkest hour, Love will still win.

Therefore I find this mass inspiring. And feeling uplifted, I don my rubber gloves and apron and set to work in the Botica. The Botica stays open on holidays, usually, because there are crowds, which means foot traffic right in front of the open doors of the Botica, which means people come in, which means that there are sales, which… Get It?

So I am enjoying my perch high on the ladder, where no one pays any attention to me at all, as the town comes to me, rather than me going to the town.

Raúl comes to get me and delivers me to the wondrous restaurant where Delfina and her sister, Rita, are having breakfast, even though it is now after eleven o'clock. They have waited for me before ordering. This is another hidden restaurant only a block or two away, and again it is extraordinary.

All of the tables are glass-topped over six inch deep boxes on legs. The boxes are divided into smaller sections, and each table is painted in a vivid Mexican pink, or rose, or turquoise, or green, or chartreuse, or yellow, or blue, or terra cotta. Inside each box is a different element of a unified theme, a distinctive theme for each table. Some are shells. Others are candies and sweets. Another is of hand-carved toys. Some are from nature. There are as many categories as there are tables. A clever person designed all of this.

But these are tables in the street-side dining room, a room meant for cocktails and dinners. Delfina and Rita wanted me to see the beauty of this room, which has large, fine mirrors on the walls, stonework as architectural details, floor to almost ceiling windows, iron barred, and beautiful comfortable chairs.

For breakfast, we move to the interior garden. Raúl stays too, and we take seats at one of the tables amidst the flowers in the courtyard. We are shaded by a cream colored canvas umbrella, once again of the local manta cloth, a breeze wafts smells of cooking to mingle with the scents of flowers and sweet, fresh air. Service is elegant, the breakfast extraordinary, and the conversation languid, relaxed, friends together.

About one o'clock we leave, and I help Perla a little more while Delfina and Raúl meet with their lawyer in the dining room. The architect was expected to deliver the soil sample official test results today, which he did, so now the case is being discussed from a strongly hopeful point of view.

I tell myself to take a walk, which I know I should do, but I am tired. I am tired from lack of exercise, having been occupied with other things lately, and skipping my several hours of daily walking. Even though my daily walks are in bits and pieces, they do add up.

Instead I do now something that I do, in my mind's eye, at home, when I am troubled and need to calm down. I lie down on my bed, in the bright daytime, at two thirty, with no plans, no responsibilities, listening to the sounds I like, I love, I treasure:

- Chita rattling and cooking in the kitchen below.
- Raúl's voice drifting up as an echo from the huge, cool, high ceilinged dining room.
- The harmonica of the blind beggar-man who is always on the corner.
- Radio music from passing cars spewing out ranchera music, loud, but muted as it reaches me.
- Wheels and motors humming outside of this big house where I am secure and safe.

This is the time of day when the children are still in school. Soon all the criadas will be meeting the children at school to walk them home. Or the parents, like this family, will go for them in cars. Everyone will come home, bursting in all lively and shouting, and talking all at once. The dog will run all around the patio, and the maids will gear up for serving comida.

Each comida takes many hours to prepare. To make the soup alone involves boiling a chicken for the broth, and then cutting and cooking as many as ten different vegetables. Each vegetable or fruit is first scrubbed with soap, then rinsed, and then peeled or cut as needed. Chita seems to shop separately for each meal.

The fruit and vegetable store is one block from here. So is Bonanza, a store we in Wisconsin would call tiny, but which here is called by everyone in town a supermarket. It is far too small and crowded to have even one cart. The check-out counter accommodates about ten items. Spices are still sold whole, fished out of large glass jars, for the teaspoon or half-stick you need for today's comida. The bag boys rotate and are between seven and ten years old. You should tip them. They will carry everything to your house, if you wish.

I have to go to Bonanza today to buy panti-liners because I am all out. Bonanza is the only store in town that might have them, except for El Gigante. From here, El Gigante is a long, long walk, almost straight uphill, getting uglier the closer you get to the ugly, ugly, ugly El Gigante itself. (If I didn't have my bad attitude towards big-box stores, I would have to admit that it is clean, well-stocked, and friendly.) I also don't like it because it represents the future, bulldozing away all that I consider beautiful to lay down the parking lots and speeding, traffic clogged highways that characterize "Our Ever Changing World". The El Gigante neighborhood is exactly like the new out-skirts of every American town, and perhaps, soon, every town in the world.

But so far I have a choice, and I do not choose El Gigante-land. I choose Bonanza.

Life around here is so much fun because I never know what to expect. Today Don Martín and Doña Delfina come for comida to celebrate the Eve of Independence Day. Don Martín has fixed my suitcase handle, and Doña Delfina has brought beautiful fancy cakes. She has standing orders with a few restaurants that like to offer elegant desserts. I had no idea that she did this as a sort of a part-time job. The cakes are flat and round, each one special and exotic.

Before comida begins, Raúl serves me a tequila in a delicate, tiny, long-stemmed glass, made of cut glass, which he carefully has removed from the glass-fronted cupboard which contains the very fanciest of glasses. I am not surprised. The lawyers were here all morning, and at the end, Raúl served them tequila. When they all left the dining room, Raúl was smiling a nice big smile, so I thought, "Ah, the news about the case is good".

Our foods are in red, or white, or green to honor the Mexican flag (except for the agua, the fruit water drink, which is mango and papaya and therefore orange colored).

The soup is red tomatoes purred, with chunks of white cheese added, and green, cubed avocados, and darker red ancho chilies, chopped. It is great.

Next comes a large dish, which is unusual because normally every course is individually plated. The dish contains wedges of red tomatoes, green zuchinnis, white onions, and carrots (sort of like red). On top is a pile of shredded boiled beef. Also we have hot tortillas. I feel happy, celebrating with this loving family, and I love that I am seated next to a boy young enough to still want his soup served in a plastic bowl with soccer balls painted on it.

Pretty Conchita has brought me a treat from school that she thinks I will love. It is a tiny cup of lime sherbet with its own teensy, tiny spoon. I can only manage two miniscule bites because it is so sweet. I am delighted with her thoughtfulness, so I say I will put it in the freezer to enjoy a little at a time, one bite each day.

We talk about mountain climbing and oddities of nature. Don Martín is so funny that it doesn't matter what he talks about, you are sure to have some laughs. The mealtime conversations are as much a treat as the food of the meals. We never run out of topics that few people seem to think about.

Tonight the president is having a cocktail party in Casa Allende (on the square, where "El Grito", "The Shout", formally started the Mexican Revolution). El Grito will be reenacted, and it is a great privilege to be there as one of the inside guests. Raúl naturally has been invited, but Raúl is a purist in his soul, and there are some parts of politics that- well, sometimes Raúl politely declines invitations.

"But you should go, Sonette. You can watch the fireworks from the balconies with the president's guests." Since Raúl has already declined, he needs to call and re-accept, except telling them to expect me instead. However, everyone who didn't receive an invitation is trying to get one now, and the lines are jammed all day, and he cannot get through. Oh, well, it will be maybe even better to be in the street with the crowd.

I have my outfit all ready to wear. It is my one white tank top, that once again I ruined, and once again Chita rescued. I had dribbled or slopped red tomato sauce on the front, and it would not wash out. Chita told me to spray it with Spray and Wash and then hang it in the bright blazing sun for twelve hours. It worked! Also I have my long, red, pleated linen skirt, white sandals, and red jewelry. I have nothing green, so this is as much honor to the colors of the flag as I possess.

I take a walk, plenty of time before the dancing starts in El Centro where platforms have been erected for regional dances to be performed. Conchita invites me into the library to listen to music with her. She fiddles around on the computer in a way I do not comprehend in the least, until she gets cumbias so I can teach her the dance steps I know, which is fun.

The family is going somewhere. I will wait until close to eight o'clock and walk the block to the platform of the dancers. Then I have promised to be back here at nine thirty to take Raulito to see the fireworks. I am too old to want to do this by myself, but taking a kid brings such experiences to life. Children make you never forget your joy.

I go to my room and dress. Another event, another opportunity, another taking part in someone else's world. But no, what happened? I am at the front door, ready to leave, and I cannot get the lock to open. The family has left. What shall I do? I struggle, rattle, push, lean into the door and try again. I try everything I have ever heard of or seen about making a reluctant lock give up and come apart.

I go upstairs. All of the renters are gone. Except Nancy. That is, I assume Nancy is at home because her door is open and the TV is on loud. I knock and holler, but I would never just walk right in. Is she asleep? In the bathtub having a hot soak? I have to give up on Nancy.

Downstairs I try again. No use. I am trapped! I am alone, except for Maya, the dog. I miss Richard. He would know exactly what to do. He would swear at the lock and fiddle with it, and then the door would yield, out we would go. Or, if he couldn't conquer the door, we would take a bottle of wine up to the roof, watch all the lights come on in the five splendid church domes we can see from the rooftop, and we would laugh about being locked in, left, just like the dog.

But Richard is not here. One good thing about divorce. You can allow yourself to remember and re-enjoy every good thing, and you never have to remember one single bad thing if you don't want to. That would be me. I have opted for the "great parts only memory". Why not? It is my choice.

Never-the-less, I am stranded, marooned. Just like Cinderella on the night of the ball, I am dressed to go to the big deal celebration, just one block away, and taking place at this very minute, but I am locked in.

Instead of a bottle of wine on the roof, I find one half of a whole wheat bun in my room. (The kitchen and all other rooms are locked.) I share the bread with Maya and pet her a lot. Now I know how my dog, Puffy, feels when I go away. While I am in the patio sharing my roll with Maya, one of the renters who live on the roof comes home, and "Yippie!" I am free.

At last I am ready to see the regional dancers. Except the stage is low, and lots of people are inconsiderately standing right by the stage in front of all the chairs, so no one can see a thing. Besides, the music is recorded and is blasting at such painful volume that I give up and go home. How will I get in?

I reach the front door just as Raúl drives up in his van. Raulito has changed his mind about seeing fireworks. He says that last year people got drunk and hit each other with beer bottles. So I decide to enjoy the festivities in a different way. That means that I make my usual torta (Raúl has unlocked the kitchen for merienda), get in bed with a novel and a Heraldo, and enjoy the music far more through my open window than was possible downtown. In fact, from one block away the music is still loud. I can even hear the announcer. I drift in and out of sleep all night long, hearing the fireworks explosions interspersed with the various musics that last until three AM. It is a remarkably pleasant experience, so much better than actually being there firsthand.

30

INDEPENDENCE DAY! PARADE OF POLISHED CHILDREN, AND FIRE SHOWERS, CASTILLOS AND COJETES

I awake and want to go to mass, but I do not have a key. Chita is at her rancho to celebrate the holidays with her family. The family sleeps late. Perla will not open the Botica today until ten o'clock. Who will let me in after mass, which ends at eight o'clock?

I want to go anyway, so I take extra money. After mass I walk and walk. It still is not time to get let in to the house, so I go to Posada San Francisco and enjoy a very expensive cup of coffee. It is worth it because I am used to a first-thing-in-the-morning cup of coffee, and I have not had any so far today. Finally I think Perla will have the Botica opened. Just as I approach the house, Raúl opens the door and lets me in.

I help Perla in the Botica until Raúl comes to get me for breakfast. At the table we are only Raúl, Raulito, and me. Just to fix us breakfast, Rafaela has come to town for the morning. (Delfina is at a breakfast party, called a junta. Conchita stayed overnight with her friend.)

I work more in the Botica until Raúl comes to tell us, "Come, Sonette, there is a parade". Every parade in town comes past the Botica, so there is no reason to go anywhere. Raúl takes me up to the balcony of his and Delfina's bedroom where Raulito is already standing outside waiting for me. Although we are on the shady side of the street it is already hot, and Raúl brings us cold cokes from his little family refrigerator under the stairs in their living room.

The parade is of hundreds and hundreds of school children. Each child is clean, fresh, immaculate, almost polished all over. Girls' hair is in slicked-back, tight pony tails, and boys' hair is expertly groomed with a razor sharp part, gelled and combed so straight that not one hair will be out of place for the rest of the day.

Each school marches together in perfect formation, the rhythm of their feet precisely matching the cadence set by teachers and principals, "Maestros y Directores" who accompany them. Uniforms are classic. Girls wear plaid, pleated woolen skirts, white crisply ironed blouses, thick woolen V-necked sweaters, bright white knee socks, and brilliantly glowing black patent leather shoes with a strap over the instep, the style known as Mary Janes. Some schools also require thick, white cotton gloves.

Boys wear the same perfect white shirts with heavy woolen V necked sweaters, often with a crest, solid colored dress pants, and black, shiningly polished dress shoes. At the head of each school group, someone carries the school flag, or a banner with the identifying insignia.

How can these children stand such clothing in this heat? September in San Miguel is not like September in Wisconsin. Today, once again, I am wearing a tank top and Levis. I am in the shade, and these children will march for hours in the full, red-hot sun with heat rising from the scalding-stone pavement. No one mummers, or loses pace, or begs for water. Dignity and pride rule over all discomfort. Wow!

We watch the endless marchers until we are hypnotized. I say to Raulito, "There must be at least fifty different schools passing by". (You can tell because each school's uniform is distinctive in some way- by the color of the plaids, or some sweaters are navy, others deep dark green, others blinding white, maybe one or two use black. Or one school uses cardigan sweaters, others pull-overs. Some substitute woolen blazers, of course with a distinctive crest.

Raulito answers that there are even more schools than this in town. For example, his own school is not included today.

At the end come men on horseback, police, military, but this makes me lose interest. Nothing could equal all those beautiful, healthy children.

We unite for comida, and I am told what to see and do today. No one will accompany me because with all these crowds, everyone will be busy in the Botica.

At six o'clock I go downtown to join the multitudes waiting to see the re-enactment of the Independence Day horseback riders. I get a perfect spot on the high, tall parapet at the edge of El Jardín. I am overlooking the street below, and finally, here they come, riding like lightening, right on past us at full-tilt and up the cobblestone street, straight up the high hill and out of sight to continue up the road on the side of the mountain.

The first two men are dressed like Allende and Hidalgo, the heros. (Obviously San Miguel is named for Allende. The nearby town, start point of the riders, is named Dolores Hidalgo.) The riders are wearing full make-up and look realistic. With them are more of their type and social class. I get very upset to see one horrible man beating his horse hard with a riding crop, hitting it on the head, neck, sides, and all to show off what a tough brute he is. I shake my finger at him, scolding, and I yell "NO, NO, NO!" in my loudest voice. I would have run after him to give him more finger shaking and another sentence or two, but I am trapped by the crowd, and he is quickly up the hill and away. Bah! We must never be too embarrassed to stand and protest against bullies!

Racing along now, behind the ones just speeding up the hill, are riders dressed to be poor campesinos. Their clothing is that of the poor rebels called "insurgents". They wear strips of white cloth as bandages, blood soaking from their wounds. I cry at this, thinking of the hardships of liberty. These were men who wanted their families to have a chance, to be free, and I feel the drama of it in my heart. These are not costumed actors from far away. Like the play in El Teatro Juarez, these are real people whose own families are represented today.

While waiting for the parade to begin, I saw two old, wrinkled, shabby little men trying to earn a little something by selling packages of home-roasted pumpkin seeds. One man has a little wooden box filled with cellophane and scotch taped packages. The box is held around his neck by a ribbon, nightclub cigarette-girl style. Another is selling balloons, red, or white, or green. I buy packages of seeds and one balloon. Now I will go looking for a little poor kid who might like to have a balloon.

I find a little boy, who seems likely to not have many things bought for him, give it to him, and he is delighted. Next I walk to where poor beggar women sit all day long on the sidewalk while their tiny children sleep or quietly sit alongside them on the sidewalk. I give them the packages of seeds, which the mamás immediately rip open, thanking me, and give to the children to eat. No one hesitates. They are hungry.

The crowds will stay downtown now, waiting for the castillos to be lit. Castillos are towers made of bamboo or some type of thin, light-weight wood. There are always three, jabbed into holes dug for them right in the center of the street in front of La Paróquia. The towers have frames sort of like open boxes attached to the central poles, with bits of wood twisted into pinwheels mounted on the outsides of the boxes and on the tops. Fastened to these frames are fireworks of the kind that create a spray of burning golden sparks. When lit, the chain of burning starts from the bottom and inches upward, causing the moveable parts to spin and whirl, looking like flaming pinwheels about to fly off. And indeed, some are constructed so that they will zoom away, sometimes whirling right into the crowds below. Finally, the topmost spirals will twirl faster and faster until they launch themselves straight up into the sky.

The spectacular nature of this event will be amplified by having La Paróquia as a backdrop. The hundreds of peaked arches carved in the pink granite façade of the towering church are usually illumined by a multitude of lights. For very special occasions, more showering golden fires will pour from strategic parts of the church, creating a waterfall of burning orange. Then, once the castillos and the church fires burn themselves down to only a glow, rocket fireworks will be launched.

Sky-bursting fireworks are not as common here as they are in the USA because unless you are on a rooftop, your vision will be blocked by trees and the narrowness of streets. However, for this important day of the year, no holds will be barred.

During the interval between the horseback riders and the fireworks, the dancers are to perform on the platform again. The music starts, again unbearably loud, and a few souls once again stand up all around the stage, selfishly and unconcernedly blocking everyone else's view of what would have been a spectacular show. I may as well go home until I hear something to indicate the start of the fireworks.

From home I can hear the announcer and the dancers' music. As it gets dark and the music stops, I decide it is time to return to El Jardín. The crowds are dense, polite, jovial. I walk to one of the pillars supporting the arches over the sidewalks on the side of El Jardín. One pillar has just enough of a wide base for me to ascend, plant my feet carefully so as not to topple, and by leaning back into the pillar for balance, I have a vantage above the sea of tightly-packed families to view all of the beauty of castillos, church, crowds, and overhead fireworks. I have the best "seat" in town. I am also the only one (still hot in a tank top and skirt) who is not wearing a fleece-lined winter jacket, or a heavy woolen sweater, or at the very least, a thick shawl.

Cojetes will pop all night, I know as I get into bed. Cojetes are little rockets set off just for the delight of hearing BANG, endlessly, from every, or many, parts of town. As you try to fall asleep, you have to decide that BANG, BANG, bang-bang-bang, BANG is just another part of the fun. And it is.

31

BOTICAS AND BIRTHDAYS, ALMOST TEMPTED TO BE FRIENDLY, CHEATED AND TRICKED, AND PROBABLY NOT FOR THE LAST TIME EITHER

I like lots of old things. I like old ladies, I like old wooden barns in Wisconsin that the earth is starting to reclaim. I like birthdays, and I like Raúl's Botica.

Today is my daughter's birthday. Only the answering machine picks up my call, but it is alright. Suspecting as much, I talked to Mary yesterday, just to hear her voice. But I do get another call today, from my son. My credit card company just called him, saying that twenty thousand dollars had been charged in two days on my credit card at electronics stores here in Mexico. It is all right, they accept his stand that this is fraud, and the company will issue us new cards.

However, I am still nervous, get the number of the company's international fraud security office, and reconfirm that yes indeed, or no indeed, I did not charge any such thing. Someone in a restaurant that I do not care to publicly name in a book must have copied the number while registering my bill. The company says, "Fine, do not worry". I say, "I know where and when it had to happen. You can start your investigation there." "Do not take any action yourself. Do not get involved. We have our own teams of investigators. We handle everything ourselves", the fraud unit tells me. It is hard to agree, for a second, but I see the wisdom of their words. But no more credit card for my use until I get back home. I should have enough money in travelers' checks to be ok.

Speaking of travelers' checks, I urgently need pesos. I have invited Lita for one dinner, and Raúl and family for another. Every Casa de Cambio was closed last time I tried, because of The Big Day, and before, and after.

Still, I think of my daughter and our motto, "Oh, well, move on, live in the moment".

Every day I have stated the same thing, "I work in the Botica". It is about time to describe the Botica.

At first visit, in the days of Abelardo, the Botica looked to me like a tired, shabby, old drugstore. I didn't care at all what it looked like, because I had no interest in drugstores any more than I had in their drugs. I only ever went to the Botica to get Abelardo to go for a walk, the same as little kids used to ring a neighbor's doorbell, "Can Anna Marie come out and play?"

On Saturdays or Sundays I liked to stop by the Botica, knowing that Abelardo would throw aside his duties, and we would go out to "Dar el Paseo", which meant to wander aimlessly through town, chancing upon friends who would join us, and having a great, slow-paced time. It never occurred to me that Abelardo was leaving a real job. So my interactions with his Botica were peripheral.

Since then, I have come to see the Botica through new eyes. Let's start by standing in the street and taking an outside look. The street slants downward towards the corner, making it necessary to take a giant step up in order to pass through two wide doors, after the heavy wooden panels have been removed for customers. The left step up is not too big, but the right door is higher up from the sidewalk, and to step up and in is a stretch.

While still outside, looking to the right, you can see through the front open door all the way through to the side open door, so your view includes all the foot traffic and creeping cars in the street beyond. To the left of the front doors, as a window facing the street, is a glass fronted display case. This contains a large plaster foot, probably once white, with a few brown bandages indicating Doctor Scholl's bandage treatments. The foot, its healing, covered wounds, and the packages of Band-Aids displayed, have never changed, during my entire life-time.

For years I considered this neglect, until I came to see that although a flourishing business, the mystique of the Botica is that it never changes. You don't have to walk through the doors to get a very good idea and feel for this place. Glancing inside, you will see customers leaning against the old, green frames of the glass fronted display cases, and elbows resting on the glass topped counter. The feet of patrons will indicate the variety of those who patronize the Botica. Tired, calloused, brown bare feet in sandals. Athletically clad walking, or running, or tennis shoes in clean white socks. Tourist sandals on bare feet belonging to tanned, bare legs. Black leather oxfords under black dress pants, most favored by waiters, traveling salesmen, and the like. Children's shoes on children's little feet, or bare little brown feet next to plastic slipper clad grandmothers' old, wrinkled, tired feet.

There are two swinging doors, counter top high, at each end of the counter, for use by the family owners and employees. Behind the counter are wooden shelves very like library catalogue drawers, with the same little brass card holders, into which have been fitted typed or hand-written titles of contents. There is a collector's item vintage cash register. The floor behind the counter is made of elevated wooden slats, to give a little bounce over the mercilessly hard stone floor beneath.

Behind all, and running up the wall to the ceiling, are tall, narrow, wooden shelves, painted the same chipped light green as forever, and with the vertical groves, circular caps and fronts of joints, that bespeak "Victorian" On the walls, and placed here and there, are holy images, like Mary, or saints. Even the calendar is religious.

The shelves contain "The Collection". I have described the porcelain frascos, some still containing the original medicaments from Italy, and there are the tiny glass bottles with glass stoppers, lettered by hand to explain their liquid contents.

There is a door, accessed by a few wooden steps, through which one passes into the back rooms, the sink, the bathroom, and presumably where drugs are securely kept and made into requirements requested in the prescriptions people bring in from their doctors. I do not intrude upon these spaces, so I can only suppose.

The over-all effect is timeless and comforting. Everyone here will help you, will care about you, will remember you. For tourists there is film, shampoo, cologne. For children there are cookies and pink meringues in glass jars. For the tired and thirsty, there is a sliding fronted, upright display case of cold sodas and juices. For friends, there is time for chatter and well-wishing, receipt of invitations, a quick stop for a hello while passing by.

Raúl has been offered hefty sums for this Botica in its entirety, especially its contents. There are collectors who lust after acquiring such a treasure, intact, unimaginable. But the Botica is a part of the family, of the life, of the earning of a living, and most of all, an enabler to keep on as "A Great House".

To be "A Great House" means to stay intact in every way. And this requires a thriving, original, unchanged business in your own home, fronted to the street, frequented by all, known to the town, and thoroughly respected. It means that mamá y papá are always "at home". It means that the lavish, long, lingering meals can be counted upon. Dad or Mom will never be "away at work, can't make it home". It means that children can be trusted to the nanny or criadas because they can step into the Botica at any moment to share a surprise, or a hurt, or whatever else needs just one moment of attention, but such an important moment. It means that everyone in the family is invested in success. It means that your children will go away to the university to study pharmacology and business, but they will come back. They will take up their places as the future mamás y papás of that Great House. They will ensure the next generation, and the next. They will want to live in, love, and preserve "The Great House", your house, your cherished, blessed, special, San Miguel life.

I scrub the woodwork, and I see myself coming through the door for Abelardo. I clean the glass cases, and I hear Raulito bouncing in from the street. I wash the shelves, and I hear the thumping and clacking of doggie nails on the wooden slatted floor as the dog is called to sit on the counter and shake hands with a friend. I wipe down the cellophane covered packages and replace them on the freshly cleaned rack, and I am offered a cool diet coke, and I listen to Perla answer questions about how to construct a home altar, or what her sons study in school. This is how I work in the Botica. It is old, the Botica is timeless, and as I say, I like old things.

Antonia and Eliseo have arrived. I remember them from during my last trip, when they came to sell Levis during Semana Santa. Eliseo has cooked us a delicious breakfast.

I have to go to the bank after cashing travelers' checks. Since it is always a problem to get change, I must carry small bills and coins, especially because I invited Doña Lita to take her out to dinner tonight. We are celebrating. Thursday was her birthday, and tomorrow is mine. When I was at her house to bake bread, she admired my apron, so I will buy one for her for her birthday. On her real birthday, her son gave her four dozen roses! Roses are very religious, being Mary's flower, so Lita arranged them all around a statue of the Virgin Mary in the living room. Then her son took her for pizza and birthday cake. After that she got to stay overnight at her granddaughter's house.

At three o'clock, because comida has never been served on a Saturday, I plan to go for a walk. I am on my way out when I think, "But what if"? I go back to the kitchen, just to be sure, and there is Chita, preparing the meal. Any other Saturday I would have been so happy. But today my dinner date with Lita is for seven o'clock. I can't eat now and then have a dinner that soon. So I tell Chita, "Please make my portions tiny, like for a baby". She says "ok", but I needn't have worried. Business is so great in the Botica that all hands are needed to help, so the family enters the dining room only for a quick few minutes, eating one at a time in shifts.

Conchita has returned from the sleep-over, and she comes to get me for another parade. We stand on her parents' balcony again, and here comes a police car as fast as it can go, which is pretty slowly, with its screeching siren on at full blast. A foghorn is saying, "Clear the streets! Get onto the sidewalk!" No one jumps, but people slowly obey.

For ten minutes, nothing happens. Finally The Antique Auto Parade, looked forward to by many and highly advertised, approaches. It consists of eight cars, mostly model Ts, driving in a circle around our block over and over as fast as they can, which is not much because of all the turning at right angles. Each time around, the antique cars are preceded by the screaming, screeching police car. Once the so-called parade participants give up, the police car driver and passengers are having too much fun to stop. They go around and around our block, probably as many times as they think they can get away with it, and finally they call it quits as well. I suppose one takes fun where one can get it.

Right around the corner from us is a paper shop. I set out to buy a sheet of wrapping paper for Lita's apron. It costs ninety cents American money for one solitary sheet of tissue paper. I do not buy it. Instead for forty cents I can purchase one meter of thin gold ribbon.

While in the paper store, I spot the kind of collapsible Japanese paper lanterns that I was hoping to find as a gift for Mary for her classroom. They are around a dollar each, so I buy three. Perfect gifts to carry in a suitcase.

I think it is time to get dressed up and walk to Lita's house to pick her up and walk together back to the downtown for dinner. But I am too early and don't want to ring the bell. I decide to keep walking to the garden hotel named Jacaranda to see what they are listing for movies in their pretty private theater. You can sit at an elegant table and be served a glass of wine and popcorn to enjoy during the film, and all for seven dollars.

The listing for this week is all old Alfred Hitchcock . Here is what happens. On the way there an American man, about my age, is walking behind me on the sidewalk. He starts to pass by stepping down into the street, but a car comes by, so he gets back up, still behind me. I turn in at the hotel, and so does he. He is staying there.

I look at the posters and the movie list, and so does he. He introduces himself and we talk. He is attractive and nice. I can tell he is hoping that we could both see a movie together, as a way to get acquainted. He asks which one I am likely to see. It almost tempts me to be friendly, but I am not here for that. I get asked out all the time back in the States, and my answer is always a polite version of, "No". Dating, even in the most mild form in a safe, elegant, public place, I just cannot do it. Romance, marriage, dating, all of the couple stuff that I thought would bring such happiness turned out to be the most hurtful experiences of my life. No more of that. I can't.

I am happy singly, and I don't mean just not married. I mean no dates of any kind at all. I am pretty sure that this very appealing gentleman will check out the theater and look for me for a couple of nights, just in case I change my mind. It would be so innocent, nothing more than passing a few pleasant hours, but it is not in me. I cannot do it.

When I arrive at Lita's and knock, she is ready. This is better. Lita is fifteen years older? Or ten? Or five? I don't know, but I feel completely relaxed. She was divorced too, a long time ago. As pretty and fun as she is, she probably also had many opportunities to start something new also, and like me, she is happy now with family and friends, "y nada más", and nothing more.

We arrive at the beautiful restaurant at seven fifteen, and it is full. The maître d' takes our names, and we wait in the inside patio of the old hotel courtyard, sit at one of the pretty tables, and enjoy drinks before a table in the front opens up for us. We don't care how long it takes. We are having a great time already.

After not much of a wait, the waitress comes to take us to our seats for dinner. I pay for our drinks and a tip, and we follow her. Our meal is everything we hoped it would be, and we are happy with our little birthday party. Happy until I have already walked Lita back to her house, then walked myself back to my house, and crawled into bed.

"Wait a minute!" I think. I am sure that I was charged way too much. This will niggle at me all night, so I get out of bed, get pen and paper, write down everything that we ordered, compare to what I paid, and Darn! The bill should have been 159 pesos, but I paid 285. I am mad at them for cheating me, and I am upset with myself for not checking the bill more carefully.

For one thing, they must have re-charged me for the drinks before dinner, for which I had already paid, plus tip. For another thing, they probably used the tricks I myself have warned my students to watch out for:

- "Mix up" the bill "by mistake" and have someone else's order on it.
- Write down the correct orders, but put the wrong prices.
- Write the bill correctly, but add it up wrong.

Bah. The restaurant is closed by now, and I paid everything in cash, because of my stolen credit card numbers. And by the way, this is the same restaurant where my numbers were stolen. I have no proof of anything, but I know that I am right because Lita and I ordered exactly the same everything. I decide not to go back and make a fuss, because all they have to say is that they don't have a record, and it was paid in cash, do I have a receipt? No, I did not take a copy of the receipt with me. It is not ordinarily done as orders are just scratched down, not printed out on a computer.

Well, so much for that.

But no one likes being tricked. I start to think about The Bad Romance, and being tricked in that too. Am I just a gullible fool? Is that what it means to be innocent? No, No, No, stop that, Sonette! You are here to get over all that. All one has to do is learn and move on. In this case, pay more attention before paying the bill.

32

CHICKENS FOR THE PRISON,
STEAKS FOR SONETTE

I awaken and do my usual leisurely, agreeable routine and then dress for taking a walk to be followed by mass in the golden chapel with the dead saint. I find myself high on a street I have never explored before. No one is in sight except, even higher up, a young couple. I have found something I want to paint, so I am standing still drinking the scene into my eyes. But I am distracted because the young man keeps looking at me in a way that makes me feel menaced. I think that he wants to rob me, but the young woman does not. They talk back and forth, constantly glancing at me, he on the "Yes" side with his body language and facial expressions, and she on the "Against". But she is weaker, and I quickly turn and walk away as fast as I can without running. When I get a strong feeling, I obey it.

I have invited the family for breakfast after mass, which means noon, at Mesón San José. It will just be Conchita and Delfina though because this morning Raúl and Raulito are at the prison where they go once a month as volunteers for a special program. Today they are giving a fair with games and prizes. I bet this is Raulito's idea. They will not finish until at least one o'clock.

Delfina is working in the Botica, and Conchita is not ready. I go to mass alone, saying I will return to pick them up at the Botica. As I arrive and enter the chapel, so does Lita. We sit together. I want to include her in the breakfast invitation, but I do not because I want to pay special attention to Conchita. I walk Lita a couple of blocks to her son's química, some kind of laboratory he owns, because it is close by, her feet hurt and she cannot make it home. He will take care of her.

Just as I enter the Botica, Perla holds out the phone and says it is for me. I imagine it is Bob or Mary (because of my birthday) but we talked a lot already on Friday. The caller is Juan Alfonso, whom I met at Estela's breakfast and again later at the art lecture. He and his wife Camilia are inviting me for comida today. He will come by car and pick me up at three o'clock.

I thank them and say "I will be out in front at three o'clock, ready to jump in" because a car cannot stop even for a moment on these busy streets. I would walk, but I have no idea where they live. But first, go to breakfast with Delfina and Conchita.

At Mesón San José I get Conchita started on topics that interest her. She comes to life, happily telling about her school. I like hearing it all because I like and love Conchita, and also because what she tells about school is interesting. I feel glad because usually we adults do most of the talking, and now Conchita can have a turn at leading the conversation. Kids don't always want to be the center of attention, and I can remember how I preferred to be the listener at my mother's events, but Conchita is growing up, and she is a great person.

Since this is becoming sort of "Conchita's Day", she suggests going to a young teens store. I am delighted to get to accompany Conchita and mamá. The store is a tiny, narrow corridor. As I have explained, there are almost no Great Houses left functioning as such. They may still have a family living in a part of the house, but large portions will have been rented or sold for use as banks, restaurants, offices, and stores. This "Young Miss Store" probably was a hallway in a Great House.

The walls, an arm-span apart, are covered with glittery ornaments, hair decorations, fancy socks, slippers covered in embroidery, or flowers, or plastic emblems, stamped colors and designs, jewelry of every sort, teen lip glosses, frilly underwear, dressed up eye glasses with rhinestones or colors, or sunglasses with lenses shaped like hearts. There is so much to see and touch and dream over. I have stepped into a girls' world of pink, and purple, and every color of glitter and glitz.

Conchita's original quest was for school uniform socks. Not exciting, but a good reason to be here.

We still have time for one more stop before I have to stand on the corner waiting for Juan Alfonso's car. Conchita is the most thoughtful girl. You can see why I love her and her sweet nature. She says, "Sonette, do you want to accompany me to the Bureau of

Tourism? I need materials for my History of San Miguel report for school, and you can find nice things for Mary's classes. I will help you." "Oh, yes, thank you, what a great idea." I reply, and we walk to El Jardín to find maps and folders, brochures, posters, and at Conchita's urging, I am even given free travel videos that Mary's classes will be sure to love.

We return home in time for me to stash my loot in my room, and I make it to the corner by a minute or two before three o'clock. On the dot, Juan Alfonso's car pulls up, with Camelia and the children accompanying him. The kids are also named Juan Alfonso and Camilia. While together, it is not hard to differentiate between the double naming, since I can address the person I want, child or parent, by looking at him or her. But writing is a little harder. I call the young ones Hijo or Hija, son or daughter, which is correct, meaning junior and.....? What is the English for a girl junior? No idea.

We drive way past El Gigante and out into the countryside. Our drive takes us down what should be more properly called lanes, smaller and dustier than roads. It is beautiful, and I am delighted to be out in the country. We arrive at a beautiful house surrounded by acres of green, mown grass. This is exceedingly rare and denotes luxury. There are a few pretty trees, a large in-ground swimming pool, a huge cabana the size of a house by the pool, and a few other out-buildings.

We enter the house which is airy, bright, and starkly decorated in the minimalist style. But the atmosphere is anything but barren. This family is warm and hospitable. I quickly am delighted by the intelligent and lively conversations. Juan Alfonso is the private pilot for someone important who flies back and forth from Mexico to Texas, and other parts of the USA, I believe. We could easily converse in English, but I am happy that we use Spanish.

Immediately I am offered wine, nuts, and French chocolates. Camilia moves to the open kitchen to prepare guacamole, rice, two fresh sauces, and whole green onions for grilling. Doors and windows are wide open. We sit in the breezy living room while curtains billow from the entrance to the patio where Juan Alfonso grills steaks.

We move to the patio and sit in the slanted light of the afternoon sun at a table, refreshed by the soft, sweet country air, and begin our dinner. The steaks are the most tender and juicy that I have ever had. Delicious! Also we have hot tortillas, and everything is seasoned by our delightful new friendship.

It is a warm and perfect day, blue of brightest sky dotted with puffy white clouds. I notice that the whole large compound is ringed by mesquite trees.

Somehow they have found out that today is my birthday, and in my honor Camilia has made an American dessert, her own apple pie with ice cream. They all sing to me the Mexican birthday song, "Las Mañanitas". It is touching and fills that tiny spot of emptiness that comes from being away from your own family on your birthday. God gives us many families in endless, unexpected ways.

Both children want to show me their rooms. Each is so indicative of the bright and shining personality of the one who lives there. Juan Alfonso hijo has a large photo of his Foreign Camp, a camp experience with seventeen different nationalities. His dad is letting him invite two of the boys to come here and spend the entire Christmas vacation, and both boys have accepted with permission and blessing from their families. One boy is from Egypt and may invite Juan Alfonso hijo to go to their home in Egypt for a few months. The other is Japanese. What exciting plans.

Next year Camilia hija will go to Foreign Camp. She is slender and beautiful and has the lead role in "Beauty and the Beast" which will be presented at the Teatro Angelita Peralta, but unfortunately that will take place after I have left. She wants to go to Hollywood and be a movie star.

Without the children we talk about many things. Juan Alfonso and Camilia thank me for tips I pass along from ideas I have been given or what I have learned from experience regarding hosting foreign children or sending your young ones to live abroad with a family.

The parents call Juan Alfonso hijo to the table to hear about the Creative Arts Teams that I started and established at the high school where I taught. He is very intelligent and creative, and such kids always need reassurance that who they are is valuable, respected, and normal. There is far too much honor accorded to brute strength and money, although the exaltation of competitive team sports that dominates American schools is not the problem in

Mexico that it is in the States.

Camilia wants to start their son's foreign experiences by sending him to be an exchange student in the USA before letting him go to Egypt or Japan. I write down how to contact the exchange company that I used for many years, and I describe the special care they take with the host families and exchange students, give the parents tips, and explain some of the perils and how to avoid common misunderstandings. For this, they are grateful.

They drive me home, and I go to bed happy with my day, my new friends, and my Mexican birthday party, complete with a family serenade, Las Mañanitas.

33

HEAD IN BOX, BLOOD IN JAR,
AND STARVATION AND SOCCER

I awaken at seven, tired, but at seven fifteen I decide to jump up, put on clothes, and rush to mass. But today I do not like the "sermon" at all. My guess is that this is an obligatory story read from the big Catholic book that has to be used by the priests, that is my guess. Usually the sermons are, as I have said, about love and forgiveness and spring from some little story in the Bible. But today's reading is grisly and totally out of character. I wonder if our sweet, kindly priest believes this story, or does it apply in any way to life's betterment, or is he forced to follow certain rules about what must be read on which day that give no lee-way? Here is the story.

A certain saint in 325 AD was killed for his faith. When those in charge of such murder-executions chopped off his head, people ran to get sheets in order to trap his blood. Evidently this was a common practice, both the chopping and the blood catching. The people got a lot of blood and put it in a clean jar.

The chopped off head, and the jar of blood, were kept on the altar of the town's church. Head in box, blood in jar. Every so often, the blood would revive itself, turn red again, and fill up the jar.

At one time when the blood was reviving, Mt. Vesuvius erupted, and the lava was headed right for the town. The priest took the container of blood close to the lava, with the entirety of the townspeople following, which made the lava turn and by-pass the village or city, whichever it was.

I believe in the power of prayer, but I do not believe in the power of blood in a jar, or power of a chopped off head. Oh, well, to each his own.

I return home, sort of in a hurry, to use the bathroom. A man is waiting at the door to be let in. I tell him that I have no authority to let him in. Later I find out that Raúl came to admit him, and he is the workman whom I have seen every day working away on the constant restoration of this very house. I am ashamed for not recognizing him.

I find him and apologize, but it would be way too insulting to say, "I did not recognize you". I say, "I think I should have let you in, and I am sorry that I did not. I was not sure if I am supposed to let people in or not." (If I sound overly cautious, that is because other workmen have stolen tools in the past, I have been told, and I don't want to be responsible for anything that could happen. Still, I feel very rude and mean. This is how you can get, about daily in-house workers, if you are not careful. You do not see them enough as real people, so that out of their work stations, you do not even recognize them. At least I can forgive myself for not having become friendly, since I would never try to become friends with a man. It is almost always misinterpreted, no matter what.) I should have first said, "I recognize you, but I am not authorized." However, as I admit, I was not alert at all, and away from his accustomed spot, I did not realize who he was.

We have breakfast. I help in the Botica, until 2:30. While working, I reconsider yesterday's conversation with Juan Alfonso and Camilia. I phone Juan Alfonso and, thankfully, I reach him. I start by thanking them for the wonderful visit and birthday party.

Then I say, "I suggest that you do not send your son to the USA to be an exchange student. He already speaks excellent English, and American schools are two years behind Mexican private schools. He would be really bored, and since he is still slender and small for his age, he could not be put two grades higher, where all the boys would be so much bigger, dating, heavily into physical contact sports. Juan Alfonso hijo is artistic and intellectual, and advanced in science. I do not think school in the United States would be a good match for him."

I continue, "Instead, I believe that he would gain more from returning with one of your son's Christmas guests to Egypt or Japan. To me, Japan sounds safer, but you can investigate and make the best decision. It will be more of a challenge, he will learn a truly foreign language, make future business contacts, learn a new culture. A Japanese or Egyptian family is also likely to guard him with extreme care, whereas in the States, kids are given a lot of freedom. Talk it over with Camilia."

Right away he agrees with me, saying they hadn't thought about all that. He will discuss it with Camilia, and I feel relieved. I have done the best I can, and now it is their family's decision.

Raúl comes to get me for comida. While at the table, we each tell about our Sunday. During the afternoon, the family went to relatives for a dinner party. I was invited too, but of course I could not accept two invitations at once.

The really interesting story comes from Raúl and Raulito. While we women were at breezy, cheerful, yummy Mesón San José, Raúl and Raulito were at the prison. Here is how it works. Raúl gets to see the prisoners who are in AA. When any prisoner has an anniversary, of being free from drugs or alcohol, Raúl is allowed to make a celebration.

Raúl goes twice per month, or more, to hold Sunday morning meetings. Raúl always supplies the food, so they have a very loyal following of prisoners with an excellent reason to attend. Yesterday it was the Saint's Day of the Saint of Prisoners. (This makes much more practical sense than the dead saint's head in a box on the altar.) Raúl brings Raulito whenever he is allowed to do so. Yesterday's party consisted of Raúl bringing cooked chickens for everyone, and then father and son spent five hours cooking tacos!

Everyone loves a party, everyone loves Raúl and Raulito, and everyone loves good food. But for the prisoners, the opportunity Raúl gives them for food and encouragement is one hundred times more important to them than any of us can imagine. Here is why.

In prison, the men are given tiny rations. Everything else must be purchased or brought to you by your relatives. There are some jobs available for earning money, but pay is horribly low, and food is expensive. The men really are starving to death. Only thirty-one of the one hundred and sixty prisoners ever have visitors to bring them food.

As we hear of the woes of the prisoners, we eat our own abundant comida, which is:

- Lime aid.
- Watermelon.

- Chicken soup with pastas that are tiny dots, as if they were punched out by a paper hole cutter for your three-ring binder.
- Hog back (chicharón) with chopped tomatoes, and green sauce over the chicharón, and an avocado sliced on top.
- Beef shredded in a sauce made of boiled purple chiles.
- Beans.
- Rice.
- Tortillas, hot and all-you-can-eat.
- Coffee.

We talk about Raulito's friendship with the prisoners. He plays soccer with two of them, which they love. Raulito and Delfina are going to buy special T shirts so the prison can have a soccer team with uniforms. It is all Raulito's idea. He is a great kid!

Each prisoner is given one plate and one cup. If he loses it or it breaks, no food until he can earn another, I don't know how. When it is so-called "meal time", everyone runs with his plate because the food runs out before everyone is served, and those who are last get nothing. Bah, once again, bah!

After comida it is time to get jolly again. What can I do? I am helpless once again about suffering that I cannot control or change.

So I get out all the clothes, and socks, and jewelry, and shoes that I still possess and am ready now to give these away too. Chita helps me. I ask her to divide it all, one half for Rafaela, and one half for herself. Chita is excellent at this. She knows who can use and fit into what, and what each person will like the most. Chita says she is still very happy with what I gave her on my last visit, and she wears these items regularly to show me how nice they look.

When I am ready to walk out the door for the final time, I will leave every scrap of everything except what I bought as gifts for home, which is almost nothing. My Sea Bag (Richard's old Navy canvas bag), will collapse into my suitcase, I will push my few purchases into the remaining spaces, and that will be it. In my travel purse, I will have a novel, sweater, toothbrush and toothpaste, lipstick, passport, airline and bus tickets, a few single one dollar bills, and a few pesos that I have saved for tips en route.

And driver's license, a pen (for filling out forms), and one last notebook. Now I can relax and enjoy what remains to me of this visit.

34

SUBLIME VIRGIN WITH DIAMONDS, SOPHISTICATED EVIL BY LOCAL WITCHES, AND OUTRAGE OVER BROKEN PROMISES

When I depart for mass, I take with me the gift I have gotten ready for the old lady, the anciana, who sweeps the church garden with a twig broom and opens and closes the chapel gates. Every day she wears the same "outfit" which is: very old hurackes (an old style of poor field worker type sandals), no socks. A long checkered dress, over that a checked apron, a striped shirt someone gave her (she says a rich friend), and I think she wears a sweater under the shirt.

Each time I go to mass I take two five peso coins. I put one in the collection and give the other to her. I have brought with me a very pretty flannel jacket of soft blue and pink checks, and I put it into a large, new, plastic woven bag that I had bought to take home as a gift. I add several pairs of socks, several knee-high nylons, a nice pair of leather loafers, a new cover-all apron, and a new fly swatter (for mosquito season). It gets below freezing here in the winter months, and no one has heat. Certainly old, poor ladies do not, and there is no heating system at all in the churches. So I am thinking about her need for something warmer during the cold months. Then, just to be cute, I add a stuffed toy bunny. It looks so friendly and perky.

I give La Anciana the bag, which she accepts, the same way she always accepts my coins. Not excited, not expecting, not seemingly anything. She just takes it.

The sermon of the mass is the re-building of the temple of Jerusalem, which doesn't particularly inspire or interest me. But after the service, something nice happens. I have stayed in the chapel to wait in line with the others who want a word with the priest. When it is my turn, I give him three hundred pesos for his fund which he uses to feed poor, homeless, street children. He beckons for me to come farther into his giant study (I think it is shared by the other priests too) to stand in front of the statue of the Virgin of Loretto.

The statue, until now, has been on display on the altar. He explains many fascinating things about it, and he is so joyous about sharing all this with me. Here is what he tells, in a devoted, loving, and sweet way.

The Count of (somebody, I can't remember the name) donated this virgin. I would call it a statue, but Catholics call them all The Virgin. It was made in Spain in 1590 or 1650, thereabouts. He points out the beautiful faces of the Mother and Baby Jesus, made of porcelain. He proudly says that even The Virgin's delicate, porcelain the hands are there, but you cannot see them because of her dress and The Baby's fancy wrappings.

The dress is made of heavy white satin covered with real gold, fancy ribbons, and braids. The veil is blue and maybe twenty feet long, covered with real diamonds and golden six-pointed stars. There is no ceiling in the "house" where she has been displayed until now, but in the interior of the giant church which surrounds the house, the ceiling is about forty feet up and is covered also with golden six-pointed stars which have mirrors in the center. On the dress there are lots of ropes of real pearls, and there are also many real diamonds attached to the dress. Around the face part of the veil, there are borders of real diamonds and real rubies. Over that, but set back so you can view all the splendor, she wears a white lace mantilla.

The Virgin wears a triple crown. The priest explains that Bottom means Virgin, Middle means Mother, and Top means Queen of the Universe. I try to harmonize my own ideas with the Catholic beliefs that are being explained to me. So my agreeing goes like this: Virgin means purity, which means innate perfection. Mother means multiplication of spiritual self-existence. "Queen of All the Universe" means Divine Principle governing all that exists. That is how I hear ideas, by thinking, "This idea sounds unusual. What do I have in common with this idea that someone else is presenting?"

The Baby Jesus also wears a crown. In another sermon I remember the priest telling us of the sacred nature of the babyhood of Jesus. This makes sense to me too in illustrating the tenderness and love of what the Creator feels for His/Her creation. The babyhood of Jesus would express his complete trust and dependency on God, just as a baby trusts and depends upon its father and mother for care and love.

The priest goes on to explain that this Virgin is only on display during the period that I have been here, culminating in being carried through the streets. Now all the fancy furniture, flowers, all the decorations of the chapel, which is believed to be an exact replica of the Virgin Mary's house, have been removed until next year.

When the kindly old priest has finished, I give him the money, and of course I thank him for all the comfort and inspiration he has given me in the masses. Then I ask him to please have mercy on all the doves which live in tiny cages in the damp, dark, clammy hall outside of the chapel, and to please let them go. He says he cannot because they were gifts from people who wanted the birds' singing to beautify the mass. (To me this is not beautiful, it is pathetic and tragic.)

I say, "Then please put them in the garden, in the sunlight." He replies that usually they do, but the woman who moves them is gone because she is sick. When she returns, she will start moving the cages outside each day.

This is his final chance to educate me, and I ask him about when one is supposed to kneel. I don't want to disregard something that seems so important to the members of the church. He says that when you cross in front of the altar, you only have to nod your head unless the candle is burning. If it is, you are supposed to kneel on one knee. (I will get mixed up and forget which is which, but I will kneel or nod whenever I am pretty sure that I am doing so according to the rules.)

Before I can take my long and beautiful walk, I have to go home to use the bathroom. If I lived farther away, I have no idea how I could function.

After one hour, I have finished my walk and return home to find Rafaela. I tell her that everything on Nita's bed is for her, including plastic bags for carrying it home. She is very happy.

I wash clothes by hand in the laundry room because Rafaela is cleaning my rooms. I hang the clothes to dry on the roof, and I go to the Botica where I carefully wash the antique windows which have been etched in an old-fashioned design. All this activity before it is time for breakfast!

Raúl and I are the only ones for breakfast, and he tells me all about the witchcraft that is currently practiced in San Miguel. There is a strong and dangerous group of followers, and he has had personal experiences with them. They are serious and evil, not to be taken lightly. I remember when I wanted Abelardo to take me out of town to walk to the tops of the high hills, hills that to me were mountains, outside of San Miguel. He said, "No, Sonette, there are caves where the three witches live up there. You must not go."

I took Abelardo's warning and concern as just another cute bit of superstitious lore. The way the witches in those days worked apparently involved someone going to them and asking for love potions or else bad-things-to-happen potions for people one hates. The bad potions were powders to be sprinkled over your disliked person's food. My guess was that they were poisons. The love potions featured getting your intended to drink a nasty concoction involving your own saliva. But you must be the first one he sees after partaking of this, because he will love whoever he sees the moment he finishes his loathsome drink. Good Grief! Ay, Caramba!

Abelardo took me horseback-riding, out in the dessert among the cactus. And bike riding on giant wheeled, black iron bicycles, which were so tall I had to mount or dismount by standing on rocks or a curb, riding with all teeth rattling and chattering over the cobblestones, until I realized that San Miguel is not for bikers. But he never did take me hiking in the mountains. So I never saw the caves, and I never saw the witches.

Richard and I did climb the highest hill once, when we were first dating, or maybe already married. The view was spectacular, and the only bad thing that happened to us was that I did not know enough to bring along anything to eat or drink. Richard had brought one orange each and a bottle of wine. We drank it all, from the summit, because we were so thirsty. I had no idea that wine made you even thirstier, and we practically ran to town in search of a drink. I remember going to the only place we knew of that served water, because it was owned by Americans. It was called Jayco, and all they had on the menu were waffles with strawberries, and whipped cream, and pecans, and syrup (which we loved). And Coca Colas with fresh limes, and water, oh, at last, water!

Raúl says that today's witches are nothing like that. They are sophisticated, have ceremonies and rituals, and are dangerous enemies. I believe him, having read before I came to Mexico about anti-Catholic witches, or something like that, who are modern day and completely hideous in thought and in practice. Anyway, these are the strange topics that I find interesting, and far enough apart from my experience that I don't feel more than just part of a curious discussion, sort of like gossip about people you don't even know. Interesting, but you don't much care.

Now we adjourn to Raúl's private family rooms where he shows me the second of the albums about their recent three month tour of Europe this summer, just before Nita and I arrived. They even went to the Olympics. Raúl likes to take his family to every Olympics as a good excuse to go all over the world, plus he loves the thrill of the Olympic hul-a-baloo, pageantry, and probably the skills of the contestants.

Finally it is the day to go shopping for gifts for home, now or never, and I go to the market. For my girlfriends I buy spices: Cinnamon in stick form, or are they roots? Or branches? Or bark? Cloves, large peppercorns, and anything that you would not see in a store. Three small bottles of tequila. (In my ignorance I buy cheap ones because of the price, and also because I think my friends don't drink tequila anyway, so how would they know if it is good or bad? I don't.) A large plastic pitcher for Chita, the one other prize in La Tumbla that she would have liked, she said.

I deposit these in my room and go back to buy hand-crafted toys and decorations for Mary's Spanish classes. I used to buy lots of these and give them as prizes to my students on Spanish Bingo Days. (Ha, ha, you should have seen the odd prizes I gave, some of which are still talked about to this day.) But prices for toys are high now, I am surprised to see. Instead I buy myself a necklace and bracelet for ballroom dancing. They are made of little shiny beads like we used to put on straight pins and wear stuck through our white-blouse-Peter- Pan collars in Junior High School. The young woman who sells the beaded jewelry makes them right before your eyes. Both together cost seven dollars.

At eight pesos each I buy ten paper maché chile peppers and the other ingredients it takes to make salsa. My son-in-law loves to make his own salsa. He will love this gift, I am positive. Mary loves pan dulces. It costs a bit more for "pan dulces" (large rolls with sugar decorations) but again I buy ten, one of each different kind. The chocolate covered donut with colored sprinkles is not really a pan dulce, but it looks so mouth-wateringly realistic that I buy it too.

A beautiful hand-painted tray for…? Maybe Terry, Jason's mother? Joanne, Jason's step-mother likes tequila. (Remember that I think what I have bought is fine, not terrible as later everyone will tell me when they make fun of my choice.)

My suitcase will not be occupied by the Sea Bag now. I will be lucky to fit all of these giant, bulky gifts into both the suitcase and the Sea Bag too. I must be sure to weigh my luggage before I leave here, because for sure I will not pay another fifty dollars overweight charges like on the way coming here!

I take my purchases to my room and on the way see Rafaela. She loves all the clothes and jewelry and is very happy. And I am too, because my shopping is done, everything I need to do has been accomplished, and it is time for comida.

Chita has been making all of my favorites. We have an unusual soup, cauliflowerettes in tomatoes and limes. Delicious, and Chiles Rellenos, my heavenly delight of the food world.

Our talk, because of Rita having fled New Orleans, is on what is being reported on Mexican TV news and in the Mexican newspapers. There is outrage here, and I agree, over the Mexican army going to the USA to pass out food while here at home there is "necesidad", lack of sufficient food to eat, even right here in San Miguel. It is considered beyond wrong because whatever food there is here in Mexico should be passed out to the Mexican citizens who are starving. That is the reason so many try to cross the border, find work, and scrimp and save to send all their money home to feed the whole poverty stricken family.

Also on Mexican TV everyone saw Bush say that any Mexicans (in the US illegally) who would go fight in the war for the US army would be granted American citizenship. So one Mexican young man did go and was killed in action. Instead of honoring the promise, the United States rounded up the young man's whole family, deported them, sent the soldier's body to Mexico, and gave the family a check for ten dollars! There is outrage about this all over the nation.

Also, Mexicans were told if they were in the States illegally and went to New Orleans to clean up, they would be granted amnesty. Instead, after working for twelve hours, without being given food, or water, or pay, they were put in a bus, driven to the border, and deported. These things are not publicized in the USA, so Americans don't understand how much ill will is being generated. What a mess.

As usual, I may as well enjoy myself, since I can't do anything about the insults to humanity that we all agree are wrong. It is already six o'clock, so I'd better start painting right away. By eight thirty I have finished. I am satisfied. The painting gives me a good feeling. Yea!

35

MAYAN CODICES AT MY FINGERTIPS, BIRTHDAY CAKE WITHOUT FACE PUSHING, DRAGONS, MERMAIDS, AND CATS

Although I awake in plenty of time to go to mass, something tells me not to. And a good thing it is, because at eight AM Nita arrives. I am so glad I am still here at home because she is excited to tell me all about her trip, and I am so happy to have her back.

Nita took an all-night bus, nine hours. The bus is a deluxe sleeper! First they have a movie and sandwiches. Then everyone turns out the lights and goes to sleep because the seats are wide and comfortable and recline to an almost bed, even with a foot rest coming up for your legs and feet. Nita is a champion sleeper, so she has arrived refreshed. The bus went from Monterrey to Querétaro, and then she took a cab here- a one hour ride for only twenty-five dollars. Wow.

We are called to breakfast. We talk for hours with Raúl. He tells us about ancient Mayan codices and shows me the deluxe, large, heavy volumes they have right here in their enormous library. I have heard of these, the way one does of a legend, but never thought I would get such a chance as this to see, not just one, or a piece of one, but a whole set of color illustrations, reproductions, and tomes of text. I stay on and read for two hours more. Finally I have to stretch and go for a walk.

Nita and I are invited for comida at Lita's. When we arrive we see that her son, two granddaughters, and two great grandchildren are also here, as I guess they are every day. We start by sitting in the living room, visiting, enjoying margaritas, and Lita's peanuts that she cooks herself from some special recipe. I have never known anyone who prepares homemade peanuts. Of course they are superb.

Then we have my other favorite of favorites, chicken with mole.

(Anything with mole is my favorite.) We have consume with limes squeezed into it. Rice, beans, chamote, green sauce, and tortillas. Lita serves us the tortillas in the following way. The doorbell rings, and it is the señora who stops at Lita's house and other houses every afternoon at this time delivering fresh tortillas. For a huge stack of (maybe forty?) tortillas, homemade, it costs thirty cents. This is the only food that is really cheap. Why so cheap?

There is "necesidad", lack of work, lack of income, lack of crop harvests because of lack of water because river water is being diverted to those more powerful. It is a terrible chain that makes lack a serious problem in "los campos", out where people must grow their own food. A woman like this, who makes her own tortillas each morning and walks door-to-door selling them is working very hard to earn a pittance in the only way available to her. I don't know this woman's particular story, but here is the common one.

A family has access to a small parcel of land, too small and rough to be called a farm. The family plants corn, beans, and maybe squash. Corn is planted with a stick and harvested by hand. The dried kernels are taken to the local mill as needed for making masa, corn dough. To make masa is a long process, probably begun each day pre-dawn.

Tortillas are patted out by hand, one at a time, and cooked over an open charcoal fire on a comal, which is a flat metal plate. These are the tortillas that señoras from el campo make and bring to town to sell. This may be the origin of the tortillas we right now are being served for lunch. Lita is lucky to have them delivered each day right to her door. The seller is lucky to have a customer. But it is heart-rending to think of the work involved for such a tiny monetary gain. (Some people, back in the States, tell me, "Sonette, you think too much.")

For dessert we have one of the few cakes I really enjoy, a typical white Mexican birthday cake. Instead of frosting, it has an inch or two of thick whipped cream covering it, and fresh red strawberries dotting the top and sliced to fit in between the layers. No one pushes the birthday person's face into the cake, as is commonly done to the glee of all, even the victim. Since it is a celebration of Lita's birthday, we are all too dignified to do face pushing, I guess. I suppose that is the reason to neglect this hilarious custom. All we do is sing and then eat.

After this happy afternoon of such good-will and friendliness, it is time for me to make my last purchase. At the start of this visit I entered the mask store. Now it is time to return for Bob's gift. I select two bright shining "lizards". These are delightful, fanciful, dragonesque. They are long, twisty pods with the seeds still inside, from I don't know what tree, but where I live the Catalpa trees drop similar pods. To see the creative mind that turns old, dried pods into gloriously painted, serpentine dragons with teeth, eyes, and little legs is a visual treat. Some even have other animals riding upon their backs, so naturally I pick those. It is hard not to want them all, but I make myself select only two. These can be nailed right through our lath-and-plaster walls to hang anywhere Bob wants them.

My son-in-law is Jason, whose step-father, Ken, has a wonderful sense of humor, so I buy him a paper maché mermaid which is very humorous with her sneaky smile and two white pointy breasts. He will love it. What a conversation piece! Jason loves cats, so I buy him a deluxe tiger which looks like a man in a flat tiger suit with a tiger mask head.

When I get back home, I sit in the kitchen for a long visit with Chita. I show her the books of Mayan codices and explain the little that I know about them. Chita is very smart and quick to understand a great deal. She is not wasted in her job. She is more than the cook. She is the manager of the running of the household, helper with everything, and entrusted with the safety of the house with all the details those jobs require. Everyone not only loves Chita; they are grateful for her wisdom and work. Everyone respects her, greatly respect her. And with good reason. Being appreciated is something we all want, hope for, enjoy. And being respected is something we earn.

Chita leaves her perusal of the codices to make soup and juice for Raulito. I finish another painting, this time of a fountain in back of La Paróquia. I am pleased. Nita comes into the room, and I enjoy hearing more about her trip before I get in bed to read.

36

BIG BAD TEETH, AND THE NINE DAYS ROSARY

Nita and I sleep until eight thirty, very late for us, and when we awaken, we say, "Que rico!" "How delicious!"

Nita goes to the kitchen, makes her first-thing-upon-arising-oatmeal, and leaves for the dentist. I wait and join the family for our usual elaborate breakfast and endless conversation, which means we are all still at the table when Nita returns. She is very angry, and justifiably so. Her new bridgework is all wrong and makes her look ridiculous. Nita is a very pretty woman, and these teeth are too big, too white, stick too far out, and who would not be upset by that. We all say, "You are right. Do not accept this. You are so pretty, and the dentist has ruined you. Go back. Insist. Do not give up."

Encouraged, justified, she returns to the dental office. Eventually they agree and do a good job so once again Nita becomes her lovely self, smiling, the Nita we love. The Nita she deserves to be. The Nita she really is.

Now that she is fine, we all gather for comida. It is so good, featuring two of my favorites, papaya, and red enchiladas, and of course, much, much more.

Now it is five o'clock, and the family leaves for hearing the last of nine days of attending the rosary! A friend has died, and that is what everyone has to do, in memory of the deceased. While they are gone I lose all track of time by making another painting. It seems like I just started, and now it is late. They are all back again.

37

PRE-PAMPLONADA TOURTURE CHAMBER, LAVISH RESORT OF THE MISTRESS OF CORTEZ, OR THE HOWARD JOHNSON MOTEL? AND THE PRESIDENT'S ATTENTION

Always, right after someone leaves, there is a little let-down. First, the flurry of getting ready, then finally able to leave, at the last possible moment, but to still be on time for the plane or the bus. And last, silence. The person is gone.

Nita is leaving for another trip. Again, she has invited me, and I have declined, but with sincere thanks. Starting at ten PM last night, Nita bustled around our room, but not much really got done. She told me she wanted to awake by seven and leave by eight fifteen. I am the one who, nervous for her sake, awakes at seven, and I tell her that this is when she wanted to get up.

I always accompany Nita for her oatmeal time, both of us sitting in the kitchen at the tiny table, starting the morning together. Nita has showered and dressed, and finally she has packed. I am the only one getting the jitters about the progress of the clock, but not much progress towards leaving. Nita takes her time making and eating breakfast, until I say, "Shouldn't you be getting a taxi?" "Oh", she waves her hand, "I will send Chita." This means walking to the Jardín, finding a taxi, and then riding for blocks in zig-zags with the driver to the Botica, because we are on a one-way street going the wrong direction for easy pick-up. "I will send her pretty soon", she says. It is already eight fifteen, the time she had planned to leave, the luggage is still upstairs, and no taxi.

Just then Raúl hollers that he will drive her to the bus station. It is a far drive, to my way of thinking. Her bus leaves at eight forty. More last minute things keep happening until finally they leave. They will make it with one or two minutes to spare, no doubt, and no one will be worried at all. I wish I were not so American in that respect.

Driving the car does not mean walking to the car and getting in. It involves hollering for Chita to drop everything and come to the front of the house to open and close the huge outside doors. The doors glide on their ancient, curved, embedded, iron rails, the same as the churches' enormous old, old gates.

There is about one inch to spare to back the van straight out to the street. Then wiggle, wiggle, left, right, left, right, and finally Raúl is positioned correctly for starting out. Because of the removal of the previous street, and the widening of the sidewalks, it was a scary thought that perhaps Raúl's car would not be able to make it in and out of the house anymore. It is ok, because it turns out that it can be done, but no one except Raúl would attempt it.

Now Nita's bags can be loaded and she can get in. Even though the side doors of the van slide, it is still almost impossible to enter until the car is out of the confines of the entryway. When Raúl returns, he will have to honk for Chita, and she will have to run even faster to open the great doors, because until Raúl has tucked the car away entirely, all traffic will be stopped and rapidly backing up on his narrow front-door street.

A few will honk, as if anything else could be done to speed up the process and get out of the way faster.

Nita's destination is Guadalajara where she will attend a First Communion. She will be back Monday at six PM. I leave Tuesday at eight AM. We will just have time for "Hello" and "Goodbye".

Because of La Pamplonada, the rest of us are leaving sometime today for Leon. Raúl had said we were to stay at a beautiful hacienda that Cortez built for La Malinche. Nita says, no, we are going to the Howard Johnson Motel. Raúl has business in Leon, that is why the change. I am all packed for the trip to the motel, and this time I am taking only clothes that are wrinkle-proof, which means very thin and tiny garments.

I don't know when breakfast will be, or when we will leave, so I shampoo and dress. Nothing happens. I paint for a while. I make a plan for before we leave. To buy cloth, trapo, to use for packing my take-home souvenirs. Ceramic light switch covers for my house, and ceramic knobs for Mary's kitchen cupboards. Go to the bank. Even take a walk if I still have time. Maybe I should buy one more pen. I packed lots of pens, I was sure, but I only found three in my suitcase. The three are used up, and I will need one for filling out forms at the airport, and maybe I will write more too.

Last night Raúl gave me a tour of rooms in this house that I had never seen. There were storerooms, the six roof-top apartments, all the clothes washing areas (which I did know about already). So there are always people in residence, with much coming and going, whether we are paying attention or not.

Every day at comida, Conchita has begged to stay for La Pamplonada. She is of the age when huge crowds mean excitement, and her friends get to stay in town. This year they are old enough to want to be part of seeing what goes on without their parents. They are not thinking of the ugly treatment of the bulls. They are kids, growing up, and excited about taking part in their town's spectacles and adventures.

When I was in a car a few days ago, I can't remember why, we drove towards El Gigante. On the side of the road, in a dusty open field, sat a sort of a metal cattle-car. I say, sort of, because it had no slats for ventilation. It was painted red, had locked doors all over the sides, and had only small windows at the tops of the doors. "Do you see that, Sonette? That contains the bulls. They are waiting for La Pamplonada."

This was a horrific revelation. It was already unbearably hot in the sun, if you stood outside the bull container, even with the breeze that might move over your skin slightly. But inside that red metal container, with no ventilation, I cannot even guess how hot it must have been. The bulls were left standing, confined in that torture chamber.

I asked how often they were let out. "Only when they are taken into the towns and let out into the streets to run for La Pamplonada." This is such horrible cruelty that it makes my stomach churn. "These are the bulls that travel to all the towns giving La Pamplonada. They must not see people or light until they are let out."

I already know of this practice about bull fighting, that they must never see a man on foot until the bull fight, so that they don't realize how weak their killer is. However, at least bull fight bulls are raised on ranches, attended to by men on horseback. Bulls for the matador are also confined in darkness before being let into the ring so that they will be blinded by the sun and confused by the roar of the spectators, giving the matador and his ceremonial team a great advantage. But at least those bulls, during their confinement, presumably have air and water.

I want to leap out of the auto, run to the evil bull car, find a way to unlock the doors, get water, get the police, go downtown and alert everyone. "Do you know what is being done to the bulls? Help! Find a way to at least get the bulls into a field, or cut holes in the terrible doors, do anything possible to rescue the animals from their useless misery!" But I know that I can do nothing. This is the system. No one would help me. The police and town officials already know. The only ones who might care are people like me, helpless.

The day passes, and we do not leave San Miguel. Raúl comes to tell me that we will leave the next morning instead. The reason is that the president is coming to town, bringing with him a woman who is a friend of Delfina's. His wife? This woman is a relative or friend of Delfina's. Raúl and Delfina will quickly make copies of all the documents relating to the court case about the digging. If this woman will help, maybe something will be resolved, action will be taken.

They decide to prepare a "short form" about their case. They will be working until late tonight. If they can get their papers into this woman's hands, she will pass it to the president for his immediate and personal attention. President of what? I wonder. The state? The nation?

"Be packed and ready to leave by eight AM.", Raúl instructs.

38

LA PAMPLONADA HERE, LA PAMPLONADA IN SPAIN, BULL FIGHTS WITH ABELARDO, AND HELP, I AM TRAPPED WITH THE BULLS!

I am ready right on the dot at eight AM. I go to the kitchen, where Chita is preparing her morning beet juice. Every morning she uses the vegetable juicer, identical to the one my mother used when I was growing up, to prepare herself a glass of beet juice, or carrot juice, or something using other vegetables. She would gladly make the same for me, but seeing the juicer brings back revolting memories of my mother following me all around our house every day with a glass of the disgusting stuff, relentless in her pursuit of me, until I finally, gaggingly, drank it. To my mother, it was nectar from heaven. To me, it was another of the trials of being the daughter of a health-nut (although I eventually became very much a replica of my mother and her habits, all except for carrot juice.)

Chita long ago stopped offering me carrot juice, but I believe she makes an additional morning glass for Delfina. Chita prepares week-day breakfasts for the family early, carries everything to their private quarters so the kids will be fed before school, the trays being delivered right to everyone's bedrooms as they wake up. Sometimes I am down here in the kitchen with Chita as she prepares and delivers, and I also see what returns, eaten or uneaten. That is how I know who eats or likes what. Mainly the kids like pancakes, French Toast, and sugary cereals. Today though, everyone is still asleep.

While we visit, Chita carefully dismantles the complicated structure of the juicer, cleans it until it looks store-shelf ready again, and replaces it in the original box of purchase, just as she does with every one of the many appliances she uses daily.

I had not really expected that we would leave as early as eight o'clock, but I was told, so I did it. I am not bothered by this in any way. It doesn't matter to me what we do. I care about most: One, being in Mexico with this family, and Two, that things go right for them.

I have put more clothes, shoes, an umbrella, writing paper, envelopes, another broach, and a few other things in a bag for Rafaela. Whenever she comes here next, it will be waiting for her. To Chita I now give more clothes, shoes, and my "racket radio". I have not wanted to relinquish my racket radio. It has been my trusted friend on years of travels and satisfies my requirements as a noise muffler. It is ideal because One, It is not too big and heavy. Two, It has a cord so won't run out of power. Three, It is of sufficiently inferior quality to bring in strong static between the few stations it can access. I turn on the static loudly to muffle the awful noises of someone else's TV next door, or having my room right next to the elevator or ice maker, or hearing loud talking in the corridor all night. Now that I think of it, I'd better take it with me when we go to Howard Johnson's and give it to Chita when we get back.

I won the struggle with myself, wanting to keep it, by argument and logic. I rarely travel anymore. Chita's family does not have a radio. Why should this one sit in my closet, unused, waiting for maybe years before I take the next trip? I have money. I can buy another radio.

The same with my big pedestal fan, but different reasons for wanting to store it here for my someday return. It is large and cumbersome and therefore hard to get here from the USA. The other fan I brought, although brand new, arrived broken.

The arguments for leaving it for Rafaela are more compelling. She and her children live in a little almost windowless house (because of safety from robbery and because windows cost money) which must be boiling hot in summer. She lives with her parents, and now I realize that aunts and uncles live there too, again because of lack of money. Rafaela and her children have a little room "For just the three of us, señora", and she feels exceptionally lucky about that.

People who are so jammed together would surely enjoy a little air, especially since this fan is on a pedestal and rotates. There would not be interior doors, too expensive, so a breeze might help the whole little house. I will also give them an extension cord and outlet adapter because their house may not even have one outlet per room.

As I am thinking about this, Rafaela arrives with her sweet daughter. I give them the bag of clothes etc. that I have prepared, show them the fan, and instruct them that the minute I depart, Rafaela should put the fan in the storage space that the family allows the maids to use and take it home on the bus the same night. Rafaela and her daughter are completely delighted.

We have a great family breakfast, eventually. Raulito and Conchita arrive dressed for La Pamplonada, which means white T shirt and Levis, with a red scarf around the neck. (I do not notice that I too am dressed for La Pamplonada, in Levis and a white tank top, and I for sure do not understand what this will mean later on today.) The T shirts of the kids were purchased at the "Real" Pamplonada in Spain. Raulito wears his red kerchief around his neck, and Conchita wears hers as a belt. We are now dressed exactly like all the thousands who have come from far and wide and are now crowded into the downtown.

Raúl and Delfina have also dressed for the occasion. The kids are delighted that we have not left. Raulito gobbles his breakfast and asks to be excused. Conchita eats nothing, and both run off excitedly to meet their friends. The parents and I linger, savoring breakfast and conversation.

After a while Raúl leaves, returns to Delfina and me in the dining room, and says, "Sonette, would you like to see La Pamplonada? Come to our sala, it is on TV."

The hotel plan seems forgotten. Instead of watching on TV, I go outside to see the real event for myself. The young men and women who started arriving yesterday have also been drinking since yesterday. The streets are thick with discarded plastic cups and empty wine bottles. All these out-of-towners appear to be city people, men and women with harder eyes, a more sophisticated life-style, used to drinking heavily, who use "party" as a synonym for drunkenness. As with any confirmed hard drinkers, especially when they are still in their twenties, have good jobs, nourishing food, expensive cars and clothes, they do not show the effects of alcohol in sleepiness or slurred speech. But you can tell. These are not men and women who ever had a chaperone on a date. These are not sweethearts for whom novia means that the girl you choose to date will become your sweetheart, your fiancé, and then your innocent bride. There is nothing innocent left in theses strangers.

I think I am going to see the parade and join the crowd swarming through the narrow street. Although no one is even thirty years old except for me, this does not resonate. I continue on with them. Finally I realize that the parade is over, and everyone is pressing forward to El Jardín which will be the scene of the running with the bulls.

I still am not concerned. I walked around yesterday and saw the moveable barriers being put up. The barriers are tall, metal, made of horizontal bars, very much like the gates at my Iowa farm. I assume that these fences will separate and protect the watchers from the players. My plan is to find a good watching spot. There are police on horseback among us now. Every so often, a policía cries out, "Make way for all who want to enter! If you are going, go through now!" The crowd parts, to the degree that packed humanity allows, and young men squeeze forward to participate.

I continue to work my way forward, getting no resistance from the crowd, thinking that being little, I will find a good spot where I have a view in the front, or maybe high up, like for the fireworks, where I can see over all the tall people's heads. I can see people who arrived much sooner than I clinging to the bars of windows on the plaza, standing on the centuries old stone sills, and I start to understand the damage that will be done, and I see why residents do not like La Pamplonada.

Now the crowd parts wider, allowing the truck pulling the red metal torture chamber that contains the bulls. They will park at the street entrance, where in full view of the crowd, the bulls will be released, one by one. What I have not realized, is that I, yes, I, am within the area that holds only the young men who have traveled all this distance and squeezed their way into this very spot, because they are the ones who will at any moment be shoved into the streets along with the bulls! Caramba! I want out!

Getting out is no simple matter, and I don't know if I have minutes or just seconds to escape. People have filled the surrounding streets and are pushing forward with all their strength to get to the front, to be in the very spot where I am now. Now I understand how people can get trampled and crushed. The ones in the back push in order to come forward, and those at the front have nowhere to go, no way to signal, "Stop! We can't move anywhere! You are crushing us!" But I must get at least far enough into the jammed tangle of bodies, and arms, and legs to at least have a few people as a buffer between me and the soon to be released charging bulls, even if I can't escape completely. I do want to watch the spectacle, but at last I fully comprehend why Raúl said, "We invite you to our sala to watch it on TV." Oh, to be in their little nest of a living room at this very moment.

Here is how I make my escape. I stand sideways and insert the fingers of my right hand an inch or two between two of the bodies pressing me towards the bulls. I wiggle my fingers, wiggle, wiggle, until I can get my arm in up to the elbow. This brings me chest to chest with a stranger, and now I am in his way. He tries to make room for me to get behind him. I feel around for the next body, insert fingers again, wiggle, wiggle, pick up my right foot, push my toes, and then the whole shoe, into the slight space where legs belong to different people, then push in with my calf, then continue pushing with my leg, and this brings my... anyway, this brings me impolitely close to another young man who does his best to let me slide past. Finally, the crowd is less jam-packed, I can worm my way out, and I am free! "Good for you, Sonette", I congratulate myself.

I have to walk in a very long route in order to return to the house. There is no possibility of taking the direct streets. People now fill every conceivable area of standing room. Instead of taking the one block of street from where I find myself, the street that goes straight to Raúl's house, I have had to circle the edges of the whole downtown. And at last I am back.

I enter through the Botica. Perla and her husband are watching the scene on TV while Perla waits on clients. Business is booming. Raúl has been looking for me. Maybe Perla calls to tell him I have safely returned, because now he comes to the Botica to bring me to the sala. No more going out for a little while!

Rafaela and her daughter have been included and are already seated in front of the television and watching. Raúl serves me a tequila, for this most Mexican of days, and Rafaela jumps up, runs to the kitchen and fetches me sliced limes and salt.

To my relief, what I see now is not cruel. The only thing bad about this part for the bulls is that when they are released (and they do not burst forth, enraged and looking for a man to gore), they have to be dragged with a rope down the ramp from their confinement, and then given a nudge or a slap to get them going. The bulls are blinded by the sun, people are darting in front and around them, and it looks to me like the bulls would just like to run and discover an opening somewhere, speed through it, and high-tail it to the freedom and quiet of the dessert.

Instead their hoofs slide on the cobblestones, causing them to zig, zag, stagger, wander, and occasionally run. The men, so thrilled to be here on this momentous day, wave their red handkerchiefs as close to one of the bulls as they can, hoping to be chased, wanting badly to have a meaningful encounter. The worst thing anyone does to a bull is to slap it on the flanks, and not to hurt, just to make contact, to show their bravery, to be seen on TV by the folks back home. Raúl says that the other men would hit anyone who actually tried to hurt the bulls. This is intended to be a show of manly bravery, not of cruelty. And if I did not know of the suffering caused by callous confinement, I would not see this event as worse than a rodeo, in fact, less harsh than a rodeo, I suppose.

The danger to the men who are "fighters", or more properly, "runners", is from slipping and hitting one's head on the hard cobblestones of the street. In a bull-fight, horns have been sharpened to razor points to draw the matador's blood, if perchance the fight goes that way. These bulls' horns have been ground so as to be blunt. But a bull is a bull, and getting kicked or butted is a definite risk and danger. Bulls will use their horns to push a youth into a fence or wall, and keep pushing.

La Pamplonada, this part of it, doesn't seem anywhere near as bad as what someone had told me previously, and we are sort of enjoying the spectacle, as an interesting cultural phenomenon, when a fine looking fellow, maybe still in college, is tossed high by a bull, and right before our eyes, smashes his skull upon landing. Sirens, an ambulance is at hand, ready to help all who may get wounded, white coated rescuers, but later it is announced that sadly, the young man has died. I am a mother. I was a teacher. I think of his mother, all those who loved him, his exuberant, high spirits and male energy, his car with maybe a jacket waiting for him, the place his friends planned to eat and celebrate tonight. All of it is too terrible.

Those still running around the square, the crowds, are not aware of what has happened. Maybe even his friends have not seen him fall. The event goes on.

Finally it is time to force the dehydrated, panting bulls back into their unthinkable confinement. Is there water waiting for them at least? One at a time, the bulls are lassoed by the horns. It takes tugging and pushing to force the terrified, confused, dehydrated animals to stumble up the ramps to their awful prison quarters in the truck once again. The slots provided for each bull are so miserably small that the poor creatures must turn their horns to a sideways tilt in order to fit in. How could an animal thus twisted and wedged get his head into a position from which he could drink water, if any were offered? Who are the monsters in charge of such accommodations? Isn't the heat, the loneliness, and the day after horrid day of confinement sufficiently distressful without the added misery of being twisted and wedged? How do people even think of ways to inflict the pain they cause? And why?

I am trying to think of what I can do. Letters to the editor? Explain that American tourists do not like such cruelty, and that could cause a loss of vacation spending? But there are no Americans in sight. Americans do not attend this event. So that argument wouldn't work. What to do? How can I help?

Raúl decides to show me the video of his own running with the bulls, the "real" one, in real Pamplona, in Spain. He participated fourteen times! That means fourteen trips to Spain. Raúl loved the running, got banged around by the bulls, and like all young men thought that the dangerous horseplay was fun. Nice, clean, rough fun.

Before Raúl can show the video, he has to use his cell phone to call Raulito to come home and fix the player. Just like most parents, we turn to our children for electronic problem solving. I go up to my room until they will call for me.

As I leave, Delfina is busy making photocopies to take to her friend, who turns out to be the wife of President Fox! President of Mexico! Evidently she and Delfina are close friends, so this is an opportunity to expedite their case and save the house from collapsing. Yippee!

Nothing seems to be happening regarding the trip to Leon, so I may as well start another painting. I plan to make two small paintings as thank-you cards to put into envelopes with the money I will give to Chita (one hundred dollars US) and to Rafaela (fifty dollars). Raúl still hasn't decided if we are going to Leon, and because it still could happen, maybe, I am drinking very little water in order not to need a bathroom on the way.

In fact, I am happy to not go, to stay right here, but that is not the issue. Whatever we do, we will have a great time. Sometimes one needs to be forced into something new, and then it turns out to be wonderful.

Business is good at the Botica. Raulito has the idea of selling cups of ice from their refrigerator, and his enterprise is going nicely. Next year he plans to have a table for selling ice downtown.

Outside the streets are packed, all strangers, almost all with a bottle in hand, many having already passed out and been dragged to safety by their friends. But most are still staggering around, presumably enjoying the deafening music, wandering and walking.

Conchita comes for me and says that comida will be pizza in the Botica. Business is so good that no one can leave. We eat our pizza, celebrating all the customers and therefore prosperity.

At last Raúl shows me his videos of La Pamplonada in Spain. That one is very different from what happened here today. All the bulls are let out at once, and it only takes two or three minutes of fast running to get into the bull ring. The bulls do not attack the men who are running with them, but the street is narrow, crooked, and slippery. The bulls skid and crash into the runners, men slip and get kicked, and sometimes an animal can't get back onto his feet, which means his flailing and thrashing is dangerous for those trapped near him. Finally all the bulls have run into the ring where later that day they will all be killed by the Matadors in the well-known spectacle that takes place all over Spain every Sunday afternoon at four o'clock. Ugh.

I can't be a hypocrite though and pretend it is not fun to go to a bull fight. Abelardo used to take me, and the pageantry, enthusiasm of the spectators, music, ritual, suspense, drama, and fear all combined to make it an event very difficult to reject. Going anywhere with Abelardo was fun, naturally because we were so comfortable in each other's company, but also because Abelardo was well known and had many friends.

Being with Nita reminds me of those "Abelardo years" in that wherever we went, we were welcomed, greeted, kissed by the young women and embraced by the men. We usually sat in the sun, to start, while lengthening shadows crept towards our section, covering us with the relief of shade on a hot afternoon. It is not always bull fighting season, and one of the few things I do not remember is how often we were able to attend. But I can never forget the smells of the hot dirt in the ring, beer being peddled, people eating snacks, and the feel, so invisible yet tangible, of when a multitude of people all focus on the same thing.

I don't think Abelardo liked the hurting associated with the ritual any more than I did, but we both knew that these killings, bloody and cruel, were less a cause of suffering than the slaughter involved in bringing us the steaks we enjoyed at El Patio in our elegant late supper-and-dancing evenings. Especially you could understand our attendance if you would have to know that what passed for entertainment in those days could be a crowd gathering to sit on a curb and watch someone change a flat tire, or to gather on roof-tops and take sides, cheering for one or the other of drivers who met on the not-yet-one-way streets. Both drivers would exit their cars, tell the other that he should be the one to back up while traffic behind each piled up, making it impossible for either to relent. Sometimes people would even hang around to watch someone get a haircut.

One of Abelardo's, and mine, and his friends' favorite entertainment was going to the old Bougainvillea restaurant, facing the Jardín, when it rained. Unsuspecting customers would enter to buy a cone from one of the two places in town that sold ice cream. The refrigerated chest was located conveniently in front of the tables where we hung out, making one cup of Nescafe last for hours. The patron of course had to be innocent enough to not know that touching the freezer chest, as one does in making a selection between the two or three flavors available, would guarantee you of receiving a hair-raising, scream producing shock. Everyone at all of the tables, which had become suddenly silent, would then erupt into laughter. Of course the victim would catch on, laugh too, and join a table to wait for the next unsuspecting ice cream seeker to wander in. This was our fun. Now it may be more evident why the entertainment offered by bull fights could attract even animal lovers, such as I.

But that was then, and now that today's La Pamplonada has finished with the bulls (and I still being a lover of entertainment), I would like to go to el Jardin to hear the many wonderful bands that are now playing, but the same crowds are still in full force everywhere in town, despite that all the bars are filled with revelers. Every parking space in town is full, there are strangers sleeping in opened trunks, people leaning against cars while they talk, eat, and of course drink, and mill around aimlessly, waiting until it is time for a late dinner in a restaurant with lots of others of like dispositions, I suppose.

I see that el Jardín around the bandstand is stuffed with swarms of people who are dressed just like me, but who are not at all just like me. So instead I circle around the Jardín and walk towards the Instituto. When I have almost arrived, although I do not have the Instituto as a destination, only that it is a landmark on my taking a walk, a very pregnant woman with her little daughter at her side approaches me and asks me for work. Any American would be a likely prospect, and she says that she and the child have not eaten all day.

She looks too well-fed and confident for this to be true, but after all, she has asked for work and not a hand-out, so just perhaps, in case maybe her story is true, I cannot pass by and offer her nothing. I decide to offer food to both herself and her little girl, certainly not money. I take them to a nearby modest restaurant. I am carrying very little money. The menu says twenty-five pesos for three tacos. That is the cheapest thing available.

I empty my pockets and show the maître d' (a sign that this restaurant is more upscale than I thought) that I have exactly twenty-five pesos. I say, "Please add rice and beans, and bring two glasses of water and two plates. I will return later and bring money for the rice and beans and the tip". He says, "Muy bien, señora", and I sit with the mamá and daughter while they are served.

The three year old is delightful but does not eat much. The mother doesn't act starving either. On one hand, though, children who are excited rarely eat. The mother wraps up what is left to take home and asks the waiter if she can keep the plastic cups, so although the story of not eating all day was not true, still they had a need, and once again, I would rather be a sucker than brush off someone's plight. Twenty five pesos is only two dollars and fifty cents.

We leave the restaurant, and the little girl jumps up onto me, causing me to catch her in a hug, and she covers my face with kisses.

When I get home, the Botica is still going strong with customers, so I make ham, cheese, onion, and tomato tortas for everyone and take them to the Botica to be eaten in nibbles while attending to the many customers coming in and out.

We did not go to Howard Johnson's in Leon, we survived La Pamplonada, the house did not even shudder, let alone collapse, Conchita has had a thrilling time milling around with her friends, Raulito has breezed in and out and everywhere all afternoon and evening, and the day is about to end. All is well.

I am not yet sleepy and go up to Nancy's apartment, knock on the open screen door, and she and I take wine and cheese up to the roof. We watch the lights go on illuminating all the church domes that surround our block, enjoy the twilight, talk, relax, and put a nice end to the long eventful day.

39

LEBANESE LAMB, AND LAMB, AND LAMB, BALLROOM SHOW IN THE SALA, AND ESQUIMOS IN THE MARKET

When I awaken, it is from a delicious sleep that lasted until nine o'clock! This is an event, in my way of life, because the last time I slept that late was three or four years ago when I was here, in this very room, in this exact bed. That means I awaken to my favorite sounds of clanging, banging bells, every church in town going hard at it in a Sunday-come-to-mass cacophony.

I leisurely dress and walk to eleven o'clock mass in the golden chapel. I am delighted to see that the tiny cages with birds in each one have been hung from trees in the sunlight in the courtyard of the church! Oh, joy! But after mass, the ancient lady to whom I gave the jacket, and sweater, and socks, and shoes, and coins snatches up the cages and begins to put the poor creatures back into the dungeon of a clammy, dark, dank hallway.

I ask her to please leave them out, but she says, "No, señora, the cat will open their cages and kill them. There is no one to put them away for the night. I have to do it now." Nothing I say makes any sense to her. All she knows is that birds belong in cages, and cages belong hanging on the rack inside, where she has always put them, with no more thought than putting silverware in a drawer.

To my surprise, when I sit down in the chapel, here comes the whole family to join me. That iss so nice. And I like the topic for the day. It is the parable of the father who asked his two sons to work in the vineyard. One said ok but did not go. The other said, no, he didn't want to, but then he went anyway and worked all day. The sermon that followed was about doing what is right even when we don't want to.

This helped me a lot because I have been having a struggle with myself. I knew that I should leave every bit of everything for the maids because they have so little, and I can get more of anything. The struggle was my last possession, except for what I must wear on the airplane. It was my London Fog coat. It is perfect for travel, with a zip-out lining, waterproof, and fits perfectly. Plus it is machine wash and dry!

It gets cold in San Miguel in winter. Although I did give it to Chita, with instructions to give it to someone else who needed it if she didn't need it, I have been feeling ashamed about being reluctant to let it go. That is why this sermon helped me. I didn't exemplify a free and generous spirit, but still, I did do the right thing. In the end, it is actions that count. I guess that is the message.

Since meals are never served on Sundays at home, we are all going out to a restaurant, but not until after Raúl and Raulito drive out to some barren spot to fly their giant model airplane. When they finally come back though, they want to see the video I brought of Allen and me dancing.

Allen is my dance partner. In addition to our weekly Friday and Sunday four hour ballroom parties, we practice for three hours every Tuesday morning at the village hall near my house which has a large meeting hall with a new wooden floor. Since our practices enable us to put on dynamite, glitzy, flashy shows for retirement homes and service organizations, free of charge, we are allowed the use of the bright, airy town facility, to move all the rows of chairs away, dance, dance, and dance, and finally to return the seating to their original lines.

Allen set up his tripod camera just before I left so that the family could witness the answer to, "So, Sonette, what do you do with your time back in Wisconsin?" This is the last possible moment for the whole family to gather and watch. Naturally they all praise our costumes, our show, our ability. And then it is time to get ready for the dinner.

I dress up in my red pleated skirt, white tank top, red jewelry, and white sandals, my stand-by dress-up outfit. Conchita has new shoes, the latest thing, high heels all covered with beads and sequins. With these she wears the favorite of this town, tight jeans, and a pink glittery T shirt, plus a jean jacket. She looks darling.

We drive up to El Mirador, The Lookout View, to a Lebanese restaurant. Raúl has made a great choice for my last Sunday here, a perfect place for a celebration. We ask to be seated on the terrace, overlooking all of San Miguel. Everyone considers it to be freezing except for Raúl. All wear sweaters and jackets, except Raúl is fine in his handsome new shirt. And I, of course, have not been in Mexico long enough to have lost my thick Wisconsin blood, so I am enjoying the early evening breeze in my tank top, since to me it is still hot. At the only other table occupied, all are swathed in "It's cold!" clothes. But no one wants to miss out on dining with such a spectacular panorama at our feet.

I order the combination and share as much as possible with everyone. It is delicious and enormous. Lamb in grape leaves, lamb in rice, lamb ground and cooked and served like a piece of pie, lamb wrapped in rolled cabbage, and lamb in zucchini squash. Also whipped garbanzo paste, diced tomatoes with cucumbers, and cilantro, and onions, and lime juice, and black olives.

We talk about the breads of many countries, and then I offer, "Only Esquimos don't eat bread, right? They live on ice and only eat what comes from the sea?" Raulito answers with, "When they come here..." What! Esquimos come to San Miguel?! I did not know that Esquimos went anywhere at all, let alone to Mexico. I am astonished. "...when they come here, they take lots of pictures in the food markets. They are amazed by all the colors and varieties of foods." Now there is a scene I have never contemplated! Esquimos in a Mexican market filming videos!

Mosquitoes have begun to gather around us. No one but me is noticing because they are all bundled up against the "cold", but I am getting bitten. We move inside to free me from the biting and to warm everyone else up. Conchita and Delfina order Baklava, Delfina and Raúl request Turkish coffee because it is included with their dinners. Raúl gives his to me because he doesn't like coffee. I find it delicious. It is very strong and sweet, and at the bottom are a lot of grounds which I intend to eat with a spoon because that is how I am, eating crunchy things like the shells of shrimp and apple seeds and other parts of food that others think make me a crazy woman.

Before I can dip my spoon into the cup, Conchita stops me. "No, no, that is for telling your fortune." Raúl tells Conchita "No", on having our fortunes read, and we relate fortune telling experiences and the pros and cons. I say that even if you say it is just for fun, yet sometimes predictions can influence your actions and beliefs. It is better not to. The so-called foretelling can rule you with "maybe". We all skip the reading of the coffee grounds.

I have worn flat sandals, and Delfina and I walk down the steep twisty streets and stairs and alleys towards the Jardin. While we do this, the kids are driven home by papá, and ideally they should be finished with homework by the time we arrive. We get back way too fast. Conchita has to memorize a two page typed poem! This seems utterly impossible to me, even under the best of circumstances, and late (to me) on a Sunday night is the absolute guarantee that it can't be done by starting now. Also, she has to do a project for Mexican history involving glue, pictures, and writing with a stick of thick, glowing, pasty ink. I help her with the poem, and to my amazement, she completes everything.

Raúl had to correct his math, which he has finished. After all of the school projects, we settle in the family's sala to watch videos of their extensive European trip this summer. These sure are night people! I am the kind who always wanted to finish my home assignments right after school on Friday, or it would ruin my week-end thinking about them. And I always went to bed by nine o'clock on school nights, even in college. Is it Mexico vs. USA, or is it night people vs. day people? Maybe both.

What a full and fun day. It is obvious that the family is spending every precious minute with me because tomorrow is my last day here. Before dawn Tuesday I will get into the van for the last time.

40

NIGHT WORRIES, A PACKING REVELATION,
NITA ALMOST DIES

I awaken thinking that my worst problems today will be getting my e ticket printed and figuring out how to pack. I have abandoned the worries that kept me awake most of the night since I have no answers but prayer.

First, the worry. The bulls. I can't stop thinking that the terrible, unventilated metal boxes they are pushed into for transport are often parked directly in the sun all day, and the bulls are left standing in that torment for forty hours at a time. The temperatures inside would kill a man, and it is amazing that the bulls don't die too. Maybe some do. The cruelty of it is absolutely unnecessary, and horrific, and is terribly disturbing to me. Right at this moment, their prison of a transport vehicle is, and has been, parked up by El Gigante, waiting to proceed to the next town for the next La Pamplonada. Since the events are only given on Sunday afternoons, the in-between time is spent in nothing but penned up, sweltering, thirsty misery.

Why do I make so much of this? Why can't I just say, "I can do nothing. It isn't my problem." I cannot stop thinking about it.

The second worry. What should I wear on my return bus ride and flight? Airports will be hot, buses and airplanes freezing cold. What should I put into my carry-on? This is one of those worries that seem idiotic once you finally go to sleep and then awaken in the light of day.

As I said, I still believe that these will be my most difficult issues today, packing, and trying to calm down about the bulls.

My plan had been to roll up the sea bag and stuff it into my suitcase. Since I had given everything away, theoretically the sea bag would be "bailando", dancing around, banging and crashing inside my suitcase, and looking very strange when opened for inspection at the airport. But I ended up purchasing large last minute souvenirs for everyone, so I will go to the plastic store and buy bubble wrap, put the presents in the canvas sea bag, and hope for the best. In my suitcase I will have my left-over paints, the paintings that I have made while here, and very little else.

I decide to turn the sea bag inside out, to get out lint or anything that might be stuck in there, and, OH MY, OH MY! There at the very bottom, wedged into the folds, is a paper, a sort of card. It reads "You have been selected for examination by the Department of Homeland Security" and a lot of blah, blah, blah.

That explains everything! The broken and missing pencils. (The cores of lead pencils is lead, and lead is on the "suspicious list".) The brand new tubes of paint that had turned to glue. (X-ray machines cannot see into paint, no matter if you x-ray until the paint is cooked, because the tubes are lined with lead. Refer to lead being suspicious.) The broken handles on some of the brushes. (Maybe because the other art items were suspicious?) The new shoes with the high heels ripped and rumpled up. (Bombers apparently transport scary weapons in the heels of shoes.) The broken, brand new fans. (Having motors, I suppose a fan motor could be altered to do some dastardly deed. Why the blades were ripped or snapped remains a puzzle. The quality of thought of the inspectors? A long and boring day and a way to pass the time? Anger at having done so much inspecting which yielded nothing at all?)

It explains my luggage being "lost". It explains my being held at the airport for hours of filling out "lost" luggage forms. It does not explain why they couldn't have just taken my luggage and said, "It is being held for inspection. It will be delivered to you when we are finished."

Did some kind of authorities investigate my likelihood of being a solo or a group member of a terrorist gang? Bah, and Bah, Bah, Bah. Don't quite a few people pack lead pencils in their luggage? And if tubes of paint are so dangerous, why aren't they just prohibited? And why not outlaw shoes, especially ladies fancy, high heeled dress shoes?

(When I arrive at home, my son will explain it all to me in this way. "Mom, it was the paints and brushes that did it. Artists are often liberals, and as such they are already under suspicion by way of being non-conformists and therefore capable of any lunacy.")

Now I think I am done with odd things for today, and my biggest issue will be giving away the last of my hand painted cards, possessions, and money. How much money will I need for my trip home? Just about nothing, I decide. My son will pick me up at the airport, I have my tickets, and that should be that.

I have time before breakfast to finish my last painting. I am pleased with the result. It will be dry in time to pack. I have the last struggle with myself over leaving my two best pairs of Levis for Rafaela's children. The jeans fit me to perfection. Oh, what to do? The answer is obvious, once again. I can buy more. The pants are perfect for Nita's son and daughter. Did I mention that humble Mexican dwellings do not have closets? No room, and not much to put in them. A couple of nails on the wall suffice for the little that anyone possesses.

Chita has been doing everything she can to cook all of my favorites at once. I chat with Chita in the kitchen. Once I had asked her how they did things at her house. I said, "Desayuno y comida igual que aquí?" "Breakfast and lunch the same as here?" I meant, "Same hours? Same family gathering?" She thought I meant, "What is eaten?" and answered, "No, no tanto." "No, not as much." "Why is it different?" I continued, meaning in what ways, not in what was served. She answers, "No nos alcanza", which means "It doesn't stretch to us", or we would say, "We can't afford it". I am embarrassed to have asked questions that could be so misinterpreted. Of course they can't afford anything remotely like what we have here.

Rafaela has told me that her family lives on the beans, squash, and the corn that they grow, corn which must be dried, ground, and cooked into tortillas. The only other food they can buy comes from what Rafaela earns from scrubbing and cooking here in this house. She loves her job, is grateful for it, is well treated, and spends her days in a loving, harmonious, and beautiful atmosphere. Yet her job could not pay very much, considering that she is responsible for paying the utilities, school expenses, bus fares, children's necessities, and the necessities of her parents, and aunt, and uncle, and last of all, if any pesos are left, she can buy maybe some instant coffee, or bread, or a bit of fruit. Chita's family is the same.

I want to give the very last of everything, which I have bagged and set aside, to Chita before Nita returns. Why? When Nita returns, I will see her for only a few hours, go to sleep, awaken, and leave, perhaps not to return for years. My time must be free to spend entirely with Nita, to the degree she chooses. And, it does not go well to give too much to servants in front of others. It just doesn't.

I ask Chita to come to my room for the last of her gifts, the main one being the card I painted for her, with the money. When Chita opens her card, with the one hundred dollars (in pesos, of course), she is speechless. Shyly she thanks me, telling me that it is too much and praising the card-painting. The painting is a small-sized depiction of the courtyard, since living here, as such a vital part of the family's daily life, this is her house too. We finish putting the last of what I have given to Chita into her room and are just closing the door when in sweeps Nita, all joyous and radiant. Perfect timing.

Breakfast begins. I memorize every bite, every flavor, smell, texture, clank of spoon, swallows of juice, aromas from the kitchen, Chita's clearing, cooking, serving, the wonderfully perfected ritual which I will soon taste only in the bank of my memory.

- Orange juice.
- Tiny bananas which are golden inside.
- Scrambled eggs with carefully chopped ham, onions, jalapeños, and tomatoes.
- Freshly, laboriously made sauce.
- Hot tortillas, nestled in their napkin wrapped basket, passed from one hand to another.

In her excitement, Nita wants to sit right down in the kitchen and tell in glowing terms about her trip to Guadalajara. The visit was staying at someone's home for the celebration of the First Communion of twin nine year old boys. The house, described by Nita in wonderful detail, was enormous. She recounts everything she experienced and observed, just the way I like to tell stories myself, and she is excellent.

There were guests of one hundred adults and two hundred children. The mountain of gifts consisted of one hundred presents, each containing doubles of whatever had been selected as the finest that could be given for such important boys of such an important family on such an important day. And then Nita describes the gifts. I try to conceal my mounting horror at the excess, the needless smothering of children with too much to ever use while right in this room stands Chita at the sink, washing dishes, and feeling glad and lucky to have her job.

During our many kitchen visits, Chita confided to me some while ago that her sister is pregnant, and as soon as the nineteen year old boyfriend heard the news, he has never been seen or heard from again. I have told Chita that in that case the man would not be a reliable father anyway, and all that would happen would be more babies, the boyfriend re-appearing and disappearing, and no marriage or home provided anyway. So this will be a "family baby", everyone will treasure it and love it, and a baby is never anything but the most precious of all gifts, and to rejoice, rejoice, and it will all work out. This helped her a lot, because the whole family was struggling with shame and fear.

So things are ok at Chita's home, where the sister and child will continue to live, all are now excited about the coming blessing, yet the cost will be something. How does hearing of the one hundred gifts, in duplicate, sound to Chita? I suppose she is used to it, things have been this way all of her life, there is always someone poorer than you, and there is always someone richer. Chita does not join in our conversation, never does unless asked, but she too seems pleased that Nita had such fun, went to such a party, and that we can live it vicariously right her in the cozy kitchen.

Nita heads for Raúl's and Delfina's apartment where she will tell them all the news that they will appreciate about her visit. Conchita has come to find me, and we go to the little study next to the giant library. On this computer Conchita can locate any kind of music, and I teach her more steps of how to dance the Cumbia.

It is ironic, because I learned this complicated dance in Wisconsin by including students of immigrant Mexican families as dance partners for my Spanish classes. This was a two-fold purpose project. One, to learn the dance as part of culture study and active fun. Two, to integrate the shy, "outsider" Hispanic kids with the well-established and popular kids in my classes. The project was a success in every way, with my students begging for their new dance friends to return again and again. I don't know if any real friendships formed, like calling each other on the phone type of friends, but very friendly relationships like "Hi", in the hallways and conversations in passing, camaraderie in the lunch rooms, giving the Hispanics a chance to be important and to feel included. Anyway, here I am in San Miguel, bringing the Cumbia to Conchita.

Delfina peeks in the door, sees us, and we show off the dancing that we can now do together. Like any mother, Delfina is glad to see her daughter happily learning to social dance, a skill that can be put to use at parties right away because although Conchita has not started to date yet, being too young, Cumbia can be danced by girls together as much as with a boy. The girlfriends do not know this dance either, so Conchita can teach them. Soon enough, the boys will be asking Conchita.

For comida Chita again shows her skills and caring by serving the ultimate:

- Guyava drink.
- Papaya.
- Vegetable soup.
- Chile rellenos.
- Rice.
- Several varieties of sauces so I can eat my fill.
- And my beloved, fresh, hot, aromatic, soft, stacked in their basket, tortillas.

Raúl has announced that we will all be going to a restaurant tonight, after they put the huge, heavy wooden panels over the doors of the Botica and bolt them from the inside, in honor of my last night here. I decline, gently, saying that last night was our restaurant party, it was fantastic, and it cost a great deal. So it is ok with me to spend tonight all together here at home. Raúl nods, and I can see that I said the right thing. The family have devoted days to spending every minute with me, begging me not to go, to change my reservation, just stay a couple of weeks more, please.

It is good to be urged, good that I believe they really mean it, good that this is a sign that my presence is fun for them as well as for me, good that I have not been a burden. There is not the slightest possibility that I would stay since Mary will be returning to her teacher job, and I will get to care for my little, tiny, precious baby grandson. But my heart will still be here, if not during the busy days ahead, then as I climb into bed each night, as I awaken to morning sounds outside my open bedroom window, even though I will be hearing robins and chipmunks instead of church bells, and kitchen clattering, and ranchera music from the radio.

Thinking of my travel day tomorrow, I cross the street to La Colmena, the bakery. For the last time I pick up a dented metal tray, take a pair of metal tongs, and select whole wheat rolls for myself and bolillos for the family. I will make sandwiches of tomatoes and mustard tonight and take them with me for the bus ride and maybe for the wait in the airport.

Nita says to walk with her to the bakery across town that stays open until ten o'clock. It is already well after eight, when La Colmena closes. Conchita comes too, and we drift slowly down the narrow streets, streets that angle, fan, and dead-end, so that you must be very sure of the route. Nita says we are to buy tuna empanadas for merienda, her idea. Except when we arrive, Nita forgets about empanadas and spies chocolate covered donuts, pan dulces, and already made Jellos in plastic cups.

When we sit down for merienda, Nita eats only donuts, pan dulces, and Jello, all very high in sugar. I say that I don't want any desserts and start to make myself a cheese torta. This makes Nita very angry. "These are not desserts, Sonette. These are bread, bread, bread, don't you know that?" Pan means bread, and dulce means sweet, so to Nita, the operative word is bread, not sweet. We have discussed Jello before, which was before I knew that I better not criticize her food choices, even though I believe that sugar is harmful for anyone, particularly for a diabetic. Nita has said, "I am not eating sugar. I am eating Jello!" When I responded, "But Jello is made of sugar. The only ingredients are gelatin, food coloring, artificial flavoring, water, and lots of sugar. I know, because I have made it." Nita humphs, "No one makes Jello. There isn't any recipe. You buy Jello in the bakery." And that is why I keep quiet about so much sugar and nothing else for her evening meal.

Chita comes to the rescue. She sees that there is nothing on the table that I want to eat, and that if I try to make a torta now, this special evening will be ruined. She quickly steps into the dining room and says, Señora, Raulito, there are chile rellenos left from comida. I will bring them to you." Hurray, and Thank you, God. Nita is trying to make peace, I guess, because now she says she will also have some fruit and a quesadilla. The fruit she selects is one of the sweetest, but I am feeling far too critical, nosy about commenting on what is really only my friend's business, and nothing I or anyone could do or say would help in the slightest anyway.

When we finish, I give the children their last gifts, Mickey Mouse for Conchita (the family takes her to Disney World because she loves Mickey Mouse), and Frankenstein for Raulito, which is perfect for a boy who still likes toys but is almost too old for anything but monsters, aliens, warriors, and the budding man types of things.

It is ten thirty, and before we leave the table, Raúl says, "Let's all go watch videos of our trip to Europe this summer." Ok, fun, we do, and after enjoying the last entertainment of the night, I kiss everyone, as always, promise to be ready for breakfast at seven AM (when it is still dark), and to have all my baggage ready to sling into the car and speed away to the bus station in Querétaro. I climb the stairs and go to bed. Everything is already prepared for departure, so all I have to do is set the alarm and fall asleep. Which I do.

At four AM I hear sounds from Nita. Because of last time, I don't dare tell her she is snoring and ask her to please turn over. It is true that I am the noisy and troublesome one night after night, and Nita never complains. The sounds get strange though, like hard grunts. I decide that she is having a nightmare. The grunts get so loud that I decide to wake her up. When I turn on the light, Oh, No!

Nita is lying on her back, rigid, arms and legs straight as sticks, mouth drawn into a grimace, teeth firmly clenched. She is in a diabetic coma.

I run to Raúl's and knock, and yell, and he comes right down. He runs up the stairs with me to look at her. I say that once she told me about when this happened in Canada, and her son had to help. When she came to, sugar was all around her mouth because he was trying to get sugar into her, but he couldn't. When the paramedics arrived, they injected glucose. The paramedics were still taking care of her when she awoke.

Raúl unlocks the kitchen, which means first returning to his apartment for the key. We don't know how much time we have to save her. We grab the sugar bowl from the little table and also cut an orange in half. We cannot get sugar on to her tongue nor into her mouth. Thankfully her clenched teeth are parted just enough that I can hold the orange and squeeze slowly, dripping juice through the little gap. Every time she swallows, I squeeze and drip a little more. I am afraid that she could choke, but what is my alternative?

Raúl has his cell phone and calls brother-in-law Carl, the doctor. Carl says to call the ambulance, but only the Red Cross comes. It seems to take a long while. At least the streets are mostly empty at this hour, and the Red Cross van has an unobstructed path.

When the paramedics (or volunteers, whatever they are) arrive, they have no idea what to do. They ask me. Me? How would I dare to make a decision? I am only guessing about the whole thing.

The Red Cross men do have a diabetic kit of some kind, but they do not know how to use it. They only brought it because Raúl described what type of emergency this is when he phoned them. Again, they expect me to test her! How? Their kit is nothing like Nita's state-of-the-art Canadian kit. I don't have the slightest idea how to use that either. True, every day I have seen Nita prick her finger, poke something at the blood, stick the stiff paper back into the machine, and tell me what the number of her sugar is. I have tried my hardest not to be involved in all of this sickness, diabetes, terrible predictions and conditions. I do not think this way, and do not want to. If Nita had ever asked me to to help her use her apparatus to check her blood sugar, I would have helped. But I was not asked and never seemed to be needed. The little bit that I do know could be all mixed up and exactly wrong for this situation.

I am urged to get her kit and figure it out. I try, but the papers have a coated end, and a not-coated end. Which do you put blood on? Where does one insert the paper sticks into the machine? How? Up or down? What if I can do it, who here will be able to read the results? This kit uses Canadian measurements which are different from how these things are charted here in Mexico. All I know is that I do not know.

The team phones the hospital to find out how to take their own blood-sugar reading with the apparatus they have brought. When the reading is finally taken, after much conversation to figure things out, they say, "It is surprising that she is still alive". The blood sugar count is so low that it doesn't even register.

I tell the "medical team" that apparently she gets injections of glucose. Will this kill her if I am wrong? They decide to try. I am enlisted to hold the bag of glucose high over her head while they inject a needle that is attached to a tube which is attached to the bag. Nita starts to slowly come to life. I don't understand it. Glucose and orange juice have a lot of sugar. Isn't she in a coma because of too much sugar? Shouldn't glucose make her worse?

Nita's body is drenched with sweat. The sheets and blankets are sopping. As she awakens, Delfina and I get her changed into a clean, dry nightgown. I take her to the toilet, get her a drink of water, Delfina strips the bed, and I wrap her in fresh warm blankets. It is now five thirty. Delfina and Raúl go to their rooms to try to get one hour's sleep. I lie on my bed and wait for seven o'clock.

At six fifteen I decide to get up and get ready. Raúl did not sleep. He has been in the Botica making drinks for everyone. He brings me a glass, "For the shock." It is the dark tonic that the old ladies buy and slug down at the Botica first thing in the morning. "What shock?" I ask. "El susto", (The Scare). "Oh", I say, "No, thank you, but I don't need any. I was not scared". It is true. I feel fine, and I did not feel scared. Baffled, helpless from the medical point of view, but not scared.

We go to the breakfast in the dining room, leaving Nita to rest from her coma, the high-sugar-insulin-overdose, the emergency-glucose-induced sleep. When she awakens from such episodes (which family members say are frequent), Nita refers to them as her "delicious sleep". Since Nita is always unconscious during these episodes, it does not occur to her that the frenzied, frantic efforts of everyone else to rescue her are not delicious experiences for anyone else. But of course everyone else is always so thrilled that they discovered her in time to help that whatever troubles and dramas are caused is pale by comparison of having our dear Nita be ok.

Naturally the breakfast talk is of what happened in order to explain to the children who are all dressed up and ready to ride along on my being driven to Querétaro. Chita has been awake preparing breakfast, so everyone has been aware of the racing footsteps through the night, strange voices in the house, lights on in the wrong places at the wrong times, and all must be told in detail.

Although we are all still not understanding the chemistry of the attack and the remedy, in a few years, when I remarry, I will learn that when a diabetic eats too much sugar, it causes the night sugar level reading to soar. Therefore Nita sometimes injects herself with too much insulin in order to compensate. The insulin over-dose makes the body crash, dramatically, and possibly is deadly if not treated. I guess, this is my guess, of what I understand. Don't think I am some kind of medical textbook that could not possibly be wrong. I am often wrong all over the place.

In Canada about once a year, I believe, Conchita and Raulito visit La Tía for a month at a time. They love La Tía unreservedly. In Canada the insulin problem causes much disruption. "It is not her, Sonette. It is the diabetes."

I eat my last breakfast, huevos rancheros, covered with salsa like soup. This is Chita's parting gift to me. She catches me alone, for a hug good-bye, and softly whispers, "You are like an angel for us, señora. We wait and wait for you to come back. There is no one like you, no one." I tell her that I love her, she is like a daughter, and she is my friend. There is no one like her either.

"The Good-bye Day"

This morning, I go up to see if Nita is awake and to say good-bye.

Nita is smiling and comfortable. She is oblivious to anything except that she had another "delicious sleep". Chita will stay with Nita while the family takes me to the airport.

It is time. Nita has survived, is safe, is happy. My trip has come to an end, and as planned, I am leaving. We will get into the van, and Raúl will drive me to the beginning of my journey home. Delfina tells me, assures me, embraces me, to say to be sure to return again next year. Delfina and the children will accompany us in the van, we will spend the hours before the flight squeezing in last minute sight-seeing, one last Mexican meal on Mexican soil, we will treasure every drop of friendship, but ultimately I will still have to board the plane.

As for next time, as for the future, I never know where I will be. The wind will blow me, and that is where I will go.

The End of Trip Two.

Coming Soon, Trip Three & Trip Four.

ABOUT THE AUTHOR

Sonette Chanson Tippens has combined careers. She started her professional career at age eleven as a dancer in stage shows, and toured Canada and the Midwest with well-known productions.
To this she added being a circus aerialist, high school art and Spanish teacher, inspirational speaker, published newspaper and magazine writer, and now adds author of books as she recounts her own experiences of Mexican life from inside "A Great House" in a Mexican Colonial town.